Contents

D1377957

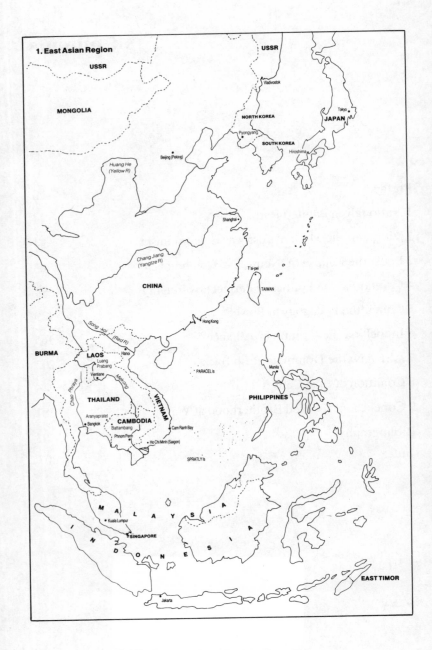

1. East Asian Region

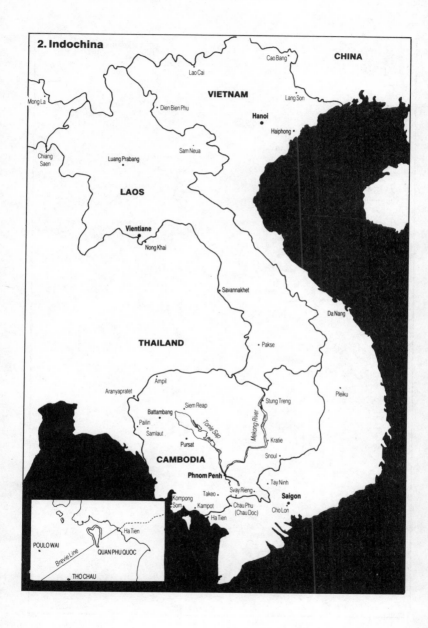

2. Indochina

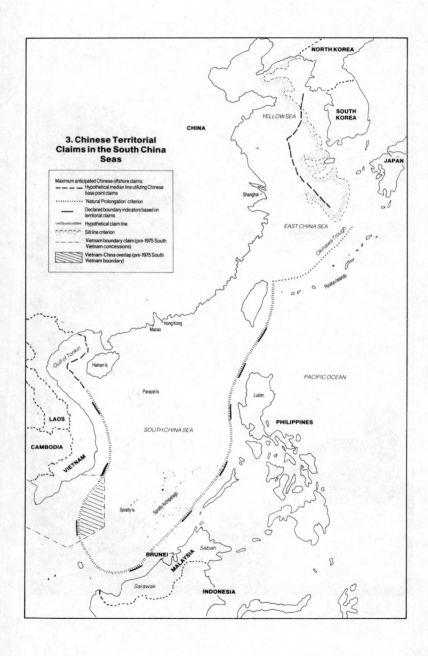

3. Chinese Territorial Claims in the South China Seas

Maximum anticipated Chinese offshore claims:
- — — — Hypothetical median line utilizing Chinese base point claims
- ·········· 'Natural Prolongation' criterion
- ———— Declared boundary indicators based on territorial claims
- ⊥⊥⊥⊥⊥⊥⊥ Hypothetical claim line
- ≷≷≷≷≷≷ Silt line criterion
- —·—·— Vietnam boundary claim (pre-1975 South Vietnam concessions)
- ▨▨▨▨ Vietnam-China overlap (pre-1975 South Vietnam boundary)

NORTH KOREA

SOUTH KOREA

CHINA

JAPAN

YELLOW SEA

EAST CHINA SEA

Shanghai

Okinawa Trough

Ryukyu Islands

Hong Kong

Macao

Gulf of Tonkin

Hainan Is

PACIFIC OCEAN

Luzon

LAOS

Paracel Is

PHILIPPINES

CAMBODIA

VIETNAM

SOUTH CHINA SEA

Spratly Is

Spratly Archipelago

BRUNEI

Sabah

MALAYSIA

Sarawak

INDONESIA

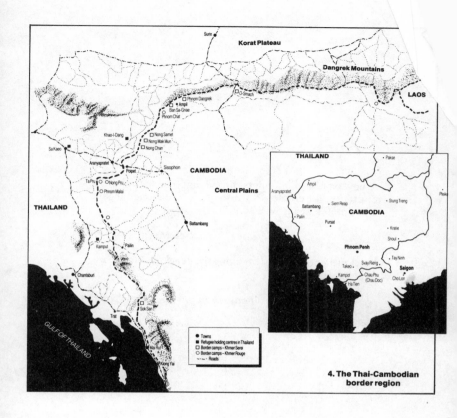

4. The Thai-Cambodian border region

Towns
Refugee holding centres in Thailand
Border camps – Khmer Serei
Border camps – Khmer Rouge
Roads

Korat Plateau

Dangrek Mountains

LAOS

Surin

Phnom Dangrek
Ampil
Ban Sa-Gnae
Phnom Chat
O-Smach

Khao-I-Dang

Nong Samet
Nong Mak Mun
Nong Chan

Sa Kaeo

Aranyaprate
Popet
Sisophon

CAMBODIA

Central Plains

Ta Pru
Nong Pru
Phnom Malai

THAILAND

Battambang

Kamput
Pailin

Chantaburi

Sok San

GULF OF THAILAND

Trat

Mai Rut
Klong Yai

THAILAND

Pakse

Aranyaprate
Ampil

Battambang
Siem Reap
Stung Treng

Pleiku

Palin

Pursat

CAMBODIA

Kratie

Snoul

Phnom Penh

Takeo
Svay Rieng

Tay Ninh

Saigon

Kampot
Chau Phu
(Chau Doc)

Cho Lon

Ha Tien

'A new prince, of all rulers, finds it impossible to avoid a reputation for cruelty, because of the abundant dangers inherent in a newly won state.'

Niccolo Machiavelli, *The Prince*

'Patriotism is useful for breaking the peace, not for keeping it.'

Thorstein Veblen, *An Inquiry into the Nature of Peace*

Preface

After thirty years of war, sustained by both local antagonisms and outside involvement, peace came to Indochina in 1975. Because the victorious parties in Indochina were all Communist, it was generally expected that relations between them would be 'fraternal' and peaceful. But, unknown to most of the world, strains and fractures had already appeared in the 'militant solidarity binding the three peoples in friendship and brotherhood'; and after victory this solidarity soon ruptured. In December 1978 Vietnam invaded Cambodia to topple Pol Pot's regime, and Communist China responded in February 1979 with an invasion of Vietnam intended to 'punish' Hanoi. Laos found itself caught in the middle of a feud between its erstwhile allies. This was the Third Indochina War. The first two had been 'wars of national liberation', but in the Third Indochina War the victorious 'liberators' turned on each other. Although the harsh domestic policies of Pol Pot's Democratic Kampuchea regime had been widely condemned, in non-Communist Southeast Asia opinion over this conflict went strongly against Vietnam. The 'heroic' liberators of yesteryear now stood condemned for attacking their fellow-Communists in Cambodia.

Two days after the Chinese attacked Vietnam the *New York Times* ran an editorial entitled 'The Red Brotherhood at War'. It said, gloatingly: 'They are singing "The Internationale" on all sides of the Asian battle this week as they bury the hopes of the Communist fathers with the bodies of their sons.' The 'hopes of the Communist fathers' had been that, since war was caused by capitalist imperialism, international socialism would bring peace. These ideals now lay shattered by the new conflicts in Indochina. By contrast with the bellicosity of Communism revealed in Indochina, the *New York Times* concluded, the United States was a 'force for peace' which should 'assert itself' more strongly throughout the world. While offering a thinly disguised vindication of America's own war in Indochina, this statement did highlight a grave weakness in socialist political theory. There can be little doubt that the rhetoric of 'national liberation' and 'socialist internationalism' provides a poor guide to events in Indochina since 1975. On the other hand, the shrill denunciations of 'international communism' to be heard from the right provide, in our view, even less illumination.

All governments claim the highest motives for their own participation in wars, and all wars produce their myths and mythmakers. It took a long time for the myths to be stripped away from the American justification for its military intervention in Vietnam. It finally came to be called a 'reporters' war', because of the degree to which journalists began to bypass official US explanations and search for the facts themselves. They realized they were being lied to, and subsequent investigations of the conduct of the war, such as William Shawcross's brilliant book *Sideshow: Nixon, Kissinger and the Destruction of Cambodia* (1979), have shown the extent of Washington's ruthlessness and duplicity, and the immensity of the tragedy that it contributed to. There are few who have read Shawcross's book who would relish America 'asserting itself' in this fashion once more.

But today the prodigals have returned to the fold and State Department briefings on the current dispute in Indochina are respectable once again. The new cold war has successfully revived an anti-Communist reflex among many commentators, who have simply dusted off the clichés about 'Communist expansion' that were current two decades ago to explain the Vietnamese invasion of Cambodia. The contradictions and oversimplifications in this view are immense, but this has not prevented it from gaining wide popularity.

It is in the face of this new cold war interpretation of the Third Indochina War that we have written this book. But in writing it we were not looking for a re-affirmation of 'old truths', whether they be held by the left or the right. We wanted, above all, to explain why Communist states had gone to war with each other in Indochina. What, exactly, happened in Indochina after 1975? Why did the Communists defy the earlier expectations of both their supporters and denigrators? What happened to 'socialist internationalism' in the paddy-fields and forests of Indochina? What explains the strange ideological bedfellows that were prompted by this conflict? Why is it that the right-wing Republican Reagan is able to come to some accord with the Communist Deng Xiaoping, but not the

GRANT EVANS was born in Berri, South Australia, in 1948. Author of
The Yellow Rainmakers (Verso 1983), an investigation into US allega-
tions of Soviet use of chemical weapons in SE Asia, he lectures in the
School of Sociology, University of New South Wales, Sydney.

KELVIN ROWLEY was born in Albury, New South Wales, in 1948. He is a
lecturer in Social and Political Studies at Swinburne Institute of Technology, Melbourne.

Grant Evans
Kelvin Rowley

Verso

Red Brotherhood at War
Indochina since the Fall of Saigon

Evans, Grant
Red Brotherhood at War.
  1. Indochina – Politics and government
  I. Title II. Rowley, Kelvin
  959.704'4 DS526.7

First published 1984
© Grant Evans and Kelvin Rowley 1984

Verso Editions
15 Greek Street London W1V 5LF

Filmset in Times Roman by
PRG Graphics Limited, Redhill, Surrey

Printed in Great Britain by
The Thetford Press Ltd
Thetford, Norfolk

ISBN 0 86091 090 3
      0 86091 795 9 Pbk

Communist Le Duan?

A major stumbling block to an understanding of events in Indochina is the influence of nationalism. On both sides of the cold war divide nationalist assumptions are taken for granted. It is rarely acknowledged that nationalism is a relatively recent historical phenomenon, one that needs to be explained rather than taken for granted. For too many commentators, the justice of a cause is determined exclusively by subjective national preferences rather than by any objective criteria. This might be psychologically satisfying, but is is politically dangerous. It is the road to chaos. In a world bursting with nationalist passions, we think there is a lot to be said in favour of the internationalist standpoint of classical liberalism and socialism. It is, basically, the perspective from which we have written this book. But modern nationalism is too important a phenomenon to be ignored; indeed, in our view, events in Indochina are incomprehensible without an understanding of it. It is this consideration which explains our lengthy opening chapter on the pre-1975 period in Indochina. Briefly, in our view, nationalism is a product of the modernization of traditional societies, and is a powerful force in both Communist and non-Communist states. Our interpretation of events in post-1975 Indochina rests on this approach rather than on an acceptance of the assumptions of any particular nationalism.

We also argue that the assertions of the new cold warriors that Vietnam is an aggressive, expansionist power are wrong. In this book we show that, far from being the active instigator of the crisis in Indochina, Hanoi was largely reacting to unanticipated external pressures, especially from Pol Pot's regime. Hanoi was nonetheless capable of responding with considerable ruthlessness to these pressures. While the conflict thus arose from essentially regional causes, we also show that China and America played a more active role than is usually realized. This whole explanation is more sympathetic to Hanoi than current fashions would dictate. But truth is important, and fashion is not. If our analysis is correct, much current Western thinking about Indochina is based on dangerously false illusions.

Given our perspective on Indochina, it also goes almost without saying that we are highly critical of Chinese policy in the region. The fog of misunderstanding, on both the left and the right, concerning Chinese foreign policy is so dense that we have felt obliged to devote a considerable amount of space (chapter V) to unravelling it and examining its historical roots.

We had originally intended to cover internal political developments as well as international relations. But this would have more than doubled the size of what is already a long book, so we have restricted our coverage to the latter. Nevertheless, writing this book has driven home to us the extent to which the internal and external policies of states form a seamless web of cause and effect. Thus, while our focus is on international politics, we have found it necessary on many occasions to venture into an analysis of domestic politics. This is especially true of Pol Pot's Cambodia, for in our view the crisis in Cambodia lay at the very heart of the Third Indochina War, but, to a lesser degree, it is also true for other governments.

Throughout this book we have often written of countries, cities and governments as if they were one and the same thing ('Vietnam', 'Hanoi', 'The Socialist Republic of Vietnam'; 'America', 'Washington', 'The United States', and so on). This is, of course, no more than a literary convenience. Since in most cases we are actually referring to the handful of people responsible for the management of a state's external relations, we should perhaps apologize to all those citizens of countries and cities who have no responsibility for the decisions made in their names. Even in the most democratic states, foreign policy is the area of government most removed from popular control.

There are other apologies we will not make. Our interest in Indochina arose originally out of our involvement in the anti-war movement in the 1960s. The new cold warriors claim that events since 1975 clearly vindicate America's military intervention, and that those involved in the anti-war movement have much to answer for. In one sense, we are 'answering' for the movement by writing this book.

In a more important sense, however, we see nothing to answer for. No doubt many naïve and silly things were said (and done) back then, but it was right to have opposed the Vietnam war, and it is right to oppose similar military interventions in the Third World today. In our view, there is nothing in the tragedies that have beset Indochina since 1975 to provide retrospective justification for the ill-conceived military intervention by America and its allies. That commitment proved disastrous, not only for the servicemen sent into a war they did not understand, and for their families, but also for the people of Indochina. It caused untold destruction and suffering, and achieved nothing. Finally, we might recall that after the First World War there were some people who chose to explain their military defeats in terms of a 'stab in the back', and hankered after a re-match from a position of strength. We hope that the new cold warriors do not need to be reminded of the outcome.

We have used the familiar 'Cambodia' rather than 'Kampuchea' throughout this book, even though the latter has been adopted by the United Nations and many governments, including our own. The choice is pragmatic rather than political – 'Cambodia' is more widely recognized, and it is arguably as good an English rendering of the Khmer name as 'Kampuchea'. For similar reasons, we have used 'Peking' rather than 'Beijing'. However, in discussing Pol Pot's party we have used its own chosen rendering of 'Communist Party of Kampuchea' (CPK). We have done the same with the regime it established, 'Democratic Kampuchea' (DK).

We have tried to discharge our debts to published sources in our notes and in the bibliography. We began work on this book late in 1979 and between us we have spent many months in Vietnam, Laos, Cambodia and Thailand. Many people have given us encouragement and assistance, and we would like to thank them all, especially Anthony Barnett, Chantou Boua, Peter Cox, Ben Kiernan, Gavan McCormack and Richard Tanter. We would also like to thank our editor at Verso, Neil Belton, for his encouragement and assistance. Thanks also to Bronwyn Bardsley and Roger Wilkinson for all their help with the typing. For their tolerance of our obsessions while writing this book, we would especially like to thank Elizabeth Astbury and Archara Rowley, and our parents. Since we have cast general aspersions on reportage on Indochina since 1975, we should pay special tribute here to Nayan Chanda, whose coverage of the region throughout this period has been outstanding. But none of the people we mention here bear any responsibility for the opinions we express. Warts and all, this is our book.

Grant Evans
Kelvin Rowley

Melbourne,
Australia,
December, 1983

1

Nationalism Painted Red

Two explanations are commonly put forward in the West for the new round of war in Indochina after 1975. One, espoused particularly by the right wing in the United States, is that it was due to the aggressive 'internationalism' of the Vietnamese Communists and to the failure of the American intervention (like Ronald Reagan, they continue to believe that America's war in Indochina was an 'honourable' one). In their view, no sooner had the Communists conquered South Vietnam than they turned their energies to the subjugation of neighbouring Laos and Cambodia, doubtless at the behest of Moscow. America, paralysed by guilt, stood helplessly by and did nothing to save these new victims of Communist aggression.

Few Indochina experts would agree that things were as simple as this, and we shall show how wrong this interpretation is in chapter II which deals with Vietnamese policy since 1975. But in this chapter our basic purpose is to provide a historical background, outlining events up to 1975. And we shall do this by focusing on the second common explanation, which is more influential among specialists on the region and Western liberal commentators. This explains the new conflicts in terms of the triumph of ancient and deep-rooted national antagonisms over the ideological bonds of internationalist Communist solidarity.

Such an interpretation certainly has some basis in the rhetoric of the antagonists themselves, who have not hesitated to find an ancient pedigree for contemporary quarrels. In September 1978 the Pol Pot regime produced a *Black Paper* depicting the current conflict as the culmination of five centuries of Khmer struggles against relentless expansion by the Vietnamese. Almost devoid of Marxist-Leninist rhetoric, it explained the conflict in purely nationalist, indeed, essentially racist, terms. It was, according to the *Black Paper*, the 'true nature' of Vietnam to be an 'aggressor, annexationist and swallower of other people's territory'. This was

1

indignantly rejected by Hanoi as a 'crude falsification' of history, but faced with the Chinese invasion of February 1979, the Vietnamese leaders responded by invoking, in less crude but distinctly similar terms, Vietnam's 'two thousand years of struggle against Chinese domination'.

Ancient Traditions or Colonial Transfomation?

This explanation of the conflict in terms of historical antagonisms has gained wide acceptance among commentators who otherwise rarely find themselves in agreement with the Communists. For example, in his book *Before Kampuchea* (1979), Milton Osborne, an authority on Cambodia of impeccably liberal credentials, entitled the chapter on relations with Vietnam 'The Hereditary Enemy'. Like Pol Pot, Osborne bases his case on the undisputed historical fact that the ancient Khmer Empire has been whittled down in modern times by the expansion of the Thai kingdom in the west and Vietnam in the east. He therefore rationalizes Khmer anti-Vietnamese racism by claiming that it is the result of Vietnamese expansionism. Cambodia's dilemma was 'how . . . to contend with a geographical neighbour whose population was so much gr?ater in size and whose leaders for centuries had pursued policies leading to the progressive absorption of Cambodian territory'.

For Osborne, the fact that the Vietnam-Cambodia border was the meeting point of two distinct cultural and political worlds was central to the conflict. The Thai-Cambodian border, by contrast, was not. 'Thailand and Cambodia had on frequent occasions in the past been in conflict,' he writes, 'but there was no basic cultural division between the two countries.' The Khmers did not think of the Thais as 'fundamentally and irretrievably racial enemies'. But in the case of the Vietnamese, he argues, they did. The explanation for this attitude, and the conflicts it gave rise to, lay in Cambodia's ancient origins as an Indianized state, and Vietnam's as a Sinitic state: 'A basic and essentially unbridgeable gap existed between Cambodians and Vietnamese. The population of each country represented two conflicting cultures; the Cambodians an Indianized culture and the Vietnamese a Sinicized culture. The differences between these cultures had very practical implications. When the Vietnamese absorbed Cambodian territory they sought to transform it into something that was "standard" Vietnamese. They sought to do this behind clearly demarcated frontiers. The Cambodians, even when they had been powerful, had not thought in these terms, neither had the Thais. For the Thais and Cambodians, both beneficiaries of Indian ideas on statecraft, frontiers were regarded as porous and shifting and new populations that might come under the control of the state as the result of conquest were not of necessity to be moulded into some pale imitation of the conqueror.'[1]

It was, according to Osborne, this traditional conflict that re-emerged after 1975 and destroyed Communist solidarity. With the Vietnamese invasion of 1978, the Pol Pot government experienced 'the ultimate proof of their countrymen's traditional fears' of the Vietnamese.[2]

A clash between modern nation-states is thus explained in terms of traditional cultural differences. But a common culture has never prevented neighbours from feuding, indeed it has often provided the excuse for slaughter. As Khien Theeravit has observed, despite their common culture, 'the Siamese and the Khmer kingdoms were often at war with one another.' Furthermore, when they went to war against their co-religionists they 'observed no rules of warfare and espoused no martial modes of conduct. More often than not, they demonstrated savagery in the conduct of warfare.'[3] And Pol Pot's regime did not adopt the rather casual approach to border questions that might be expected from a 'beneficiary of Indianic ideas on statecraft'.

Moreover, the vicissitudes of politics and war in modern times simply do not coincide with the enduring patterns of cultural differences. Why, for example, did China support 'Indianic' Cambodia against 'Sinitic' Vietnam in the conflict of 1977-8? To answer this question, we have to analyse the modern political conjuncture, not traditional cultures.

Such reasoning usually takes 'tradition' as a kind of historical *deus ex machina* which explains everything and does not itself need to be explained. However, traditional culture is not the spontaneous emanation of mysterious racial instincts but the product of concrete historical experiences and institutions. It is maintained by constant efforts, and serves the interest of specific groups. This general point has been made by Barrington Moore in terms that can hardly be bettered: 'The assumption that cultural and social continuity do not require explanation obliterates the fact that both have to be created anew in each generation, often with great pain and suffering. To maintain and transmit a value-system, human beings are punched, sent to jail, thrown into concentration camps, cajoled, bribed, made into heroes, encouraged to read newspapers, stood up against a wall and shot, and sometimes even taught sociology. To speak of cultural inertia is to overlook the concrete interests and privileges that are served by indoctrination, education, and the entire complicated process of transmitting culture from one generation to the next . . . . We cannot do without some conception of how people perceive the world and what they do or do not want to do about what they see. To detach this conception from the way people reach it, to take it out of its historical context and raise it to the level of an independent causal factor in its own right, means that the supposedly impartial investigator succumbs to the justifications that ruling groups generally offer for their most brutal conduct. That, I fear, is exactly what a great deal of academic social science does today.'[4] These remarks are particularly relevant when we find 'tradition' cited to explain the behaviour of the Pol Pot group.

Nevertheless this interpretation remains popular. It appeals to the common belief that 'nations' are 'natural' political communities (based perhaps on race or traditional culture) of great antiquity, yearning for political expression. But it ignores the fact that in pre-modern Europe and elsewhere, 'nations' did not exist in the contemporary sense at all. Affairs of the state were the exclusive preserve of a ruling aristocracy and the mass of the common people were wholly excluded from 'the political community'. They were subjects rather than citizens. It was only with the onset of those sweeping changes loosely summed up as 'modernization' that a belief in the principle of nationality took root in Europe. As Hans Kohn puts it: 'Modern nationalism originated in the seventeenth and eighteenth centuries in north-west Europe and its American settlements . . . . It became a general European movement in the nineteenth century.'[5] And, in the twentieth century, it has spread to the non-European world, largely as a result of the disruption of traditional systems of political domination by European expansion.

Nations are political communities created historically by successful nationalist movements. There are two basic elements in the process. The first is the creation of a modern state - a sovereign power with a centralized bureaucracy, uniform and impersonal laws, and a monopoly over the legitimate use of force, ruling a territory and population strictly defined in law. The second element is the incorporation of the lower classes into this system of political domination. This is facilitated by a common language and culture (which may or may not be associated with common racial features). But these ingredients are neither necessary nor sufficient. We should also add that nationalist changes can be brought about 'from above', as rulers adapt and reform existing states, or 'from below', as revolutionary forces mobilize the population behind their struggle to create a new state.

Nationalism arises therefore, not from traditionalism but from its breakdown. Arguments and interpretation based on 'antiquity of nations' merely pander to the mythology of modern nationalism, the mythologies by which the rulers of nation-states seek to gain legitimacy and mobilize popular support. There are thus no such things as 'true nationalism' and 'false nationalism', though they are favourite rhetorical devices among political propagandists of all sides. There are just many conflicting varieties of nationalism, some of which emerge victorious, and some of which prove unsuccessful.

Triumphant nationalists, as a rule, like to see history written in terms that show the justice and the inevitability of their victory, and the correctness of their political line: in short, successful nationalism uses history as a legitimating myth. Unfortunately, much contemporary scholarship is devoted to elaborating the mythology rather than analysing the anatomy of nationalist politics. Nevertheless, the Indochinese present is conditioned by the past, and an awareness of the historical background is essential to an unravelling of the tangled web of events since 1975.

At the core of the explanation of the Vietnam-Cambodia war in terms of 'historical animosities' is the assumption that the conflicts of the post-colonial era are a resumption of the rivalries of the traditional states of pre-modern Indochina. There is no doubt that the ancient 'Indianized' states of Angkor (ancient Cambodia), Champa (in what is now South Vietnam) and Lane Xang (in what is now Laos) were the main casualties of these conflicts. Nor is there any reason to dispute that the 'Confucian' Vietnamese state was one of the most successful participants in these conflicts. This success reflected the superior ability of Vietnam's centralized bureaucratic state to mobilize resources, compared to the 'Indianized' states, where political authority was, in Max Weber's terminology, 'patrimonial' rather than bureaucratic. Although legitimized by custom and religion (Therevada Buddhism), authority was exercised by dignitaries who depended for their position wholly on the personal favour of an autocratic king.

The most visible sign of the success of the Vietnamese state was the great 'march to the south', begun in the fifteenth century. This movement was a result of a combination of peasant migration precipitated by population pressures in the heartland of Vietnamese civilization, the Red River Delta, and the superior strength of the Confucian state. By the seventeenth century the Vietnamese had destroyed the kingdom of Champa, and Vietnamese settlers were moving into the Mekong Delta, at that time a thinly populated area of the Cambodian empire. This historic process has given rise to the image of the Vietnamese as an inherently expansionist people, yet it can be more readily understood in terms of demographic pressure within an agricultural society with a basically stagnant technology and a state more powerful than its neighbours. There is no need to invoke mystical racial characteristics or cultural imperatives.

Given current ideological requirements, many commentators have neglected to mention that the counterpoint to the growth of Vietnamese power in the east was the rise of the new Therevada Buddhist kingdom of Thailand in the west. Although Champa lost out principally to the Vietnamese, both Angkor and Lane Xang lost more territory to the Thais than to the Vietnamese. Thus, when it produced a white paper on Thai-Cambodian relations in September 1983, the Heng Samrin government was able to produce a chronicle of 'expansionist acts' by the Thais that is every bit as impressive as that produced by Pol Pot to indict the Vietnamese. And, in our view, it is every bit as irrelevant to the present conflict.

It should also be noted that throughout these centuries, subjected as they have been to pressure from both sides, rulers in Cambodia (and Laos) have pragmatically sought support from either side according to how they have calculated their own interests. In the light of these shifting alliances, attempts to claim that traditional alignments created 'natural enemies' (or natural allies) in the region do not stand serious examination. The most important development shaping modern Indochina has been the experience of European colonialism, rather than the pre-colonial heritage. It was French rule that brought Vietnam, Laos and Cambodia together as one political unit – the Indochina Federation was without precedent in the traditional political institutions of the region.

It also brought about a major transformation of society in Indochina. The most fundamental change was the commercialization of agriculture: under French rule the Mekong Delta became a major exporter of rice. French capital also poured in to establish plantations, mines and railways. From the statistics that are available, it seems clear that economic development accelerated under the

French; but it was a very lopsided process, and its benefits were distributed very unevenly. Few, if any, filtered down to the ordinary people – Vietnamese peasants and coolie labourers were among the poorest in all Asia – but a commercial middle class grew up in the main towns, especially Saigon. A numerically small working class, centred on the towns, the plantations and the mines, also emerged.[7]

The impact of French colonialism was extraordinarily uneven. Development was concentrated in Vietnam, where it wrought immense changes, whereas the traditional social and political structure of Cambodia remained basically intact, and Laos was left to stagnate as a backwater of the Federation staffed by no more than a hundred French officials (there were tens of thousands in Vietnam).

French colonialism destroyed the traditional Confucian system of rule in Vietnam. Although the Confucian examination system was allowed to linger on until 1919 as an alternative route into the bureaucracy, the French quickly introduced their own Western-style education system to train Vietnamese officials. It need hardly be added that they were assigned to lowly tasks, under the watchful eyes of their French superiors.

Both Cambodia and Laos had been acquired by the French for primarily strategic reasons. They were to serve as a buffer, protecting the more valuable coastal provinces of French Indochina from hostile powers. The French were also competing with the British for a southern route to China, which they hoped control of the Mekong valley would provide. Inevitably, it brought them into conflict with the Thais, outraged by their loss of influence in Cambodia and Laos, and distressed by the success of the French in rolling back the territorial gains Thailand had made in happier times. But the Thai king was also hard pressed by the British in the west, and it took all his skill to juggle the British against the French to avoid an outright annexation of his kingdom. As a result of his successes, Thailand lost territory to both the British and the French but came through the colonial era as an independent state – the only country in the region to do so.

In Cambodia the traditional social and political structure was still largely intact in 1945. Private titles to land were established, but French commercial penetration was limited; some rubber plantations had been established in the east of the country, but the French preferred to work them with Vietnamese coolie labour. Since the French used Vietnamese to staff their colonial bureaucracy, they did little to provide the Khmers with a Western-style education. As a result, unlike Vietnam, there was virtually no indigenous intelligentsia or working class. Also in contrast to Vietnam, the traditional monarch survived as a focus of national politics, under the watchful eyes of the French protectorate.

French rule disrupted life even less in Laos than it did in Cambodia. Since the break-up of Lane Xang, Laos had really been a confederation of small principalities, with regionally based aristocratic families wielding political power. The king, based in the royal capital of Luang Prabang, exercised little real power; symptomatically, the French established their administrative capital elsewhere, in Vientiane. Peasant life was barely touched. Only the merest handful of Lao aristocrats were given any education by the French. The principal headache of the French in colonial Laos was fractious hill tribes who resented French attempts to bring them under the control of lowland authorities. In Laos as in Cambodia, the hallmark of French rule was stagnation rather than modernization.

French rule also brought an end to Chinese hegemony over the states of Indochina. In the face of French annexations, Tu Duc, the last traditional ruler of Vietnam (more strictly, of its surviving northern rump, Tonkin) had turned increasingly to the Chinese for support. But when, in keeping with long-established precedent, he sent a formal mission of tribute to Peking in 1880, the French seized on this as an intolerable act of defiance and used it as their excuse for the conquest of Tonkin. In 1885 the French forced the Vietnamese to ceremonially melt down the seal of investiture granted by the Chinese emperors to the rulers of Vietnam. The Chinese invaded in protest, but were quickly defeated, and in 1885 signed a treaty with the French by which they formally renounced suzerainty over Vietnam. This was a dramatic instance of the general process by which European imperialism shattered the traditional Sino-centric pattern of relations between states in South-east Asia.

It was also as a result of the assertion of French power that the borders of Indochina were for the first time given precise legal demarcation. The borders of Laos and Cambodia with Thailand were determined in various treaties between the French and the Thais from 1867 to 1925. The borders between China and Vietnam and Laos were laid down in Sino-French negotiations in the 1880s and 1890s. On the other hand, the boundaries between Laos, Vietnam and Cambodia were decided simply as internal administrative divisions within French Indochina, and they were adjusted on several occasions for official convenience; only after World War II were they accorded the status of international borders. As a result of the colonial experience, therefore, the Indochinese countries found themselves with borders to whose determination none of them had been a party. This was to prove an explosive legacy in the era of victorious nationalism.

Vietnam: Anatomy of Nationalist Revolution

Modern nationalism emerged in the Indochinese countries as a response to colonial rule. The earliest and the strongest movement emerged in Vietnam. There was already in Vietnam that loose sense of national identity that could be termed proto-nationalism: and it was here that the transforming impact of colonialism was greatest. The basic anatomy of modern nationalism can be seen most clearly in Vietnam.[8]

Vietnamese resistance to French rule went through several distinct stages of evolution. With some variations, a similar pattern can be found in many colonial nationalist movements. Opposition began immediately after conquest, as a movement of traditionalist royalism. Members of the old ruling class felt the immediate impact of French conquest most fully, for it was they and not the common people who experienced political dispossession. Many of them sought salvation through a restoration of the full power of the Vietnamese throne, a vigorous reassertion of traditional Confucian values, and the expulsion of disruptive foreign influences. From the 1860s onwards, local Mandarins organized military resistance to the French in many parts of the country. At times they succeeded in tying up tens of thousands of French troops, but by 1895 the movement had basically been beaten.

The second phase was one of Westernization. As early as the 1870s, some members of the Vietnamese upper class were consciously rejecting the Confucian tradition in favour of Western culture. This trend was strengthened by the defeat of the traditionalists, which seemed to prove conclusively the practical superiority of European civilization, and by the growth of a semi-Westernized merchant class in the port-towns. Educated Vietnamese drank deeply of Western culture, looked to Western political models for the future of their own country and, at least prior to 1914, submitted to Western tutelage. Those who sought reforms couched their demands in moderate and respectful terms, and accepted the timetable decided on by the French.

This phase ended with World War I. Within Europe and beyond it, World War I shattered beyond repair the unquestioning confidence in the superiority of European civilization that had provided the intellectual and emotional underpinning of imperialism. After the war, the colonial reformers turned in more radical directions. In Vietnam, fewer and fewer were willing to follow French timetables.

Vietnamese opposition to French rule entered its third phase with the birth of modern nationalist movements after World War I. These were at first narrowly based, drawing their support from the urban, educated classes, and they were profoundly influenced by events outside Vietnam – not only the First World War, but also the Chinese (1910) and Russian (1917) revolutions. The Russian revolution, in particular, seemed to offer a way forward to those who wished for the benefits of modernization but opposed Western imperialism. By the 1930s the two main groups contending for the leadership of the Vietnamese nationalist movement were the Vietnam Quoc Dan Dang (VNQDD), which modelled itself on Jiang Kaishek's Guomindang in China, and the Indochinese Communist Party (ICP), which was led by Ho Chi Minh and looked to the Soviet Union for its political model.

This third stage can be termed that of 'elite nationalism'. Subjection to alien rule had implanted the idea that the Vietnamese were one people, a nation with a common past and a common destiny – and that it should take this destiny into its own hands, against French resistance if need be. But this idea remained restricted for the time being to the better-off classes. In terms of their social backgrounds, there was little to choose between the leaderships of the Communists and the anti-Communist nationalists. Both drew heavily on the children of middle- and lower-ranking Confucian officials, educated and Westernized by the French, and usually employed as minor civil servants or school teachers until they became professional political agitators. The social gulf between them and the peasant majority remained vast, and their mass following minimal.

Attempts by these elite groups to pressure the French into granting independence by means of propaganda and persuasion failed dismally, and by the end of the 1920s many of their members were in prison. When persuasion failed, the nationalists tried force, the VNQDD in particular proving adept at terrorist tactics. But while the nationalist groups were small and politically isolated they could be dealt with effectively by police repression. Vietnamese elite nationalism, even when it took a violent turn, presented no serious immediate threat to French rule in Indochina.

Given the evident intransigence of the French, the only way the nationalists could defeat them was by rallying wide popular support. Here again, European experience provided the model for those out to overthrow European rule. The nineteenth and early twentieth centuries in Europe witnessed the emergence of mass political movements and the democratization of political life. Whereas previously the only opinions that had counted in politics were those of various groups in the ruling classes, now the views and interests of the common people – the peasants, the working class and the middle classes – had to be taken into account as well. Liberal democracy, Communism and Fascism all emerged in Europe as different responses to this entry of the common people onto the political stage. And despite their divergences, they all seemed to point to one fact of central importance – success in the new arena of mass politics depended on building an effective party organization propagating an ideology with popular appeal. The era of mass politics has been one of party-politics and ideology, and this has proved as true in the colonies as in Europe itself.

Thus the fourth stage in the development of nationalism in Vietnam was the transition from elite nationalism to 'mass nationalism'. It was a stage of party-building and popular mobilization against colonial rule, which took place in the 1930s and 1940s against the background of the Great Depression and the Second World War. It also witnessed the development of a struggle between the Communists and the non-Communists for the loyalties of the common people.

The anti-Communists won a sizeable following among the mercantile classes in the port-towns, particularly Saigon, and among the commercial landlords who dominated the rural economy of Cochin China, closely interconnected as they were with mercantile interests in Saigon. While they succeeded in attracting many prominent Vietnamese into their ranks, the anti-Communists remained essentially a conservative party of the well-to-do minority. Their great failure was that they made little effort to win the support of the peasantry, the largest class in Vietnamese society. It is not unreasonable to describe these groups as 'bourgeois nationalists'.

If their social base was narrow, they also lacked a coherent ideology and the organizational discipline necessary for success in modern mass politics. The political ideas of the bourgeois nationalists ranged from liberal democracy to overt Fascism. Most wanted the French to go, or at least to hand over power to them, but beyond that they basically wanted to change the status quo as little as possible. Even their anti-French stance underwent revision as conflict with the Communists intensified, and by the 1950s many of them were looking to the French for protection from the Communists, while the French found them a congenially moderate alternative to Communism. But this *rapprochement* with the French in the middle of the war of independence only served to weaken further the already dubious patriotic credentials of the bourgeois nationalists. They also suffered from chronic factionalism, and were unable to establish a stable political organization that could sink enduring roots. In many ways, they simply did not progress beyond the amateurish politics of the elite nationalism of the 1920s.

Their Communist rivals, on the other hand, did make this transition. They succeeded in building and maintaining a disciplined organizational structure of cells and branches, which effectively linked the rank-and-file members in villages and factories to the national party leadership. They also possessed the advantage of having a leader of outstanding personal capabilities, Ho Chi Minh. And unlike the traditional Confucian state, to which it is sometimes compared, Communist organization penetrated deep into the lowest levels of the social structure. The Communists were also notable in the ruthlessness with which they dealt with rivals and opponents. In the state to which this movement gave eventual birth, a highly centralized government would be linked to a strong grass roots organization by a tightly disciplined party apparatus.

The Communists had considerable success in mobilizing working-class support. But, in terms of its social composition, the Indochinese Communist Party was hardly the 'party of the proletariat' it claimed to be. The industrial working class was still very much a minority group in Vietnamese society: and the Communists achieved their key success where the bourgeois nationalists failed, in the countryside. By exploiting agrarian grievances – landlordism, usurious money-lenders, corruption and the abuse of power by local officials – they succeeded in gaining a following among the peasants in many areas of the Vietnamese countryside: while in many others they were, if not supported, at least feared and respected. While the urban working class did play some role, the Communist revolution in Vietnam was basically a peasant uprising organized by intellectuals from a middle-class (and even aristocratic) background.

In the early 1930s the Communist movement was ravaged by police repression, and it was their leading role in the resistance to the Japanese occupation of Indochina during World War II that brought the Communists to the forefront of the nationalist movement. A similar pattern can be detected in a number of European countries that underwent Fascist occupation, with the result that this was the period of fastest growth in the history of the international Communist movement. In May 1941, the ICP formed the 'Vietnam Doc Lap Dong Minh' (League for the Independence of Vietnam), better known as the Viet Minh, whose objective was Vietnamese independence, and launched an armed struggle against the Japanese – in other words, it was aiming at the expulsion of the French as well as the Japanese. As the most effective anti-Japanese force in Indochina during World War II, the Viet Minh managed to attract the support not only of many Vietnamese nationalists, but also of Free French forces and even the American OSS, who at one point provided Ho Chi Minh's forces with weapons.[9]

When the Japanese surrendered in August 1945 the Viet Minh seized power in Hanoi and proclaimed the Democratic Republic of Vietnam (DRV). The puppet emperor retained by the French, Bao Dai, agreed to abdicate in favour of the DRV. The French, however, were unwilling to accept the loss of Indochina. They returned in force in 1946, and the First Indochina war began. The French aimed at securing all of Indochina, and tried to rally anti-Communist forces in Cambodia and Laos as well as Vietnam to their cause. The war between the French and the Viet Minh thus ranged through all of Indochina until the French defeat at Dien Bien Phu in May 1954.

The French had been by no means alone in their struggle against the Communist-led nationalist movement in Indochina. While there were many Vietnamese who supported the Viet Minh, there were many others who were mortally afraid of them. Thus the remaining traditional monarchists, many bourgeois nationalists and most Catholics rallied to the French-sponsored Bao Dai government. The 'war of national liberation' between the Viet Minh and the French was also, to a significant degree, a civil war between left-wing and right-wing Vietnamese; and when the French left Indochina that conflict had not been resolved.

The French had another ally in the United States of America. Alarmed at the spread of Communist influence in Asia, the USA had early turned against the Viet Minh. Immediately after the outbreak of the war in Korea in 1958, it began providing large-scale military assistance to the French forces in Indochina, and from then until 1954 the US treasury paid 80 per cent of the cost of France's war in Indochina.

The battle of Dien Bien Phu took place on the eve of a major international conference at Geneva to settle the Indochina and Korean crisis. All the major powers, including the USA and Communist China, attended. The Viet Minh delegation, led by Pham Van Dong, was eager to taste the fruits of victory, but was persuaded to accept a compromise by their Russian and Chinese allies. Instead of the authority of the DRV being accepted throughout the whole of Vietnam, the Viet Minh accepted the 17th parallel as a temporary demarcation line, Viet Minh forces regrouping to the north and pro-French forces to the south. Elections were to be held within two years to decide the future of the country. But the elections were never held; the reunification of Vietnam was delayed twenty years, and only achieved by war.

The Second Indochina War

The origins and nature of this Second Indochina War are often misunderstood.[10] It was certainly not, as the US government claimed in the 1960s, an external attack by Communist forces on the 'independent state of South Vietnam' established at the Geneva Conference, for no such state was established at Geneva. Although they had withdrawn their military forces to the north of the 17th parallel, the Viet Minh had been a genuinely nation-wide movement, and many of their civilian cadres and supporters had remained behind in the south.

Nor was it simply a popular uprising against an unrepresentative and repressive government in South Vietnam, as many liberal critics of the Americans argued. The insurgency in the south was not autonomous, but fully supported by the Communist north. In reality, the war was a struggle between the two streams of nationalism that had developed in Vietnam under the French – bourgeois nationalism centred on Saigon, and the mass nationalism of the Viet Minh, which had created the regime in Hanoi.

From 1954 to 1959 the leadership in Hanoi had looked to peaceful methods of reunification, but these were spurned by the government in Saigon. This led to some tension with the Communist cadres in the south, who were faced with a mounting campaign of repression by the Saigon regime and wanted to go over to a policy of armed opposition. In 1959, the Hanoi leadership decided to back armed struggle in the south. At the 3rd National Congress of the Vietnam Workers' Party – the name then being used by the Communist Party – in 1960, a number of southern cadres were promoted to leading positions. Among them was Le Duan, who had been pushing the southerners' case for a change of tactics since 1957. He was elected to the crucial position of general secretary of the party.

The National Liberation Front of South Vietnam, was formed in December 1960 to lead the struggle. A popular front organisation modelled on the Viet Minh, it became popularly known to Western readers as the Viet Cong. From that point on the fighting in the south escalated rapidly into full-scale war.

The creation of a separate state in the south was primarily an American strategy to prevent the Communists from consolidating the gains they had won on the battlefield at Dien Bien Phu and at the negotiating table at Geneva. Recognizing that Bao Dai was a discredited figure, the Americans threw their weight behind his last prime minister, Ngo Dinh Diem. A conservative Catholic of Confucian background, he was an elitist of strongly authoritarian convictions. He disliked the disorder of liberal democracy and rejected in principle the idea of government based on 'mere numbers'. 'Society,' he told Bernard Fall, 'functions through personal relations among men at the top.'[11] This was not the man to successfully lead bourgeois nationalism into the era of mass politics.

At first, Diem had surprising success. In the first two years of his rule, he succeeded in breaking the power of the Cao Dai and Hoa Hao sects, which controlled much of Saigon and the southern countryside. Then he turned to the more difficult task of eradicating the Viet Minh infrastructure. In doing this he relied on straightforward police-state methods, for which he was roundly criticized by Western liberals. But Diem's real problem was not his reliance on dictatorial methods – the Vietnamese Communists were not squeamish about the methods they used – but the fact that his dictatorship had a precariously narrow base of support. It was a dictatorship of Catholics, many of them pro-French refugees from the north, over a predominantly Buddhist population. Even within the Catholic community, all effective power lay within one family clique. Even more importantly, it began as and remained an urban-based regime, closely tied to commercial interests in Saigon: as time went on, and much of the southern countryside effectively passed into the hands of the NLF, it became more and more dependent on external economic, political and military support.

The Americans were caught in an insurmountable dilemma in Vietnam in the early 1960s. Their presence in the country was already more blatant than the French presence had ever been, and Communist propaganda was tellingly exploiting this to depict Diem as a 'puppet' of American imperialism. To deepen their involvement would be to further undercut the credentials of the 'nationalist alternative' to Communism. But when they gave Diem his head, he pursued policies based on such narrow interests that he actively alienated support and drove people into the Communist camp. After a wave of Buddhist demonstrations against his regime, Diem was murdered in a military coup in 1963. But the subsequent military regimes in Saigon were never able to overcome the heritage bequeathed by Diem.

The rapid deterioration of the military situation in South Vietnam after Diem's death led to an escalation of the American involvement. This wrought immense destruction in both North and South Vietnam, but it did nothing to solve the fundamental political problems of the Saigon regime and in key ways it compounded them. Massive reliance on the USA undermined its nationalist credibility, and the torrent of dollars led to spreading corruption that sapped the morale of government supporters. The rise of the 'PX millionaires', as one-time President Nguyen Cao Ky called them, made the war into a blatantly self-serving enterprise for the wealthy in Saigon. The result was that many people who loathed the Communists were simply unwilling to fight for the southern regime when it came to the crunch.

And, of course, the crunch did come, in the early 1970s. The illusion that American military power would smash the Communists and lead to a quick and easy victory was shattered by the Tet offensive in 1968. [12] After that, the Americans began to negotiate seriously for a withdrawal: having undermined the nationalist credentials of their Vietnamese allies by massive intervention, they now gambled everything on 'Vietnamization' of the war. The American presence was scaled down progressively, and a complete withdrawal of their forces was negotiated in 1973 – an agreement hailed as 'peace with honour' in Washington and 'treachery' in Saigon. Once the Americans were out, the ceasefire in South Vietnam collapsed almost immediately, and in early 1975 the whole political-military structure of the Saigon regime unravelled with such speed and completeness that even the Communists were taken by surprise. Essentially, the bourgeois nationalists of Saigon had never been able to progress beyond the elite politics of the 1920s. In 1975 they were finally overwhelmed by the mass nationalism forged by the Viet Minh in the 1940s.

Cambodia: the Roots of Warrior-Communism

In Vietnam, the development of a modern nationalist movement in response to colonialism can be seen in relatively 'pure' form. It took place over a lengthy period of time and, though overlapping to some extent, the different phases stand out as chronologically distinct. In Cambodia and Laos, the impact of colonialism was milder, and modern nationalism developed more slowly. When it did develop it was strongly influenced by events in Vietnam, and the different phases of the process were 'telescoped' together in a confusing fashion.

In Cambodia, the French were content to declare a protectorate over the throne, set up a skeletal colonial administration, and thereafter to leave the country relatively undisturbed. It was not until the late 1930s that the first stirrings of nationalism were felt in Cambodia. At that point the country's political life was still centred in the royal family, and consisted almost exclusively of court intrigue in Phnom Penh. Given the close relations between the monarchy and the French, the first nationalists were of necessity also anti-monarchist. But they had little support. When the Japanese decided to install a nationalist, Son Ngoc Thanh, in power in Phnom Penh, the youthful King Norodom Sihanouk was easily able to depose him, with the help of the returning French. Sihanouk asserted that, contrary to Thanh's hope, the Cambodian people were not ready for independence.

As the war between the Viet Minh and the French intensified, the turmoil inevitably spread to the Cambodian provinces of Indo-china. Through Sihanouk the French recruited Khmers to fight against the Viet Minh; and the Viet Minh encouraged anti-French nationalists in Cambodia. Soon groups of Khmers Issaraks ('Independent Khmers') emerged, and were waging guerrilla war-fare against the French and Sihanouk. One wing of the Issarak movement, led by Son Ngoc Minh, remained strongly pro-Viet Minh, but the other, led by Son Ngoc Thanh, turned increasingly against the Viet Minh as well as Sihanouk. At first the Issarak groups were small and easily contained. But as the military situation turned in favour of the Viet Minh, their Issarak allies grew rapidly and became a serious threat to Sihanouk's position. By the early 1950s they probably had more than 5,000 men under arms and, with Viet Minh backing, controlled large areas of the countryside.

Sihanouk then made a dramatic reversal to distance himself from the falling star of French power and to cut the ground out from under his nationalist opponents. Although earlier an opponent of Cambodian independence, in 1953 he launched himself as the champion of a 'Crusade for Independence'. After some hesitation, the French decided that he was a more congenial prospect than the

Issaraks, and hastened to grant independence to his government. Fighting continued in Cambodia thereafter, but in 1954 the Geneva Conference recognized Sihanouk's government. The Issaraks received no recognition.

Sihanouk thus emerged as the man who had won Cambodian independence from the French, and (in contrast to Bao Dai in Vietnam) he succeeded in focusing emergent nationalism on the throne and the traditional political system. Following Geneva, Sihanouk proceeded to deck out his traditionalist monarchy with the trappings of mass nationalism, and he re-established an effective monopoly over Cambodian political life. Although he formally abdicated from the throne, formed his own political party, Sangkum, and began to issue nebulous rhetoric about 'royal socialism' and the 'people's community' his rule was still grounded on traditional values. He was still revered as a sacred figure and, not surprisingly, he concentrated on maintaining the traditional political role of Therevada Buddhism rather than building up an effective bureaucratic state apparatus. Personal loyalty to the ruler was the paramount consideration, and Sihanouk's secret police dealt swiftly with anything he took as an 'insult' to his royal person.

The continuity of traditional monarchic political and religious institutions linked pre- and post-colonial Cambodia, and after the departure of the French Sihanouk interpreted regional politics in terms of the rivalries between the old kingdoms. He pointed to the contrast between the glories of Angkor and the sad state into which Cambodia had fallen in modern times. This he explained, not in terms of the socio-economic or political weaknesses of the Khmer Empire, but in terms of its geographic position and the evil designs of its enemies. As proof of this analysis, he took border disputes with both Thailand and South Vietnam.

Immediately after the Geneva Conference, Sihanouk had flirted with the idea of aligning himself with the West. But this effectively meant joining the Southeast Asia Treaty Organisation (SEATO). He feared that this would mean the subordination of Cambodia to its more powerful anti-Communist neighbours with (as he saw it) designs on Cambodian territory – South Vietnam and Thailand. The USA was willing to defend Cambodia's territorial integrity against Communist forces but not against right-wing regimes. On the other hand, Sihanouk found that the Communist bloc was willing to give him unequivocal assurances on this point, Communist China in particular coming to the support of his government. Sihanouk therefore opted for a policy of neutralism, and found that while the USA was not willing to tolerate such a policy, especially in the light of its growing commitment to South Vietnam, it was positively welcomed by the Communist countries. Sihanouk thus found himself pushed in a 'pro-Communist' direction in his foreign policy, although he feared and detested Communism.

Combined with the populist trappings he adopted, this had led to much confusion about the basic nature of Sihanouk's regime. Sihanouk's main purpose was to perpetuate the monarchy that had ruled his country for centuries, and the ideological and socio-economic forces that sustained it. Aware of the dangers of backwardness, he developed a modern educational system, and sought foreign aid to foster urbanization and the growth of commerce. This barely touched the rural sector, which remained one of the most backward in all Southeast Asia, but it did lead to the growth of the middle class in Phnom Penh, and the emergence of modernizing nationalist groups, which soon split into left and right.

Analysis of Cambodian politics has been hopelessly confused by the widespread notion that Sihanouk was (and still is) a 'charismatic' figure.[13] This is nonsense: the basis of his popular support was not personal magnetism but the strength of royal institutions in a strongly traditionalist Therevada Buddhist society. Sihanouk clung to the ideal of the benevolent despot worshipped by the peasants (who he liked to refer to as 'my little people'). Bureaucrats, businessmen, generals and politicians always filled him with suspicion; they represented 'vested interests', not 'the people'. Their existence was tolerated, as a rule, but Sihanouk took every opportunity to restrict their influence in Cambodian politics.

To see Sihanouk's rule in perspective, it may be useful to compare it with the reign of King Chulalongkorn in Thailand (1868-1910). Chulalongkorn was basically successful in carrying through a 'revolution from above'. He transformed a traditional patrimonial regime, essentially similar to Sihanouk's, into a centralized bureaucratic state, taking the British colonial administration in Burma as his model. Of course, this transformation was by no means total, and even today the Thai bureaucracy is riddled with networks of patronage rooted in the traditional pattern – but this should not obscure the central reality of the transformation he brought about.

Chulalongkorn also actively promoted commerce and capitalist development within his kingdom. Ultimately, the modernization of state and society in Thailand proved incompatible with the patrimonial regime that initiated it. The autocratic power of the monarchy was destroyed in the revolution of 1932. This gave military, bureaucratic and business groups in Bangkok a strong voice in the government, while the monarchy, with vastly diminished powers, was retained to integrate the traditionalist peasantry into the new political system. This arrangement proved durable enough to survive all the subsequent political upheavals in the region.

But Sihanouk did not bring about any comparable 'revolution from above' in Cambodia. After 1954 he continued to deal with the new bourgeois politicians in Phnom Penh in the way absolute kings usually deal with court intrigue – by a judicious combination of patronage, manipulation, espionage and repression. At first he favoured the right, and persecuted the left; then, in 1963, when he thought that the right was growing strong, he turned to the left; and then in 1966, just when the left appeared to be consolidating its position, he dropped it to reinstate the right once more. The result was that attempts to promote both capitalist and socialist modern-ization were enveloped in a system of royal patronage, favour-swapping and increasingly blatant corruption, and came to nil. The social and political frustrations of the would-be modernizing elites were concealed beneath the veneer of obligatory king-worship, and thick layers of tourist-brochure cliches about the 'kingdom of smiles' from romantic Western observers. The world was therefore quite unprepared for the ferocity with which these frustrations finally erupted after the Sihanoukist system collapsed in 1970.

In a sense, Lon Nol's coup of March 1970 was analogous with the 1932 revolution in Thailand. But Cambodia had not passed through the equivalent of Chulalongkorn's 'enlightened despotism'. The weakness of both state and bourgeoisie meant that the outcome would be very different.

In the end, Sihanouk's position was undermined by the escalation of the war in Vietnam, rather than by indigenous social forces. One of his main concerns in the 1960s, amply justified by what happened in the 1970s, was to keep his country out of the war. To this end, Sihanouk had been willing to turn a blind eye to the Communist infiltration of troops and supplies into South Vietnam via the 'Ho Chi Minh trail' through the forests of Laos and eastern Cambodia, provided that the Vietnamese kept away from populated regions. He also allowed them to purchase rice supplies in Cambodia. Sihanouk was also willing to turn a blind eye when the Americans began secretly bombing Vietnamese forces in eastern Cambodia in 1969, but publicly protested when they began bombing Khmer villages as well.

However, this de-stabilized Sihanouk's government internally.

In 1966, the right had been returned to office in Cambodia, and they were thoroughly alarmed by what they saw as Sihanouk's pro-Communist and pro-Vietnamese foreign policy. Then when American bombing of their border sanctuaries pushed the Vietnamese deeper into Cambodia in 1969, the right was panic-stricken, and Lon Nol and Sirik Matik organized the coup of March 1970.

Sihanouk's fall reflected the tensions among elite groups in Phnom Penh rather than an upsurge of popular discontent. Greeted with general enthusiasm by the well-to-do in Phnom Penh, it caused consternation in the provinces. Traditional loyalty to the monarchy remained strong in rural Cambodia in 1970, and where it had broken down the peasants had turned to alternatives more radical than those offered by the group of men who had seized power in Phnom Penh. When Sihanouk, furious at his 'betrayal' by Lon Nol and Sirik Matik, joined with the left to form the National United Front of Kampuchea (NUFK), the fate of the Lon Nol regime was, in effect, sealed. It was faced with a war between town and countryside in an overwhelmingly rural society.

Sihanouk was soon to find that the Khmers Rouges were not as easy to manipulate as the old Phnom Penh left had been. The Khmer Rouge leaders welcomed Sihanouk's followers into the ranks of the NUFK, but they kept Sihanouk out of the country as head of a 'government in exile' in Peking, and progressively stripped him of his political influence inside Cambodia. By 1974-5, Pol Pot was organizing purges of active Sihanoukists from the ranks of the NUFK. Between them, Lon Nol and Pol Pot smashed the institutional structure of the traditional monarchy and wiped out many of its key personnel. Stripped of power, Sihanouk lost his divine status and much of his popular support as well.[14]

As soon as he seized power in 1970 Lon Nol had attempted to drive the Vietnamese Communists out of their Cambodian sanctuaries. They responded by inflicting a series of devastating defeats on his ill-prepared army, from which it never recovered.

As in the First Indochina War, the policy of the Vietnamese Communists in the areas they occupied in Cambodia was to keep a low profile, to encourage and arm local insurgents, and to withdraw when these groups appeared capable of standing on their own. In 1970-71, much of the main-force fighting against Lon Nol's army was carried out by the Vietnamese, but from 1972 it was mainly in the hands of the Khmers Rouges. The Vietnamese happily assumed that because of their shared 'anti-imperialist' objectives and the 'fraternal bonds' between Communists in Vietnam and Communists in Cambodia, there would be no serious conflict between their interests and those of the national liberation movement they were encouraging in Cambodia.

The Lon Nol government started out badly, and rapidly went on to worse. Within a matter of months it controlled only enclaves around Phnom Penh and the provincial capitals, and along the main roads linking these enclaves. By 1972 it was already clear that the government was doomed unless major changes took place. But the Americans clung desperately to Lon Nol and the overthrow of the regime in 1973 was only averted by American saturation bombing of Khmer Rouge forces closing in on Phnom Penh. However, with USA disengagement from Indochina from 1973, aid to the Phnom Penh regime was scaled down in 1974. The regime collapsed in April 1975, even before Saigon fell. Then the NUFK came to power in Phnom Penh with Sihanouk as nominal head of state and real power lying in the hands of the Khmer Rouge leaders.

In Cambodia, the relatively mild impact of colonialism resulted in the belated development of the nationalist reaction. This, combined with Sihanouk's remarkable political agility, ensured the survival of the traditional monarchy into the post-colonial period. When the monarchical regime collapsed under the pressures generated by the escalation of the war in Vietnam, Cambodia disintegrated from the top downwards. But the peasantry was still deeply traditionalist, and the system was overthrown by elite intrigues rather than a popular upheaval. At the same time, the backwardness of Cambodia virtually ensured that elite nationalism would be a débâcle.

The Khmers Rouges, then, came to power in much the same fashion as the Vietnamese Communists, as a group of radical middle-class intellectuals at the head of a peasant army. But they rose to power from a position of almost complete isolation in little more than five years, against the background of massive disruption caused by the impact of modern warfare on an archaic social and political structure. Unlike the Vietnamese, the Khmer Communists were not able to draw extensively on the intelligentsia and the middle class as well as the peasants for their cadres – the intelligentsia and the middle class were small, and largely rallied to the Lon Nol regime.

Instead, they were obliged to rely almost exclusively on poorly educated peasant soldiers. A sprinkling were veterans of the Issarak struggles of the 1950s, but the great majority were disorientated village youths who had been plunged in a matter of months, or even weeks, from a traditional village society into a savage modern war. In other revolutions, cadres from such a background have often been noted for their crudeness and brutality, unless guided and restrained by more sophisticated leaders. In Cambodia, such leaders were few and far between, and the suddenness and destructiveness of the war amplified the problem. Furthermore, among the Khmer Rouge leaders were some who sought to exploit this reservoir of potential brutality to the hilt for their own ends rather than restrain it. The outcome was that the Cambodian revolution climaxed in the most complete triumph of the peasant-warrior over the modernizing bureaucrat in the history of Communism.

Laos: The Paradox of Extreme Backwardness

For all its backwardness, Cambodia had both a centralized state and a relatively homogeneous population living in an area with a distinct geographical identity as a basis for nationalism. By contrast, in Laos the population consisted of a diversity of ethnic groups scattered across a rugged mountain terrain. Even today, less than half the population are Lao; the majority of the population thus consists of 'national minorities'. The mountainous topography tends to divide Laos into a number of separate geographical (and economic) zones, and internal communications were largely non-existent until recently. On the eve of the French conquest, the royal family in Luang Prabang exercised little real control and effective political power lay in the hands of regionally based aristocratic families. This 'feudal' fragmentation of power in Laos was preserved by the French, and gave rise in due course to the most anarchic of the modern nationalist movements. If in Cambodia, the Khmer race seemed to provide a 'natural' basis for the nation, in Laos the central problem was that the construction of a nation required the integration of the most diverse ethnic groups, and Lao nationalism had to avoid at all costs the xenophobic inflection taken on by Khmer nationalism.

As in Cambodia, the growth of nationalism in Laos stems from 1945, when the Japanese overthrew the French and installed a Lao government. Here, even more than in Cambodia, politics still consisted exclusively of the rivalries between members of aristocratic families. Only a handful of Lao (mostly from the aristocracy) received any higher education, even in the post-independence period, and the middle-class intellectuals who played such an important role in the Vietnamese and Cambodian revolutions were almost non-existent. But Laos too soon found itself a battleground for the French and Viet Minh forces during the First Indochina War. As a consequence, it underwent the whole evolution from a traditionalist royalism to a mass nationalism modelled on the Viet Minh within a single generation. This resulted in a situation where the competing streams of nationalism, primarily royalists and Communists, (bourgeois nationalism being for all practical purposes non-existent in Laos) were all lead by rival members of the royal family. The mystique of royalty in a Therevada Buddhist society, monopolized by Sihanouk in Cambodia, was in Laos shared between different groups, including the Communists. The main problems they confronted did not arise out of the modernization of Lao society – that process lying almost wholly in the future – but out of the traditional dilemma faced by Lao rulers (and other rulers of weak states with more powerful neighbours). The question was whether to turn to Vietnam for support and some kind of political model, or to Thailand, or to opt for a neutralist course of balancing one carefully against the other. But with the Communists gaining control of North Vietnam and Thailand aligned with the United States, these questions turned Laos into a battleground of the cold war.

The first nationalist movement was the Lao Issara ('Free Lao') movement created in August 1945 by the premier of the Japanese-installed government, Prince Phet Sarath, along with his brother, Prince Souvanna Phouma, and their half-brother, Prince Souphannavong. In September, in the wake of the 'August Revolution' in Hanoi, they declared the complete independence of Laos from the French, and placed the king under house arrest when he objected. But the Lao Issara were capable of putting up only scattered resistance when the French returned, and its leaders were soon forced to go into exile in Bangkok. But Souphannavong tried to rebuild his forces, and he soon developed contacts with the Viet Minh.

In 1949, the French granted nominal independence to the royal Lao government. Many of the exiles were satisfied with this, and returned to Vientiane. But Souphannavong and the more radical members of the nationalist movement retreated into the mountains of Laos to continue armed resistance. In August 1950 Souphannavong, along with a number of hill-tribe leaders, such as the Hmong chief Faydang Lobliyao, formed what came to be called the Pathet Lao ('Nation of Laos') to fight for complete independence, and in the following year they formalized their alliance with the Viet Minh.

In Laos, the Geneva Conference provided for a neutralist government under Prince Souvanna Phouma, for regroupment zones for the Pathet Lao forces in Phong Saly and Sam Neua provinces, and for the peaceful reunification of the country along lines similar to that envisaged for Vietnam. The agreement ran into difficulties because of the antipathy between the rightists in the RLG (Royal Lao Government) army, who had fought with the French, and the Pathet Lao, but the general expectation was that, notwithstanding the Pathet Lao, these could be integrated into a national coalition government.

But Laos was by now a battlefield in the cold war. As with South Vietnam and Cambodia, the USA wanted Laos to become part of its anti-Communist SEATO alliance. There were anti-Communists in Laos who wished for the same thing, and the Americans were soon given the opportunity they wanted. Shortly after the formation of SEATO, Souvanna Phouma's defence minister was assassinated, precipitating a cabinet crisis that led to the government's resignation. This was followed by a right-wing government which quickly opened the door to American economic and military aid for the RLG. Under these circumstances, negotiations with the Pathet Lao stalled, and armed clashes between the RLG and Pathet Lao forces became common.

In the teeth of American opposition, Souvanna Phouma returned to power in 1956, committed to a policy of neutralism and reconciliation with the Pathet Lao. After long negotiations he formed a coalition government in 1957. But the USA was adamantly opposed to this coalition, viewing it as a thinly disguised Communist take-over (along the lines of Eastern Europe in the late 1940s). It forced Souvanna Phouma to resign by withholding the economic assistance on which the RLG had become dependent, and by instigating a closure of the Thai border. A new rightist government was formed, but it proved unable to consolidate its position in the face of opposition from the neutralists and the Pathet Lao.

A period of political chaos ensued, ended by a re-convened Geneva Conference in 1961. This bought Souvanna Phouma back as the head of a tripartite coalition. But the USA refused to stop supplying the CIA-funded 'Secret Army' of Hmong leader 'General' Vang Pao, which continued to operate behind Pathet Lao lines. The neutralists split over the issue, the Pathet Lao leaders abandoned

Vietiane, and Souvanna Phouma and the other neutralists who remained in Vietiane became the captives of the right, led by Phoumi Nosovan. From 1963, after teetering on the brink on many occasions, Laos slid into full-scale civil war.

The extreme backwardness of Laos did not provide Phoumi Nosovan with a bourgeois social base enabling him to play the role of a Ngo Dinh Diem, or even a Lon Nol, for Laos. Nor was it possible for the RLG to exploit traditional religious loyalties to the throne in the manner of Sihanouk. Whereas the appeals of sanctified royalty covered the great majority of Cambodians, the political reach of specifically Lao culture hardly extended beyond the lowland population. Over half the population fell outside this cultural universe and were hostile to its encroachments. Such narrowly based nationalism only served to perpetuate the alienation of the hill tribes from the Lao government. Nosovan thus found himself as little more than a local strong-arm man whose power was dependent on external patronage.

The USA threw its weight solidly behind the right-wing controlling the RLG from 1963. Secret bombing of Pathet Lao areas commenced in 1964, and over the next decade, every town, and most villages, in the Pathet Lao-controlled zone was destroyed. But the extreme factionalism and disunity of the rightists meant that the USA took over more and more RLG administrative functions, to the point where the American ambassador was popularly known as the 'second prime minister', and there were many who thought that in reality he was the first prime minister. But this did not transform the RLG into an operational government; it simply undermined its legitimacy, to the point where its own military commanders refused to accept the 'interference' of the central authorities in their regional domains. The RLG thus reproduced the fragmentation of power characteristic of traditional Laos.

Unlike the Lao right, the Pathet Lao had been operating in the mountains since 1949. Since they had no chance of building up a broad movement in this environment unless they transcended narrow tribal loyalties, they appreciated the vital importance of ethnic integration for nation-building in Laos. Since at least 1950 they had been at pains to incorporate a wide spectrum of tribal leaders into their power-structure and in the end this foresight paid off handsomely. While the top leadership of the Pathet Lao was always predominantly lowland ethnic Lao, the majority of their troops were recruited from minority groups. It makes sense to say that the Pathet Lao leaders finally defeated their opponents by forging a Lao national coalition to overwhelm an ethnically Lao government.

This, of course, would be an over-simplification. Naturally, control of tribal groups did not always fall the Pathet Lao's way. The Hmong around the Plain of Jars, under Touby Ly Fong, for example, supported the French and later provided the main recruitment base for Vang Pao's 'Secret Army'. But his traditional Hmong rival, Faydang, became a founder of the Pathet Lao. And the way they incorporated their Hmong followers was a good practical illustration of the differences between the two sides. Vang Pao's followers gave their loyalties to him and the Hmong people; few of them cared less what happened to the RLG. On the other hand, Faydang's followers became members of ethnically mixed Pathet Lao regular units, where much energy was devoted to building up a multi-racial 'national' spirit.

While the Lao right turned to Thailand and the USA for support in the civil war, the Pathet Lao turned to Hanoi and the Communist bloc. The main Pathet Lao base areas were close to the Vietnamese border, and they were given both logistic and political support by the Vietnamese. While they were under the protection of the North Vietnamese army, these bases could never be militarily destroyed by the RLG. The Viet Minh also provided an organizational and ideological model for the Pathet Lao. Since the Vientiane regime had done little to establish a national educational system, many Pathet Lao cadres received their first education in party schools, and if they went on to higher education, they went to Hanoi, Peking or Eastern Europe. Pathet Lao nationalism was thus not bred of the extreme isolation that one might at first expect. It was always tempered by a degree of Communist cosmopolitanism, and never degenerated into the backwoods chauvinism that was soon to emerge in Cambodia.

In one sense, it is impossible to over-state Vietnamese influence on the Pathet Lao; yet, in another sense, this is done all the time. The Pathet Lao modelled itself on the Viet Minh, and accepted Vietnamese assistance, but it was a Lao national movement under the leadership of a member of the Lao royal family. For all its failings, the Pathet Lao administrative apparatus was run by Lao nationals for Lao nationals, which was more than could be said for the RLG. It was never an instrument of Vietnamese 'colonialism' in Laos, as is often alleged. If the Vietnamese had really wanted to colonize Laos, the best way would have been to annex it militarily and administer it directly – most of the population, after all, probably objected to lowland Lao control as much as they would have to lowland Vietnamese control. Instead, the Vietnamese provided support and encouragement, and waited patiently while the Pathet Lao movement got off the ground.

While it took the Pathet Lao many years to build up a fighting force capable of seriously threatening the RLG, it could never topple it as long as the USA was fully committed to the RLG. The outcome of the war in Laos thus depended less on success in the battlefield – although the war was increasingly going the way of the Pathet Lao after 1968 – than on the ability of the Vietnamese to negotiate an American withdrawal from Indochina. As soon as this was achieved, the civil war in Laos came to an end, and as the USA scaled down its assistance the anti-Pathet Lao forces disintegrated.

While international political forces have played a vital role in all three Indochinese countries, this has been especially the case in the weakest of them. The forces of modernization that produced a revolutionary upheaval in Vietnam and a collapse of the traditional political order in Cambodia had hardly been felt in Laos. The civil war that resulted from the collapse of Souvanna Phouma's second coalition government was almost wholly the result of external forces rather than of any internal social and political explosion. The lowland peasantry remained largely indifferent to both sides, and it was the Pathet Lao's ability to mobilize more successfully among the minority groups that was finally decisive.

When a ceasefire was signed in 1973, the Pathet Lao controlled 80 per cent of the countryside. A new coalition was formed under Souvanna Phouma, and in 1974 Souphannavong returned to the capital to take up his government post. From this point on the Pathet Lao steadily assumed control of the government as the right wing disintegrated. Vang Pao's 'Secret Army' continued the war against the Pathet Lao in the countryside, but suffered a major defeat in April 1975. Coinciding with the fall of Phnom Penh and Saigon, this threw the remaining rightists in Vientiane into a panic, and many fled the country. By June, almost the entire wartime RLG leadership had debarked to Thailand. The RLG army, which had still been controlled by the right, disintegrated, and was officially disbanded in June, followed by the complete demise of the RLG in December 1975, when King Savang Vatthana signed a letter of abdication in favour of 'the people's democratic system'.

At Souphannavong's suggestion, both the ex-king and Souvanna

Phouma were appointed as advisers to the government – a conciliatory gesture designed to promote national accord that was in
striking contrast to the policies being pursued in Cambodia. But
then, in Laos the leap into political modernity had been so com-
pressed that the transition from monarchism to Communist mass
nationalism had taken place under the leadership of a member of
the traditional royal family. The unification of the country under
the Pathet Lao was thus in a real sense a family reunion as well.

Nation-building and Communism in Indochina

Liberals in nineteenth-century Europe believed that when oppressed nationalities were freed from foreign domination, and when
the principles of national self-determination were applied throughout the world, sovereign nation-states would live in peace and
harmony. This optimistic vision of international peace has been
badly battered by the bloody torrent of imperialism, chauvinism
and militarism that has so far constituted the international politics
of the twentieth century – so much so that one recent historian of
nationalism has likened it to a fairy-tale in which the Sleeping
Beauty is transformed into Frankenstein's monster.[15] However,
the optimistic vision has lived on in socialist and Communist
theories of international relations. According to Marxist theorists,
the clash of sovereign nation-states is due to the competitiveness
and the imperialism of capitalism. It is a product of the self-interest
of ruling classes, not of the working classes. When socialism re-
places capitalism, therefore, the promise of international harmony
will be realized.[16] In Indochina, the promised day arrived in 1975.

Ultimately, this view rests on the premiss that states are essentially instruments of class rule. It neglects the extent to which state
power is actually used to create political communities, and to
defend them against external attack, irrespective of the class nature
of the state. We have argued here that nationalism is essentially a
movement for the creation of a modern state based on such a
community. It aspires to a government based on notions of popular
sovereignty rather than authority sanctified by time and tradition,
or divine will.

Looked at from one angle, nationalism is an empty rhetorical
vessel, given a concrete social and political content by the successful
nationalists themselves. The institutions of the nation-state can
serve a variety of social ends, and nationalists have conflicting

visions of the national community they attempt to build. Nationalism thus comes in a variety of forms – left-wing and right-wing;
pluralistic, dictatorial and totalitarian. Thus, paradoxically, we
have seen that in Indochina the spread of the ideal of 'national
unity' ushered in a period of civil war. Both sides insisted that they
alone were the 'true' nationalists, and that their opponents were
'traitors'. What was decisive here was not abstract arguments about
who were the 'true' nationalists; it was which side was able to
mobilize the population and, finally, impose their particular view.
In Indochina, the groups capable of doing this were the Communists.

Communism did not come to power in Indochina as a party of
working-class socialism, but as the radical wing of the nationalist
reaction to colonial rule, as a movement of middle-class and peasant
nationalism. This was typical of the successes Communism experienced elsewhere in Asia (and other Third World countries as well).
The Indian ex-Communist M.N. Roy wrote in 1951: 'Communism
in Asia is essentially nationalism painted red . . . . The Leninist
program was to regard nationalism as an ally; now communism
plays the role of nationalism, and appears in its most extreme form,
having a corresponding share of all its vices – racism, cultural
revivalism, intolerance, jingoism and resistance to western bourgeois influence. This nationalist degeneration is a general feature of
postwar communism, and assumes its most pronounced form in
Asia.'[17]

Roy is in error here only in describing nationalism as a 'degeneration' of Communism. In Asia, Communism was rooted in
nationalism from the start. And since nationalism meant above all
the political mobilization of the masses for purposes of state, it is not
surprising that the triumph of nationalism has added a further
element of popular passion to clashes between states. In this
context, there is no good reason to expect that Communist states
would be basically different from non-Communist ones. Indeed,
their genesis as revolutionary organizations for the politico-military
mobilization of the masses might be expected to make their colli-
sions in the international arena all the more explosive – quite
contrary to the theory of 'socialist internationalism'.

Yet even today many Western anti-Communists still refuse to
recognize the reality of Communist nationalism. In a recent article
on 'Vietnam under Communism', Stephen Morris castigates the
idea that the Vietnamese Communists are nationalists as
'nonsense'. He quotes Le Duan expounding on the Communist

Party's dedication to 'internationalist' virtues, and from this concludes: 'Today, as Vietnam rests securely within the Soviet bloc, one may wonder how anyone could have thought that the Vietnamese Communists were using "Communist means to nationalist ends". Indeed, long before the alignment with the Soviet Union became public, there was plenty of evidence of Vietnamese Communism's "internationalist" goals . . . . That is why Vietnam today is not only colonising Cambodia and Laos, but also training Communist geurrillas from Thailand, and using its stockpile of arms to supply Communist guerillas in El Salvador.'[18]

The allegation concerning El Salvador is beyond the scope of this book, but we shall be dealing with the other issues. For the moment, we wish to emphasize the assumption underlying Morris's argument. We would not disagree if he was to argue simply that events since 1975 had decisively rebutted the claim that the Vietnamese revolutionaries were nationalists rather than Communists, but his claim is a different one. It is that because Communists are 'internationalists', they cannot be nationalists. The only true nationalists, then, are the anti-Communists; Morris dismisses nationalist rhetoric of Communist leaders as a 'fraud' and a 'lie'. We do not accept this – it is no more than an assumption that Communism and nationalism are mutually exclusive. Finally, as we survey events in Communist Indochina after 1975, we may observe that if they are supposed to be manifestations of international solidarity and cooperation (of any kind), we would hate to see the consequences of really deeply rooted nationalist antagonisms in this region.

Notes

1. Milton Osborne, *Before Kampuchea: Preludes to Tragedy.* Sydney 1979, pp. 165–6; see also his article, 'Cambodia and Vietnam: A Historical Perspective', *Pacific Community*, vol. 9, 1978. The director of the Institute of Asian Studies at Chulalongkorn University in Bangkok offers a similar perspective: Khien Theeravit, 'Thai-Kampuchean Relations: Problems and Prospects', *Asian Survey*, vol. 22, 1982, p. 562.
2. Osborne, p. 174.
3. Theeravit, p. 562. Although the historical record shows that these states were just as warlike as others, the romantic myth of the 'gentle Buddhist kingdoms' persists. This is one reason why people were so unprepared for the brutality of the victorious Khmers Rouges. In fact, it could be said that they were simply updating the traditional conduct of Buddhist rulers victorious in war (execution of the defeated rulers and their followers, sacking of the enemy capital, and enslavement of their subjects). However, we shall argue below that the Khmer Rouge practices arose out of a

modern revolutionary upheaval, rather than traditional precedents.

4. J. Barrington Moore, Jr., *Social Origins of Dictatorship and Democracy*. London 1967, pp. 486–7.

5. Quoted in K.R. Minogue, *Nationalism*, Baltimore 1970, p. 17. In a recent survey, Cornelia Navari writes: 'The pre-nineteenth-century state did not serve nations; it did not even serve "communities". It served God, the Heavenly Mandate, the Law of Allah; it served hereditary rulers – the dynasts and the dynasties who were portrayed as God's vicars and whose appointed task was to carry out that mandate . . . . The fact of what language any dynast's subjects spoke was irrelevant to that task, and the particular cultures of his people only mattered to the degree to which they impeded that mandate.' Navari emphasizes that although the idea had earlier roots, it was not until the nineteenth-century that the idea that states ought to be based on nations became widespread in Europe and 'it was only in 1918 that any government made being a nation-state the basic criterion of political legitimacy and the basic condition of treating with other governments.' ('The Origins of the Nation-State' in Leonard Tivey, ed., *The Nation-State: The Formation of Modern Politics*, Oxford 1981, p. 14.) One of the best discussions of the whole matter, in a European context, is E.H. Carr, *Nationalism and After*. London 1946.

6. It is all too typical of the rhetoric denouncing Vietnam's 'traditional expansionism' that it has not been accompanied by any serious attempt to explain its social roots – Pol Pot's claim that the 'true nature' of the Vietnamese is that of a crocodile is crude racist rhetoric. None of those who echo his line repeat this, but nothing better is offered. For a serious discussion of the issue, see M.G. Cotter, 'Towards a Social History of the Vietnamese Southward Movement,' *Journal of Southeast Asian History*, vol. 9, 1968.

7. The most recent account of the economic and social impact of colonialism on Indochina is Martin J. Murray's *Development of Capitalism in Colonial Indochina 1870–1940*. Berkeley and Los Angeles 1980. Writing from a neo-Marxist perspective, Murray rather unconvincingly tries to show that French exploitation led to the stagnation rather than the development of the Indochinese colonies. We would also note that it is a book about Vietnam rather than Indochina as a whole: Cambodia and Laos are hardly mentioned. An earlier account, painted in rosy hues, is Charles Robequain, *The Economic Development of French Indochina*, London 1941.

8. The best overall account is William J. Duiker, *The Rise of Nationalism in Vietnam 1900–1941*. Ithaca and London 1976. For a broader picture see Peter Worsley, *The Third World*, 2nd edn, London 1967.

9. See the recent account by the head of the OSS's Indochina mission: Archimedes Patti, *Why Vietnam? Prelude to America's Albatross*, Berkeley and Los Angeles 1980.

10. The literature on this period is, of course, immense. Much of it focuses on the American involvement. One of the best recent syntheses focusing on the other side is William J. Duiker. *The Communist Road to Power in Vietnam*, Boulder, Colorado 1981.

11. Quoted in Bernard B. Fall, *The Two Viet-Nams: A Political and Military Analysis*. London 1963, p. 237.

12. Since the notion that Tet was really a victory for the Americans, and that everyone has been misled on this point by biased left-wing reporting, has become popular among the New Right, it might be worth quoting the judgement of Nguyen Van Loc, the South Vietnamese prime minister in 1967–8, who left Vietnam in 1983 after undergoing eight years of 're-education': 'We lost the battle for the South in 1968 . . . . By 1975 the Communists had to push only in a few chosen areas to gain

total victory.' (Quoted by V.G. Kulkarni, *Far Eastern Economic Review*. 2 June 1983).

13. The term is taken from the writings of Max Weber, but is grossly misused in this context. Weber used it to refer to the extraordinary qualities of a leader who gathers disciples by force of character and conviction, to overthrow traditional institutions. By this account, the charismatic leader is a revolutionary, a popular demogogue, or a military hero, not a traditional monarch. Indeed, according to Weberian typology, Sihanouk's regime was based on a patrimonial traditionalism, and Weber argued that it was in the wake of the breakdown of such regimes that charismatic figures were likely to be thrown up. For one of the few analyses that recognizes Sihanouk's traditionalism, see Michael Vickery, 'Looking Back at Cambodia 1942–76' in Ben Kiernan and Chanthou Boua, eds., *Peasants and Politics in Kampuchea 1942–81*, London 1982.

14. Here again it is of central importance to understand that Sihanouk's regime was traditionalist rather than charismatic. His popular following depended on the real exercise of power rather than his personal characteristics. In the Therevada Buddhist Kingdoms, 'the King was viewed as a course of power that ensured the prosperity of the land . . . . It is important to note that royal legitimacy . . . could not simply be asserted. It was also necessary that the King undertake acts that established that he indeed had such power.' (Charles F. Keyes, *The Golden Peninsula: Culture and Adaption in Mainland Southeast Asia*, London 1977, p. 68.)

15. Minogue, pp. 7–8.

16. See, for example, the Second International's famous Stuttgart Declaration of 1907 on 'Militarism and International Conflicts': 'Wars are . . . inherent in the nature of capitalism; they will cease only when the capitalist economy is abolished, or when the magnitude of the sacrifice of human beings and money, necessitated by the technological development of warfare, and popular disgust with armaments, leads to the abolition of this system.

'That is why the working classes, which have primarily to furnish the soldiers and make the greatest material sacrifices, are natural enemies of war, which is opposed to their aim: the creation of an economic system based on socialist foundations, and which will make a reality of the solidarity of nations.'

(Quoted by James Joll, *The Second International 1889_1914*,2nd edn, London 1974, pp. 206–7.)

17. Quoted by Rupert Emerson, *From Empire to Nation:The Rise to Self-Assention of Asian and African Peoples,* Cambridge, Mass. and London 1960, pp. 373-4.

18. Stephen J. Morris, 'Vietnam under Communism' in *Commentary*, September 1982, p. 46.

2

Vietnam: The Myth of post-war Expansionism

Following the fall of Phnom Penh to Vietnamese forces in January 1979 the London *Economist* wrote: 'This invasion by Vietnam will not reassure the Asian neighbours of Vietnam's burgeoning little Communist empire. The Vietnamese are Southeast Asia's Prussians; a people whose aggressive insecurity, or maybe plain aggression, creates insecurity around them.' The editorial comment, entitled 'Ho's will is done', claimed that the invasion fulfilled 'the lifelong goal of the dead leader'. Thus the *Economist* saw the invasion as a long premeditated action spurred on by an aggressive Vietnamese foreign policy and national psychology. A similar opinion was expressed by former US Secretary of State Henry Kissinger in the 1982 instalment of his memoirs, *Years of Upheaval:* 'The Vietnamese . . . outlasted French occupation, all the time nurturing the conviction that it was their mission to inherit the French empire in Indochina. Lacking the humanity of their Laotian neighbours and the grace of their Cambodian neighbours, they strove for dominance by being not attractive but single-minded. So all-encompassing was their absorption with themselves that they become oblivious to the physical odds, indifferent to the probabilities by which the calculus of power is normally reckoned . . . . Our misfortune had been to get between these leaders and their obsessions. Our Indochinese nightmare would be over; Hanoi's neighbours were not as fortunate. Propinquity condemned them to permanent terror.'[1]

These speculations about an aggressive national psychology in Vietnam contrast with Morris's argument – outlined in Chapter I – in terms of Communist 'internationalism'. But they do converge on the thesis that once the war in the south was over, Hanoi, unilaterally and without provocation, adopted aggressive policies towards its neighbours and other countries in the region.

Before examining this question, we should clear up the matter of

Ho Chi Minh's 'will', referred to by the *Economist*. This has been claimed by a number of right-wing authors to be a call for the establishment of an 'Indochina Federation' ruled from Hanoi and embracing Laos and Cambodia as well as South Vietnam. This is simply untrue. On 10 May 1969 Ho signed a 'Last Will and Testament', written, he explained with distinct Confucian overtones, 'in expectation of the day when I shall go to rejoin the venerable Karl Marx, Lenin, and our revolutionary elders'. It was a call for unity, discipline and a high standard of morality in the Vietnamese Communist Party, and for a continuation of the struggle to reunite Vietnam. On international affairs, he addressed himself to the Sino-Soviet split: 'Having dedicated my life to the service of the revolution, I am all the more proud to see the international Communist and workers's movement expand, and I suffer all the more because of the dissension that at present divides the Communist powers. I want our party to do its best to contribute efficaciously to the re-establishment of good relations between the Communist powers, on a Marxist-Leninist and international proletarian basis, always in conformity with the demands of the mind and heart. I firmly believe that the fraternal parties will one day be reunited.' And he concluded: 'My ultimate desire is that all our party and all our people, closely united in combat, will raise up a Vietnam that is peaceful, unified, independent, democratic and prosperous. Thus we will make a worthy contribution to world revolution.'

There was no mention at all of Laos and Cambodia, or of the 'Indochina Federation' which this veteran anti-French leader allegedly wished to create. Consistent with this, Le Duan was able, at the VCP's 4th Congress in 1976, to boast that Hanoi had already 'succeeded brilliantly' in fulfilling Ho's will by bringing about the unification of Vietnam – without mentioning Cambodia or Laos in this context.[2]

Vietnamese Foreign Policy after the War

For a more realistic perspective we must recognize, first of all, that the end of the war in Vietnam had considerable implications for regional politics. Even if it had no designs on its neighbours, a Vietnam that was no longer pouring its energies into civil conflict promised to be a major new power in the region. With a population in excess of fifty million, Vietnam was the most populous state in mainland Southeast Asia and the third largest Communist state in the world. With a regular army of 680,000 troops, hardened by decades of warfare, Hanoi was a military power to be respected. Whatever its professed intentions, therefore, it is not surprising that the governments of Southeast Asia viewed Hanoi with some apprehension after its victory in 1975 – especially those who had backed the USA in Indochina.

However, it was soon apparent that the Vietnamese government's main concern was not military adventures abroad but the rebuilding of their war-shattered country. The need was overwhelming. Forty years of war had left Vietnam with a per capita income that was about a quarter of that of Thailand, and about a thirtieth of that of the developed capitalist countries. Furthermore, the cutting of American aid to the south precipitated an immediate crisis. Colonial Vietnam had been an important exporter of rice (this came mainly from the fertile provinces of the south; the densely populated north had itself relied on imports from the south). Years of war had destroyed this capacity, and the rapidly growing population had become increasingly dependent on outside supplies of food – from the West in the south, from China in the north. The country's economy was clearly fragile, and would have to be handled with care if it was to be nursed back to health.

The general guidelines of the government's policies after the war were summed up in Le Duan's Political Report to the 4th National Congress of the VCP in December 1976. It had been sixteen years of war since the previous congress, but now the country was unified and at peace. The general mood of optimistism, even euphoria, at the congress was therefore understandable.

The section of Le Duan's Report dealing with foreign policy was comparatively brief. Imperialism, he said, was a declining force while the socialist camp was growing stronger day by day, as were the struggles of national liberation and working-class movements around the world. These factors added up to an 'irreversible trend' which meant that Vietnam would be able to undertake the construction of socialism under 'new and favourable conditions'. In his analysis, nationalism, socialism and internationalism were harmoniously fused. Victory in the 'war for national liberation' had removed obstacles to national reunification and 'takes the whole country towards socialism'. At the same time, he affirmed the international significance of the national revolution: 'The Vietnamese revolution is part and parcel of the world revolution. Our people's victory in the patriotic war of resistance against US aggression is closely associated with the wholehearted support and great assistance of our brothers and friends from all continents . . . . Our people's victory is a worthy contribution to the common victory of the world revolutionary forces.'[3]

Elaborating on this 'internationalist' foreign policy, Le Duan called for a strengthening of relations between Vietnam and 'all the fraternal socialist countries'. In this context, he judiciously balanced praise of the Soviet Union with praise for the People's Republic of China, which, he said, 'is rapidly building a powerful socialist country'. He made no mention of the Sino-Soviet split, but said that Vietnam was committed to 'restoring and consolidating solidarity, and promoting mutual support and assistance' among socialist countries. He warmly praised the 'great historical victories' in Laos and Cambodia, and called for a strengthening of the 'special relationship' between these countries. This emphasis on international solidarity certainly contrasts with the Maoist espousal of national 'self-sufficiency', but there is no justification for reading it as a policy of foreign expansion.

Towards the non-Communist countries of Southeast Asia, Le Duan's position was one of studied ambiguity. On the one hand, he sought to promote peaceful coexistence among Communists and non-Communists in the region. Vietnam was, he declared, 'ready to establish and develop relations of friendship and cooperation with other countries in this area'. On the other hand, he also spoke of Vietnamese support for the 'just struggles of the peoples' for democracy, independence, peace and 'genuine neutrality' (this he specified as meaning 'without military bases and troops of the imperialists on their territories'). This implied threat to back local Communist insurgents was not inspired by a doctrinal commitment to the 'export' of revolution. It was aimed at frightening Southeast Asian governments into minimizing the military presence of Hanoi's recently defeated antagonist, the USA.

These hints from Hanoi were particularly alarming for Thailand and the Philippines: they had been members of the US sponsored Southeast Asia Treaty Organization (SEATO) along with the now-defunct Saigon regime; they had committed troops to the struggle against Communism in Indochina, and allowed US airstrikes in Vietnam, Cambodia and Laos from their soil. However, the other main states of the region – Malaysia, Singapore and Indonesia – were hardly less vigorous in their hostility to Communism. It is not surprising that Hanoi viewed all of them with some suspicion, and was inclined to view the Association of Southeast Asian Nations (ASEAN), which brought them all together, as a covert military alliance directed against Vietnam.

However, Le Duan's Report made it clear that the VCP leadership assigned first priority to national reconstruction, not international objectives. The party, people and government of Vietnam should, he said, 'make the most of the favourable international conditions so as to rapidly heal the wounds of war, restore and develop the economy, develop culture, science and technology, consolidate national defence, build the material and technical basis of socialism in our country'.

The second five year plan, adopted at the 4th National Congress, was intended to make the country self-sufficient in food once more by the end of 1980. Surplus labour from the towns would be absorbed into productive employment on state farms in New Economic Zones (NEZ) to be opened up in the western Mekong basin, near the Cambodian border. Rice production was expected to rise to twenty-one million tonnes of paddy, and the process of industrialization would get under way. Overall, the planners expected a growth rate of 15 per cent per annum in Vietnam's gross national product as the country recovered from the ravages of war. But since, as Le Duan put it in announcing the plan, 'accumulation from internal sources is non-existent', the whole strategy depended on an influx of foreign aid to finance investment. Subsequent developments have shown the 1976 plan to have been excessively optimistic. But, for our present concerns, the main point is that it was geared towards peaceful economic development, not military preparations. As one writer put it: 'The Second Five Year Plan, which was principally a development plan, had discounted defence development . . . . Vietnam certainly expected a long period of peace after the liberation of Indochina in 1975, and it assumed that defence would no longer need the priority that it had during the previous three decades, and thus allow the unfettered pursuit of economic goals of reconstruction and development.'[4]

The army was not demobilized, but it was largely reoriented to peacetime tasks, rebuilding the shattered communications network in the country and clearing land of unexploded bombs and shells so that it could be brought back into production. The Vietnamese plan of 1976, therefore, did not anticipate 'expansion' into Cambodia or conflict with any of the country's neighbours.

The foreign ministers of ASEAN responded to the changed situation in Indochina at their annual conference held in Kuala Lumpur on 13–15 May 1975 by expressing their desire 'to enter into friendly harmonious relations with each nation in Indochina'. On 24 July

President Marcos of the Philippines and Prime Minister Kukrit Pramoj of Thailand reaffirmed this position in a joint statement which said that foreign military bases in the region were temporary and agreed in principle that SEATO 'had served its purpose' and should be phased out. Already, on 5 May, the Thai foreign ministry had announced the cessation of US operations from Udon airbase in northeastern Thailand and a programme for the scaling down of the US military presence in the country. These moves smoothed the way for talks on establishing diplomatic relations between Thailand, the Philippines and Vietnam.

Interestingly, all of the ASEAN states had recognized the new Cambodian government on 18 April, the day after the fall of Phnom Penh, but took no common action on the new South Vietnamese regime – the Provisional Revolutionary Government (PRG). This presumably reflected the (accurate) belief of Thai intelligence that the Khmers Rouges were not puppets of Hanoi and that immediate recognition could keep Phnom Penh from moving in the latter's direction.

Yet the ASEAN foreign ministers' conference showed that they were not unanimous about what approach ASEAN countries should take toward Communist Vietnam. Obviously feeling that Thailand and the Philippines may have been over-reacting to events, Indonesia's Adam Malik cautioned that adjustments 'should not be inspired by negative notions of fear and uncertainty or of perceived "vacuums" in power relationships'. Singapore's Sinathamby Rajaratnam pointedly noted that it was wrong to assume that the USA was withdrawing from Asia, and warned that ASEAN should not give the impression that it was ready to do anything to win the favour of the Communist governments of Indochina.

While ASEAN was juggling with the consequences of the Communist victories in Indochina, it was Hanoi's nominal ally, China, which revealed itself to be the most alarmed. When the Philippines' President Marcos made the first visit to Peking by an ASEAN head of state on 7 June, he was fêted by Deng Xiaoping, who warned him that an American withdrawal from the region would lead to increased Soviet activity, and praised the Philippines' 'unremitting effort to safeguard national independence and defend state sovereignty'. Deng urged the ASEAN countries not to over-react to developments in Indochina. He repeated his warning to the Thai prime minister at the end of June. The Chinese clearly did not wish to see an American military withdrawal from Thailand and the Philippines, as well as Indochina.

But Thailand and the Philippines persisted with their generally conciliatory policies toward Vietnam and continued to scale down their relations with the USA. No doubt their actions were influenced by the fact that the Soviet Union's policy toward ASEAN was generally sympathetic, seeing the Association as a laudable attempt at political and economic cooperation in danger of being pushed into playing a military role by the USA. Indeed, some ASEAN leaders were inclined to see the Soviet Union as a moderating influence on Vietnam, helping to allay the latter's fears that ASEAN was another SEATO.

From Hanoi's vantage point the regional situation had improved considerably by early 1976. Agreements to establish diplomatic relations with ASEAN states had either been reached or talks were progressing well, and SEATO had been formally abandoned in the previous September. Following the formal reunification of the north and south, Vietnam moved to consolidate its relationship with ASEAN. On 5 July the Vietnamese foreign minister, Nguyen Duy Trinh, said that his government was prepared to establish and develop relations of friendship and cooperation with other Southeast Asian countries on the basis of the following principles:

1. Respect for each other's independence, sovereignty and territorial integrity, non-interference in each other's internal affairs, and peaceful coexistence.
2. Not allowing any foreign country to use one's territory as a base for direct or indirect aggression and intervention against other countries in the region.
3. Establishment of friendly and good neighbourly relations, economic cooperation and cultural exchanges on the basis of equality and mutual benefit, together with settlement of disputes through negotiations in a spirit of mutual understanding and respect.
4. Development of cooperation among the countries in the region for the building of prosperity in keeping with each country's specific conditions and for the sake of independence, peace and genuine neutrality in Southeast Asia.

The deputy foreign minister, Phan Hien, set off on the same day to visit the capitals of all the ASEAN states, as well as Rangoon and Vientiane, in what was a generally successful effort at cultivating friendly relations. At a press conference in Singapore Phan Hien said he had taken note of assurances that ASEAN was not a military alliance, and was not influenced or directed by any foreign country.

Relations with America in the Aftermath of the War

Until January 1977 the White House was occupied by the man who had presided over the end of the US débâcle in Indochina, Gerald Ford. Henry Kissinger, the architect of the American escalation of the war into Cambodia in 1970, the invasion of Laos in 1971 and the bombing of Hanoi in 1972, remained secretary of state. Neither of these men were known to hold the slightest sympathy for the Vietnamese government. But Hanoi hoped that, with the war behind them, relations with the USA could be developed to offset Soviet and Chinese influence.

Vietnam made its first diplomatic move in September 1975. Prime Minister Pham Van Dong announced that Vietnam was ready to establish normal relations with the USA on the basis of the Paris Peace Agreement drawn up in 1973. For the Vietnamese, this entailed the fulfilment of promises made by President Richard Nixon in a letter to Dong on 1 February 1973, which offered aid to the value of $3,250 million for post-war reconstruction without any political conditions, in addition to other forms of aid to be agreed on between the two parties. For his part, on 26 March 1976, Kissinger stated the US terms as being: (i) accounting for US servicemen missing in action (MIAs); (ii) 'the need for assurances of Hanoi's peaceful intentions towards neighbouring countries in Southeast Asia'. He said the Vietnamese could raise any issue they liked, including their demand for aid, although he 'would not hold out much prospect for that'.

Unofficial contacts had been made some months before in Paris between Vietnamese officials and American oil companies over the resumption of offshore oil exploration in the South China Sea, a move that would transgress the embargo on trade and business with Vietnam imposed by the US government following the fall of Saigon. The Vietnamese aim was clearly to play to powerful business interests in the hope of gaining some leverage within American political circles.

But 1976 was presidential election year in the United States. In the Republican Party, the right wing was out in force and the incumbent, Gerald Ford, was trying to hold onto his position in the face of the challenge from Ronald Reagan by beefing up his anti-Communist posturing. In March 1976, therefore, he was railing against the Hanoi leadership as 'a bunch of international pirates' to enthusiastic Republican crowds. This was hardly a promising atmosphere for Hanoi to make its bid for improved relations with Washington. In late April, after goading by Reagan, Ford declared: 'I never said we would seek to normalize relations or recognize North Vietnam.'

The US government's demand that the Vietnamese account for all 753 Americans listed as still missing in action was impossible to fulfil. The Vietnamese replied that they would help in this project, but indicated that they could hardly be held responsible for all American MIAs in Vietnam. As Hanoi saw it the USA was attempting to renegue on what they argued were Washington's obligations under the Paris Agreement.

The MIA issue was a potent one in the hands of the right wing in Congress, particularly in an election year, and many congressmen seemed to believe that Vietnam was still holding some of these MIAs prisoner. But this claim was rejected in a December 1976 report by a US House of Representatives Special Committee, which said that there was no evidence that any of the missing men were alive or being held prisoner. With this controversy apparently cleared up there were no major obstacles left to a normalization of US relations with Vietnam. But the real significance of the MIA issue soon became clear. The right wing intended to use it as a means of delaying rapprochement indefinitely.

The MIA issue was used by the USA to veto Vietnam's application in November 1976 for United Nations membership because of its allegedly 'brutal and inhumane' attitude to the question of the missing men. Similarly, in September, the USA had been the only member to vote against Vietnam's application to take over the seat of the old southern regime at the World Bank; here the US had no power of veto, though it did have the power to obstruct loans.

The Carter administration took over the White House in January 1977 and it seemed at first to be offering a more conciliatory line. Although he had no previous involvement in foreign policy, Jimmy Carter himself had a reputation as a liberal. It was said that Andrew Young, the new US ambassador to the UN, only took the job on the proviso that he would not have to veto Vietnam's application for membership. Accordingly, the Socialist Republic of Vietnam was admitted to the United Nations on 20 September 1977.

The new administration relaxed its embargo on trade by permitting foreign ships or aircraft servicing Vietnam to refuel in the United States. A presidential commission, headed by Leonard Woodcock, landed in Hanoi in mid-March for talks on the prospects of normalization between the two countries. Then, on 24 March, President Carter said that he would 'respond well' to suggestions of possible US aid to Vietnam but that it would have to be viewed as 'normal' assistance and not as reparations. The prospects for normalization looked bright.

At that time, however, the differences between the right wingers and the moderates within the Carter administration had not come into focus. The former were represented by National Security Advisor Zbigniew Brzezinski, the latter by Secretary of State Cyrus Vance. Even in the beginning, Carter was unable to keep the rightists under control, and they increasingly came to dominate the American foreign policy process. In 1977–8, American foreign policy over nuclear weapons, relations with Moscow and military involvement in the Third World evolved rapidly in a more belligerent direction; and in 1979–80 most of the liberals departed from office (Young was dismissed in July 1979, Vance resigned in April 1980). It was thus under the Carter administration that the stage was set for Ronald Reagan's presidency and the new cold war.[5]

The mood of the Carter administration was signalled to the Vietnamese in 1977 by a Vance supporter, the Assistant Secretary of State for East Asian and Pacific Affairs, Richard Holbrooke. He spoke of Nixon's promises of aid to post-war Vietnam as 'an outmoded historical curiosity that keeps arising and complicating the discussion'. Nixon had originally made these promises to Hanoi only to get the USA out of a difficult spot, and once the war was over they were not worth the paper they were written on, but the Vietnamese continued to pin high hopes on them. The Ford administration had denied their very existence; now the Carter administration chose to release the text of this 'outmoded historical curiosity', and to refuse aid on the grounds that the Communists had violated the Paris Agreement of 1973.[6] Far from paying reparations, the Americans were actively trying to obstruct international aid to Vietnam.

Nor did the Carter administration normalize diplomatic relations with Hanoi. At first, their excuse for not doing so was the MIA problem. Then they cited the rapidly deteriorating political situation in Indochina. The real reason – apart from anti-Communist hostility towards the Hanoi government, a factor of increasing importance – was that they feared this might jeopardize America's developing relationship with China. Both the liberals and the right wingers were agreed on this. Carter himself wrote in his memoirs: 'The China move was of paramount importance, so after a few weeks of assessment, I decided to postpone the Vietnam effort until we had concluded our agreement in Peking.'[7]

Vietnam and China: the End of Hanoi's high-wire Diplomacy

Hanoi's failure to break through to the West was especially serious because its relations with China deteriorated rapidly after the end of the war. Both China and the USSR had committed themselves heavily to North Vietnam prior to 1975. Vietnam had been the largest single recipient of Chinese foreign aid; on the other hand, the Soviet Union had supplied 70 per cent of Hanoi's foreign aid throughout the war. Ho Chi Minh's high-wire diplomacy had sheltered Vietnam from the stormier blasts of the Sino-Soviet dispute. After 1975 this became impossible, and the Vietnamese were steadily forced to take sides.

Following the fall of Saigon, Peking's attacks on Moscow became more strident. In June 1975 Deng Xiaoping declared that the USSR was replacing the USA as the main threat to peace and security in Southeast Asia and that the Soviets 'insatiably seek new military bases in Asia'. It was an obvious warning to Vietnam. Le Duan travelled to Peking in September and was received by Mao Zedong. He signed an aid agreement but resisted Chinese pressure to break relations with the Soviet Union. From Peking Le Duan went on to Moscow where he also signed an aid agreement covering the 1976–80 period. A joint communiqué was issued by the Vietnamese and Soviet delegates expressing agreement on all substantive issues. That no similar statement had been issued in Peking was the first sign of serious differences between Vietnam and China.

Peking then began to publicize its territorial claims over the South China Sea, which overlapped and conflicted with those of Hanoi. The 'territorial waters' claimed by the Chinese People's Republic stretched along almost the whole coast of Vietnam and to within twenty miles of the coast of the Malaysian state of Sarawak. China's claims overlapped with claims by Malaysia, the Philippines, Taiwan, and Indonesia as well, but it was Vietnam they affected most of all.

The dispute in the South China Sea revolves around control of some 127 scattered and largely uninhabited tiny islands. The

Paracel Islands are 150 miles southeast of Hainan Island (China) in the north, and 550 miles to the south are the Spratly Islands, which lie off the coast adjacent to Saigon.

Control over these islands had been exercised by the South Vietnamese regime since the French exit from Indochina in the early 1950s. But Vietnamese sovereignty had never been accepted by either Taiwan or Peking. Indeed, Woody Island in the Paracel group had been occupied by Chinese forces since 1947. In late 1973, when President Thieu attempted to bolster his regime's nationalist credentials by provoking China in the Paracel Islands, China retaliated by forcefully expelling the ARVN forces in January 1974 and occupying the whole group. During this action China staked its claim to 'indisputable sovereignty over these islands [that is, both the Paracels and the Spratlys] and the seas around them'. With their struggle for unification still incomplete the North Vietnamese and the Provisional Revolutionary Government were forced to respond cautiously to the Chinese action: 'Disputes handed down by history,' said a northern official, 'often very complex ones, sometimes arise and need to be examined carefully. The countries concerned must settle these problems through negotiations.' The Chinese claims, however, were repeated by Peking's delegate to the 3rd UN Law of the Sea Conference in June 1974. These assertions of Chinese sovereignty in the South China Sea foreshadowed the later China-Vietnam conflict even before Saigon had fallen.

Shortly after the fall of Saigon the PRG announced the capture of 'beloved islands in the fatherland's waters', meaning the takeover of six islands in the Spratly group formerly occupied by southern Vietnamese soldiers. Peking remained silent. However, following Le Duan's Moscow visit, the October issue of *China Pictorial* carried an illustrated article on Chinese exploration in the Paracels and reaffirmed its claim to islands in the South China Sea. The November issue of the Vietnamese army journal responded that whereas in the past 'our people's right to be its own master' had concerned only the north, it was now the armed forces' duty to protect the sovereignty and territorial integrity of the whole country, including 'the islands and continental shelf'. Later that same month the Peking *Peoples' Daily* set out China's most extensive and detailed claim to sovereignty in the South China Sea. Refraining from naming Vietnam, it noted that 'some of the islands still have not returned to the hands of the Chinese people', and it affirmed China's determination to recover them: 'We will absolutely not allow anyone to invade and occupy our territory on any pretext.

The South China Sea islands are China's sacred territory. We have the duty to defend them.'

The issues, however, were not simply those of nationalist irredentism on the part of either Hanoi or Peking. Much larger political and strategic questions were at stake. Peking was also involved in a similar situation in the East China Sea, where its claims overlapped not only with those of Taiwan and North and South Korea, but also with those of Japan, which in turn had overlapping claims with the USSR. At a global level this area was even more explosive than the South China Sea. Thus it is not surprising to discover that, on 4 January 1974 the Chinese government simultaneously condemned the Thieu regime over the South China Sea islands as well as the Japanese and South Korean governments for their proposed 'Joint Development Zone' in the East China Sea. Peking viewed its maritime dispute with Vietnam in this wider context, which reinforced its intransigence.

China's growing assertiveness towards the offshore areas coincided with preparations for the first major working session of the UN Conference on the Law of the Sea in 1974. At this and subsequent conferences China has been one of the most militant supporters of extensive sovereignty over coastal waters. Its support for a 200-mile exclusive economic zone was vigorous from the outset.

The tangled problems of the Law of the Sea were further complicated by exploration for offshore oil in both the South China and East China Seas. American companies had been conducting surveys for the southern regime (and Hanoi had wished to do likewise in the Tonkin Gulf) but by 1975 there had still been no substantial finds. Nevertheless, the area is considered to have good oil potential in the long term. Naturally both China and Vietnam would like these resources for their development efforts, but the fact that exploration and exploitation of them has not been pursued jointly in disputed areas indicates that there are deeper issues at stake. An expert on these questions has written: 'To put the oil factor into meaningful perspective, it should be viewed as one element in a more comprehensive Chinese effort to consolidate a position of regional primacy.'[8] Not only would Chinese maritime supremacy in the South China Sea severely limit Hanoi's economic prospects but it would also make Vietnam very vulnerable to Chinese political pressure. Thus the dispute was not simply a crude two-sided grab for oil wealth (though in part it is just that), but also a Chinese demand for political submission on the part of the Vietnamese – and it was clearly understood as such in Hanoi.

More broadly again, control of the South China Sea as a vital strategic waterway would enhance China's global power. It would also play a vital role in the Sino-Soviet dispute. The Chinese have been aware of the fact that the Soviet navy must pass through this waterway en route to and from its base in Vladivostok, and so control of the South China Sea islands is very desirable in military terms. Very early on *Pravda* accused China of pursuing an expansionist policy and of using force 'to lay its claim to the Paracel Islands which the Vietnamese people consider their own territory'. Thus, from its own global perspective, the USSR found it necessary to support Vietnam's regional needs.

The dispute between China and Vietnam simmered on into 1976 when, with the death of Mao and the struggle against the 'Gang of Four', Chinese politics once again plunged into turmoil. While the Hanoi leadership apprehensively awaited the outcome of the power struggle in its giant neighbour it sought to widen its options by further developing relations with non-Communist countries. The unfolding domestic crisis in Vietnam added to the urgency of these diplomatic efforts.

Rapidly Diminishing Options

Prospects for the Vietnamese economy had begun to look gloomy by the end of 1976. Insufficient aid from both East and West meant that the country's industrialization plans had to be drastically scaled down. China had halted its wartime gift of 500,000 tonnes of rice per year and cut its supply of consumer goods.

Meanwhile agriculture suffered a series of set-backs. There were shortages of fertilizer and fuel, keenly felt in those areas of the south where modern farming methods, using high-yield varieties of rice, had been established. Since the urban population was able to offer few goods in exchange for farm produce, and the official purchase-price of rice was kept low, the peasants lacked market incentives to produce much beyond their own needs. In 1977 the situation worsened, with acute shortages pushing the black market price of rice up to ten times the official purchase price.

Abnormal weather conditions aggravated these problems. Drought and then typhoons wreaked havoc in the north in 1977, causing Vietnam to use more of its precious foreign exchange to import food. Crop failures were even more disastrous in 1978. The year began with droughts and flooding, while crops in the Mekong

Delta were hit by an insect plague. Then, between August and October, the whole country was battered by the worst typhoons and floods for sixty years.

Food shortages intensified. The monthly rice ration was cut to one kilogram, the rest of the month's ration being made up with wheat, flour, potatoes and other substitutes. In the free market, prices continued to spiral upwards. Undernourished, the people were unable to maintain their working capacity, and labour productivity declined further. Poor nutrition, coupled with shortages of imported drugs and medicines, led to a deterioration in public health. Three years after the war, many Vietnamese found to their bewilderment that their standard of living had declined seriously with the coming of peace.

Hanoi's first response was to intensify diplomatic attempts to breakthrough to the West. Pham Van Dong toured Europe early in 1977 soliciting aid and technology while offering a liberal and flexible foreign investment code to foreign capitalists. He gained only a small aid package from France while other European countries indicated that they were reluctant to deal with Vietnam until the USA had normalized relations with Hanoi.

In the midst of this domestic crisis the Khmers Rouges launched their first full-scale attacks on Vietnamese border villages. These attacks severely disrupted the New Economic Zones in which the government had been hoping to absorb the urban unemployment into productive activity. Many had been reluctant to go to the NEZs in the first place, their poor living standards leading some to refer to them as 'Vietnam's Siberia'. The Khmer Rouge attacks sent thousands of their inhabitants fleeing back to Saigon with tales of horror, and making the urban population still more resistant to government pressures to move to the NEZs.

Simultaneously, the new Peking leaders showed they were as intransigent as the former 'Gang of Four'. On 30 July 1977, eight days after Deng Xiaoping had been officially rehabilitated once more, China's foreign minister, Huang Hua, delivered an address which said that the issues in the South China Sea were nonnegotiable: 'The territory of China reaches as far southward as the James Shoals, near Borneo, of Malaysia . . . I remember that while I was still a schoolboy, I read about the islands in the geography books. At that time, I never heard anyone say that those islands were not China's . . . The Vietnamese claim that the islands belong to them. Let them talk that way. They have repeatedly asked us to negotiated with them on the [Paracels] issue; we have always declined to do so . . . As to the ownership of these islands, there are historical records that can be verified. There is no need for negotiations since they originally belonged to China. In this respect Taiwan's attitude is all right; at least they have some patriotism and would not sell out the islands. As to when we will recover the islands, this will have to wait until the time is ripe.'[9] Barring total capitulation by Vietnam to China's position, this statement set the stage for permanent tension between the two countries.

Vietnam's Ethnic Chinese and Refugee Crisis

Throughout 1977 tension between Hanoi and Peking had also grown over Vietnam's attitude to its one and a half million ethnic Chinese (referred to as the Hoa), 250,000 of whom resided in the north. As in many other Southeast Asian countries, the overseas Chinese in Vietnam maintained a distinct Chinese culture and retained family links with China itself. Most had come as labourers or traders in the early stages of modern commercial expansion in Indochina, and by the mid-twentieth century some Chinese played a prominent role in commerce and banking in many Southeast Asian countries. Before 1949 Peking had insisted that the overseas Chinese were all Chinese citizens. If they took out citizenship in their country of residence, they were deemed to have taken out dual citizenship rather than to have renounced Chinese citizenship. Chinese governments claimed extra-territorial rights, the right to intervene in other countries to protect its overseas citizens.

With the coming of independence after World War II, nationalist governments throughout Southeast Asia often passed legislation deliberately favouring indigenous racial groups, or restricting the activities of the Chinese. In most countries they were obliged to renounce dual citizenship – they could become either a citizen of China or of their country of residence, but not both. In this context the Communists reappraised China's traditional posture of extra-territoriality. In the 1950s, at Zhou En-lai's initiative, the People's Republic of China formally renounced its claim to this right as part of its adoption of the principle of equality between nations.[10]

In Vietnam, the PRC was able to reach agreement with the Communist north over the question of the ethnic Chinese in Vietnam, but not with the Saigon regime. In 1955 the central committees of the two Communist parties concluded that Chinese nationals in the north would be administered by Vietnam, would enjoy the same rights as Vietnamese citizens, and would be encouraged to voluntarily adopt Vietnamese nationality after 'sustained and patient persuasion and ideological education'. The agreement did not specify the time needed for the process of naturalization, though the Vietnamese have subsequently claimed: 'The Chinese ambassador in Vietnam in 1956, Lo Kwei-po, said the time necessary for turning the Hoa into Vietnamese citizens was from eight to ten years or a little longer.'[11] Even this, the Vietnamese argued, was too long compared with practice elsewhere.

In the interim, the Chinese in North Vietnam were in a privileged position. In 1980 a 71-year-old Hoa refugee from the north recalled: 'We had the best of both worlds. The Hoa in the north had all the rights and privileges of Vietnamese citizenship and none of its disadvantages. From about 1970 the Vietnamese had been trying to get us to become citizens, but few of us regarded it to be in our best interests. We would even vote in their elections. We were regarded as Vietnamese in all respects, except that we were not subject to the military draft.'[12] This was a valuable prerogative during the war and the Chinese were naturally not anxious to be assimilated.

Government pressure on the Hoa to assimilate increased in North Vietnam in the mid-1960s as a result of the Chinese Cultural Revolution, when some Hoa began their own 'Red Guard' activities and denounced the Vietnamese party as 'revisionist'. Worried about potential PRC manipulation of the Hoa, in 1970 the North Vietnamese government began downgrading history and language lessons in Chinese schools; some years earlier Chinese signs began to disappear from shops in Hanoi and Haiphong. However, compared with the actions taken by the southern regime, and to be taken throughout Vietnam after 1975, northern policy toward the Hoa before 1975 was moderate and tolerant.

In 1956 the southern regime of Ngo Dinh Diem had compelled the Hoa to take Vietnamese citizenship on pain of expulsion from Vietnam. Peking protested against this in May 1957, saying that the Vietnamese measures were 'a brutal encroachment upon the legitimate rights of the overseas Chinese in South Vietnam'. Hanoi supported Peking – though it is significant, certainly in retrospect, that this is the only statement Hanoi ever made with regard to the status of Chinese in the south before 1978. The NLF, however, made a number of statements between 1960 and 1968 saying specifically that 'all decrees and measures of the US puppet regime regarding Chinese shall be abrogated', and that 'Chinese residents have the freedom and right to choose their nationality.'[13]

When the Vietnamese Communists marched into Saigon on 30 April 1975 the Hoa problem remained unresolved, a fact dramatized by the festoons of Chinese national flags and portraits of Mao Zedong which greeted them in Saigon's sister city Cholon. This was probably no more than an attempt by the Hoa to get on the good side of their new Communist rulers, but in the context of increasingly strained relations between Hanoi and Peking it was not successful. Instead it intensified Vietnamese Communist suspicions about the national loyalties of the Chinese in Vietnam.

In January 1976, in an attempt to gauge the depth of the problem, the Vietnamese government ordered the Hoa to register their citizenship, whereupon the majority registered as Chinese, repudiating their compulsory adoption of Vietnamese citizenship in 1956–7. Apparently alarmed, the government ordered them in February to re-register their citizenship once again, this time according to their status under the Diem regime. Those who persisted in registering as Chinese were dismissed from their employment and had their food rations reduced. Later in the year all Chinese newspapers in the south were closed down, followed by Chinese-run schools.

Vietnam's later explanation of its actions in 1976 were disingenuous, to say the least. Of the process of registering foreign residents – and presumably referring to the February one – they claimed that 'not a single Vietnamese of Chinese origin turned up for registration'. And in response to Chinese demands for the abrogation of Diem's decree they said: 'Since the Vietnamese Party and government have never recognized the policies of the puppet administration, to make a statement abrogating any of their decrees is out of the question. But the fact that Chinese residents have become Vietnamese of Chinese origin, Vietnamese citizens, is an objective historical reality which has existed for over twenty years and which nobody can deny.'[14]

These verbal gymnastics were a product of the fact that Vietnam had chosen to ignore the understanding of 1955 that enjoined them to consult Peking on the future of the Hoa in Vietnam after liberation; as well as the later undertakings given by the NLF. Vietnamese policy in 1976 was influenced by its rapidly changing relations with China, and by fears that the latter could use the Hoa to pressure Vietnam into conforming with its policies. The Hoa issue was perceived by Hanoi as a test of Vietnamese sovereignty, rather than as a simple internal matter.

In 1976 relations between Vietnam and China were still cordial, and it appears that most Hoa in the south had resigned themselves to the actions of the Hanoi government. But when the conflict between the two governments came to a head, the Hoa would be caught in the middle.

Peking made no comment on the Hoa issue throughout 1976, indeed through to mid-1977. Possibly this was because the Chinese leaders were too preoccupied with their own internal factional struggles. But in February 1977 editorials in the *People's Daily* and *Red Flag* showed a revived interest in the overseas Chinese. In the same month, Hanoi was using the opportunity of a general census to consolidate the action taken a year before. Then, after the first major Sino-Vietnamese border clash in April 1977, the Vietnamese government began to apply more pressure on the Hoa in the north, particularly along the border. As one refugee explained: 'In 1977 the authorities tried to get the Hoa living on the border to adopt Vietnamese citizenship. Those who refused were forced to choose between returning to China or moving inland away from the border.'[15]

In June 1977 Chinese Vice Premier Li Xiannian brought up the matter of the Hoa in Vietnam with Vietnamese Premier Pham Van Dong. He reprimanded Dong for 'not consulting China' on the issue and warned that 'every country has the duty to protect the legitimate rights and interests of its nationals residing in other countries.'[16] Li implied that all Hoa were Chinese nationals even where they had taken out Vietnamese citizenship, and this was taken by Hanoi as a challenge to its sovereignty. Along with the simmering dispute over the South China Sea, and the rapidly deteriorating situation on the Vietnam-Cambodian border, this set the two countries on a collision course.

Thus when Peking initiated a new, active policy toward the overseas Chinese in late 1977 it caused more alarm in Vietnam. Hanoi's fears were galvanized when the new policy was outlined in the *People's Daily* of 4 January 1978. It spoke of the overseas Chinese as 'part of the Chinese nation . . . with their destiny closely linked with that of the motherland', and of Peking's intention to 'strengthen the work on overseas Chinese affairs' and 'unite with those overseas Chinese who belong to the bourgeoisie' and 'work energetically among them . . . to form a broad patriotic united front' for the goal of the four modernizations. This was a sharp move away from Zhou's policies of the 1950s. Then on 26 February at the 5th National People's Congress in Peking, Chairman Hua Guofeng declared that China opposed any attempt to compel overseas Chinese to change their citizenship.

Hanoi's worries became particularly focused on the political loyalties of the Hoa community in the south. Here Chinese businessmen had always monopolized the wholesale trade and export-import firms, and as a group held tremendous economic power, having often successfully obstructed attempts at economic reform under the Thieu regime.[17] The same problem had been encountered by the new Communist regime in its dealings with this commercial oligarchy. A Vietnamese Communist Party magazine gave the following analysis of the situation in the south in August 1978: 'The bourgeois of Chinese descent . . . controlled nearly all important economic positions, and especially firmly controlled three key fields: processing, distribution and credit. At the end of 1974 they controlled more than 80 per cent of the installations of the food, textile, chemical, metallurgy, engineering and electrical industries and nearly achieved a trading monopoly – wholesale trade 100 per cent, retail trade more than 50 per cent and export-import trade 90 per cent. They completely controlled the purchase of rice and paddy . . . . Since they controlled the supply of goods to the market, they could manipulate prices . . . through their import-export network and transport network and through the network of medium and small traders of Chinese origin . . . . They built a closed world based on blood relations, strict internal discipline and a network of sects, each with its own chief, to avoid the indigenous administration's direct interference. Each sect had its own budget, school, clinic, journal, headquarters and cemetery and a monopoly over a special branch of activity. This was truly a state within a state . . . '[18]

An inflation rate of 80 per cent in 1977 and the continuing problems of food shortages and hoarding convinced the Communists of the continued power of the southern capitalists. Hanoi now feared they could be won over to Peking's foreign policy objectives, and this, combined with the serious dislocation of the southern economy as a result of conflict with Cambodia, made Vietnamese leaders fearful of a Chinese-inspired disruption of the country from within and without. Following Phnom Penh's refusal to respond to a substantial peace proposal from Hanoi on 5 February 1978 the VCP Central Committee held its portentous 4th Session at which it took two strategically intertwined decisions: the first was to find a way of toppling Pol Pot; the second was to break the back of the Chinese-dominated oligarchy in the south.

The attack on 'bourgeois trade' in Saigon/Cholon was launched on a Friday (24 March) as many of the big traders were preparing to leave for a weekend at the beach resort of Vung Tau, about seventy kilometres southeast of the city. As many as 30,000 businesses were nationalized; the young Communists who were mobilized to carry out the operation claimed they uncovered hoards of goods and gold bars. Thousands of other small businessmen and retailers were, however, allowed to continue operations. The measures were extended to the whole of the south in April. Then, on 3 May the introduction of a new national currency to replace the formerly separate northern and southern denominations further eroded the economic position of the rich traders and tightened the government's grip on the economy. Those rendered unemployed by these measures were obliged to leave the cities for the NEZs on the Cambodian border; many preferred to leave the country.

The number of people leaving Vietnam in the first three years after 1975 averaged about 35,000 per year. This figure more than doubled again in the first six months of 1979. Most of these were the 'boat people' who headed for Southeast Asian countries or Hong Kong; and in 1978–9 they were overwhelmingly Hoa. To the 'boat people' must be added approximately 250,000 Hoa who crossed into China between April 1978 and the summer of 1979.

The Communist leaders in Peking claimed that the Vietnamese were 'ostracizing, persecuting and expelling Chinese residents'. In reply *Nhan Dan*, of 29 May 1978, asked why China was taking such great interest in 'a handful of Vietnamese bourgeoisie of Chinese descent' while ignoring the fact that thousands of Chinese in Cambodia had been persecuted, massacred and expelled. But the Vietnamese government's emphasis on the class basis of the outflow does not explain the fact that over the following year twice as many Hoa crossed into China from the north as left as boat people from the shores of the south.

In contrast to the south, the Hoa in the north had maintained close contacts with China, and they had not been directly confronted with the issue of citizenship. But in 1978 all that changed, as one refugee explained: 'In early May 1978, Xuan Thuy (who had represented Hanoi at the peace negotiations in Paris) replied to a Radio Peking broadcast accusing Vietnam of persecuting the Hoa. In his reply he noted that China and Vietnam had agreed after 1954 that the Hoa people would all gradually become Vietnamese citizens. This announcement, which the Vietnamese radio repeated over and over again, came as a shock to us. It had never before been made public. What worried us most was the draft, which we regarded as a sure road to death. It also meant that those Hoa with relatives in China would no longer be able to visit them. This was important for economic as well as for sentimental reasons. According to practice Hoa were able to visit China every three years. Those who went could bring Vietnamese goods to China and Chinese goods back to Vietnam for sale on the blackmarket, so it meant an economic loss as well.'[19]

In this atmosphere alarming rumours of suspicious origin – the Vietnamese and the Chinese blame each other for spreading them – about war between China and Vietnam, and about what might happen to the Hoa if they remained in Vietnam, triggered a sudden exodus from the north. The Hoa rush from the north was facilitated by a land rather than a sea border (few southern Hoa who objected to Vietnamese Communist rule were tempted to flee to Pol Pot's Cambodia). Having begun, the 'movement out of Vietnam and into China could not be stopped', writes Bruce Grant, 'because it was fuelled by a potent mixture of rumour, panic and the increasingly virulent propaganda war between Peking and Hanoi. Once started it became self-generating. The shock-waves from the northern exodus to China almost certainly spread to the Chinese community in southern Vietnam, just as the nationalization measures and currency reform in mid-1978, which hit the Chinese-dominated business community in Southern Vietnam hardest, also had an unsettling effect on the Chinese in the north.'[20] At this stage the Vietnamese authorities were still attempting to discourage Hoa people from leaving the north because they made up a significant proportion of the skilled workforce, especially in the mines and in the port city of Haiphong.

In the south many Hoa had responded enthusiastically to China's championing of their right to revert to Chinese citizenship. They hoped that as foreign nationals they would fare much better economically, avoid the draft, and be able to leave the country just as French and Indian nationals in the south were doing. Their considerations had little to do with ethnic or nationalist loyalty to China. The Vietnamese government, however, did not perceive it this way and demonstrations by Hoa in Cholon in favour of taking out Chinese nationality in the days immediately preceding the nationalization of big business in the south could only have confirmed Hanoi's fears about them.

When the PRC announced on 26 May 1978 that it was sending ships to Vietnam to collect 'victimized Chinese residents' an estimated 200,000 Hoa in Cholon applied for exit permits. But having created the demand for repatriation among the Hoa the Chinese then refused to go ahead because Vietnam would not concede publicly that 'Chinese nationals' were being 'ostracized and persecuted'. This left the Vietnamese leadership feeling even more insecure about the Hoa's allegiances, while at the same time exposing the Hoa who had applied to leave to government reprisals. The final result was that Hanoi saw the whole affair as part of a Chinese plot to de-stabilize Vietnam. It was in the wake of this incident, and amid increasing tension on the Vietnam-Cambodia and Sino-Vietnam borders, that the VCP's Politbureau decided in June 1978 to 'clearly identify China as the main enemy of Vietnam'.

When China closed its border to refugees in July 1978, the Vietnamese quickly saw it as an attempt to maintain 'a small Chinese nation in Vietnamese territory' which it could use for 'trouble-making and disturbances'. Consequently, from September onwards, Hanoi covertly cooperated with overseas Chinese syndicates operating out of Hong Kong, Taiwan and Singapore to facilitate the removal from Vietnam of Hoa who had already demonstrated their 'disloyalty' by wishing to convert to Chinese citizenship and leave the country. Since the boat people had to buy their way out with bribes, there was considerable profit in the business for the officials involved.[21]

The Vietnamese government's participation in organizing the exodus naturally lifted the number of departures dramatically. There was a brief pause over December 1978 and January 1979, but following the Chinese invasion a surge of anti-Chinese sentiment throughout the country caused the number of departures from both the north and the south to skyrocket. Many of the Hoa left because they knew that in the mounting conflict between China and Vietnam, the Chinese in Vietnam would inevitably be the meat in the sandwich. Others were swept along in the panic. And, especially from mid-1978 onwards, large numbers of people – both Hoa and, to a lesser extent, ethnic Vietnamese – hoped to escape from deteriorating economic conditions.[22] Whatever their reason for wanting to go, they all knew that emigration through official channels would be far too slow and protracted; they wanted to leave immediately, not in five years' time, and signed on to what journalists jokingly referred to as 'Rust Bucket Tours Inc.'.

But it was no joke. To get out as quickly as possible, the boat people were willing to take great risks. They were fleeced by unscrupulous entrepreneurs and corrupt officials, and the cost of their escape attempt did not end with payments of money and gold. They usually set out in small, overcrowded and dilapidated boats intended for coastal rather than deep-sea use. Few of them had any seafaring or navigational skills. They often ran out of food or water because of misjudgements of time and distance, and many of the boats broke down in mid ocean. Many of those who sailed for Thai or Malaysian coasts died in brutal attacks by pirates operating in the Gulf of Thailand.

It was claimed in 1979 that between 40 and 70 per cent of the boat people died making their escape. Such figures were the basis for the charge that the Vietnamese government was committing genocide against the Hoa – that they were deliberately using the ocean as a 'poor man's gas chamber'. Of course, the very nature of the exodus makes it impossible to get precise figures, but it is clear that these claims were vastly inflated. The real mortality rate of the 'boat people' was much less – probably less than 10 per cent. But even this reduced estimate is appalling – it means that for the four years 1976–9, 'more than 30,000 human beings died unnecessarily at sea'.[23]

The exodus of boat people probably damaged Vietnam's international image more than its invasion of Cambodia. Even in 1978 the outflow had already seriously jeopardized Vietnam's developing relations with the ASEAN states who had to bear the main burden. All of these countries had their own overseas Chinese problem and by 1979 many people in ASEAN saw Vietnam's actions as an attempt to de-stabilize the rest of Southeast Asia. Characteristically, this sentiment was given its most forceful exposition by Singapore's foreign minister, Rajaratnam, in July 1979: ' . . . once you go to the causes of [the exodus] you enter the secret world of wild Vietnamese ambitions and their even wilder dreams . . . . It is a military exercise to further the ambitions which the Vietnamese have concealed from us but not from their own people or their allies . . . . Their ambitions are hegemony in Southeast Asia . . . . In other words each junkload of men, women and children sent to our shores is a bomb to de-stabilize, disrupt, and cause turmoil and dissension in ASEAN states. This is a preliminary invasion to pave the way for the final invasion . . . '[24]

One of the most important effects of the refugee crisis was that it drove the ASEAN states to coordinate their policies towards Vietnam and Indochina, and thus undermined Vietnamese diplomacy in the region, which had taken full advantage of differences between the ASEAN countries.

By July 1979, when Rajaratnam was predicting that the worst was still to come, the refugee crisis had in fact already peaked. At the Geneva Conference that month the UN Secretary General was able to say in his closing address that: 'the Government of the Socialist Republic of Vietnam has authorized me to inform you that for a reasonable period of time it will make every effort to stop illegal departures.' In the following three months the number of refugees leaving Vietnam fell dramatically – a fact that undermined the credibility of the Vietnamese government's protestations that it had no control over the exodus – and since then departures have steadily dwindled. In the middle of 1979 boat people were leaving Vietnam at the rate of nearly 57,000 per month. By 1983, this had fallen to around 3,000 per month. And increasingly, they were leaving less for political reasons than to escape from Vietnam's poverty to the affluence of the West.

The Fateful Meridian

As the conflict with China and the domestic crisis in Vietnam intensified, so too did the fighting with Pol Pot's forces. In June 1978, when the VCP leadership decided to clearly identify China as the main enemy of Vietnam, they also decided that they would have to intervene in Cambodia to destroy Pol Pot's regime. Military preparations for the invasion began. In the meantime, Hanoi initiated a final desperate effort to normalize relations with the United States. On 11 July, Deputy Foreign Minister Phan Hien announced in Tokyo that Vietnam would drop all preconditions to normalization of relations with America. The Carter administration refused to acknowledge the change, insisting that they had not been notified officially of any change in line, and that they 'wanted it in writing'.

In fact, a major struggle was taking place within the US administration over foreign policy at this time. Carter's National Security Council adviser, Zbigniew Brzezinski, believed that the USA should take a tough line against the Soviet Union by playing the 'China card' against Soviet influence in Asia. In Indochina, this meant backing China and, by extension, Pol Pot, in their dispute with the pro-Moscow government in Hanoi. Carter's Secretary of State, Cyrus Vance, argued for a more flexible diplomacy in dealing with the USSR, in particular, in favour of maintaining *détente* rather than deliberately aggravating cold war tensions. In March 1978 Holbrooke, a Vance supporter, had argued against Brzezinski that the USA should not tie itself too closely to Chinese policy in East Asia and that it was in the interests of the USA to try and stabilize

Southeast Asia by normalizing relations with Hanoi. But by the middle of the year, it was clear that Brzezinski rather than Vance was setting the pace in America foreign policy.

By mid-1978 Vietnam was in deep economic crisis, was once again at war, and its need for assistance from the outside world was more desperate than ever. Following years of Soviet pressure to join the Council for Mutual Economic Assistance (COMECON), the Vietnamese finally became a member on 29 July 1978. In the following week China ended all economic and technical aid to Vietnam, recalled its remaining technical personnel, and lashed out at the Hanoi leadership for pursuing 'regional hegemonism', serving as the 'Cuba of the East' and 'junior partner' in a Soviet attempt to gain control of Southeast Asia.

In the USA Brzezinski used the Vietnamese move to bolster his case concerning their subordination to the Soviet Union. His adviser on China, Michael Oksenberg (notorious for his remark that Vietnam is 'the cesspool of civilization'), suggested that the Vietnamese may be secretly obligated to give the Soviets base rights at Cam Ranh Bay. Holbrooke quickly countered with a CIA report rebutting this charge, and as a result Holbrooke was authorized to begin talks with Vietnam's deputy foreign minister, Nguyen Co Thach. These talks began in New York on 26 September; apparently the Vietnamese once again demanded reconstruction aid, but quickly dropped the idea in favour of normalization without conditions; it was obviously a final faint-hearted try.[25] Both sides having agreed in principle to normalization, Thach then pressed for a signing in November, clearly so that it would precede any Vietnamese move against Cambodia. Holbrooke stalled, saying that progress would have to await congressional elections and that a signing might be possible in November – so long as there was no change in Vietnam's relations with the Soviet Union, and no action over Cambodia.

But Vietnam could not afford such vague commitments. It was under pressure from within and without, and in Hanoi the arguments for pushing ahead with the diplomatic-military timetable decided in June were mounting. By October it was clear to the Vietnamese that the hardliners in the US administration were predominant and that any further delay would only allow Peking time to try to polish up Phnom Penh's international image, while allowing it to continue the damaging border war.

On 3 November 1978 Vietnam signed a 25-year treaty of friendship and cooperation with the USSR. The pact contained six economic agreements, and a military clause obliging the parties to consult in the event of a threat of attack against one of them. This was obviously an attempt by Vietnam to insure itself against Chinese retaliation following the offensive against Phnom Penh it planned for December.

The same day Cyrus Vance finally acknowledged that Vietnam had dropped all its preconditions for talks with the United States. But this was too late to influence the course of events: the Soviet-Vietnamese treaty was pounced on by Brzezinski, and thus when Holbrooke and Thach met later that month to try to finalize normalization Thach discovered that the USA had toughened its preconditions. Vietnam would have to guarantee that it would not invade Cambodia, and, according to the USA, desist from sponsoring illegal immigration, and from provoking a Soviet-backed war with China. Thach denied all of the insinuations in these demands. With this the two men packed the uninitialled documents back into their briefcases and, with grim faces on both sides, the meeting broke up.

A month earlier Prime Minister Pham Van Dong had conducted his goodwill tour through the ASEAN capitals in an attempt to drum up support for Vietnam in its dispute with Cambodia and China. He apologized to his hosts because Hanoi had trained and supported guerrillas 'in the days when we needed to please the Chinese'. According to the *Economist* Dong also spoke of 'possible cooperation with Malaysia and Thailand in providing intelligence against the guerrillas'.[26] However, these overtures to ASEAN were unsuccessful. But such diplomatic set-backs could not stop the Vietnamese determination to deal with Pol Pot.

It was evident that the optimistic 'peace' plans of 1975–6 for Vietnam's post-war reconstruction lay in ruins. But there is no evidence that this was due to fanatical expansionism on the part of Hanoi. Their overriding priority was the development of a desperately poor country. In their relations with the West in the period immediately after the war, the Vietnamese were gambling diplomatically for high economic stakes, and they lost. Here they can be faulted, not for Communist dogmatism, but for pinning too much faith on conciliatory trends in post-war America. Their relations with the ASEAN countries had been developing favourably, until they were torpedoed by the twin crisis over Cambodia and the boat people in 1978–9.

But it was above all in its relations with 'fraternal' socialist countries – Cambodia and China – that Hanoi's calculations went most completely astray. The VCP leadership in 1975–6 had been looking forward to growing international cooperation among the Communist nation-states of East Asia. Instead, by 1978, the 'Red Brotherhood' had been torn apart by a new, fratricidal war. Only in Laos were Hanoi's post-war expectations more or less fulfilled.

Notes

1. Henry Kissinger, *Years of Upheaval*, London 1982, p. 12.
2. Communist Party of Vietnam, *Fourth National Congress Documents*, Hanoi 1977, p. 11. The text of Ho's will has been reprinted in the appendices to Le Duan, *This Nation and Socialism are One*, Tran Van Dinh, ed., Chicago 1976.
3. Fourth National Congress, pp. 149–50.
4. D.R. Sar Desai, 'Vietnam's Quest for Security' in Sudershan Chawla and D.R. Sar Desai, eds, *Changing Patterns of Security and Stability in Asia*, New York, 1980, p. 222.
5. Fred Halliday, *The Making of the Second Cold War*, London 1983, ch. 8.
6. *In Years of Upheaval*, Henry Kissinger gives his account of the 1973 negotiations. With characteristic panache and duplicity, he turns them into an occasion for American self-congratulation: 'No other major nation has been so uncomfortable with the exercise of vast power as the United States . . . No other society has considered it a national duty to contribute to the rebuilding of a defeated enemy.' (pp. 37–8) In the event, of course, the Americans never actually made the 'contribution' of which he is speaking at all. Even from Kissinger's account, it is evident that he was motivated by more than a 'sense of national duty to the defeated enemy'. In 1973, far from having been 'defeated', Communist forces in Indochina were close to victory, and America was searching desperately for an 'honourable' way to abandon its doomed allies. Kissinger's solution to the problem was to withdraw American forces, and, in effect, offer Hanoi a massive cash bribe to not take advantage of the situation thus created. He made it clear, he says, that the Vietnamese would get their money only if they did not take over South Vietnam; this was an attempt to buy with cash what could not be won on the battlefield. Hanoi never accepted these conditions, and it is doubtful that Kissinger ever really believed that they would.
   The American claim that the Vietnamese Communists violated the Paris Agreements is true enough, but misleadingly beside the point. All sides violated the Agreements, which were not intended to be a long-term solution to the problems of Indochina, but a face-saving way for the USA to extricate itself. To the extent that President Ford was able to declare with a straight face that 'it's not our war' as the anti-Communist regimes collapsed across Indochina in 1975, the 1973 Agreement had served its purpose. (For a study of the Paris Agreements, see Gareth Porter, *A Peace Denied*, Bloomington 1975.)
7. Jimmy Carter, *Keeping the Faith*, London 1982, pp. 148–95.
8. Selig S. Harrison, *China, Oil and Asia: Conflict Ahead?*, New York 1977, p. 194.
9. In King C. Chen, ed., *China and the Three Worlds*, London 1979, pp. 272–4.
10. For a more detailed discussion see Stephen Fitzgerald, *China and the Overseas Chinese: A Study of Peking's Changing Policy 1949–70*, Cambridge 1972.
11. Hoang Nguyen, 'When the Hoa Become Peking's Political Cards Against Vietnam' in *Vietnam Courier*, ed., *The Hoa in Vietnam*, dossier 2, Hanoi 1978, p. 12.

12. Quoted by Charles Benoit, 'Vietnam's "Boat People" ' in David W.P. Elliot, ed., *The Third Indochina Conflict*, Boulder, Colorado 1981, p. 144.

13. See Pao-min Chang, 'The Sino-Vietnamese Dispute Over the Ethnic Chinese', *China Quarterly*, no. 90, 1982, p. 197.

14. Hoang Nguyen, pp. 14–15.

15. Benoit, p. 143.

16. Pao-min Chang, p. 204.

17. Former southern President Ky has since related the methods he used to control the rice market: 'The rice trading system in (south) Vietnam lay in the hands of ten moguls, most of them Chinese. They could arrange any price they liked . . . . I ordered the ten businessmen to report to my office, and without giving them a chance to speak, I lined them up in front of my desk and told them: "I am perfectly aware of your intention to overthrow the government by dumping rice. Now let me tell you something. If I fall you won't stay alive." As they watched I wrote down their names on ten pieces of paper and put them in my cap. "I'll give you one week to re-supply the market with enough rice at a reasonable and stable price", I warned them. "If you cannot do this by the deadline, I shall draw lots and the first man whose name I pick out of my cap will be shot . . . I shall [continue] to do this until there is enough rice for everyone". The result of this undemocratic approach was astounding: within three days the markets were filled with rice and its Price was frozen.' (Nguyen Cao Ky, *Twenty Years and Twenty Days*, Stein and Day, New York, 1976, p. 102).

18. *Vietnam Courier*, no. 78, November 1978.

19. Benoit, p. 145.

20. Bruce Grant, *The Boat People: An 'Age' Investigation*, Melbourne 1979, p. 87.

21. On the involvement of the Vietnamese government, see Barry Wain, *The Refused: The Agony of the Indochinese Refugees*, Hong Kong 1981, ch. 4: cf. also Gareth Porter, 'Vietnam's Ethnic Chinese and the Sino-Vietnamese Conflict', *Journal of the Concerned Asian Scholars*, vol. 12, 1980.

22. Reading accounts of the Vietnamese exodus, one could be excused for imagining that it was a historically unique event. Sadly, this is not the case. This account of the Irish response to the Great Famine of 1846 has a familiar ring to it: 'Emigration, formerly a last desperate remedy, was now the first thing thought of; and there was an almost hysterical rush to leave the country, to escape from the "doomed and starving island", to find safety elsewhere. In earlier years, emigrants' sailings had been confined to spring and summer; and intending emigrants had made their preparations carefully. But, from the latter half of 1846 onwards, the panic-stricken crowds were clamorous to be off without delay. The traffic continued throughout the year; and thousands of hapless refugees put to sea with only the scantiest of provisions for the voyage, and without either means of subsistence or prospects of employment on their arrival.' (J.C. Beckett, *The Making of Modern Ireland 1603-1923*, 2nd edn, London and Boston 1981, p. 344). Of course, these Irish 'boat people' were fleeing from a crisis created by capitalism rather than one created by Communism, and few in the West care to recall such matters now. But the scale of the economic dislocation was greater, and the proportion of the population that responded by emigrating was much higher than in Vietnam.

23. Wain, p. 83.

24. Cited by Frank Frost, 'Vietnam, ASEAN and the Refugee Crisis', *Southeast Asian Affairs 1979*, Singapore 1980, p. 361.

25. Gareth Porter, 'US and Vietnam: The Missed Chance', *Nation*, 20 October 1979.

26. Economist, 18 November 1978 and 12 January 1979.

3

Laos: the Eclipse of 'Neutralist' Communism

The cessation of American aid to Laos in mid-1975 effectively ended the Lao sojourn within the Western sphere of influence, while the complete Pathet Lao takeover in December of that year registered Laos' decisive shift into the 'socialist camp'. It is common wisdom among most journalists and academics writing about Indochina that from that point on Laos became a Vietnamese 'colony'. Arthur J. Dommen, author of a major study on Laos before the Communist takeover, now calls the country 'a satellite of Vietnam' and the Vientiane government a 'puppet' of Hanoi.[1] Another specialist, Martin Stuart-Fox, has written of Laos: 'All major areas of decision-making from foreign policy to economic planning and military security are dependent on Vietnamese direction'.[2] Indeed many have been argued that Laos was Vietnam's prototype for the formation of the 'Indochina Federation' – composed of Vietnam, Laos and Cambodia. No one has put this view more forcefully than Dommen: 'The stationing of Vietnamese troops in Laos today is obviously aimed at defending the independence, sovereignty, territorial integrity and cultural construction not of Laos, but of a Greater Vietnam, envisioned by Ho Chi Minh's successors and supported by the Soviet bloc. This Greater Vietnam will make Laos far more a part of Vietnam than the Indochinese Federation Ho envisioned when his preoccupation was with the expulsion of the French . . . . Vietnam has replaced France as the colonial power in Indochina.'[3]

No one is denying that the relationship between Laos and Vietnam is an unequal one, a relationship in which Hanoi has more influence than Vientiane; the most cursory study of the political resources the two regimes can marshal quickly establishes that elementary fact. But many writers blur all the crucial distinctions between outright annexation, federation, colonial rule, and the formation of alliances between sovereign states in their discussion of Lao-Vietnamese relations. In the passage just quoted, Dommen appears to imagine that the formation of an 'Indochina Federation' is the equivalent of annexation by a state he calls 'Greater Vietnam', and that this is what has happened in Indochina. Faced with such a flight of fancy, it is necessary to make a few elementary observations. In the first place, neither of the political entities to which Dommen refers actually exist – the Lao People's Democratic Republic is recognized by the United Nations, the United States, China and a host of other governments as a sovereign state with, among other things, the right to form alliances with other sovereign states if it pleases; but there are no institutions that can be labelled 'Indochina Federation' or 'Greater Vietnam'.

If we concentrate on the formal relationships – which are by no means unimportant, and all that international law, for example, can take into account[4] – these statements are demonstrably untrue. They are no more than careless rhetoric masquerading as political analysis. But if we put aside the muddled terms they use, the basic points that authors like Dommen and Stuart-Fox appear to be making are two-fold. The first is that despite its formal equality, the government of Laos has in fact come under the informal control of the Vietnamese government. The second is that this control is exercised to the detriment of Laos. In other words, it is alleged that the relationship is of the type that some writers have termed 'neo-colonial'.

To document this claim would require a more detailed empirical study than any of these authors have undertaken. From the start, however, it needs to be emphasized that the point at issue is not one of inequality, of Vietnamese influence in Laos – it is one of Vietnamese control and exploitation of Laos. The allegedly malevolent nature of Vietnamese power has to be demonstrated, not merely asserted or assumed.

Certainly, it cannot be disputed that the relationship between the two governments is a close one. It was the Lao prime minister and secretary general of the Lao People's Revolutionary Party (LPRP), Kaysone Phomvihane, who first spoke of the 'special relationship' between Vietnam and Laos in a speech to the 4th Congess of the VCP in mid-1976: 'In the history of the world revolution, examples of the radiant spirit of proletarian internationalism are not lacking, but never has there been anywhere an alliance of militant solidarity so especially durable. Thirty years it has run, and yet it remains clear. This solidarity and durable alliance places high value on the spirit of independence and sovereignty as well as the values of each people. Each joins forces with the peoples of the other two countries to help in combat and carry off victory, accomplishing at the same time the noble historical mission before each of our nations and before the revolutionary movement of the world. The relations between Vietnam and Laos have become special relations of great purity, imprinted with an exemplary and rare fidelity, which has consolidated and developed more and more each day.' Dommen, no doubt, would see this speech as no more than a vassal paying homage to his master at court. Yet, as we shall see, Kaysone's speech was probably a rare example of highblown political rhetoric expressing real beliefs.

Most critiques of the Lao-Vietnam 'special relationship' assume that there is a 'natural' antagonism between Lao nationalism and Vietnamese nationalism, and that the alliance between the two countries involves the subordination of the former to the latter. Much of this has been based on woolly assertions about 'historic antagonisms' between the two countries and ethnic differences, but no one has really argued this point of view at length, and like so much else it remains a background 'taken-for-granted' assumption.

In fact, there is little evidence for it. Laos is so ethnically fragmented that to a large portion of the population, there is little to choose between lowland Lao and lowland Vietnamese rule. And, as we saw in chapter 1, mass nationalism came to Laos quite recently, largely as a result of the activities of the pro-Vietnamese Pathet Lao. The idea of 'historic antagonisms' between the Lao and Vietnamese nations has even less foundation than the corresponding claims about the Khmer and Vietnamese nations.

One of the few empirical studies to address itself to this question was a Rand Corporation study by Paul Langer and Joseph Zasloff in the 1960s. They concluded: 'A widely held thesis holds that the Lao dislike the Vietnamese. Our research points to a more complex relationship. For one thing the typical lowland Lao rarely exhibits the acute, virulent nationalism and xenophobia so common in contemporary Asia and so often directed against the neighbouring people. Among the broader population, therefore, anti-Vietnamese feelings do not appear to be intense. It is true, however, that many members of the Lao elite fear what they perceive as Vietnamese aggressiveness, as well as organization and drive . . . . The feeling of inadequacy vis-à-vis the Vietnamese is particularly evident among those educated Lao who were once placed in positions subordinate to the Vietnamese by French colonial officers, whose administrative policies tended to discriminate against the Lao.'[5] The last sentences, of course, refer to the American-backed RLG elite, not the Pathet Lao elite.

Our experience indicates that the ethnic antagonisms that do exist between the Lao and the Vietnamese are no more serious than those found between different groups in a country like Australia, or between the ethnic Lao and the various hill tribes, or indeed between the various tribal groups themselves. Such feelings only become politically significant in specific conjunctures, and then only if they are promoted by some organized political group, party or government which exploits them politically. The Lao right wing, for example, encouraged anti-Vietnamese sentiments, the Communists do not. If anything, a major theme of the Pathet Lao government is ethnic reconciliation.

What is extraordinary about the long relationship between the Vietnamese and Lao Communists is that it is hard to find a single instance where the two movements were at loggerheads with each other. From 1949 onwards the Pathet Lao leaders were supported militarily, politically and diplomatically by the Vietnamese at every turn: they were supported when they decided to enter the coalition government in 1958 and when it collapsed under right-wing pressure they found Vietnamese support waiting for them when they escaped back to the mountains. The Vietnamese supported them in military actions and diplomacy surrounding the Geneva negotiations on forming a new coalition in Laos in 1962, and again during the Paris negotiations. Indeed, at critical times, such as in the late 1950s, it is certain that the Pathet Lao base areas only survived because of Vietnamese support.

Of course, the Vietnamese had good national reasons for giving this support because the base area provinces of Sam Neua and Phong Saly were on its border, and when the Vietnam war started in earnest in the early 1960s the Ho Chi Minh trail, which wound its way down along the Lao-Vietnam border, was a critical supply route for guerrillas in South Vietnam. Thus the Pathet Lao liberated zones acted as a buffer for the Vietnamese Communists. But the fact that the Pathet Lao has had Vietnamese support for such a long time does not make it a 'creature' of Hanoi. The studies made throughout the long civil war by Langer and Zazloff indicate that the relationship is one of cooperation and coordination of actions, rather than one of Vietnamese domination.

The general absence of substantive conflicts naturally inclined the Lao Communists towards the Vietnamese version of Marxism. The traditional social structure of Laos, like that of Cambodia, had produced no substantial intelligentsia, as had the Confucian system in Vietnam, and the French had concentrated their educational resources for Indochina in Vietnam. This predisposed the Lao towards a degree of dependence on the Vietnamese Marxist canon, and therefore there never appears to have been any basic ideological clash between the two movements.

Thus the national interests of the Lao and the Vietnamese Communists have tended to converge historically rather than diverge, and it is for this reason above all that Kaysone could speak with such confidence of the 'radiant spirit of proletarian internationalism' binding the two countries. However, the glow would most certainly fade if their national interests did ever seriously diverge.

It was therefore predictable that the Vietnamese and Lao governments would cooperate closely after 1975. Two months after the founding of the LPDR Kaysone led a government and party delegation to Hanoi (on 5–11 February 1976), following which the two countries pledged to strengthen economic and cultural cooperation, and Vietnam offered to help Laos train economic, scientific and other technical experts. The treaty of friendship signed in July 1977 simply extended this by stressing a desire to increase economic and trade cooperation between the two countries. The pledges of mutual assistance were largely one-way: Vietnam offered Laos duty-free access to the Port of Da Nang and interest-free loans to Vientiane over 1978–80. In 1983 *Nhan Dan* gave further details of Vietnam's aid. It had pledged, from 1976 to 1985, 1.3 billion Dong (US \$146.7 million) to cover the rebuilding of Sam Neua township and two smaller towns; the repair of 300 kilometres of roads; provision of 900 specialists; and the training of half of the 10,000 Lao students who go abroad. 'Almost half' of this aid, the paper said, would have to be reimbursed. This is not exactly standard neo-colonial practice.

The treaty also said that Laos and Vietnam would 'cooperate closely in increasing their capability of defending and protecting their independence, sovereignty and territorial integrity'. This undoubtedly served Vietnam's regional diplomatic objectives well. By this stage the dispute with Pol Pot was well under way, and at the same time Vietnam was coming under mounting pressure from China over the South China Sea. The treaty with Laos secured their one friendly border, blocking what Hanoi saw as a possibility of complete 'encirclement' by pro-Chinese forces.

However, it also needs to be recognized that the Lao government itself had a strong interest in military cooperation with Vietnam.

The LPDR is a weak state, with a long and virtually indefensible border with Thailand. Relations between the governments in Bangkok and Vientiane, and the atmosphere along this border, were tense in 1977. The Vientiane government also faced harassment from several hundred right-wing guerrillas, mostly followers of Vang Pao operating in the mountains of central Laos and out of refugee camps in Thailand. An immediate result of the treaty was the launching in late 1977 of a major offensive against the remnants of Vang Pao's 'Secret Army', which appears to have been crushed by early 1978.

The treaty legitimized the presence of Vietnamese troops who had been stationed in the country for many years. It is the presence of these troops that is regarded as the main proof of Vietnamese domination in Laos. The exact figures have never been revealed, but they were undoubtedly substantial. According to an allegedly senior Lao government official, who defected to Thailand in 1979, Hanoi's troop strength in Laos was between 24,000 and 30,000 at the end of 1977, and was subsequently lifted to 50,000 as regional tensions grew. At present most of these soldiers are based near the Lao-Chinese border. In our visits to the country in the early 1980s we never observed any combat soldiers in Vientiane. So this deployment is not that of a military force there to intimidate the Lao population, as a 'neo-colonialism' theory would suggest.

A large number of the soldiers are also engaged in construction work throughout the country. In Xieng Khouang, where the link to Vietnam is being upgraded so that vital fuel supplies can be trucked into the province from Vietnam, we saw them at work on road construction. These troops were unarmed, unlike an army of occupation. Throughout their long presence the Vietnamese army has shown sensitivity to the feelings of the local population. Indeed, over the many years of Vietnamese presence in Laos, there have been remarkably few reports of their harsh treatment of the local population. The Vietnamese army appears to be acting similarly in contemporary Cambodia, where their experience in Laos seems to be standing them in good stead. Former Lao prime minister, Prince Souvanna Phouma, who resided in Vientiane until his death in January, 1984, was sanguine about their presence. In late 1980 he said: 'The day we have peace, the Vietnamese will go back to their country . . . there are American and French soldiers in West Germany. Did West Germany lose its independence? I think not. It's the same thing.'

The 1977 treaty also said that the two countries 'would build the

Vietnam-Laos border into a border of fraternal friendship', and later an agreement was signed delineating the border. There should have been few problems with this – the areas on both sides had long been under the control of political groups cooperating with each other, and both agreeing that the border established by the French should be accepted. The French had taken the watershed of the Annamite mountain chain as the border, and both sides presumably accepted this in principle. But the region has never been thoroughly surveyed, and some modern maps show the border cutting across the headwaters of certain rivers.[6] Since some of these flow to the Mekong (through Laos) and others to the Gulf of Tonkin (through Vietnam), adjustments according to the principle established by the French would be roughly mutually compensatory. However, no attempt has been made, so far as we know, to give any definitive delineation of the border, and the agreement has not been published.

Despite this, Hanoi was later to praise border relations with Laos as a 'model for good neighbourliness and friendship' – doubtless thinking of the problems it had encountered with China and Cambodia over these matters. Dommen, on the other hand, presents a typical Western assessment: 'The text has never been published, but presumably it legalizes "adjustments" in Vietnam's favour that the former royal government had been unwilling to concede. There are already reports that Vietnam is colonizing the disputed border areas in Xieng Khouang and Savannakhet provinces.'[7] Neither Dommen nor anyone else has ever presented any evidence to support these assertions.

We have not visited the border area in Xieng Khouang but according to Japanese journalists who have, and to Hmong refugees we spoke to who had lived along the border since 1977, Dommen's assertions about colonization are untrue. With regard to Savannakhet province we gleaned an interesting snippet of information about the border. A church minister from Savannakhet said that the number of Christians in the province had increased since the treaty because a village formerly on the Vietnamese side of the border which had Christians in it had since come under Lao jurisdiction. Thus the only detail we have of the border 'adjustments' made under the 1977 agreement indicates that they favour Laos. No doubt, however, adjustments elsewhere have been made in Vietnam's favour as a trade-off.

Even though the signing of the treaty was motivated from Vietnam's side by its deteriorating relations with China and

Cambodia, this was still being kept under wraps by Hanoi in 1977 in the interests of 'international proletarian solidarity'. Thus a joint statement by Laos and Vietnam spoke of the need 'to strengthen their militant solidarity and relations of cooperation with the USSR and China', and the treaty called for 'militant solidarity, lasting cooperation with and mutual assistance to fraternal Cambodia'. Laos's immediate concern was the extreme right-wing Thanin regime in Bangkok and its desire to break the Thai monopoly over its access to the sea.

From the beginning this had been a stated aim of the LPDR and access through Cambodia had figured in its calculations. In December 1975 Phoumi Vongvichit, deputy prime minister and foreign minister, spoke of a plan to cooperate with the Vietnamese to build roads to the sea. Then he continued: 'Apart from Vietnam, we may have passage to the sea through Cambodia. After building highways reaching Pakse and Cambodia, we may go as far as Kompong Som port in Cambodia. Prince Sihanouk has said that we can tell him where we want facilities and build them as we wish. If this is done we shall have many routes to the sea. We shall choose the route which permits us to pay less for the transport of goods. This will make it unnecessary for us to kowtow to anyone, as we did before . . . '

A government delegation to Phnom Penh, at the request of the Cambodian government, followed on 15–18 December. The delegation, led by General Sipraseuth, held talks with Prime Minister Penn Nouth and other Khmer leaders in what was said to be 'an extremely friendly, cordial and warm atmosphere'. The main focus of the talks, however, seems to have been the continued US presence in Thailand and demands that Lao and Cambodian rightists be prohibited from establishing bases there. No doubt Sipraseuth discovered during his stay in Phnom Penh that neither Penn Nouth nor Prince Sihanouk had any say in the running of Democratic Kampuchea. Nothing ever came of the plans for Laos to use the outlet of Kompong Som.

There is no doubt that Hanoi was successful in creating the 'special relationship' it desired between the SRV and the LPDR. But it is misleading to view this as a colonial relationship, between master and subject. Vientiane had good reasons of its own for fostering closer cooperation with Hanoi. A more fruitful approach is to focus on the geopolitical position in which the new Lao government found itself after 1975. We also need to consider the LPDR's relations with Thailand, China and Cambodia, as well as Vietnam, to get a balanced picture.

As a small and weak state, Laos has frequently found that its destiny has been decided for it by the actions of more powerful states. Its strategic location in Southeast Asia did not allow it to retreat into isolation: Laos has the dubious distinction of sharing borders with all the major states of the region – China, Vietnam, Thailand, Burma and Cambodia. Involvement in their disputes was inescapable, though Laos itself had little to gain from other peoples' quarrels. Neutralism has always been a tempting option for Lao politicians, but rarely one they could afford.

Laos and Thailand

Thailand's power in relation to Laos is neglected by almost all contemporary commentators on Indochinese politics. Before 1975 the Bangkok government had exercised considerable influence among Royal Lao Government (RLG) politicians, had actively supported the RLG in the civil war by allowing US air strikes to be flown against the Pathet Lao from Udon airbase in the northeast of Thailand, and when the ceasefire was announced in 1973 it had at least 20,000 Thai military 'volunteers' fighting in Laos against the Communists. The Communist victory, therefore, abruptly reduced Bangkok's influence in an area it had come to regard as its own. However, even though the Thais were pushed back to their side of the Mekong River they still held a powerful political weapon – the ability to blockade landlocked Laos.

Thailand provides Laos with its main outlet to the world market. Furthermore, Thailand itself has always been Laos' main trading partner. Over 1973–6, for example, 65 per cent of Lao exports were absorbed by Thailand, and goods from Thailand accounted for 98 per cent of Lao imports in 1973. On the other hand, Laos figures as a very minor partner in Thailand's overall trade. On top of this a great deal of informal trade has always been conducted back and forth across the border, and because internal communications within Laos are so poor sections of the Lao economy are more closely integrated into the adjacent Thai economy than the Lao economy.[8] The cumulative effect of this is that Bangkok possesses a great deal of economic power over Vientiane – greater than anything Vietnam has ever exercised or is likely to exercise for the forseeable future.

Ironically perhaps, it was Bangkok's power of blockade that dictated the timing of the formation of the Lao People's Democratic

Republic in December 1975. The Lao economy was already a shambles at the end of 1975 because of the instability caused by the drawn-out nature of the Communist takeover after the formation of the coalition government in April 1974. The cessation of US aid in mid-1975 had caused runaway inflation, so when the Thais closed their border with Laos on 18 November because of frontier clashes the economic impact on the Lao economy was immediate and crippling. For the population in the Mekong River cities and the former RLG zones it brought unprecedented austerity. The crisis forced the Lao Communists to call the National Congress together in early December, although they had not been expected to assert complete control until the elections already announced for April 1976. 'The hardening of Thailand's attitude,' *Le Monde* commented, 'the prolonged closing of the frontier formed by the Mekong and the halt of deliveries of fuel and foodstuffs have no doubt driven the Laotian Communists to close their ranks and to provoke a political transformation which will allow them to deal rapidly with economic problems.'

Because of Thailand's actions during the civil war, the Lao Communists had good reason to be wary of Bangkok's intentions towards the new regime. However, from the beginning of 1976 moderates began to get the upper hand in Thai politics. The border was re-opened at several points in January and in March the Thai authorities set a deadline of 20 July for the US Military Assistance Command Thailand to leave the country. In April the liberal leader of the Democratic Party, Seni Pramoj, took command of the coalition government in Bangkok, and indicated that he favoured a policy of *détente* with Communist Indochina. Improved relations with Laos quickly followed. The two governments signed a communiqué on 3 August which stated that relations between them would be based on the five principles of peaceful coexistence first enunciated at Geneva, and contained clauses covering a range of commercial and political agreements.

This *rapprochement* was strongly opposed by the right-wing Thai parties and the military, who overthrew the Pramoj government in October 1976, installing a government led by the reactionary judge Thanin Kraivichien. This dealt a body blow to Thai-Lao relations and over the following year border trading points between the two countries were restricted, while mutual recriminations about border incidents were traded back and forth between Vientiane and Bangkok.

The establishment of the Thanin regime in Bangkok coincided

with a rapidly deteriorating economic situation in Laos, which in 1977 reached crisis proportions. A mild drought in 1976 became a severe one in 1977. A joint study by the Lao agricultural ministry and the United Nations Development Programme in September 1977 estimated that the harvest was down 40 per cent nationwide compared with the previous year, and an appalling 95 per cent in some provinces in the south. Only large infusions of international food aid staved off famine throughout the country. In this situation the hostile policies of the Thanin regime were seen as a direct attempt at bringing the government in Vientiane to its knees. The Thanin regime also provided a safe haven for right-wing Lao resistance groups who could make sabotage raids into Laos from base areas in Thailand.

It should not have been surprising, therefore, to find the Pathet Lao actively moving, in mid-1977, to solidify its ties with its long-time ally, Hanoi. Already, at the end of 1975, Vietnam had acted swiftly to help the Lao overcome the difficulties imposed by the first blockade when it trucked vital supplies across the Annamite mountain chain from Da Nang to Savannakhet. At this time the Soviets had also brought in vital supplies by air. Both of these countries immediately came to Vientiane's aid again when it came under pressure from the Thanin regime. When Laos and Vietnam signed their treaty of friendship and cooperation in 1977, an accompanying statement clearly identified Thailand's policies as a motivating factor on the Lao side: 'Since the October 1976 coup the Thai administration has pursued a hostile policy towards Vietnam and Laos, resorted to the application of economic pressure against Laos, oppressed and terrorized Vietnamese nationals and failed to implement the joint communiqués signed between Vietnam and Thailand on 6 August 1976, and the joint communiqué signed between Laos and Thailand on 3 August 1976 . . . . The fact that the administrations of a number of ASEAN member-countries are actively strengthening bilateral military alliances under the anti-Communist label will lead to a danger of transforming ASEAN into a de-facto military alliance.' While this latter reference apparently alluded to joint Thai-Malaysian operations against guerrillas in southern Thailand, Vietnam, and Laos in particular, obviously felt that such actions could just as easily be turned against them.

Cambodia and Laos

The geopolitical location of Laos meant that it inevitably stressed the need for Indochinese cooperation. We have already noted Vientiane's interest in access to Kompong Som port. As the conflict between Vietnam and Cambodia intensified, the Lao government attempted to act as mediator. Indeed the LPDR maintained an embassy in Phnom Penh right up to the fall of the capital to Vietnamese troops on 7 January 1979 – which earned it a spray of bullets from Pol Pot troops during their rapid departure from the capital.

Relations between Phnom Penh and Vientiane never degenerated into the acrimony that passed between Phnom Penh and Hanoi. The overriding reason for this was their shared border with Thailand. As the *chef du cabinet* of the Lao foreign ministry, Soubanh Srithirath, explained in early 1979: 'We could limit the very minor problems we had with Cambodia. Vietnam could not. The politics are different there. We have a border with Thailand. Vietnam does not . . . '

Another important general reason for the absence of Khmer-Lao antagonism was the fact that Cambodian nationalism was not formed in relation to the Lao, and vice versa. Both nationalisms were defined relative to their two powerful neighbours, Thailand and Vietnam. Not even in the deranged historical fantasies of Pol Pot did the ghost of the old Lao kingdom of Lane Xang loom menacingly on Cambodia's northern border (although Sihanouk had invoked it in moments of extreme exasperation). Lao-Cambodian relations from 1975 to late 1978 were relatively calm, though not untroubled. In one of the Pol Pot regime's saner diplomatic moves, Phnom Penh donated food aid to a desperate Laos in mid-1977. The political capital this won in Vientiane was dearly bought – many Khmers themselves were close to starvation at the time.

By late 1977 the border war between Cambodia and Vietnam was in full swing. A delegation headed by President Souphannavong and Foreign Minister Phoumi Sipraseuth was dispatched to Phnom Penh over 17–21 December in a bid to avoid an open rupture between their Communist neighbours. On the day before the delegation arrived Phnom Penh radio had broadcast an account of Lao history which said that, like Cambodia, Laos had been a victim in the past of 'the expansionist ambitions of the Annam feudalists from the east and the Siam feudalists from the west'. The Lao, it said, had every reason to establish common cause with Cambodia against Thailand, but more particularly against Vietnam. Needless to say, the Lao delegation had little success in smoothing the Pol Pot regime's quarrel with Vietnam.

The differences between the two governments were obvious from Souphannavong's opening speech in Phnom Penh, when he spoke of the Lao Party continuing 'the splendid work of the Indochinese Communist Party, jointly with the Cambodian people and the Vietnamese people . . . ' This favourable reference to the old ICP directly challenged the line of the Pol Pot leadership, who were currently attacking the Vietnamese for supposedly advocating an Indochina Federation. Souphannavong also went on to speak of the Lao-Vietnamese treaty of friendship, and the treaty on the delimitation of their frontiers, as good examples of how neighbours should conduct their international relations. This also was a position categorically rejected by the leaders of the Democratic Kampuchea government. There had also been reported clashes on the Lao-Khmer border, which both sides had denied at the time, but clearly Souphannavong had these in mind as well.

The only journalist who ever got near the Lao-Khmer border region was Nayan Chanda, who visited Pakse in November 1978. He reported that it was clear from his talks with local officials that the situation on the border had been deteriorating since the end of 1976. The Cambodian donation of 3,000 tons of rice in mid-1977 was the last time that Route 13 across the border had been used, after which the Khmers Rouges dug trenches across the road and laid mines. At the same time, strengthened Khmer Rouge border patrols began shooting at Lao fishermen on the river, and anyone else who strayed too close to the frontier.

In mid-1978 several Lao soldiers were killed and the Cambodian ambassador in Vientiane, Sam San, visited the border area and saw the bodies. He expressed regret over the deaths 'caused by mistake', but the incidents continued. Phoumi Sipraseuth visited the border a number of times and instructed Lao soldiers not to return the fire so as not to aggravate the situation and thereby embroil Laos in a costly conflict. Chanda also reported: 'In conversation with local officials, it was revealed that in pursuance of their good-neighbour policy, the Lao authorities had sent back (at least until the end of 1976) a large number of refugees who had fled Cambodia. Asked when they decided to stop sending refugees back, one source said: "When we realized that all the returned refugees had been executed. When we tried to send some refugees back they pleaded with us to kill them rather than send them back to Cambodia. Then we realized things over there were really bad".'[9]

Within a fortnight of the Lao delegation's departure from Phnom Penh in December 1977, Cambodia broke off diplomatic relations with Vietnam and made the dispute between the two Communist countries public. The USSR and most Eastern European countries, including Albania, immediately condemned Phnom Penh. The LPDR, on the other hand, continued to chart a neutral course in the dispute. Claims by the Japanese press and Reuters that the Vietnamese had placed a division of troops on the northern Cambodian border in southern Laos were strongly denied by Vientiane on 17 January 1978: 'The Lao Party and government . . . have always been persistent in pursuing their policy of solidarity with Vietnam and Cambodia . . . there has never been any military operation carried out by Vietnamese forces through Lao territory.' A day later Prime Minister Kaysone sent identical letters to both the Vietnamese and Cambodian governments expressing his wish that they would 'make joint efforts to settle the disputes at an early date by holding negotiations on the basis of respect for each other's independence, sovereignty and territorial integrity'.

The belligerence of Phnom Penh made this 'neutralist' stance increasingly difficult to sustain. The Vietnamese peace proposals put forward on 5 February 1978 were welcomed in Vientiane, but their rejection in Phnom Penh ensured the final divergence between the two countries. By mid-year a joint statement by Kaysone and Souphannavong said 'we support Vietnam's stand for the settlement of differences' through negotiation, a course Cambodia still rejected.

Meanwhile the Lao were increasingly viewed as Vietnamese puppets by the Pol Pot regime. Elizabeth Becker relates: 'When I was in Pol Pot's Cambodia (in December 1978) officials there said Laos had been "Vietnamized" and the Lao race threatened with extinction due to forced marriage with Vietnamese. This proved outlandish but worth mentioning because the Pol Pot regime believed it and acted accordingly.' She added: 'The Lao, in fact, have preserved their own culture much better than Cambodia did under Pol Pot.'[10]

China: the unavoidable Enemy

One of the first foreign policy tasks of the LPDR in 1975 was to stake out a new form of neutralism in relation to the Sino-Soviet dispute. The task fell to Phoumi Vongvichit, who said in 1975: 'At present there are several countries which cannot get along with each other. However they can get along with us. This is because we have used correct diplomatic means . . . My policy is to win more friends while decreasing the number of enemies . . . as a friend, I hope that you two will be able to get along sooner or later. I side with neither you nor him . . . ' Such studied aloofness from the implications of this dispute was in the end no more possible for Laos than it was for Vietnam. As regional tensions mounted, Laos was inexorably drawn into the conflict.

Up to 1978 Vientiane's links with Peking were cordial but distant. When the conflict between Vietnam and China came to the surface the Lao initially tried to keep their distance in much the same way as they had over the Vietnam-Cambodian conflict. But as all the disputes became interlocked so the Lao eventually had to shift their position. The reluctance of a number of Lao leaders to accept a more partisan role in the gathering political storm can be seen in remarks made by Kaysone in March 1978 when he said that 'a number of individuals are influenced by psychological warfare tactics employed by the enemies' and by 'narrow-minded national-ism'. This expressed the persistent neutralist current in Lao politics, and possibly some resentment at what the Vietnamese had led them into. No doubt many Lao approached the impending conflict in Indochina with trepidation: after all, it was unlikely that they could have any decisive influence on the course or outcome of events; yet they would have to bear the consequences, whatever they might be.

As 1978 proceeded Vientiane's position on the politics of the region became tougher. In late June, Radio Vientiane broadcast that 'the unity between the army and the people must be further strengthened, as well as the army's international unity with the Vietnamese army and people.' In the following month an editorial in *Sieng Pasason* marking the anniversary of the treaty with Vietnam said that the Lao government would 'stand by the side of the Vietnamese people' and was 'determined to smash all divisive schemes of the imperialists and international reactionary forces' (the latter term a Vietnamese code-phrase for China). At the same time Kaysone made a thinly veiled attack on China by saying that 'imperialists and international reactionaries have incited dissension among our people of various nationalities' and called for struggle against schemes 'trying to incite the nationalities to carry out prolonged resistance against our revolution'. Kaysone repeated the charge in August. Peking reacted strongly, accusing Moscow and Hanoi of trying to 'poison relations between China and Laos'.

It was at this point, when the regional barometer was about to explode, that differences within the LPRP on the country's strategic options came briefly into public view. At a gathering of party functionaries to celebrate the 33rd anniversary of Lao independence day, Souphannavong gave a speech which, while praising the Russian Revolution and celebrating the founding of the Indochinese Communist Party, went on to say that 'imperialists and the international reactionary forces are attempting to sow divisions between Laos and other socialist countries, especially Vietnam'. But most significantly he went on to add: 'More seriously still, recently they spread the rumour that Lao traitors in exile . . . now have a new supporter, that is Great China, and that China would attack Vietnam and then Laos. This is very wicked and dangerous propaganda aimed at sowing bedevilment and anxiety among our people to make them lose confidence in the line and policies of our party and state, to sow division between the Lao people and the Chinese people and, finally to sabotage our revolution.'

This speech cannot be read (as some have) as an anti-Vietnamese statement, nor as a pro-China one; it is either a statement of the position of Lao 'neutralist' Communism directed at the staunchly pro-Hanoi stance of Kaysone, or a veiled attack on great power pressure by China itself, accusing it of spreading rumours of its support for anti-government activity similar to those which had circulated in Hanoi and had recently panicked the Hoa there to flee to China.

There had never been a solid pro-Peking faction in the leadership of the Pathet Lao. Deputy Premier Vongvichit had often been rumoured to be pro-China, in much the same way as Truong Chinh has been in Vietnam. There is no real evidence for this (prior to 1975 Kaysone was often depicted as pro-Chinese and Vongvichit as pro-Soviet). Again, in October 1978, Vongvichit said: 'As to the Vietnam–China and the Vietnam-Cambodia conflicts, we want them to end and that peace should prevail in Indochina and in Southeast Asia. We believe that the differences in views, the conflicts can be settled in a peaceful way. This is why we back the proposal of the Vietnamese comrades to settle conflicts through negotiations.' But both China and Cambodia had at this stage rejected such proposals.

The debate within the LPRP, however, is a longstanding one within Lao politics – between a neutralist tendency and one arguing for a closer alliance with powerful friends. For the right wing in the old RLG it meant closer ties with Bangkok and Washington in opposition to Prince Souvanna Phouma (at least until the early 1960s). For the Communists, the options have been a form of neutralism or a close alliance with Hanoi. In 1978 the Communist 'neutralists' were particularly worried about adding to the country's problems through antagonizing their powerful northern neighbour by identifying too closely with Vietnam. However, the gathering regional power struggle cut the ground from under their feet. They realized that neither Peking, Phnom Penh nor Hanoi would brook a policy of neutrality in the coming conflict. It was also clear to them that it would be absurd to trade the Vietnamese and the Soviets as allies for an alliance with China. Longstanding political ties with the Vietnamese, and Soviet aid and expertise, could not be balanced by the Chinese. Moreover, if Vietnam, by virtue of its size and proximity, posed a threat to Lao sovereignty, this was also the case many times over in the case of China.

Nevertheless, it is notable that the Lao government has maintained a relaxed attitude towards its ethnic Chinese community. In 1983, Chinese traders still dominated the free market in Vientiane. A Chinese school continued to operate. But the Maoist literature that had been available in Vientiane bookshops in 1980 had disappeared. In the northern provinces, the government has made no serious attempt to bar border trade and other contacts with southern China. This approach is in notable contrast to that of Vietnam over such matters.

Overall, the march of events in Indochina offered the LPDR few options. The one it finally took was both logical and predictable – indeed, the only real surprise has been the relatively lenient treatment Laos received from the USA.

The Eclipse of neutralist Communism

The Vietnamese invasion of Cambodia, or rather the political deadlock that made it inevitable, sealed the fate of Lao neutralist Communism. Immediately prior to the offensive the Thai supreme commander, General Serm Na Nakorn, claimed that most of the 40,000 Vietnamese troops stationed in Laos had been moved to the Lao-Cambodian border in preparation for an invasion. These forces were allegedly launched into Cambodia from staging areas in Laos, in a dramatic reversal of the Lao policy enunciated less than a year earlier of not allowing 'any country to use Lao territory to invade another country'. This propelled it irrevocably into the vortex of the conflict, and China could not be expected to overlook Vientiane's complicity in the invasion.

This, in turn, made the alliance with Hanoi absolutely vital to Lao security in 1978–9, for there was a possibility China could strike at Vietnam through Laos. The Lao government was increasingly pre-occupied with its northern border, for Thai pressure on Laos had eased considerably following the overthrow of Thanin on 20 October 1977. The new Thai government, headed by General Kriangsak Chomanan, was committed to improving relations with all three Indochinese states. The economic blockade of Laos was lifted at the end of November, and an agreement for the resumption of flights by Thai International Airways was signed in early December. Around the same time Kriangsak held a meeting with provincial governors in an attempt to harness them to the government's more conciliatory policy toward Laos and Cambodia. Right-wing Lao and Cambodian refugee leaders were reportedly asked to leave the country.

Kriangsak and his followers were obviously aware that Bangkok's blockade simply deepened Lao dependence on Vietnam and its other socialist supporters. The signing of the treaty between Laos and Vietnam had clearly jolted the more astute politicians into realizing that Thanin's extreme anti-Communism was only isolating Thailand.

During the Thanin period the Lao had little to retaliate with. One bargaining chip was restricting use of their airspace which, combined with a bar on overflights of Vietnam pending Bangkok's diplomatic recognition of the Hanoi government, was costing Thai International Airways dearly on its flights to Hong Kong. Not surprisingly the Airways lobbied Bangkok for a softer line on Indochina. Theoretically, the Lao could also have threatened to cut off hydro-electricity supplied from its Nam Ngum dam to northeastern Thailand. However, Laos could not afford the loss of revenue this would cause, and thus it was no real source of leverage.

The Vientiane government's only other bargaining chip was its provision of weapons and a base area for the Communist Party of Thailand (CPT). Both governments could play the game of pro-moting insurgencies. However, in 1977–8, Laos was supporting a still unified and potentially ascendant force, while the rightist Lao rebels backed by Bangkok, or at least its regional commanders, were fragmented and declining. Bangkok's fears over Lao support for the CPT were also fuelled by the consideration that the CPT was particularly strong in the northeast, a region characterized not only by poverty and agrarian discontent but also by a population that was predominantly ethnic Lao and by geographic proximity to Laos itself.

It was probably inevitable that Lao support, or otherwise, for the CPT would become an adjunct of its foreign policy. It was obvious that any substantial bargain struck between the Thai and Lao governments would involve the mutual cessation of active support for armed rebels in the other country's territory. Achieving such an agreement with the Lao was a central aim of Kriangsak's foreign policy, alongside his concern to stall the formation of an Indo-chinese bloc of states.

Accord was reached between the two governments in lengthy negotiations in 1978. The importance of this for Bangkok was underlined by the fact that a meeting to sign an agreement set for December was delayed only slightly by the Vietnamese invasion of Cambodia, while a shooting incident on the Mekong, which on other occasions had closed the border, was ignored. In Vientiane on 6 January 1979 the prime ministers of Laos and Thailand issued a joint communiqué 'ushering in a new era in Lao-Thai relations of friendship, cooperation and peaceful coexistence'. The com-muniqué also included a Lao pledge to 'terminate all support pre-viously given to the Communist Party of Thailand', whose ally, Pol Pot, was driven from his capital by Vietnamese troops the following day.

Forsaking the pro-Peking Communist Party of Thailand had been made all the easier for the Lao by Vietnam's growing tensions with China and Cambodia, and Pham Van Dong's renunciation of support for the Thai Communists during his mission to Bangkok in September 1978. The weakening of ties between Laos and China over 1978 also helped to rationalize the step. However, the Lao attitude to the CPT was primarily a direct product of bilateral nego-tiations between Vientiane and Bangkok, and their need for cordial relations.

According to CPT sources the Lao and the Vietnamese had attempted since 1976 to try to reorient their party's strategy away from armed struggle. Unable to sway the CPT's leadership towards a strategy that would accommodate continued support from the Indochinese states, Laos and Vietnam finally disowned it. In the following year the fratricidal struggle in Indochina rebounded on the CPT, shattering its constituency into warring factions – some pro-Hanoi, some pro-Peking and some independents. Since then the CPT has suffered a succession of military set-backs and mass defections, and its role in the regional power struggle, and probably in Thai politics as well, is over.

Vientiane's foreign policy orientation after 1975 was not dictated by Hanoi, but by the conjunctural interaction of all the larger states surrounding Laos. Given the LPRP's long and close working relationship with the Vietnamese it is not surprising that it should support them when the march of events finally forced a choice. Realistically, they had no other option. This, however, is not evidence of colonialism, 'neo' or otherwise. There is no evidence of Vietnamese economic exploitation of Laos – if anything the reverse situation applies. Laos is poor and it has relied on Vietnam, the USSR and other Eastern bloc countries for aid and expertise to establish the most rudimentary aspects of a socialist economy.

Indeed Vietnam's influence in this area is limited because of its own poverty. But this still did not stop Martin Stuart-Fox from arguing that 'despite the presence in Laos of hundreds of Soviet and Cuban advisers and technicians, it is the Vietnamese who effectively run the country.'[11] The only evidence he furnishes to prove this is that the Lao followed the Vietnamese in their attempt to collectivize agriculture in 1978. That this decision had a similar economic and security rationale in both countries is barely considered, while the fact that Communist governments pursue policies of collectivized agriculture (a policy attempted at some stage by every Communist government to date) is hardly proof that the Vietnamese 'run the country'. Indeed within the framework of a colonial relationship with Vietnam Laos's much greater economic liberalization after 1979 becomes unfathomable.

Arguments about colonialism or neo-colonialism do not help us understand the Lao situation in Indochina. There is no question that its alliance with Vietnam has drawn it into a quarrel it could do without – but then, in an abstract sense, Vietnam could equally have done without it. There is no question that Vietnam is the dominant partner in the alliance, but one cannot conceive of any alliance in which Laos would be the dominant partner. Disparities of power, however, do not add up to colonialism or domination. As we have seen the alliance has held mutual benefits for both parties.

Notes

1. Arthur J. Dommen, 'Laos: Vietnam's Satellite', *Current History*, December 1979, p. 201.

2. Martin Stuart-Fox, 'Laos: The Vietnamese Connection', *Southeast Asian Affairs 1979*, Singapore 1980, p. 208. The author has since moderated his position considerably; see his 'Lao Foreign Policy: The View From Vientiane', *Journal of Contemporary Asia*, vol. 11, 1981.

3. Dommen, p. 202.

4. Cf., for example, Michael Akehurst, *A Modern Introduction to International Law*, London 1970, pp. 74–5.

5. Paul F. Langer and Joseph J. Zasloff, *North Vietnam and the Pathet Lao: Partners in the Struggle for Laos*, Cambridge, Mass. 1970, p. 17. See also Joel M. Halpern and William S. Turley, eds, 'The Training of Vietnamese Communist Cadres in Laos', mimeo, 1977. Carlyle Thayer, 'Laos and Vietnam: The Anatomy of a "Special Relationship" ' in Martin Stuart-Fox, ed., *Contemporary Laos*, St Lucia, Queensland 1982.

6. J.R.V. Prescott, D.F. Collier, and D.F. Prescott, *Frontiers of Southeast Asia*, Melbourne 1977, p. 62.

7. Dommen, p. 202.

8. Bunyaraks Ninsanda, *et al*, *Thai-Laos Economic Relations: A New Perspective*, Bangkok 1977, p. 11.

9. *Far Eastern Economic Review*, 8 December 1978.

10. Elizabeth Becker, 'Laos: The Widening Indochina Conflict', *Indochina Issues*, no. 2, June 1979.

11. Stuart-Fox, p. 206.

4

Cambodia: the Politics of Perfect Sovereignty

At first glance, it is not obvious why events in Cambodia should have taken a contrasting path to those in Laos. Like the Pathet Lao, the Cambodian Communist movement originated as an outgrowth of the Vietnamese-dominated Indochinese Communist Party and the struggles of the Viet Minh against French colonial rule in Indochina. As in Laos, the backwardness of the social and political milieu was reinforced by the relatively limited impact of capitalist imperialism on the outlying parts of French Indochina. The result was that in Cambodia the revolutionary movement remained weak and dependent on Vietnamese sponsorship for many years before developing its own momentum. As with the Pathet Lao, the Khmers Rouges were accused by their enemies of being Vietnamese puppets. Both countries were strategically important to Vietnam, and the Vietnamese inevitably took a similar interest in the affairs of both Laos and Cambodia. One might, therefore, expect similar influences to produce similar outcomes in both countries.

As the reality of the conflict between Phnom Penh and Hanoi after 1975 became increasingly obvious, the view that the Khmers Rouges were Vietnamese 'puppets' passed out of fashion. It was now discovered by some commentators that the Khmers Rouges were Cambodian 'patriots' struggling against Vietnamese attempts to dominate Cambodia.

The scholar whose researches on the origins of the Vietnam-Cambodia dispute have had the greatest influence is probably Stephen Heder of Cornell University.[1] Heder argues that the conflict between the two Communist governments originated as a dispute over the Vietnam-Cambodian border. However, the border issue, not of great importance in itself, catalysed a large-scale confrontation because of the contrasting overall political perspectives of the Khmer Rouge and Vietnamese leaders. They were unable to agree over the border issue because the two sides adopted diametrically opposed attitudes towards it. Phnom Penh took an intransigent stance against what it viewed as encroachments on the soil of a sovereign Cambodia by an ancient enemy, while Hanoi pressed for concessions from Cambodia in the name of socialist internationalism. When these were not forthcoming, the Viet-namese undertook a campaign to destroy Pol Pot's Democratic Kampuchea (DK) regime and the conflict became a struggle by Phnom Penh to avert the engulfment of Cambodia by the Viet-namese.

Thus, in Heder's analysis, by 1978 the original border conflict had become almost irrelevant, the dispute by then being fundamentally over Vietnam's insistence on imposing its own version of Com-munism on its neighbours even if Cambodian sovereignty were outraged in the process. He concludes that Pol Pot's claim that the real cause of the dispute was Vietnam's desire to dominate Cam-bodia by means of an 'Indochina Federation' is valid, if exag-gerated. His central assumption is that the main factor escalating the conflict was Vietnamese pressure on Cambodia.

The early Disputes on the Vietnam-Cambodia Border, 1975-6.

According to Heder's analysis, the border disputes provided the spark that ignited the wider conflict, so it is there that we should begin. Fighting on the Vietnam-Cambodia border was first reported in May and June 1975, but no details were known. From the evidence now available, it seems that these outbreaks were small-scale, and almost all of them were initiated by the Cambodian side. They were partly a result of the confusion caused by the collapse of the Phnom Penh and Saigon governments, and partly a result of the radical upheaval taking place inside Cambodia. The Khmers Rouges closed the border with Vietnam in May 1975, and pursued and shot Khmers trying to escape to Vietnam. This appa-rently led to clashes between Khmer Rouge and Vietnamese soldiers along the border.

Some Western sources, American intelligence agencies in parti-cular, speculated that one of the major causes of conflict was that the Vietnamese were holding onto their wartime sanctuaries on the Cambodian side of the border, resisting with force the efforts of Phnom Penh to remove them. It was sometimes alleged that large tracts of eastern Cambodia remained in Vietnamese hands after

April 1975.

The Cambodian statement of 31 December 1977 gave some support to this theory, charging that the Vietnamese had 'unscrupulously installed themselves' in 'refuges' on Cambodian soil before 1975, of which they were still in occupation. It gave no indication of the extent of these sanctuaries. A more detailed account in the *Black Paper on Vietnamese Aggression* produced by Phnom Penh's ministry of foreign affairs in September 1978, however, casts serious doubts on the whole idea. According to the *Black Paper*, there were indeed clashes over Vietnamese sanctuaries, but these were limited to the period immediately after the Khmer Rouge takeover, and the Vietnamese did not hold onto the sanctuaries. The Cambodian side had 'requested' that all Vietnamese in Cambodia leave by May–June 1975, and when this had not been complied with by April(!) they forcibly expelled them. There was no attempt to consult the Vietnamese government over the issue, or to distinguish between soldiers and civilians, or between Vietnamese nationals and Cambodian nationals of Vietnamese descent.

This undoubtedly contributed to tension between the two countries. But the main cause would appear to have been the arbitrary behaviour of the Cambodian authorities, rather than a Vietnamese desire to hold onto sanctuaries that had been stripped of their original military significance by the end of the war.

However, the number of people affected by these rough-and-ready deportations does not appear to have been large. No total figure is given, but the Vietnamese were said to be 'much less numerous than before' and 'scattered in the remote regions of Cambodia, at Snoul (in Kratie province) and in the provinces of Mondulkiri and Ratanikiri'; the largest concentration of Vietnamese was in Mondulkiri where the Khmers Rouges drove out 'more than 1,000 scattered here and there in many places in groups of 10 to 100'. Far from holding on to their sanctuaries, the *Black Paper* tells us, 'The Vietnamese had to leave Cambodia and go back home.'

The *Black Paper* also tells us that there were clashes as a result of Vietnamese encroachments on Cambodian territory. At two villages Vietnam 'sent its nationals to settle in Cambodia's territory' while at a number of other places 'Vietnamese houses were built with some columns in the Vietnamese territory and some others in Cambodian territory'. These attempts at colonization were backed up by 'unceasing' Vietnamese provocations 'all along the border' – an assertion documented by a claim that the Vietnamese initiated *one solitary clash* on the land border in April 1975.[2]

The most serious clashes at this time were not on the land border, but on the Wai Islands in the Gulf of Thailand. These islands had been occupied by the former Saigon government, although they were claimed by Phnom Penh, and the Vietnamese Communists had recognized the validity of the Cambodian claim in 1966. Shortly after it took over Saigon in 1975, the Provisional Revolutionary Government dispatched troops to relieve the ARVN troops stationed on the largest island in the group, Paolo Wai. In the meantime, however, Khmer Rouge forces had already taken over Paolo Wai and attacked the Vietnamese islands of Phu Quoc and Tho Chau. In late May and early June, they were driven out of these positions by the PRG troops. In August 1975, following talks between the two sides, the Vietnamese handed Paolo Wai back to the Cambodians. In 1978 the Pol Pot government claimed this was a clear-cut case of Vietnamese aggression, but it is explained more plausibly in terms of the confusion and lack of communication resulting from the near simultaneous collapse of the authorities in Phnom Penh and Saigon.

The problems that arose along the Vietnam-Cambodian border at this time were readily settled by negotiations. In early June 1975, Phan Hien met with lower ranking Cambodian officials at a border town. His proposal that provincial liaison committees be set up to resolve any local problems or, where this did not work, to report the dispute to higher authorities, was accepted by the Cambodian side.[3] Immediately after this, Pol Pot, as general secretary of the Communist Party of Kampuchea (CPK), led a delegation to Hanoi, and in August his opposite number in Vietnam, Le Duan, reciprocated with a visit to Phnom Penh. On Le Duan's return, the Vietnamese party daily *Nhan Dan* announced that 'a complete identity of views' had been achieved on 'questions of interest to the two sides'. The border liaison committees were established shortly after the June meetings, and appear to have functioned successfully throughout the rest of 1975 and 1976. The number of clashes on the border fell off sharply (the last shooting incident for some time was reported in January 1976). In April 1976 the two sides agreed to hold a high-level meeting in June to settle any remaining problems and work out a border treaty. This meeting was never held because preparatory talks in Phnom Penh in May broke down without any agreement being reached on the basis for negotiations. The full-scale meeting was suspended at the request of the Cambodian side, which then walked out of the preparatory talks. They subsequently rejected all proposals for renewing them.

There were no real problems concerning the land border. The Vietnamese Communists had already agreed to recognize Cambodia's 'existing borders' in 1967, and they reaffirmed this at the May 1976 meeting. Any ambiguities remaining in the delineation of the border were eliminated by an agreement to take a French map issued in 1954 as authoritative. It is true that the demarcation of the border was imperfect, but this did not seem to be a major problem. (To *delineate* a border is to determine where it lies on a map; to *demarcate* it is to determine where it lies on the ground.) The total area in doubt along the whole border was, as Heder notes, less than a hundred square kilometres. They also agreed on practical measures to prevent any escalation of such local incidents as might occur:

1. The two parties strive to educate their cadres, combatants and inhabitants of the border region in the spirit of strengthening solidarity and friendship and avoiding all incidents.
2. All incidents must be dealt with in a spirit of solidarity, friendship and mutual respect.
3. The liaison committees of both sides must investigate any incidents that do take place and meet to discuss appropriate solutions. [4]

In short, there was no serious territorial dispute, and both sides were agreed on the need to avoid incidents on the border and on the procedure for cooperating to minimize them. Even in the absence of a formal border treaty, this agreement should have been enough to establish a peaceful border if both sides had been willing to observe it.

There were more serious problems over the maritime border. The French had paid little attention to determining the maritime boundaries of their possessions with any precision. The various governments of Indochina had more pressing matters on their hands after the departure of the French, and nothing was done to tidy the matter up. Then, in the late 1960s, a geological survey of the Gulf of Thailand found that large areas are potentially rich with oil, transforming the ambiguities of the French legacy into potentially important and contentious issue.

At the May 1976 preparatory meeting the Cambodian side claimed that its maritime border with Vietnam was established by the 'Brevie line' laid down by the governor-general of French

Indochina in 1939, and that this had been recognized by the Vietnamese in 1967. The Vietnamese responded by claiming that the Brevie line had not been established by the French as a *territorial* boundary, but as a boundary to resolve disputes over the administration and police jurisdiction over offshore islands. In support of this they quoted Brevie's original statement, which specified that 'only the matters of administration and the police are considered here, the questions of whose territory these islands are remains outstanding'. They acknowledged that they had agreed to use the Brevie line as the basis for establishing sovereignty over the offshore *islands* in 1967. But this did not settle the question of the maritime boundary in the full sense, for it left the question of *territorial waters* still to be resolved.

The Vietnamese then proposed that the maritime border be drawn in such a way as to give them easier access to Phu Quoc island, in exchange for Vietnamese concessions on more outlying waters. It was in response to this proposal that the Cambodian side walked out of the talks. In its statement of 31 December 1977 the Cambodian government charged that the Vietnamese delegation had 'rejected entirely' the delimitation of the maritime border to which it had agreed in 1966 and introduced 'plans of annexation of a big part of the seas of Cambodia'.

To sum up, the border conflicts between Vietnam and Cambodia in 1975–6 do not appear to have been of a substantial nature. There was no territorial dispute at all over the land border, and while there were disagreements over the maritime border the waters involved were not extensive. Practical measures for dealing with any incidents that arose had been adopted and were apparently working smoothly at this time. It is true that no border treaty was signed, but many other countries have managed to live amicably enough as neighbours without such a treaty and with unresolved border problems of much greater magnitude – indeed, this is probably the rule rather than the exception for Asian and African countries. Far from provoking a full-scale confrontation, the border problems that arose as a result of the Communist victories in Vietnam and Cambodia in 1975 seemed to have been, in fact, largely settled by the middle of 1976.

Moreover, they were not problems between Cambodia and Vietnam alone. Developments on the Thai-Cambodian border roughly paralleled those on the Vietnam-Cambodian border in this period. The opening of relations between the new authorities in Phnom Penh and the Bangkok government were marred by a number of clashes between Khmer Rouge and Thai forces in May and June 1975. Here too there was confusion over a poorly demarcated border and clashes resulting from Khmer Rouge attempts to seal the border and prevent the flight of refugees. But the Thai government chose not to interpret these as an expression of official hostility by the new government, and the Phnom Penh authorities also adopted a conciliatory attitude.

When the Cambodian foreign minister, Ieng Sary, visited Bangkok in October 1975, the meeting apparently went smoothly. No treaty was signed, but the two governments issued a joint communiqué declaring mutual recognition of 'present frontiers' between the two countries, respect for each other's 'independence, sovereignty and territorial integrity', and pledging that neither side would 'resort to either the threat or the use of force in solving their differences'. To deal with any problems that did arise, liaison offices were established at the border towns of Aranyapratet and Poipet. There were some violent clashes between anti-Communist Khmer Serei guerrillas and Khmers Rouges near the Thai border in late 1975, but the border was basically quiet until early 1977.

The border between Laos and Cambodia is remote and short, and no problems were reported at the time. Later inquiries confirmed that it was peaceful until 1977 (see pp. 75-6).

Why, then, if the early border problems between the new governments in Vietnam and Cambodia had been largely settled by the middle of 1976, did war erupt between the two countries in 1977–8? Heder's answer, as we have seen, is that these incidents, trivial in themselves, catalysed a full-scale conflict because of the radically different perspectives of the two regimes towards them. These problems came to a head at the May 1976 meeting and lay dormant for some months before erupting in full-scale fighting in 1977.

There certainly were differences in their negotiating positions at these talks. The Vietnamese adopted the position that the border established by the French should be accepted as an accomplished historical fact. The disputes between governments of the pre-colonial era, and the territories ruled by them, were irrelevant to contemporary negotiations. While minor adjustments might be made on the basis of mutual consent to overcome any specific quirks and irrationalities, the inherited border as a whole had to be taken as given. Heder characterized this position as one of 'apparent flexibility', based on the expectation of 'a mutual bargaining process in which the borderline was to be adjusted and rationalized to the benefit of both sides, without either side making unilateral gains'.

This was unacceptable to the Pol Pot regime. It adopted the position that because Vietnam had made territorial gains at the expense of Cambodia in pre-colonial and colonial times, the border established by the French was itself unjust. The *Black Book* invokes the expansive territories of the pre-colonial Angkor Empire to argue that the Vietnamese had deprived Cambodia of 65,000 square kilometres of territory. While Cambodia had abandoned its claim on the 'lost territories' of 'Kampuchea Krom' – the lower Mekong Delta and Saigon – the Pol Pot regime demanded that the Vietnamese acknowledge the injustice of the frontier established by the French by conceding to the Cambodians the unilateral right to make adjustments to the border. It then tried to press the point home by demanding some minor adjustments to the land border in their favour. As Heder summarizes the Khmer Rouge negotiating stance: 'The Cambodians approached the question as the sole aggrieved party, and expected a certain recompense for their historical losses and their willingness to cease contesting them. They offered not negotiations in the regular sense, but unilateral resolutions of outstanding problems that provided such recompense in a minor way. They demanded that the Vietnamese either accept or reject their proposals and not try to tinker with them.'[5]

The Cambodians, according to Heder, walked out of the May 1976 talks because of the Vietnamese proposals, especially those concerning the maritime border, were seen as an attempt to 'undermine' this principle of granting 'recompensatory' adjustments to the Cambodian side. They claimed that the Vietnamese had accepted this principle in 1967, but there was no real basis for this claim. When the Vietnamese recognized Cambodia's 'existing borders', Sihanouk took this as an acceptance of Cambodia's right to determine the border – obviously quite a different matter. Since the Vietnamese never endorsed this statement of Sihanouk's, the Khmer Rouge argument had no basis in fact.

For their part, the 'apparent flexibility' of the Vietnamese was exhausted by this Cambodian stance. They were not willing to concede either the unilateral right to Cambodia to adjust the Vietnam-Cambodia border, or to acknowledge that it had a moral right to 'lost territories' that included Vietnam's most productive rice-bowl and most modern city. No doubt it occurred to them that to recognize the moral justice of these claims would be to lay the basis for a subsequent legal claim despite current Cambodian disclaimers on this point.

The basis of the Khmer Rouge claim that Vietnamese possession of the lower Mekong today is unjust is that it was acquired by military aggression against the old Khmer Empire. If accepted, this reasoning would enable the Cambodians to advance territorial claims against the Thais, the Lao, and even the Burmese, as well as the Vietnamese. Innumerable conflicting counter-claims could also be advanced in the names of empires or city-states (most of them as defunct as the Angkor Empire), which suffered military defeat at the hands of the Khmers at some point or other in the past. It is evident that resort to 'historical' arguments of this sort, though appealing to national pride, opens up a Pandora's Box of insoluble conflicts.

A recent textbook on international law by Michael Akehurst summarizes the general problem in these terms: 'Nowadays conquest, or at least conquest by an aggressor, cannot confer title (to territory); in the past it could. Do old titles based on conquest now become void? If so, the results could be very startling; if carried to its logical conclusion, this suggestion would mean that North America would have to be handed back to the Red Indians, and that the English would have to hand England back to the Welsh.'

Such examples could be multiplied indefinitely. The conclusion reached by most authorities is that modern notions of international law cannot be applied retrospectively to past conflicts in order to cast doubts on the validity of present-day borders. These problems are especially acute in the former possessions of European colonial powers. Akehurst observes: 'Colonial frontiers, which were established by force in previous centuries, have now, for the most part, become the frontiers of newly independent countries, who have no wish to see their frontiers called into question. Latin American and Afro-Asian countries, with a few exceptions (such as Communist China) are agreed that colonial boundaries must, under international law, continue to be used as boundaries after independence. (In Latin America this is known as the principle of *uti possidetis* - "as you possess, so you shall continue to possess".) Colonial boundaries, particularly in Africa, are often unnatural, disregarding tribal divisions and cutting through areas which form a natural economic unit, but since the newly independent states cannot agree on a radical re-drawing of frontiers, they are wise to avoid uncertainty and conflict by preserving their existing frontiers.'[6] Thus the position adopted by Vietnam in relation to the Vietnam-Cambodian border was in conformity with generally accepted international law. That of the Pol Pot regime was not.

These disagreements are sufficient to explain why the Vietnamese and the Khmer Rouge regimes were unable to work out a mutually satisfactory border treaty in 1976. But it should not be assumed that such a diplomatic stalemate inevitably leads to war. Many unresolved border problems lie dormant because the governments concerned do not think it worthwhile pressing the issue. In the second half of 1976, it appeared as if this might be the case with the Vietnam-Cambodia dispute. Despite the disagreements over a border treaty, the two sides had agreed to practical measures of cooperation to minimize any incidents on the border. Though no border treaty had been worked out with Thailand, the Phnom Penh regime had also worked out a practical arrangement with Bangkok. There was no treaty with Laos, but no problems had even emerged yet in this connection.

Thus, by mid-1976 the Cambodian regime had established working relationships along all its borders. The tensions arising out of the instability of 1975, far from being the 'spark' of a wider dispute, appeared to have been resolved. But then, early in 1977, the situation began to deteriorate along all of Cambodian's borders, especially the border with Vietnam. It was this which set in motion the chain of events that led to the Vietnamese invasion of December 1978. The question that has to be resolved is: what was responsible for overturning in 1977 the apparent stability that had been achieved in 1976?

The 'Indochina Federation'

One of the central allegations in the Phnom Penh government's statement of 31 December 1977 was the accusation that for 'many dozen years' the Vietnamese Communists had sought to 'annex and swallow' Cambodia by forcing it into a Vietnamese-controlled 'Indochina Federation' in order to make Vietnam, 'a Big Power in Southeast Asia'. The Vietnamese immediately denied these charges, saying they were 'slanderous accusations'. In April 1978 they produced a 'white paper' on *The Truth on the Question of the Indochina Federation*', describing it as 'a question which has passed forever into history'.[7]

This did not prevent the Pol Pot government from continuing to cite Vietnam's schemes for an 'Indochina Federation' as the obstacle to peace in the region. In June 1978 the Cambodian foreign minister, Ieng Sary, explained that this was not a 'normal border dispute', capable of resolution by diplomatic means, because its roots lay 'in the fact that Vietnam has the intention of swallowing Cambodia, subverting and aggressing against it, attempting to engineer a *coup d'état*, to force it to join an Indochina Federation under its domination so that Vietnam can annex Cambodia within a set period of time and take a step towards fulfilling its ambitions in Southeast Asia.'

The most detailed and authoritative version of the Khmer Rouge accusations against Vietnam was the *Black Paper* of September 1978. Although issued by Ieng Sary's ministry of foreign affairs, this document was reportedly composed largely by Pol Pot himself. It purports to document Vietnamese designs on Cambodia from the fifteenth century to the present. The matters covered range from territorial annexation in dynastic wars to the 'sordid use' of Vietnamese girls; this historical exegesis concludes that the Vietnamese 'have always sought by all means to take possession of Cambodia's territory'. A whole chapter is devoted to the question of the 'Indochina Federation', but all Pol Pot is able to offer by way of documenting Vietnamese Communist designs on Cambodia is the name of the Indochinese Communist Party in the 1930s: 'The Vietnamese Party was founded in 1930, by the name of "Indochinese Communist Party" . . . . The choice of a name of a Party has its political significance. Lenin, an eminent internationalist leader, did not give his Party the name of "European Communist Party". Thus, the name given to the Vietnamese Party means that this Party is one and the same for Vietnam, Laos and Cambodia. The choice of such a name reveals that the objective of this Party is to dominate the three countries . . . . Since 1930, in order to achieve this strategic programme, the Vietnamese have prepared their forces and trained their cadres to successively send them to Laos and Cambodia.'[8]

But even here, Pol Pot managed to get his basic facts wrong. At the founding meeting of Vietnam's first Communist Party on 3 February 1930, Ho Chi Minh specifically rejected the name 'Indochinese Communist Party' on the grounds that it was too broad. It was only in response to criticism from Moscow that this name was later adopted.[9] Far from reflecting Vietnamese designs on Laos and Cambodia, the name of the ICP reflected the idealistic vision held by the contemporary Communist International of socialist revolution sweeping away all divisions based on race and nationality among the toiling masses. In the 1930s and 1940s, a common colonial state had given some theoretical basis to the ideal of a revolutionary Indochina Federation, but the Vietnamese Communists appear to have paid no more than lip service to the idea, which subsequently collapsed along with the French colonial structure.

The ICP was dissolved in 1951, never having become a reality, to be succeeded by separate national parties. According to the Vietnamese, this is the end of the story of the 'Indochina Federation'. The *Black Paper* delegates this event to a footnote, where it is dismissed as a mere formality: 'In fact', claims Pol Pot, 'this party continues to exist.'[10] Neither version is wholly accurate. It seems that although a separate party was set up, for some time it operated under Vietnamese tutelage. A Vietnamese inner-party document, written in 1951, asserted: 'The Vietnamese Party reserves the right to supervise the activities of its brother parties in Cambodia and Laos.' It added that 'later, if conditions permit, the three revolutionary Parties of Vietnam, Cambodia and Laos will be able to unite to form a single Party: the Party of the Vietnam-Khmer-Laotian federation.'[11] If the old Comintern notion of an Indochina Federation had not been a major aspiration of the Vietnamese-Communists before 1951, as Pol Pot would have us believe, neither did it die as instantaneous a death in 1951 as the Vietnamese would now wish us to believe.

These were the years in which the struggle between the Viet Minh and the French ranged throughout Indochina, and the Vietnamese were not willing to forgo the opportunity of building up 'fraternal' movements in Cambodia and Laos. The first generation of Khmer Communists thus received their basic political training in schools run by Khmer-speaking Viet Minh. A CPK history of 1973, written by rivals of Pol Pot's group, recalled without resentment that Marxism-Leninism had been 'injected into our revolutionary movement by the international Communist movement and by the Vietnamese Communists'.[12]

The *Black Paper* claims that after 1945 the Viet Minh actively sought to recruit Cambodian support for their struggle against the French, but there is nothing to indicate that their objective was to take Cambodia over, rather than to simply drive the French out. We are also told that, as the war in South Vietnam escalated after 1959, increasing numbers of Vietnamese took refuge on Cambodian soil and that the Viet Cong used sanctuaries on the Cambodian side of the border, but again there is nothing to indicate that the Vietnamese had any objective other than winning the war in the south of their own country.

There is thus little evidence to support the central allegation of the Pol Pot government, although this has not prevented some Western commentators from taking it as a well-established fact. There is nothing to show that the Vietnamese-Communists were ever strongly committed to the idea of an Indochina Federation, although they did espouse the idea at one time. However, it is clear that they have long appreciated that the security of the revolution in Vietnam is greatly influenced by its relations with neighbouring countries. For this reason they have taken a continual interest in politics in Cambodia and Laos, and when circumstances have been favourable, have tried to encourage friendly tendencies there. The relationship is, of course, reciprocal – the Lao and the Khmers have always had an eye on what has been going on in Vietnamese politics, for similar reasons. However, Vietnam is larger and more powerful than Cambodia and Laos, and has influenced them much more than it has been influenced. Much the same, of course, can also be said of Thailand, and the explanation is to be found in the contemporary hierarchy of power among the states of the region, rather than in Comintern slogans dredged up from the 1930s.

An awareness of the simple point that a country's security depends largely on its relations with its neighbours led the Vietnamese to place considerable importance on cooperation with Phnom Penh and Vientiane, especially after 1975 when they were governed by supposedly 'fraternal' parties. The Vietnamese maintained that the basic framework for the post-war relations between the three governments was laid down in the statement of the summit conference of the Indochinese Peoples in 1970. This recognized 'the independence, sovereignty, unity and territorial integrity' of the three Indochinese nations, and specifically pledged respect for 'the territorial integrity of Cambodia within her existing borders'. Relations between them would conform to the 'five principles of peaceful coexistence'. But the statement also put a strong emphasis on long-term cooperation: 'The parties affirm their determination to preserve and develop the fraternal friendship and the good neighbour relations between the two countries, with a view to mutual support in the struggle against the common enemy and to lasting future cooperation in the building of each country according to its own way.'

According to Prince Sihanouk, who headed the Cambodian delegation of this conference, the keynote of the occasion was the celebration of the alliance that had emerged between the Vietnamese Communists, the Pathet Lao and the National United Front of Kampuchea (NUFK): 'Some "experts" in the West like to write about the things which divide our three peoples, and dwell on "traditional hostilities". But we like to think more and more about the factors that unite us. Today, above all, it is the fact that we are victims of American aggression . . . . We are three weak nations against a giant. Unless we stand together, we fall singly. It is "unite and win" against "divide and rule" . . . . This was the central idea of the Summit Conference of the Peoples of Indochina . . . . We agreed that while each component would retain its separate entity, we would combine our efforts until final victory. For the first time the Indochina put together by the French would become a living reality. For that, at least, we owe our thanks to Richard Nixon.'[13]

The Vietnamese envisaged a continuation of this wartime unity between the three movements after their joint victory in 1975. But Sihanouk has now revealed that even in 1970 the Khmer Rouge leadership saw little basis for post-war cooperation. In 1979 he wrote of his own 'trusting and affectionate friendship with Pham Van Dong and Vo Nguyen Giap', but even in 1970–71, 'the best period of our alliance with North Vietnam', the Khmer Rouge leaders spoke of 'the Yuon's [the Vietnamese] hypocrisy' and the 'need for the Khmers in the NUFK to beware of the North Vietnam's desire for hegemony after our foreseeable joint victory over the Yankee aggressors and the traitor Lon Nol'.[14]

The Cambodian statement of 31 December 1977 echoed those parts of the 1970 statement which referred to independence and sovereignty, and made no mention at all of cooperation. However, the Vietnamese reply emphasized the principle of 'all-out efforts to consolidate and strengthen our mutual trust, our sincere long-term cooperation, and our mutual assistance on the basis of respect for each other's sovereignty and territory, and non-interference in each other's internal affairs'.

This emphasis of cooperation was elaborated by the Vietnamese into the notion of a 'special relationship' between Vietnam, Cambodia and Laos. 'We insist on a special relationship,' a Vietnamese official explained in 1978, 'because there is not another example in history of such a relationship where the two people shared each grain of rice, every bullet, suffering and victory.'[15] More was involved than Communist sentimentality based on an idealized view of past struggles. The Vietnamese also hinted at their desire for cooperation in developing the resources of the area, and in matters of regional security as well. This position has at least a basis in the 1970 statement, but it was unacceptable to the men and women now in power in Phnom Penh.

According to Heder these disagreements take us to the crux of the matter. The 'basic issues' of the Vietnam-Cambodia conflict were 'the contradictions between two very different models of revolution and two very different views of the world scene' arising from the different historical experiences of the two parties. Internationally, the Vietnamese Communists looked to the Soviet Union and the Cambodians to China. But the focal point of their differences was the commitment of the Vietnamese to the principle of international cooperation between countries of the 'socialist bloc' and the commitment of the Khmers Rouges to the principle of 'self-reliance'. The Vietnamese position, he asserts, is a rationalization of 'the extension of Vietnamese influence over other countries and Communist movements'. For the Cambodian leaders, to accept any modification of their policies in the light of external circumstances was to undermine Cambodia's independence. Rejection of all compromise with the Vietnamese, Heder asserts, 'invites Vietnamese action' against Cambodia, but he reasons, this was the course into which the Khmer Rouge leaders were forced by their commitment to Cambodian independence.[16]

This argument is untenable, but at the same time it is very revealing. The idea that international cooperation involves the sacrifice of national sovereignty is naive. It rests on the assumption that the rulers of a nation-state can claim (in Pol Pot's words) 'perfect independence' – sovereign power, free of all external restraints. But in reality sovereignty is always subject to external constraint, for every national government has to come to terms with other states and their interests. In acknowledgement of this, international law recognizes that the sovereignty of states is necessarily limited by respect for the rights of other states. For the Cambodian regime to claim such absolute sovereignty that any concession to other governments is in principle unacceptable is to make any compromise solution impossible even in the case of minor conflicts; total capitulation is all that can be accepted.

As Heder suggests, such an attitude does indeed 'invite Vietnamese action' against the Cambodian regime in the event of conflict. However, the Cambodian stance was not the result of a simple desire for national independence but of an intransigence springing from a vision of independence that is megalomaniacal in its premisses. How did this emerge?

Cambodian Communism and the Vietnamese

The attitude of the Cambodian government was in part a matter of personality, the euphoria of victory, and naïvety arising from inexperience. But, as Heder emphasizes, it was also rooted in the historical experiences of the Cambodian nation as a whole, and in the experiences of its revolutionary leaders before 1975.

The Khmer Rouge leaders, Heder rightly points out, were simply pursuing many of the policies of Prince Sihanouk's government with greater vigour and less sophistication. Khmer Rouge fears that their country would be engulfed by a reunited Vietnam, their insistence that they be acknowledged as the aggrieved party in border negotiations because of the territorial losses of the Angkor Empire centuries before – all this was taken over directly from the backward-looking royalist nationalism forged by Sihanouk in the 1950s, with its vision of Vietnam as the 'historic enemy'.

But far more specific factors kept this anti-Vietnamese perspective alive among Sihanouk's Communist opponents, particularly in Pol Pot's faction. As with Laos, we have seen that much of the early impetus in creating a Communist movement in Cambodia was inspired by the Viet Minh, and encouraged by it during the First Indochina War. However, in Laos relations between the Pathet Lao and the Vietnamese remained friendly. Despite its weaknesses the Pathet Lao was a force to be reckoned with in a country characterized by a 'feudal' fragmentation of political power, and Hanoi was never seriously tempted to sacrifice its interests to curry favour with the RLG. In Cambodia, by contrast, Sihanouk's government was obviously a much more powerful force than the RLG, and the Communist movement was nowhere near as effective as the Pathet Lao. Hanoi also welcomed Sihanouk's anti-Western foreign policy. Hence, as Sihanouk's regime consolidated itself in the late 1950s, Hanoi sought to cultivate good relations with it. As the war in South Vietnam escalated, this became of greater and greater importance to the Vietnamese Communists. They urged Khmer leftists to support Sihanouk's 'progressive' government, and turned a blind eye on his attempts to suppress the Cambodian Communists.

Many aspects of the history of Cambodian Communism remain obscure, but there is little doubt that the movement was small and without a significant mass base until the overthrow of Sihanouk in 1970. The first generation of Khmer leftists included those who had linked up with the Viet Minh during the war against the French.

Following the Geneva Conference of 1954, most of them were compelled to 'regroup' in North Vietnam with the Viet Minh, and Sihanouk would not let them return to Cambodia. The handful of remaining pro-Communist activists in Cambodia formed a political party, the Pracheachon, but it never succeeded in becoming more than just one more little clique in Phnom Penh, completely overshadowed by Sihanouk and highly vulnerable to police repression.

A new generation of left-wing activists began to emerge in the late 1950s and early 1960s. They were mostly students who had been studying abroad in the 1940s and 1950s, and who had not had much contact with the Viet Minh. They were all strongly nationalistic, but beyond that their ideas diverged widely, ranging from moderate social-democratic reformism to Maoist-oriented Communism. Some, such as Khieu Samphan, joined Sihanouk's Sangkum Party, and even served in his government in the early 1960s. Others, such as Pol Pot (then still using his real name Saloth Sar), joined the Pracheachon, where they rose rapidly to positions of influence in the small and dispirited party. It changed its name to the Communist Party of Kampuchea (CPK) in 1960, and Pol Pot became the secretary general of the party following the mysterious disappearance of his predecessor, Tou Samouth, in 1962. Whereas the leadership of the Pathet Lao remained in the hands of men and women for whom Vietnamese Communism had been a formative influence, in Cambodia the leadership of the CPK was taken over by young radicals who had been only marginally influenced by the Vietnamese.

By the late 1950s Pol Pot had become convinced that the Pracheachon's efforts to work in a broad front of 'progressive' forces in Phnom Penh, inevitably centred around Sihanouk, were achieving nothing. He was convinced of the revolutionary potential of the peasantry, and favoured abandoning politics in the capital in favour of guerrilla warfare in rural areas. In 1963 he and his supporters left Phnom Penh to pursue this strategy. This met with little success among the Khmer peasants, and they were obliged to establish their camp among the primitive *montagnards* in the remote and rugged northeast of the country. It was not until 1968 that they felt strong enough to pronounce that the 'armed struggle' had been launched. Even so, it remained a guerrilla movement in its earliest possible stage – small and poorly armed bands whose main activity was raiding isolated police stations and small guard posts in attempts to acquire weapons.

Events at the other end of the country in 1967 helped foster the illusion that the CPK was a force to be reckoned with. From the revolt at Samlaut and the government's reaction to it, some writers have been inclined to accept that a pre-revolutionary situation had developed in Cambodia; the CPK was capitalizing on agrarian unrest and emerging as a major threat to the Sihanouk regime. We are not persuaded by this argument. The revolt was based on localized grievances and it failed to spread precisely because the exploitative relationships that have sparked off peasant rebellions elsewhere had not yet developed extensively in the Cambodian countryside. [17] Resentment at the atrocities with which the Phnom Penh government had suppressed the revolt turned the Samlaut area into a redoubt for local anti-Sihanouk guerrillas, who were apparently joined by some of the leftists fleeing Phnom Penh. But it was only after the fall of Sihanouk that they joined forces with Pol Pot's group. Pol Pot and the CPK leadership were geographically isolated in the north east, and played no role in these events. Their forces remained small and ineffective on the eve of Sihanouk's overthrow. There are widely conflicting figures on this, but it was probably only several thousand at the most and may have been no more than a few hundred. [18]

Sihanouk reacted so vigorously because he feared that the Vietnamese were behind the activities of the Cambodian Communists. Pol Pot's efforts to foment 'armed struggle' in Cambodia thus immediately jeopardized Hanoi's good relations with the Sihanouk government. According to Pol Pot's *Black Paper*, the Vietnamese had consistently opposed his tactics from the beginning. They had argued that Cambodia was not ripe for a peasant revolution and that the Khmer Communists should support the 'national-democratic revolution' (that is, Sihanouk's government), and accused Pol Pot of being 'ultra-leftist and adventurist'. As the war in South Vietnam intensified, the 'Ho Chi Minh trail' through the jungles of southern Laos and eastern Cambodia became increasingly important to the Vietnamese Communists, and their disagreements with Pol Pot's group intensified.

Pol Pot personally led a CPK delegation to Hanoi in late 1965 to thrash out his differences with the Vietnamese party leaders. By all accounts, the talks went very badly. The *Black Paper* relates that the Vietnamese 'dragged on the discussions' and made a 'stand-up attack' on Pol Pot's position, but he would not budge. He then went on to Peking, and it was in the wake of this trip that he 'clearly discerned the true nature of the Vietnamese'. [19] Relations between the CPK leaders and Hanoi deteriorated once more after the events of 1967–8, and Pol Pot went to Hanoi for another bout of acrimonious and unsuccessful talks in 1969. Again, he adjourned to Peking afterwards, and was there when Sihanouk was overthrown in March 1970.

Though they were allies, tensions between the Vietnamese and the Khmer Communists continued through the war of 1970–75, becoming particularly acute from 1973. The Vietnamese succeeded in negotiating the Paris Agreements with the Americans, bringing about a ceasefire in South Vietnam (temporary) and in Laos (permanent). The Americans also pressed for a ceasefire in Cambodia, but this did not materialize. Since they were convinced that the Khmers Rouges were Hanoi's puppets, the Americans took this as proof of Vietnamese bad faith. According to the *Black Paper*, throughout late 1972 and early 1973 the Vietnamese pressured Pol Pot to negotiate, but he refused. However, this version of events has been denied by the Vietnamese. The *Black Paper* relates that on this occasion Pol Pot accused the Vietnamese of collaborating with the Americans and rejected negotiations with Lon Nol and the USA on the grounds that it was all part of a Vietnamese plot to 'swallow' Cambodia – a line of reasoning that threw the Vietnamese into a 'towering rage'.[20]

In 1973 the Americans agreed to sign agreements covering Vietnam and Laos, and then launched a bombing campaign that dropped more than 250,000 tons of bombs on Cambodia in six months (compared to the 160,000 tons of bombs dropped on Japan in six years of war) before Congress, to Kissinger's fury, halted it. Pol Pot attributed all the resulting devastation to the 'selfish egoism' of the Vietnamese and their 'betrayal' of his cause. Sihanouk wrote that when he returned to Cambodia in 1975, he was impressed by the 'bitterness and even hatred' the Khmer Rouge leaders bore towards Hanoi over this 'sellout'.[21]

Pol Pot's belief that negotiations were just a trick on the part of the Vietnamese (even if they were not involved directly) was based on more than simple irrational prejudice. Many of the old Issarak fighters had now joined the Khmers Rouges, and many of them were convinced that they had been betrayed at Geneva by the Vietnamese (and, presumably, by the Chinese and Russians as well). Pol Pot evidently shared this perception, which was reinforced by his own unhappy experiences attempting to negotiate with the Vietnamese.

His refusal to do a deal with Kissinger in 1973, which presumably would have led to the formation of a coalition government (as in

Laos), precipitated immense destruction and prolonged the fighting in Cambodia for another two years. When the end to the fighting did come, it was without any negotiations. Pleas by the Lon Nol government in 1974 for unconditional negotiations were summarily rejected by the Khmer Rouge leaders. Even the announcement that the Lon Nolist side was laying down its arms was cut short on 17 April 1975 by a Khmer Rouge declaration: 'We are not coming here for negotiations; we are entering the capital by force of arms.' Thus, it is clear that prior to 1975, and in a context where Sihanouk's posturing over the border problem was irrelevant, Pol Pot spurned the idea of a negotiated settlement of the conflict in favour of a military resolution.

Post-1975 attitudes towards Vietnam were undoubtedly heavily influenced by these historical factors – by the dominance of Sihanouk's traditionalistic, backward-looking nationalism, absorbed even by the revolutionaries who had sought to overthrow him; by the long-standing quarrels between the Cambodian and Vietnamese Communists; and by Pol Pot's outright rejection of negotiations as a way of settling disputes. However, these background factors should not be over-stated. The peculiarities of the regime Pol Pot set up in Cambodia after April 1975 played a central role in the dispute.

The Purges in Cambodia, 1975–78

The Khmers Rouges came to power as a result of the social disintegration and political collapse that occurred when Sihanouk was overthrown and the country was abruptly plunged into the vortex of the Indochina war, rather than as a deep-seated movement of social protest and political change. The movement had grown explosively since 1970, but it was by no means united and its mass support was not necessarily secure. It had won control of the population before it had won popular legitimacy or even internal unity.

The leaders of the movement were urban intellectuals by origin, but for six years before the fall of Sihanouk they had been leading a spartan life in a military encampment among Cambodia's most socially and economically primitive people, completely isolated from the Khmer peasantry, let alone the urban centres. Here Pol Pot found his first reliable cadres, 'very faithful to Cambodia's revolution' and 'much feared' by its enemies, as the *Black Paper* put it.

At first Pol Pot had little chance to capitalize on the opportunities presented by the coup against Sihanouk and the formation of the NUFK, which joined together Sihanouk's supporters with the Khmers Rouges against the right-wing 'traitors' in Phnom Penh. His forces were small and isolated from the lowland population that was in political turmoil. Large areas of the country were temporarily in the hands of the Vietnamese, the majority of the NUFK were Sihanoukist rather than Communist, and in his view even the lowland sections of the CPK were not to be trusted, for 'some elements' among them had been 'duped and corrupted' by the Vietnamese. His suspicions on this point were confirmed when they went ahead and cooperated with the Sihanoukists and the Vietnamese. As the ranks of the CPK grew, the regional party secretaries quickly emerged as powerful figures, ruling quasi-independent fiefdoms and running their own armies. Since the central party leadership had no armed forces at its command (except by virtue of Pol Pot's position as regional secretary for the northeast, as well as general secretary of the CPK), it had to treat these potential rivals with caution and respect for the time being.

The growth of the CPK thus weakened the control of Pol Pot's faction over the party apparatus. They responded by trying to impose a highly-centralized, top-down control on the party, by breaking off cooperation with the Vietnamese, and by gradually eliminating those whom they regarded as pro-Sihanouk and pro-Vietnamese. Pol Pot had the party's 'security branch' (known as *santebal* or *norkorbal*) at his disposal. From 1972 onwards, the purges of the party and NUFK apparatus carried out with the utmost secrecy by this organization became one of the means by which Pol Pot gradually gained ascendancy over the Khmer Rouge movement.

This process was by no means complete when the Lon Nol regime collapsed in 1975. Pol Pot's faction still faced disagreements from key figures in the central party and government apparatus, such as Keo Moni, Nong Suon and Hou Yuon. Its control over the lower levels was even less secure: while the regional secretaries in the north and west of the country appear to have been supporting Pol Pot in 1975, those in the southeast of the country (Vorn Veth, So Phim and Chou Chet) would still criticize him.

In April 1975 Sihanouk, as the leader of the NUFK, became Democratic Kampuchea's nominal head of state – but the position was an honorific one that allowed him no real power inside the country, most of his supporters having been purged from the NUFK in 1973–4. He remained in exile until September and resigned his post on 4 April 1976. This was followed by the formation of a purely Khmer Rouge government, with Khieu Samphan replacing Sihanouk as head of state, and Pol Pot becoming prime minister. Ieng Sary remained foreign minister.

The DK regime lacked most of the characteristic features of modern states. The impression one gets from the accounts of visitors is that the government was little more than a temporary encampment of guerilla leaders in the city they had conquered and emptied of its population in April 1975. The formal executive of the government functioned only intermittently. Government ministers were expected to fulfil their duties on a part-time basis and they devoted most of their energies to work in the rice-fields, and no bureaucracy was established to implement policy (apart from Pol Pot's secret police), As Richard Dudman put it: ' . . . the Communist government of the country it renamed Democratic Kampuchea never really rose above the shadowy, underground insurgency it had been before it overthrew the previous United States-backed government'.[22]

The DK regime had then sealed the country off hermetically from the outside world, largely abandoning conventional diplomatic relations. Such foreign relations as the regime had were firmly in the hands of Pol Pot's group. According to a visitor in 1976, Ieng Sary ran the government's foreign relations with about half a dozen assistants, who helped him on a part-time basis, and were responsible for 'internal security' in Phnom Penh as well.[23] As general secretary of the CPK, Pol Pot was responsible for inter-party relations, liaison with the Vietnamese party in particular. Vietnamese relations with the Cambodian Communists were thus primarily relations with Pol Pot personally, until he was removed. The only other channel of communication they had was to officials in the border provinces via the border liaison committees, until their operations were suspended by Pol Pot in May 1977.

The domestic policies pursued by the government in 1975–6 were those of Pol Pot. These were summed up by their architect in these terms in his first 'press conference', an interview with Yugoslav journalists in 1978: "We are building socialism without a model," smiled the head of the Communist Party and Premier of Democratic Kampuchea, Pol Pot. "We do not wish to copy anyone; we shall use the experience gained in the course of the liberation struggle. There are no schools, faculties or universities in the traditional sense, although they did exist in our country prior to liberation, because we wish to do away with all vestiges of the past. There is no money, no commerce, as the state takes care of provisioning all its citizens. We did not have money or commerce in the liberated territory either. The cities have been resettled, because this is the way things had to be. Some three million town dwellers and peasants were trying to find refuge in the cities from the depredations of war. We could not provide enough food for them, and there were imperialist plans to organize guerrilla movements and a counter-revolution in the populated cities . . . . We evacuated the cities; we resettled the inhabitants in the rural areas where the basic living conditions could be provided for this segment of the population of new Cambodia. The countryside should be the focus of attention for our revolution, and the people will decide the fate of the cities." '[24]

Following the evacuation of the towns in April 1975, there was a purge directed against those involved in the army, police and public service of the Lon Nol regime. This was carried out partly by the CPK's security branch and partly by regional security forces, and its severity varied widely from one part of the country to another. In some parts, there were reports of 'counter-revolutionary elements' being detained for 're-education', in a primitive version of the policies being pursued in Laos and Vietnam; but in Cambodia, the more usual procedure seems to have been simply to execute such people. In some parts, the purge was so indiscriminate that refugees fleeing the country were convinced that the government's objective was the complete extermination of the old upper and middle classes, although there is no convincing evidence that this was the case.

The basic reason for these purges was probably the weakness of the new Communist regime in Cambodia. Democratic Kampuchea simply did not have the cadres and resources to maintain a more or less sophisticated system of political controls over its defeated enemies, as the Lao and Vietnamese Communists had. Such 're-education' as there was in Cambodia appears to have been in the hands of teenage soldiers, who barely knew what they were talking about, rather than skilled ideologues. Terror, on the other hand, was a method readily understood and implemented by the most unsophisticated 'peasant-warriors'. It also had the consequence of enhancing the role of the security branch and the men who controlled it within the DK regime, a point which probably did not escape Pol Pot.

At the same time, the DK leadership was attempting to build the country up as rapidly as possible by 'self-reliance' and sheer hard work. This economic strategy necessitated the imposition of a system of harsh discipline on the entire population. The violation, or neglect, of instructions was frequently punished by execution. As this system of forced labour yielded only mediocre results, the search for scapegoats intensified, and the number of 'disciplinary' killings increased. Khmer Rouge cadres we interviewed in Sa Kaeo in 1980 told us that discipline was understandable during a war – but to their surprise it became more rather than less harsh after April 1975. The 'new people' evacuated from the towns suffered particularly heavily under the regime, but the same pattern developed in the 'base areas' that had been under Communist control before 1975.

We explain the terror in Cambodia in 1975–6 primarily in terms of practical circumstances: it was the brutal response of an extremely backward state apparatus to overwhelming economic and political problems. It was, of course, a disastrous response, but that is another matter. But this explanation is contrary to the generally accepted view in the West, which follows that expressed by François Ponchaud in his book *Cambodia Year Zero*, the first serious attempt to document what was happening under Pol Pot. According to Ponchaud, the purges were 'the translation into action of a particular view of man'[25] – in short, they were the product of Communist ideology. In our view, ideology is usually the rationalization of practical action, and in this case Pol Pot's 'socialism without a model' was a perverted kind of pragmatism.

Even in April 1975 Pol Pot's policies provoked open disagreement from figures such as Hou Yuon, the minister for the interior, and Chou Chet, the party secretary for the southwest region – both of whom were promptly dismissed from their posts. Others apparently disagreed with these policies but chose to accept 'democratic centralism' and work within the party hierarchy to change them. But a majority of the CPK leadership appears to have gone along with Pol Pot's line at this time. However, by mid-1976 disenchantment was spreading among CPK cadres, including those who had previously supported Pol Pot. Refugees reported that at this time regional officials from the northern and western regions sent a petition to Phnom Penh calling for a change in policy and asking for 'the Party to have mercy on the people', and that this was supported by former Pol Pot collaborators in the central government such as the minister for information, Hu Nim.

The details of the factional struggles among the Khmers Rouges after 1975 are still obscure.[26] At first things went in Pol Pot's favour. The Khmer Rouge armed forces were unified in June 1975, and placed under the command of Pol Pot's lieutenant Son Sen. Hou

Yuon, who even after his removal from the ministry continued to be a vocal critic of Pol Pot, was arrested in August 1975 and probably killed shortly afterwards. In April 1976 Pol Pot himself emerged from obscurity to take over the post of prime minister in the government (prior to that he had held no government post at all despite his prominence in the party organization). Then the tide appears to have turned, for Pol Pot was obliged to stand down for reasons of 'ill-health' in September 1976. There were signs that the regime would move away from his policies in the closing months of 1976, but these proved abortive.

Pol Pot disappeared from public view for a year after his removal from government, but he was not inactive in this period. In fact he rallied his supporters and used his position as party leader to launch a massive, violent purge against his opponents. The turning point in the inner-party struggle appears to have been in late 1976, when two of Pol Pot's leading opponents in the central government, Keo Moni and Nong Suon, were arrested. This was followed by a sweeping purge of the central government in the early months of 1977, which spread out into a massive assault on the regionally based structures of the party-government apparatus, as well as involving renewed killings of those in the general population suspected of sympathizing with the enemy – a term that now referred to the old local Communists as well as to the surviving remnants of the Lon Nol regime. In many areas the executions of real and imagined Lon Nolists were more sweeping than those of 1975–6 and this time round those who had supported the Communists suffered the same treatment.

Pol Pot himself played a large role in these events. In his capacity as general secretary of the party, he undertook an extensive tour of the country, personally investigating the loyalty and competence of many local cadres and ordering purges. These were carried out by his lieutenants Son Sen and Nuon Chea, who had both established 'training schools' under the aegis of the CPK central committee which they had secretly used to drill purge squads, and by Kaing Kech Ieu (better known as 'Brother Duch'), who ran the secret police and personally supervised the infamous Toul Sleng interrogation centre in Phnom Penh. Ostensibly under the control of the party's central committee as a whole, Kaing reported directly to Pol Pot and Ieng Sary. Another key ally in this struggle was Ta Mok, the regional secretary for the southwest, whose troops were instrumental in crushing armed resistance in other regions, and whose cadres usually replaced the locals after they had been killed.

The purges continued throughout 1977 and 1978, with some areas undergoing the ordeal twice in less than twelve months, the beneficiaries of one purge being wiped out in the next. The climax came in mid-1978, when Pol Pot finally moved in force against the eastern region Communists. So Phim, the party secretary for the eastern region, was an Issarak veteran who had unsuccessfully opposed Pol Pot for the position of CPK general secretary in 1963. After 1975, he came increasingly into conflict with Pol Pot, and in 1977–8, resisted his demands for a wholesale purge of 'traitors' in the eastern region. In May 1978 troops commanded by Son Sen and Ta Mok launched a full-scale military attack on the eastern region. Following heavy fighting, the ill-prepared eastern troops were overrun. So Phim committed suicide rather than surrender, while some of his followers continued fighting in the jungle. Others retreated to Vietnam.

The eastern region, one of Cambodia's most productive rice bowls, then became the scene of unrivalled brutality and devastation. Captured cadres or soldiers were killed on the spot; whole villages deemed unfaithful were massacred; and tens of thousands of people (perhaps hundreds of thousands) were forcibly deported to other regions, only to be executed *en masse* when they reached their destinations. Most of the mass graves unearthed since the fall of the Pol Pot regime appear to date from this period.

It is unlikely that the human cost of Pol Pot's regime will ever be known accurately. The Heng Samrin government and the Vietnamese have charged that three million people out of a total of seven million perished. The CIA has estimated the figure at 1.2–1.8 million, with 100,000 of these accounted for by executions. For their part, the Democratic Kampuchea leaders have admitted 'excesses' but nonetheless insist that the figures were much lower. In February 1981 Khieu Samphan told us: 'We are now compiling statistics on this matter. Our estimate is that we committed excesses harming the lives of 3,000 people, but the Vietnamese agents harmed more than 10,000 people.' The DK leadership subsequently also said that 20,000 people had died as a result of food shortages in 1975. All these estimates are, of course, politically motivated. The most impartial estimate available is probably that of Amnesty International, according to which there were 'at least 300,000 people killed in purges' under the Pol Pot regime.[27] Amnesty made no attempt to estimate the number of deaths through malnutrition and over-work; our own rough 'guesstimate' is that this was probably around two million over the whole period.

Under these circumstances the Pol Pot group finally emerged as the unchallenged master of the country in 1978. The central government consisted of Pol Pot, Ieng Sary, Son Sen and their wives – CPK leftists who had followed Pol Pot's line from the early 1960s onwards – and a handful of others. Pol Pot, Nuon Chea and Ta Mok controlled the party apparatus. Khieu Samphan, who had taken over from Sihanouk as head of state in 1976, stayed on, the only one of the old Sangkum leftists who had joined with Pol Pot in the late 1960s to survive the purges. Apart from Pol Pot's faction, the entire leadership of the 1970–75 revolution had been swept away – of the seventeen Communists holding posts in the central government in 1975–6 there were only five known survivors by the end of 1978; and except for Pol Pot and Ta Mok, none of the 1975 party regional secretaries survived.

Pol Pot himself publicly re-surfaced in September 1977 when he proclaimed the existence of the CPK (the identity of the ruling party in 'Democratic Kampuchea' had actually been secret until this), introduced himself as its leader, and gave a tendentious and self-glorifying history of the party in a marathon speech of five hours duration. The following day Phnom Penh radio announced that 'Prime Minister Pol Pot' was to make a state visit to Peking; not only had he secured control over the party, he had assumed his old government post again and emerged as an international statesman to boot.

Pol Pot's bloody struggle for power inside Cambodia was linked to the question of relations with Vietnam in three ways. In the first place, since the Vietnamese opposed his political line, anyone else who disagreed with Pol Pot had to be a Vietnamese 'agent'. This is the premiss on which the account of the conflicts inside the CPK in the *Black Paper* is based. Like Lon Nol, Pol Pot had observed Sihanouk successfully rallying 'patriotic' Cambodian opinion to his side by branding his opponents as puppets of the Vietnamese, and he followed suit. By this logic, anyone opposing his political line was opposing Cambodia's 'independence', and such persons were therefore 'traitors' and, wittingly or unwittingly, 'agents' of Vietnamese designs on Cambodia.

But, for the credibility of this argument, Vietnam had to become a frightening menace to Cambodia when the struggle against Pol Pot's domestic rivals intensified. Sihanouk relates: 'Pol Pot and Ieng Sary were very much afraid of reprisals against them, but they nonetheless indulged in challenging, humiliating, insulting, incessantly wounding the Socialist Republic of Vietnam, its leaders, people and the Vietnamese race . . . . In Phnom Penh I tried to learn the whys and wherefores of the Khmers Rouges' senselessly dangerous provocation of Vietnam. I was finally able to get Khieu Samphan to explain it to me in diplomatic terms. He unabashedly told me that "to unite our compatriots through the Party, to bring our workers up to their highest level of productivity, and to make the *yotheas* (soldiers) ardor and valor in combat even greater, the best thing we could do was incite them to hate the Yuons (Vietnamese) more and more everyday." Khieu Samphan added: "Our *bang phaaun* (literally, older and younger brothers and sisters) are willing to make any sacrifice the minute we wave the "Hate Vietnam" flag in front of them.'[28] Thus, provoking conflict with Vietnam was the tactic by which the Pol Pot faction believed they could mobilize support and defeat their domestic rivals.

It is not easy to gauge the real extent of Vietnamese penetration of the CPK, given the secrecy with which the latter surrounded its affairs. The Vietnamese make no bones about the fact that they opposed Pol Pot and tried to encourage the groups they regarded as more sympathetic, but they deny any interference with the 'internal affairs' of the CPK. It seems plausible that they would have cultivated every friendly source and contact within Pol Pot's party, and that since 1966 at least, Pol Pot had been systematically eliminating such people.

It also seems clear that the spread of opposition to Pol Pot's policies among prominent CPK figures after April 1975 was based primarily on revulsion at their consequences, rather than Vietnamese influence, although Pol Pot himself could hardly be expected to admit this. Certainly, all of the leading figures eliminated in the purges of 1976–8 had collaborated to a greater or lesser degree with Pol Pot and supported his version of 'patriotism' prior to this. If they nursed 'pro-Vietnamese' sentiments, they kept them such a good secret that even the *Black Paper* had no evidence of Vietnamese penetration of the CPK other than a few insubstantial references to 'confessions' (presumably extracted at Toul Sleng). Nor did the *Black Paper* claim that Vietnam itself exerted any direct pressure from outside prior to 1977. On the contrary, it claimed that until then the Vietnamese had acted through the 'agents' inside the CPK, whose existence the document signally failed to demonstrate. Only in 1978 is there evidence that Pol Pot's domestic rivals linked up (hesitantly) with the Vietnamese – and this was in response to Pol Pot's own actions.

Nevertheless, Pol Pot and his supporters interpreted his removal from his government post in September 1976 as a Vietnamese-inspired attempt at a *coup d'état*. The subsequent purge of internal opposition was accompanied by a propaganda campaign against the Vietnamese. Even though it was accompanied by no action against Vietnam by the Phnom Penh government, this was likely to create a tense situation on the country's borders. It encouraged local border officials, especially those who may previously have compromised themselves by a cooperative attitude, to try and save their own necks by making a conspicuous display of their 'vigilance'.

Pol Pot's group also adopted a belligerent attitude to Vietnam itself. Following the victory of April 1975, they cultivated a chauvinistically distorted view of the military prowess of their army, spoke of eliminating the Vietnamese 'menace' once and for all, and of regaining the 'lost territories' abandoned by previous governments in Phnom Penh. Sihanouk relates: 'In September 1975, the first time I returned to "liberated" Cambodia at the invitation of the Khmer Rouge leaders, I was surprised to hear Khieu Samphan, Son Sen, and Co. tell me, all smiles and looking perfectly pleased, that their soldiers were "unhappy" with the Party because it would not give them the green light to recapture "Kampuchea Krom" – that is, Lower Cambodia (South Vietnam) – as well as the border districts along the Thai frontier that had once belonged to Cambodia (Aranya, Surin, etc.). Son Sen, Vice Minister in Charge of National Defence, claimed his glorious "revolutionary army of Cambodia" felt it could make quick work of General Giap's army, not to mention Kukrit Pramoj and Kriangsak Chamanond's much less imposing Thai army.'[29]

Son Sen also informed Sihanouk that the 'Vietnamese threat' was like a cancer eating away at Cambodia's body, and that the very survival of the Khmer people depended on the 'total eradication' of this cancer. On several occasions from 1976 to 1978 Son Sen and Khieu Samphan outlined to him their plans for achieving this. The 'cancer' required a 'three-part surgical operation':

1. Categorically refusing Vietnamese citizens, whoever they might be, the right to live in Cambodia. The Khmers Rouges' efforts in this direction were the physical elimination of a large number of Vietnamese residents "suspected of being agents or spies for the Vietminh or Vietcong" and the forced repatriation of all other Vietnamese residents . . . .
2. Giving all Cambodian men and women the order to work twice, ten times as hard as the Vietnamese people, in order, Khieu

Samphan told me, to make Cambodia much stronger from every point of view (military, economic, ideological). According to the Khmer Rouge leaders, this frantic work they were making their people do would turn Cambodia into an "impregnable fortress" . . . .

3. "Accepting" a large-scale engagement with Vietnam: to what end? The problem of Vietnamese sanctuaries had to be fought out; they must be eliminated. A "more just" delineation of the border between Cambodia and Vietnam was also necessary. Finally, the threat of Soviet Vietnamese expansionism had to be met head on. Without Democratic Kampuchea to stop it, it would end up spreading through the rest of Southeast Asia and even further. . . . [30]

In keeping with this vision, with the end of the war the DK government expanded its armed forces rapidly. But these ideas could not be put into practice in the 1975–6 period because Pol Pot's faction was constrained by the power of rival groups in the CPK hierarchy. Only when the purge of these groups got underway, at the end of 1976, did Pol Pot have a free hand to deal with the Vietnamese in any way he wished.

The evidence thus seems to support those writers, such as Gareth Porter and Ben Kiernan, who argue that relations between Vietnam and Cambodia since the Communist victory in 1975 can be explained more plausibly in terms of a factional struggle among the Khmers Rouges than in terms of Hanoi's supposed plans for an 'Indochina Federation'. Far from just wanting to be left alone, as Heder maintains, Pol Pot's faction was spoiling for a fight with Vietnam. The Vietnamese no doubt encouraged Pol Pot's opponents, but the extent of their involvement in the inner-party struggle in Cambodia is unknown. In any case, Pol Pot blamed them for all the opposition aroused by his harsh policies. The extermination of the internal opposition went hand in hand with a campaign of hostility towards Vietnam, and also eliminated whatever restraints there had been previously on Pol Pot's conduct towards the Vietnamese.

Tension on the Thai Border, 1977

Before dealing directly with the eruption of fighting on the Vietnam-Cambodia border, it is important to recall that it coincided with a rash of incidents along Cambodia's borders with both Laos and Thailand as well. We saw in chapter three that the situation on the Lao border first became tense at the end of 1976 and deteriorated thereafter.

The situation on the Thai border was much more serious. On 28 January 1977, Khmer Rouge soldiers clashed with Thai troops at the village of Ban Noi Parai, to the north of the frontier town of Aranyapratet. Rather than backing off, both sides apparently called for reinforcements, and the ensuing firefight spread to two neighbouring villages. Thirty Thais and an unknown number of Khmers were killed.

The Bangkok government did its best to publicize the incident, charging that a Cambodian invasion of Thai territory had taken place. Reporters were taken to see the shattered, abandoned houses and the mangled bodies, and generally accepted the Thai government's account (the only one who tried to check out the background to the story more closely was expelled from the country). Given the blaze of publicity, Phnom Penh was obliged to offer its account two weeks later. It claimed that the villages involved were on Cambodian territory, and that what had happened there was an 'internal affair' which was nobody else's business: 'The measures taken by the Government of Democratic Kampuchea in its own territory are answerable to the absolute sovereignty of Democratic Kampuchea.' It charged that the villages had been bases for right-wing Khmer Serei guerrillas, whose activities were being encouraged by the Thai military dictatorship.

It is not an easy business to establish the rights and wrongs of this incident.[31] The Thai-Cambodian border has not been properly demarcated to the north of Aranyapratet, and it runs through a flat, largely featureless landscape. Noi Parai was apparently a recent settlement, and is not to be found on maps of the area, so on whose territory it was located is genuinely uncertain. On the Thai side of the border, the province of Prachinburi had once been an important part of the Khmer Empire, and today has a mixed population of Thai, Lao and Khmer. The locals had been accustomed to moving more or less freely across the border, and the border zone had continued to be a centre of smuggling and insurgent activity despite vigorous Khmer Rouge efforts to suppress both.

Relations between the local Khmer Rouge and Thai authorities had already taken a turn for the worse before the shooting at Noi Parai. It may well be that the military coup in Bangkok in October 1976 meant that Thai army and police on the border were given a freer hand, but the immediate catalyst was a Cambodian offensive against Khmer Serei encampments in the mountains to the south of Aranyapratet. The Khmer Serei fled into Thailand, and there were several violent clashes between the Khmer Rouge soldiers pursuing them and Thai border police.

Both sides responded by reinforcing their forces all along the border, and the undemarcated zone to the north of Aranyapratet immediately became an area of tension. When the Thai-Cambodian border liaison committees met in December, both sides blamed each other and the Cambodian side bitterly accused the Thais of actively supporting Khmer Serei activity on the border. Noi Parai soon emerged as the focus of these quarrels, and the meeting broke up with the disagreement unresolved. Whoever was responsible for the violence at Noi Parai three weeks later, it seems likely that it was a deliberate provocation.

There can be little doubt that this incident marked the adoption of a more aggressive stance on the part of the Cambodians. They ignored Thai calls for further meetings of the border liaison committee, and answered Thai calls for demarcation of the border with demands that the Thais abandon their support for the Khmer Serei groups. Reports of Khmer Rouge attacks on Thai villages and clashes with Thai border police and soldiers became almost a daily occurrence over the next few months, not just in the poorly demarcated sector around Noi Parai, but all along Cambodia's western border. In August the Thai prime minister accused the Cambodians of about 400 incursions since the start of the year, and said that Thailand would have no choice but to go to war unless Cambodia desisted. Following this the number of incidents fell off, and by January 1978 a Thai military spokesman was able to declare that the border 'has been quiet of late'.

The Vietnam-Cambodia Border War, 1977-78

It should be clear from this that the problem was primarily Cambodia rather than Thailand. However, the clash over Noi Parai illustrates how readily minor clashes of obscure origin can escalate into full-scale confrontations when both sides adopt intransigent attitudes. It is tempting to assume that something very close to this must have happened on the Vietnamese border as well, and this is just what Heder does. He writes that, as the months passed after the collapse of the May 1976 talks between Vietnam and Cambodia, both sides became 'more and more impatient with the deadlock', that there was 'probably' mounting tension along the border as a consequence, and that the full-scale conflict was the result of the intransigence on both sides.

But Heder himself reports that the border liaison committees successfully handled incidents on the Vietnam-Cambodia border in the second half of 1976, which were 'apparently infrequent and small-scale'.[32] We now know that the Cambodian regime was at this time preoccupied with an intense internal struggle for power. Then, following the victory of Pol Pot's faction, the situation deteriorated along all of Cambodia's borders simultaneously. And even if Hanoi was becoming increasingly exasperated in its dealings with Phnom Penh (which is not unlikely), it is clear that it was not actions by the Vietnamese side that initiated a new level of conflict.

In the first three weeks of January 1977 Cambodian forces launched armed attacks on civilian settlements in six out of Vietnam's seven border provinces. The worst attacks were in the provinces of Kien Giang and An Giang, which run from the Mekong River to the coast. They are also opposite Cambodia's southwest region, then under the control of Pol Pot's main regional ally, Ta Mok. In May the capital of An Giang province, Chau Doc, and the coastal town of Ha Tien (population 30,000) were bombarded by Cambodian artillery. A year later, when the dispute had been made public, the Vietnamese government alleged that Khmer Rouge troops in this period 'perpetrated utterly inhuman crimes, raping, tearing foetuses from mothers' wombs, disembowelling adults, burning children alive'. However, the Vietnamese government had (in contrast to the Thai government) maintained a studious silence at the time, and one might be inclined to regard this as mere propaganda. But Vietnamese boat people arriving in other countries from this region had at the time reported heavy fighting and widespread Khmer Rouge atrocities. Later, Khmer refugees from the border area also confirmed that the Cambodian side had attacked Vietnam. For that matter, the Pol Pot regime did not deny the charges or accuse the Vietnamese of initiating fighting at this time.

It is clear, then, that it was military action by the Cambodian side that precipitated the full-scale confrontation between Vietnam and Cambodia in 1977–8. This is not our own idiosyncratic interpretation; it is a view shared by Western specialists hostile to the Hanoi government. D.R. Sar Desai, for example, gives credence to the 'Indochina Federation' allegations (though without producing any evidence to support them) and argues that 'The Pol Pot regime was certainly justified in attempting every means to avert Cambodia's conversion to a Vietnamese satellite.' Yet when he comes down to the details of the border dispute, he concludes: ' . . . the Cambodians obviously decided that offense is the best form of defence . . . .'[33] Thus, even if thoughts of an Indochina Federation still lingered in Hanoi, it was not action based on them that led to the conflict.

Heder admits that the Cambodian side was responsible for initiating hostilities in 1977. In January 1977, he says, the Cambodians decided to 'increase the pressure' on Vietnam by sending troops to 'demonstrate a Cambodian presence' in the Vietnamese-held areas to which the Cambodian side had laid claim at the May 1976 meeting. When the Vietnamese responded to this 'intensified patrolling' by reinforcing their military positions, the Cambodian side 'began to initiate military activities' on the border in April 1977. By this stage, he says, they were no longer concerned with the areas they had claimed for Cambodia the previous May, but were trying to 'demonstrate that the Cambodians had a capability to strike at Vietnamese territory'. No Vietnamese provocation or precedent is cited for any of these acts of escalation by the Cambodian side.

Heder explains this as part of Cambodia's 'negotiating strategy' in the wake of the failure of the treaty talks: 'The Cambodians probably saw themselves attempting to break the deadlock by suggesting that they were willing to make it costly . . . for the Vietnamese to rely upon their superior military strength to maintain the status quo . . . [These] Cambodian military initiatives were part of a negotiation strategy. The Cambodians were not making any new territorial claims nor were they trying to permanently occupy any of the targets of their attacks. Rather, they still believed themselves to be responding in kind to what they saw as long standing *de facto* Vietnamese aggression against Cambodian territory'.[34]

Thus, according to the topsy-turvy logic of Pol Pot (which Heder does not criticize), armed attacks on undisputed Vietnamese territory to enforce a demand for the unilateral right to adjust the border at Vietnam's expense were 'defensive' in character. It should then be no surprise to find that these military actions are interpreted by Heder as a 'negotiating tactic', even though it was Cambodia rather than Vietnam which had originally suspended the negotiations and was refusing to re-open them. For, as Heder has already explained, the Khmer Rouge leaders understood 'negotiations' to be the unconditional acceptance of their demands by the other side. And since Pol Pot believed himself to be the aggrieved party in the dispute, the refusal of Vietnam to submit to his demands, even when he backed them with military action, on Vietnamese soil, constituted 'aggression' against Cambodia.

The Vietnamese responded to these attacks by building up their border defences, but they apparently did not launch any counter-attacks in the first half of 1977. Western press reports at the time suggested major Vietnamese incursions into Cambodia in April and May, but these appear to be in error, for later accounts by the Pol Pot regime make no mention of them. According to the *Black Paper* the Vietnamese at this time were still pinning their hopes on 'plots' by their agents inside the CPK. Hoang Tung, then political director of *Nhan Dan* and a member of the VCP central committee, later claimed that the Vietnamese responded passively to early Cambodian attacks, in the hope that restraint would make a negotiated settlement easier. Following the massive Cambodian incursions in April and May, according to Tung, the Vietnamese drew up contingency plans for a military counter-attack but they were still hoping for a diplomatic solution.[35]

On 7 June they sent a conciliatory letter to Phnom Penh, proposing that a high-level meeting should be held to resolve the border problem as soon as possible. The Pol Pot government rejected this proposal on 18 June, asserting that it would be better to 'let some time elapse' before any talks took place. In the meantime, they proposed that there should be a mutual withdrawal of forces from 'disputed areas'. Cambodian attacks continued on the border (at the time Phnom Penh sent this message to Hanoi, Chao Doc was under Cambodian artillery attack).

With the failure of this initiative, the Vietnamese moved towards the option of military retaliation. In July General Giap publicly embarked on an inspection tour of the border regions. This was a clear warning to the Cambodian side to desist, but (to judge from the *Black Paper's* account) Pol Pot interpreted it as a sign that the Vietnamese had adopted a new strategy for swallowing Cambodia; with the defeat of their attempts to take over Cambodia from the 'inside' (due to the exemplary 'vigilance' of his regime), they were forced in mid-1977 to 'set up a plan of large-scale attack' to capture it from the 'outside'.[36]

Heavy fighting erupted once more on 24 September, shortly after Pol Pot's re-emergence from obscurity and just before his triumphant visit to Peking. Both sides held the other responsible for this fighting. According to the Vietnamese, the Khmers Rouges attacked all along the border of Tay Ninh province (on the northern side of the Parrot's Beak salient) with four divisions, a version of events supported by US intelligence sources. According to Hoang Tung, it was now that the Vietnamese decided to meet force with force as they launched a vigorous counter-attack, although they did not enter Cambodia. The Cambodian statement of December 1977 claimed that the *first* major Vietnamese attacks occurred at this time, an oblique admission that previous fighting had been the result of Cambodian attacks, and accused the Vietnamese of penetrating for 'dozens of kilometres' into Cambodia, perpetrating terrible atrocities against the population, burning villages, and looting thousands of tons of rice-paddy from fields and granaries. Heavy fighting continued until the end of November.

Then, on 16 December, it was unequivocally the turn of the Vietnamese to escalate the military conflict on the border. As might be expected, both sides gave wildly conflicting accounts of what happened. While agreeing that their troops had struck in force (Western press reports variously suggested from 30,000 to 60,000 infantry, with tank, air and artillery support) up to forty kilometres into Cambodian territory, the Vietnamese claimed that the attack was a response to further Cambodian incursions into Vietnam. They denied any intention of permanently occupying Cambodian territory. Three months later, Hoang Tung described their objectives: 'First of all to chase them out of our territory and then to deal a heavy blow to their divisions, to make them realize we are not as passive as they assumed and to tell them that they have to choose the other solution. It was not to mount a *coup d'état*.' Having made their point, according to the Vietnamese, they withdrew their forces back to the border in early January 1978.

If this action was intended to jolt the Khmer Rouge leaders into a more restrained stance, as open threats of war by Thailand had the previous August, it failed dismally. Phnom Penh responded by breaking off diplomatic relations with Vietnam on 31 December and finally making the whole dispute between the two Communist regimes public by launching a barrage of propaganda against Vietnam. The withdrawal of Vietnamese forces in January was interpreted by Phnom Penh as proof of Cambodia's military superiority and of the weak and cowardly nature of the Vietnamese.

In its statement of 31 December the Cambodian government declared its willingness to engage in negotiations over the border conflict 'in a spirit of friendship'. But when the Vietnamese responded with a call for the two sides to 'meet as early as possible, at whatever level, so as to solve together the border issue between the two countries in a spirit of brotherly friendship' the Cambodians refused. A statement by the Cambodian ministry of information on 3 January 1978 demanded the Vietnamese withdrawal from Cambodian soil and an agreement to respect Cambodia's 'independence, sovereignty and territorial integrity' (defined, presumably, in the eccentric manner previously advanced by Phnom Penh) as a precondition for talks. The Vietnamese would have to 'first create an atmosphere of friendship and mutual confidence' before the DK government would consent to negotiations.

Following the withdrawal of their troops in January, the Vietnamese offered again to negotiate. On 5 February 1978 Deputy Foreign Minister Nguyen Co Thach proposed an immediate end to all hostilities on the border, a withdrawal of the armed forces of both sides to five kilometres from the border, and a conference to draw up a treaty 'on the basis of respect for each other's territorial sovereignty within the existing border' and reach agreement on 'an appropriate form of international guarantee and supervision'. This paralleled the Khmer proposals of the previous June, except that the Vietnamese focused on 'the existing border' instead of 'disputed territories'. They also wanted negotiations as soon as possible and were willing to accept outside supervision, both unacceptable to Phnom Penh.

The Cambodian side refused to discuss these proposals on the grounds that they had not been transmitted to Phnom Penh via official channels (the Vietnamese embassy there having been closed). The Vietnamese then sent a letter describing these proposals to Ieng Sary via the Lao ambassador to Phnom Penh, but Sary refused to accept the note. Pol Pot himself finally went on Phnom Penh radio on 12 April to give the Cambodian response. He reiterated DK's refusal to negotiate, and proclaimed Cambodia's 'right' to 'demand the revision of border documents and changes in the demarcation of land and sea borders', and 'the resettlement of the "Kampuchea Krom" issue'. Presumably, acceptance of this understanding of Cambodian sovereignty was a precondition for negotiations.

Over the following months the diplomatic deadlock continued. In June 1978 the Cambodian foreign ministry justified the Cambodian refusal to negotiate by declaring that the Vietnamese proposals were aimed at 'misleading world opinion' and that the proposal to withdraw Cambodian troops five kilometres from the border 'automatically lets Vietnam annex a belt of Cambodia's territory five kilometres wide'. Meanwhile, the military conflict intensified, a development for which the Cambodian side openly claimed responsibility. On 10 May Phnom Penh Radio stated that after the 'victory' over the Vietnamese on 6 January 'we did not let the Vietnamese initiate further attacks against us, but kept on launching attacks against them'.

The border war with Cambodia inflicted immense damage on Vietnam in 1977–8. According to statistics released by Hanoi in 1979, 25 townships and 96 villages were destroyed by the Khmers Rouges; 257,000 people were rendered homeless, and 100,000 hectares of farmland had to be abandoned because of the fighting. Given that Vietnam itself was already in a state of crisis, this was something which the government in Hanoi could not tolerate indefinitely.

It is clear that the main responsibility for the conflict lay with the regime in Phnom Penh. There is no evidence that Hanoi was anticipating a major conflict with Phnom Penh after 1975. Vietnam advanced no territorial claims against Cambodia, unless one chooses to interpret the dispute over the maritime border in this way. The early border clashes had been resolved, and practical measures for dealing with any future ones had been adopted. It was the Cambodian side that initiated the fighting in 1977, escalated it, and then blocked any negotiated solution. When the Vietnamese finally responded in force Phnom Penh again refused to negotiate and chose to further escalate the fighting. Under these circumstances it is not surprising that the Hanoi leadership concluded that the war with Cambodia would not end until the war party in Phnom Penh had been overthrown.

The Road to Invasion

The VCP's central committee was in a grim mood when it met secretly in Hanoi to decide what to do about the Cambodian problem after it became clear that their ceasefire proposals of 5 February 1978 had been rejected. Since the Pol Pot group had blocked every attempt at a peaceful resolution of the dispute, it seemed obvious that Pol Pot had to be removed. A military invasion was one possibility, but the central committee opted for the alternative of throwing their full weight behind the anti-Pol Pot forces within the CPK and backing them with Vietnamese military force if it proved necessary.

The first public signs of the shift in Vietnamese policy towards Cambodia appeared in early April. In addition to denunciations of the Pol Pot clique and its murderous policies, Hanoi Radio now began issuing open calls for the Cambodian people to overthrow the regime. Then General Hoang Cham, who had commanded the Vietnamese forces fighting in Cambodia in 1970–72, was put in charge of the Vietnamese troops in the border region. They also encouraged the organization of an anti-Pol Pot resistance movement among the large Cambodian refugee population in Vietnam (more than 150,000 people). When Nayan Chanda spoke to Cambodian refugees at a camp in Tay Ninh province in April 1978, Khmer Communists were busy organizing a resistance movement. Many of the people he spoke to were eager to return to Cambodia to overthrow the Phnom Penh regime, and there had already been 2,000 people recruited at this particular camp. Not all were Communists. One man Chanda spoke to said that, while he was not a Communist himself, he accepted that this movement would establish another Communist government in Phnom Penh – at least, he said, 'it will be a communist government with justice, not barbaric like the present one.'

The Vietnamese had also secretly established contact with the anti-Pol Pot forces controlling Cambodia's eastern region. The *Black Paper* alleges that the Vietnamese began plotting with So Phim only in February 1978. The Vietnamese themselves later related that in January 1978 they had begun discussions with eastern region cadres about the possibility of overthrowing Pol Pot by means of a military-political uprising by So Phim's forces, for which the Vietnamese would provide military support. However, Pol Pot struck in force against the eastern region before anything concrete had emerged from the discussions. Although they were still ill-prepared, the Vietnamese threw their own troops into the fray in June, and the fighting continued until late August. Those of So Phim's forces who survived were under the control of his deputy military commander, Heng Samrin. They retreated with the Vietnamese troops and joined the resistance movement being organized in Vietnam.

The elimination of the eastern region Communists ended the possibility of Pol Pot's overthrow by an internal upheaval, and after that the conflict headed for a straightforward military denouement. Through the rest of the rainy season both sides reinforced their troops along the border. By the end of October 1978 General Cham had 100,000 troops under his command. Cambodian anti-Pol Pot forces, operating mainly as small guerrilla units, numbered somewhere between 10,000 and 20,000. Facing them were 60,000 Khmer Rouge troops, two-thirds of all Pol Pot's forces.

Meanwhile, a frantic race for diplomatic support went on. China was Pol Pot's main backer, and the Vietnamese increasingly looked on Pol Pot as a tool of Peking. Hanoi moved to protect itself from the unexpected Chinese retaliation against its actions by committing Vietnam more firmly to the Soviet bloc – joining the Council for Mutual Economic Assistance (COMECON) in July and signing a 25-year treaty of friendship with Moscow in November.

Both sides set about wooing ASEAN countries in earnest. Pham Van Dong made a tour, offering treaties of friendship to anyone who was interested. Ieng Sary patched up relations with Thailand (they had been strained by a number of Khmer Rouge forays into Thailand in April and May 1978), established trade relations with Singapore, and visited the Philippines and Japan. Chinese Vice-Premier Deng Xiaoping did the rounds in November, trying to counter Dong's tour.

On 3 December 1978 Hanoi Radio announced that a Kampuchean National Front for National Salvation (KNUFNS) had been established 'somewhere in the liberated area' of Cambodia, with Heng Samrin as president. It issued a programme calling for the overthrow of 'the reactionary Pol Pot-Ieng Sary clique' and the establishment of a regime 'tending towards genuine socialism'. Phnom Penh responded six days later, branding KNUFNS as 'a Vietnamese political organization with a Khmer name' and a tool of 'the Soviet expansionists'.

The Vietnamese finally launched their military onslaught against the Pol Pot regime on Christmas Day 1978. Twelve Vietnamese divisions – about 120,000 troops, with tanks and armoured cars – poured across the border and spread out across Cambodia with a speed that stunned observers. The attack was personally directed by the Vietnamese army chief of staff, General Van Tien Dung, who had been in charge of the final Communist offensive in South Vietnam in 1975. The Khmer Rouge forces committed some classic military mistakes. In response to some preliminary Vietnamese probes, Pol Pot had concentrated more than half of all his forces to deal with a Vietnamese offensive through the 'Parrot's Beak', or 'Fish Hook', salient of Svay Rieng and Kompong Cham provinces. General Dung then launched outflanking attacks from Pleiku and Tay Ninh (and, according to Thai sources, from positions in southern Laos) towards the provincial capitals of Stung Treng,

Kratie and Kompong Cham in the north, and along Routes 2 and 3 towards Takeo and Kampot in the south.

The success of these offensives opened the roads to Phnom Penh from both the north and the south to the Vietnamese. Only then did they attack the main Khmer Rouge defensive positions along Route 1, opening the main highway from Saigon to Phnom Penh by early January. But Phnom Penh Radio still maintained that the war was going well for the Khmers Rouges. On 5 January 1979 a broadcast stated: 'The news of the victory of our revolutionary troops . . . have been received every day and make our people happy and satisfied. It also made us trust and be confident in our heroic struggle. We are confident we must win.''Two days later the Vietnamese captured Phnom Penh unopposed. Three weeks after the attack began, the Vietnamese were in control of all the main towns and lines of communications in Cambodia. Then they began spreading out along the side roads to mop up the Khmer Rouge forces they had by-passed.

By the end of January 1979 Western intelligence sources estimated that the Vietnamese had inflicted some 30,000 casualties on Pol Pot's forces – representing a third of his total forces, and half of those he had committed to the defence of the Vietnam border. Due to numerical superiority, better weaponry and successful tactics, Vietnamese casualties were relatively light. On 30 January Pol Pot's radio (now named the Voice of Democratic Kampuchea and relocated in southern China) claimed that the Vietnamese had suffered 14,000 casualties. Given the Khmer Rouge propensity for exaggeration this should be taken as the upper limit of probability.

Despite these successes, Vietnam's victory was incomplete. Though faced with massive defeat, the morale of Pol Pot's army held; there were no large-scale surrenders to the Vietnamese. Recognizing that they were unable to match the Vietnamese in conventional warfare, many of the Khmer Rouge commanders quickly broke their forces up into small guerrilla units and retreated to the mountains and swamps, to continue the struggle at a later stage.

By the end of January 1979 Pol Pot's forces were starting to strike back against the Vietnamese. Though they had some temporary successes, they succeeded nowhere in recapturing the initiative, and Khmer Rouge leaders later characterized these operations as 'premature'. In March and April the Vietnamese seized the initiative again, launching a series of sweeps to clear Khmer Rouge forces from the rice-growing plains of western Cambodia, and forcing them to retreat into the mountains of southwestern Cambodia or to the Thai border. On 10 April the Vietnamese captured a heavily defended underground complex at Ta Sanh, which the Khmer Rouge leadership had been using as a headquarters – they were forced to leave it so quickly that the Vietnamese captured Ieng Sary's passport, along with many documents. (The Provisional Revolutionary Government's white paper of September 1983 quotes from these documents in support of its charges of Thai-Chinese collusion with Pol Pot.) In the same month, the Vietnamese surrounded Khmer Rouge headquarters at Ampil (near Ban Sa-ngae) in the northwest of Cambodia.

At one point Pol Pot's forces escaped only by retreating into Thailand. Western journalists watched as between 50–80,000 people trekked for thirty miles along roads well on the Thai side of the border before re-entering Cambodia. There were thousands of tough young soldiers herding along a captive workforce of sullen and malnourished villagers at gunpoint – 'a walking concentration camp' was how one of the observers later described this weary procession.

The military situation stabilized in May and June 1979, as the monsoon rains set in. The Vietnamese were in control of the main populated parts of the country, the eastern border region, and the central and western rice-growing plains, but security was still poor in the outlying districts.

The Pol Pot forces controlled areas in the largely uninhabited mountains of the southwest, and along the Thai border. The only significant town still in their hands was Pailin. From these bases they could still range through much of the western part of the country and through the southern mountains, and they could launch occasional raids on the highways between Phnom Penh and Battambang, and between Phnom Penh and Kompong Som. There were also units loyal to Pol Pot operating in Kompong Thom and Ratanikiri provinces, in the centre and east of the country, but they preferred to lie low for the time being. On the whole, it was clear that the Khmers Rouges' control of the people of Cambodia had been broken.

Militarily, Pol Pot's army had been severely mauled. Western intelligence sources estimated that its numbers had fallen to 35,000 by mid-1979; in six months' fighting it had lost two-thirds of its number. The size of the population remaining under its control at this time is not known, but it is unlikely to have been more than a quarter of a million. Nevertheless, the Khmer Rouge army continued to be a functioning military force, and the leadership of the DK government was still intact. Presumably, capturing them had been one of the main objectives of the Vietnamese in the attack; in this regard, at least, it must be counted a failure. Pol Pot and his colleagues all managed to escape being trapped in Phnon Penh and made it to the Thai border. Within a few weeks they had regrouped and were trying to rally support inside and outside Cambodia for a struggle against the new, Vietnamese-sponsored Heng Samrin government in Phnom Penh.

Notes

1. Heder has summarized his researches in 'The Kampuchean-Vietnamese Conflict' in David W.P. Elliott, ed., *The Third Indochina Conflict*, Boulder, Colorado 1981.

2. Ministry of Foreign Affairs, Democratic Kampuchea, *Black Paper: Facts and Evidences of the Acts of Aggression and Annexation of Vietnam against Kampuchea*, Phnom Penh, September 1978, pp. 73–4.

3. Gareth Porter, 'Vietnamese Policy and the Indochina Crisis' in Elliott, p. 94.

4. Ministry of Foreign Affairs, Socialist Republic of Vietnam, 'La Vérite sur le Problème Frontalier Vietnam-Kampuchean', in *Dossier Kampuchea*, 2nd edn. Hanoi 1978, vol. I, pp. 132-3.

5. Heder, p. 25.

6. Michael Akehurst, *A Modern Introduction to International Law*, London 1970, pp. 192–3.

7. *Dossier Kampuchea*, p. 117.

8. *Black Paper*, pp. 14–15.

9. William J. Duiker, *The Rise of Nationalism in Vietnam 1900–1941*, Ithaca and London 1976, pp. 213–16.

10. *Black Paper*, p. 19.

11. Quoted in William J. Duiker, *The Communist Road to Power in Vietnam*, Boulder, Colorado, 1981, p. 143.

12. Quoted in the introduction to Ben Kiernan and Chanthou Boua, eds, *Peasants and Politics in Kampuchea 1942–81*, London 1982, p. 21.

13. Norodom Sihanouk, *My War with the CIA: Cambodia's Struggle for Survival*, Harmondsworth 1973, pp. 182, 185.

14. Norodom Sihanouk, *War and Hope: The Case for Cambodia*, London 1980, pp. 16–17.

15. Quoted by Nayan Chanda, *Far Eastern Economic Review*, 21 April 1978.

16. Heder, p. 41.

17. The most detailed examination of these events is Ben Kiernan 'The Samlaut Rebellion 1967–8' in Kiernan and Boua. This gives qualified support for the first view. For the contrary view, cf. W.E. Willmott, 'Analytical Errors of the Kampuchean Communist Party', *Pacific Affairs*, vol. 54, 1980.

18. William Shawcross writes: 'By its own account it had 4,000 regular troops and 50,000 guerrillas, but these figures are almost certainly exaggerated. Captured documents show that the regulars were grouped into companies. Such small-scale organization suggests that they were scattered and not nearly so numerous as 4,000.

One Vietnamese leader later claimed that the Khmers Rouges numbered only a few hundred in 1970' (*Sideshow: Kissinger, Nixon and the Destruction of Cambodia,* London 1979, p. 246). Steve Heder cites a Sihanouk intelligence report suggesting a figure of 5,000–10,000 ('Kampuchea's Armed Struggle: The Origins of an Independent Revolution', *Bulletin of Concerned Asian Scholars,* vol. 11, January-March 1979, p. 14).

19. *Black Paper,* p. 22. For the Vietnamese denial, see Anthony Barnett's interview with Le Duc Tho in John Pilger and Anthony Barnett, *Aftermath: The Struggle of Vietnam and Cambodia,* London 1982, pp. 58–9.

20. *Black Paper,* p. 69.

21. Sihanouk, *War and Hope,* p. 21.

22. Richard Dudman, 'Cambodia – A Land in Turmoil', Supplement to *St Louis Post-Dispatch,* 15 January 1979. Dudman is a veteran Indochina reporter who visited Cambodia with Elizabeth Becker and Malcolm Caldwell in December 1978. Sihanouk relates: 'It is quite obvious that the Khmers Rouges never really wanted to set up an administration and a central government worthy of the name.' (*War and Hope,* p. 79).

23. Hamad Abdul Aziz al Aiya, 'Modern Kampuchea', *News from Kampuchea,* vol. 1, no. 4, October 1977. Aiya was the Peking representative of the PLO, and visited Phnom Penh in March 1976.

24. Slavko Stanic, 'Kampuchea – Socialism without a Model', *Socialist Theory and Practice,* Belgrade, October 1978, p. 67. Stanic was a member of a Yugoslav team that produced a film on life under Pol Pot's regime. Since the Yugoslav government enjoyed good relations with DK, the journalists were constrained by diplomatic considerations in their reportage. Wilfred Burchett relates his meeting with the head of the team: 'After greetings, his first question to me was: "Did you see my film?" I had not, but my wife Vessa, who was standing alongside me, said that she had seen it on French television. Asked what she thought of it, Vessa replied: "For anyone who has ever lived in Cambodia, it was terrifying. The only smiling face was that of Pol Pot." Vittorovich seemed relieved. "Then my message got through," he said. "What we saw was a thousand times worse than we could put on film or I could express in my commentary." ' (*The China-Cambodia-Vietnam Triangle,* London 1981, p. 162.)

25. François Ponchaud, *Cambodia Year Zero,* Harmondsworth 1978, p. 69.

26. For a short survey of the literature to date, see May Ebihara, 'Perspectives on Sociopolitical Transformations in Kampuchea/Cambodia: A Review Article', *Journal of Asian Studies,* vol. 41, 1981. The most valuable discussions are by Ben Kiernan, 'Pol Pot and the Kampuchean Communist Movement' in Kiernan and Boua, and Steve Heder, 'From Pol Pot to Pen Sovan in the Villages', Paper to the International Conference on Indochina and stability in Southeast Asia, Chulalongkorn University, Bangkok 1980. An abridged version of Heder's paper appeared in *Southeast Asia Chronicle,* no. 77, 1981. See also Pilger and Barnett.

27. *Amnesty International Report 1982,* London, pp. 3–4. For the CIA's calculations, see *Kampuchea: A Demographic Catastrophe,* Washington 1980.

28. Sihanouk, *War and Hope,* pp. 91–2.

29. Ibid., p. 38.

30. Ibid., pp. 45–6.

31. The most thorough attempt is by Larry Palmer, 'Thailand's Kampuchean Border Incidents', *News from Kampuchea,* vol. 1, no. 4, October 1977.

32. Heder, 'Kampuchean-Vietnamese Conflict', pp. 31–2.

33. D.R. Sar Desai, 'Vietnam's Quest for Security' in Sudershan Chawla and D.R. Sar Desai, eds, *Changing Patterns of Security and Stability in Asia,* New York 1980,

pp. 229–31. Simon W. Sheldon, 'New Conflict in Indochina', *Problems of Communism*, September-October 1978, p. 27, also writes: 'Cambodia seems to have set in motion the chain of events that led to major hostilities.' And, according to Dennis J. Duncanson, ' "Limited Sovereignty" in Indochina', *The World Today*, July 1978, p. 261: 'It is the Cambodians who have started the shooting.'

34. Heder, 'Kampuchean-Vietnamese Conflict', p. 32.
35. Nayan Chanda, *Far Eastern Economic Review*, 21 April 1978.
36. *Black Paper*, p. 77.
37. Porter, 'Vietnamese Policy', p. 39.

5

China: the Pedagogy of Power

The Chinese government responded to the Vietnamese invasion of Cambodia in the most violent terms. It accused Hanoi of 'militarism, wild aggression and expansion' and promised to do its 'utmost' to help the deposed Khmer Rouge regime 'in every way'. During his visit to the United States in January 1979 Deng Xiaoping made his famous remarks on the need to teach Vietnam 'some necessary lessons'. On his way back to Peking, he said in Tokyo that Vietnam must be 'punished severely'.

Deng's exercise in pedagogy began at dawn on 17 February, when approximately 100,000 Chinese People's Liberation Army troops poured across the 1,300-kilometre border, backed by tanks and artillery. The attack bogged down quickly, and their numbers had to be boosted to 200,000 before it was resumed. The immediate military objective of the Chinese was the capture of the capitals of Vietnam's six provinces bordering on China, four of which had fallen to them by 23 February. The decisive battle of the campaign then took shape around the town of Lang Son – situated in a natural pass through the mountains separating China and Vietnam (this strategically located town has been the site of many historic battles). The Chinese attacked on 27 February and, after bitter fighting in the surrounding hills, managed to push their way into Lang Son itself on the evening of 2 March. The battle was still proceeding in the town three days later, when Peking announced that it was withdrawing its forces. However, it was not until 16 March that the withdrawal was complete, largely because the Chinese troops methodically demolished all major Vietnamese fortifications and many buildings before pulling out.

The cost of the month-long war was immense. The Chinese admitted suffering 20,000 casualties themselves, but claimed to have inflicted 50,000 on the Vietnamese; for their part, the Vietnamese claimed that 20,000 Chinese had been killed and that the total of Chinese casualties was more than 60,000. During America's Vietnam war these northernmost provinces had been largely insulated from US bombardment because of their proximity to the Chinese border, but this same geographic fact had now exposed them to widespread devastation. Lang Son still lay in ruins when we visited it a year after the invasion. Most of the main buildings had been reduced to heaps of rubble, and much of the housing had been utterly wrecked. Some homes had been rehabilitated, but most of the town's 30,000 inhabitants still lived in primitive shanties similar to those in refugee settlements elsewhere in the region. According to the Vietnamese, the Chinese had demolished four provincial capitals (Lang Son, Cao Bang, Lao Cai and Cam Duong) and 320 villages. Two hundred and fifty thousand people were rendered homeless; 41 state farms and agricultural stations, as well as factories, mines, hospitals and schools were destroyed; 58,000 hectares of rice-fields had to be abandoned; and vast areas of forest had been burnt out.

Peking duly announced its satisfaction with the punishment it had inflicted on Vietnam. However, in an interview with Oriana Fallaci in the Milan *Corriere della Sera* in August 1980 Deng Xioaping admitted that the operation 'wasn't very successful'. It was true that the Chinese had achieved most of their immediate military objectives inside Vietnam, but the price had been distressingly high. Only in the battle of Lang Son had the Vietnamese committed one of their main force divisions (the crack 308th Division, transferred from Hanoi's defence perimeter). For the rest, 200,000 main force PLA troops had been contained by half that number of Vietnamese regional troops and local militia – an outcome that seemed to expose China's military weakness rather than show off her strength.

The Chinese clearly underestimated the capabilities of Vietnam's defence forces, which were well entrenched in a rugged terrain that they knew intimately. The PLA's equipment was generally out-of-date. The Chinese weaponry was mostly of late 1950s-early 1960s vintage, whereas the Vietnamese fought with modern weapons supplied by the Soviets or captured from the Americans. Vietnam's air superiority meant that the Chinese infantry had to attack without the protection of air cover. Chinese logistics proved inadequate – their supply trucks moved slowly on the twisting mountain roads, and they were not able to keep their troops fully supplied with ammunition. Chinese tactics also proved unsatisfactory. As in the Korean war, the PLA relied on 'human wave' assaults, which enabled well-entrenched and well-equipped defence forces to inflict devastating casualties, especially in rugged terrain that slowed the advance of the infantry. In the battle for Lang Son, the Chinese also used cavalry, which suffered heavy casualties in the face of modern, rapid-fire weaponry. The Chinese relied on bugle calls to co-ordinate their units, and Vietnamese snipers were able to throw them into confusion by picking off the buglers. Some reports suggested that the Chinese expected to be welcomed as 'liberators' by the local population, but this did not happen.

It is not surprising that the war sparked off a lengthy debate in Chinese military circles over the validity of Mao's 'people's war' tactics under modern conditions and on the need to modernize China's fighting equipment. It was also followed by the most extensive shake-up among PLA leaders for years, but this appears to have been more closely related to factional struggles in the Chinese Communist Party than to the outcome of the war as such.

Even more important than the PLA's poor battlefield performance was the failure of the invasion to achieve its political objectives. Peking's ostensible aim was simply to secure a 'peaceful border' with Vietnam. It claimed that Chinese troops had been forced to launch a 'self-defensive counter-attack' to safeguard China's territorial integrity in the face of incessant Vietnamese provocations. As Han Nialong, leader of the Chinese delegation to the subsequent Sino-Vietnamese negotiations, put it: 'Their bullying became simply intolerable.'

Ostensibly it was a border war, but the problem was a political one rather than a boundary dispute. Although it is true that certain points were not accurately delineated, on the whole this was one of the best-defined borders in the region.[1] Both sides agreed that there had been no significant problems before 1974, but from that point on incidents on the border had multiplied as relations between Hanoi and Peking deteriorated. The situation was especially tense in the second half of 1978, each side accusing the other of deliberate provocations.

That the border dispute was really a political one became perfectly evident when negotiations on the problem opened in Hanoi in April 1979. The Vietnamese side put forward a three-point proposal to deal with the border problem itself: an end to hostilities and a demilitarization of the border; restoration of normal transport and communications; a settlement of any territorial problems on the basis of 'respect for the borderline' established in the Sino-French agreements of 1887 and 1895. The Chinese side refused to consider this proposition and put forward an eight-point proposal of their own. They rejected a demilitarization of the border and demanded that territorial problems be settled 'on the basis of Sino-French conventions' rather than on the basis of the actual border-line that resulted from these agreements. They also demanded Vietnamese recognition of the Paracel and Spratly islands as 'an inalienable part of China's territory'.

As part of the settlement of the border dispute the Chinese also demanded an end to the persecution of Chinese 'nationals' in Vietnam and the restoration of 'friendly relations' between the two governments. Their second point read: 'Neither side should seek hegemony in Indochina, Southeast Asia, or any other part of the world, and is opposed to efforts by any other country or group of countries to establish such hegemony. Neither side shall station troops in other countries and those already stationed abroad must be withdrawn to their own country. Neither side shall join any military blocs directed against the other, provide military bases, or use the territory and bases of other countries to threaten, subvert or commit armed aggression against the other side or against any other countries.'[2]

In short, the Chinese served notice that there would be no end to the conflict on the Sino-Vietnamese land border unless the Vietnamese were willing to surrender sovereignty over their South China Sea possessions, withdraw from Cambodia, and end their alliance with Moscow. In a subsequent round of talks (on 5 July) the Chinese brushed aside discussion of the border itself and demanded that negotiations 'proceed from the crux of the matter – opposition to hegemonism', accusing Vietnam of setting up an Indochina Federation embracing Laos and Cambodia in coordination with the alleged Soviet 'drive for world hegemony'.

The border negotiations were thus stalemated from the beginning. The Chinese refused to discuss the Vietnamese proposals at all and rejected calls for a 'clarification' of their own position. For their part, the Vietnamese rejected the Chinese proposals on the grounds that China had no right to dictate their relations with other countries as part of a border settlement. The Chinese tried to coerce Hanoi with threats of another attack – Deng Xiaoping declared on 29 May that China 'reserved the right' to teach Vietnam another lesson if it continued its 'provocations' – but the Vietnamese refused to budge.

The talks did continue for a time, but they became simply a propaganda forum. The Chinese attacked Vietnamese 'hegemonism' in Indochina, while the Vietnamese attacked Chinese policies of 'pursuing hegemonism under the guise of anti-hegemonism'. Meanwhile, violent clashes continued on the Sino-Vietnamese border, usually flaring up at times of tension over Cambodia, most notably in June 1980, April 1983 and April 1984.

The official Chinese explanation for its invasion as a defensive response to Vietnamese 'bullying' on the Sino-Vietnam border is almost everywhere recognized as a trumped-up excuse, and indeed is hardly mentioned in most Western commentaries on the conflict.[3] It was evident that in this war the Chinese side was the aggressor, and that the aggression was openly premeditated. No incidents were alleged to which a full-scale invasion could be considered a proportionate response. In reality, the Chinese invasion was a reaction to Hanoi's overthrow of Peking's allies in Cambodia, and to its continued links with the Soviet Union. The war was not forced on the Chinese by circumstances; the Peking leadership had consciously opted for military aggression as an instrument of policy. China's objectives in attacking Vietnam were generally believed to be two-fold: first, to demonstrate to Hanoi that China was a major power whose wishes could not be defied; and second, to take the heat off Pol Pot's forces by compelling the Vietnamese to withdraw troops from Cambodia to defend their own northern border.

In both regards, it was not successful. The Vietnamese remained defiant, having dealt with the Chinese invasion without withdrawing any troops from Cambodia, where they proclaimed that the situation was 'irreversible'. Hanoi maintained its relationship with China's antagonist, the Soviet Union, and proceeded to strengthen its 'special relationships' with Vientiane and the new regime in Phnom Penh. All this served to further intensify Peking's outrage at the 'ingratitude' of the Vietnamese. The stage had been set for an enduring conflict between two supposedly 'fraternal' Communist governments.

There are some ironic parallels between the Sino-Vietnamese conflict and the Vietnam-Cambodia conflict. Vietnam had sought a 'special relationship' with Cambodia, and China was in effect demanding a 'special relationship' with Vietnam and the other Indochinese countries. Hanoi reacted so vigorously to Pol Pot's actions in part because it perceived a 'Chinese threat' to Vietnam behind them, and China in turn perceived a 'Soviet threat' behind Vietnamese actions. Vietnam had justified military intervention in Cambodia in December 1978 on the grounds of legitimate self-defence, and it is no doubt more than a coincidence that China justified its own invasion of Vietnam on identical grounds.

The political relationships involved can be conceived of as a hierarchy of power with the Soviet Union (and beyond that, the United States) at one end and the DK regime and Laos at the other end. The two countries in the middle of the hierarchy, China and Vietnam, each sought to maximize their own freedom of manoeuvre by resisting the power above them and pressuring the ones below them into an alliance. The Lao government was willing to align with Vietnam, but the factional struggle inside the CPK obliged Pol Pot to turn against it. Thus the government with the most naïve pretensions to absolute sovereignty found itself with the least room for manoeuvre. It availed itself of the option of countering Vietnam's pressure by seeking Chinese protection, and in turn Vietnam sought Soviet protection against China, and China sought American protection against the Soviet Union.

However, these parallels cannot be pushed too far. When it came to the crunch, Vietnam was willing to forgo its 'special relationship' with Cambodia when the Pol Pot government rejected it in 1975–6. By contrast, China has shown no signs of forgoing its demands on Indochina and has demonstrated its willingness to initiate full-scale war in order to force Vietnam to submit to its will. The parallels between the Vietnam-Cambodia war and the Sino-Vietnam war break down at another level too – the middle power, Vietnam, found itself under attack from both a weaker country, Cambodia, and a stronger country, China. If he had respected symmetry, Pol Pot would have tried to create a 'special relationship' with Laos but his military adventurism led him instead to attack Vietnam. Finally, whereas Vietnam's December 1978 invasion of Cambodia was aimed at the total elimination of Pol Pot's regime, and was largely successful, China's February 1979 invasion of Vietnam had a more limited objective even though the troop numbers were larger, and it proved unsuccessful.

'Great Han Chauvinism'

The Chinese response to Vietnam's intervention in Cambodia was a dramatic demonstration of the desire of the Peking government to reassert China's status as the pre-eminent power in the East Asian region. There has been a curious lack of recognition of this desire on the part of many Western commentators. In the 1950s and 1960s it was commonly assumed that because the new government was

Communist it was not really 'Chinese', and was best understood as a puppet of the Soviet Union. It was depicted as militant and expansionist, but in the service of foreign masters. The nationalist aspect of Chinese Communism became widely appreciated only after the Sino-Soviet split made it blindingly obvious. More sympathetic interpretations of Chinese foreign policy came into favour in the 1970s, but these tended to give too much credence to China's self-image as the leading opponent of 'big-power hegemonism'. The nationalism of the Chinese leadership had been recognized, but not the possibility that this might lead to an assertion of Chinese power at the expense of other nations.

The Chinese had constantly depicted themselves as the leading opponents of the power politics practised by the Soviet Union and the United States. 'All nations, big or small, should be equal; big nations should not bully the small, and strong nations should not bully the weak' proclaimed the Chinese side in the Shanghai Communiqué of 1972. 'China will never be a super-power, and it opposes hegemony and power politics of any kind.'[4] This left many ill-prepared for a situation where China would proclaim its own 'right' to intervene militarily in smaller countries which displeased it in order to teach them a 'lesson'.

Hanoi offered its explanation of Chinese power politics in a white paper issued by the Vietnamese foreign ministry in October 1979. This argued that the Chinese rulers had revived traditional 'Great Han chauvinism', believing that the retreat of Western imperialism would allow China to resume its old position as the dominant power throughout Southeast Asia. The leaders of the People's Republic of China, the Vietnamese declared, had for a long time 'dreamt of conquering' Southeast Asia, 'a traditional target for Chinese expansionism throughout the centuries'. They linked China's war with Vietnam to its border disputes with India, the Soviet Union and Mongolia, and argued: 'The Chinese leaders have appeared in their true colours as big-nation chauvinists and bourgeois nationalists! The Chinese rulers' present policy towards Vietnam, although well camouflaged, remains the same as that pursued by the rulers of the "Celestial Empire" during the past millenniums – a policy aimed at annexing Vietnam, subduing the Vietnamese people and turning Vietnam into a satellite of China.'[5]

The Vietnamese white paper reviewed Chinese policy since the Geneva Conference of 1954 in the light of this assessment, arguing that it had been two-faced. The Chinese had appeared to support the Vietnamese revolution, but all the while had been conniving with its enemies. Their real objective was to keep Vietnam divided, weak, and dependent on China. An independent, unified Vietnam, Hanoi argued, would be 'a major obstacle to the Chinese leaders' global strategy, first of all, to their expansionist policy towards Southeast Asia'. The Chinese, needless to say, hastened to deny this. They quoted past statements of praise for China from Le Duan and other Vietnamese leaders, and then took their current views as proof of grave 'degeneration' in Hanoi's ruling elite.[6]

The Vietnamese Communists had thus come to agree with the analysis of some Western China specialists, such as C.P. Fitzgerald, who had maintained that despite the Communist takeover 'the Chinese view of the world has not fundamentally changed'.[7] Maoism had updated, but not basically altered, the traditional Sino-centric view of China as the sole upholder of civilization and virtue, and lawgiver to the barbarians that surrounded it. There is some force in this argument, but it is misleading to view the foreign policy of the modern Chinese state as simply a continuation of traditional policies, as if these remained unaffected by changing practical circumstances.

As the powerful 'civilized' centre of a 'barbarian' universe, the Celestial Empire had been able to command deference from the smaller and less powerful states surrounding it. This deference was institutionalized in the tributary system and, until the coming of the French, the courts in Hue, Phnom Penh and most of the Lao principalities all paid tribute to the imperial court in Peking. The attitudes this fostered among Chinese rulers is exemplified by the message the Emperor Qianlong sent to George III in response to British requests for diplomatic representation in Peking and trading rights in China: 'Swaying the wide world, I have but one aim in view, namely, to maintain a perfect governance and to fulfil the duties of the state . . . . Our dynasty's majestic virtue has penetrated unto every country under heaven, and kings of all nations have offered their costly tribute by land and sea . . . It behoves you, O King, to respect my sentiments and to display even greater devotion in future, so that, by perpetual submission to our Throne, you may secure peace and prosperity for your country hereafter.'[8] While the tributary states were left to run their own internal affairs, the Chinese government saw itself as the arbiter of disputes between them, with the right to punish the recalcitrant. As for the idea of leaving them to establish independent economic and political relations with outside powers, as Quanlong explained to George III, this would be 'quite impossible'.

In the case of Vietnam, a modern historian has described the traditional tributary relationship in these terms: ' . . . the relationship was not between two equal states. There was no doubt in anybody's mind that China was the superior and the tributary state the inferior. The Vietnamese kings clearly realized that they had to acknowledge China's suzerainty and become tributaries in order to avoid active intervention by China in their internal affairs . . . . China felt that she could not govern this area directly; at the same time, however, she wished to avoid trouble in frontier regions . . . . Tributary status was granted by China not to a country but to a ruler. This status could be granted only after the foreign ruler had manifested his acknowledgement of China's superiority . . . . The investiture of a tributary ruler was apparently viewed by the Chinese emperor as similar to the appointment of an official within the empire. Hence investiture could be withdrawn if the ruler failed in his duty . . . . In such a case the tributary king could be punished just like any other high official of the empire.'[9] This is the system which, according to Hanoi, the Chinese leaders wish to restore today.

In keeping with this, it has been suggested that all the Vietnamese leaders really have to do to restore peaceful relations with the PRC is to 'pay tribute', to pay lip-service to Chinese supremacy while pursuing their own independent line. On this reading, the Chinese leaders are preoccupied with 'saving face' and maintaining ancient traditions. It assumes that they will be satisfied with the formalities rather than the realities of power.

We are not convinced. The traditional Chinese imperial order rested on the isolation of East Asia from the other great state systems of world history. When the maritime expansion of the European powers broke into this closed universe, the supremacy of the Chinese empire came to an end. The tributary states were stripped away and in due course the central power of the empire itself collapsed. Chinese territory fell increasingly under the sway of European imperialism. Modern Chinese nationalism developed out of this trauma. When a centralized state was re-established by the Communist revolution of the 1940s, its rulers confronted a radically different international environment, one of competing territorial nation-states. Although some of the old attitudes towards the 'barbarians' persisted, basically, the modern Chinese nationalists (including the Communists) 'were quite willing to exchange the Chinese world order for a strong Chinese nation'.[10]

The Communists have explicitly rejected the notion of hierarchy central to the old Confucian system and affirm, as we have seen, the modern concepts of state sovereignty and equality. But while there is no real evidence that they wish to rebuild the old tributary relations, there is little doubt that the old attitudes linger on in a more diffuse expectation of regional affirmation of their leading role. Only against this background can the fury of the Chinese leaders over the 'ingratitude' of the Vietnamese Communists, who, having driven the Americans out, refused to subordinate themselves towards China, be understood.

But arguments that explain present Chinese policy solely in terms of 'Great Han chauvinism' are unsatisfactory. They bestow a life of its own on the 'Chinese political tradition' and fail to identify the institutions and forces that would sustain this tradition in a radically changed context. The tributary state system is, for the present generation of Chinese, even more a matter of ancient history than the binding of women's feet. If attitudes derived from it have persisted, it is because they have been kept alive by present-day forces. Looking at the question from this angle, we can see that the analysts in Hanoi have got the answer the wrong way around. The Chinese are not practicing power politics today because they are prisoners of their imperial past; rather, the ideology of 'Great Han chauvinism' has persisted because the Chinese have been practising power politics in modern times.

We argued in Chapter I that the Communist revolutions in Asia are best understood as the radical wing of a much broader anti-imperialist revolt. Like their bourgeois and monarchist counterparts, they are engaged in the effort to modernize a traditional society and forge a modern nation state. Nationalist ideology serves to mobilize popular support for this endeavour. Having thrown off foreign rule and created a sovereign state, each nation state seeks to advance its interests and defend its security as best it can in an anarchic world of competing nation states. And all the democratic and egalitarian rhetoric in the world cannot disguise the fact that some states are more powerful than others. Their strength makes some capable of advancing their interests more forcefully than weaker states, and therefore more valuable as allies. In this situation the 'proletarian internationalist' succumbs to the logic of power politics as readily as the 'bourgeois nationalist'.

In this regard both the Vietnamese and the Chinese Communists are alike. Nationalism was a driving force in both revolutions and, having won state power, in a short space of time both had demonstrated their willingness to use it against other nations in defence of what they saw as their own national interests. But, setting aside the rights and wrongs of these particular disputes, there is still an important difference between them. Quite apart from its Sino-centric, imperial tradition, the very fact of China's vast size (its population was estimated at 985 million in 1981) prompts its rulers to have realistic ambitions of global power despite the country's poverty. Vietnam (population 55 million), by contrast, can never aspire to be more than a regional power. Thus Communist China is a modern nation state, a great power, whose relations with Vietnam, and Southeast Asia generally, have been in large part shaped by its relations with other great powers; whereas those of imperial China had been shaped largely by the isolation of the Chinese 'world-system' from the pressure of powerful rivals.

It is to a consideration of modern China's relations with the other great powers that we now turn. Essentially, the story is one of the rise of China as a great power in the context of Soviet-American antagonism. Since the outlines of this story are obscured by so much confusion and wishful thinking, on both the left and the right. It is necessary to describe them in some detail.

China in the Modern World: the Emergence of a Great Power

The Chinese Communists saw their revolution as a triumph of Chinese national self-assertion after a period of humiliating foreign domination. In September 1949 Mao declared: 'Our nation will never again be an insulted nation. We have stood up . . . . Let the domestic and foreign reactionaries tremble before us.' But, in fact, in its early years the People's Republic of China remained a weak state. It had been through a period of economic chaos and ruinous war, and its new rulers were obliged, in another of Mao's famous phrases, to 'lean to one side, the side of the Soviet Union' in international affairs.

When China was aligned with the Soviet Union, Western commentators depicted it as a militantly expansionist power – blithely ignoring the realities of Chinese weakness at that time. Since then this picture has been drastically revised in the light of the Sino-Soviet split and the Sino-American *rapprochement*. China is now commonly depicted in much more sympathetic terms, as essentially playing a passive role. Thus the Sino-Soviet split is seen as the result of Soviet 'bullying', and China's turn to the West as a defensive reaction to Soviet expansionism.

Such an interpretation accords with common cold war prejudices, but it obscures the reality of China's growing assertiveness as an independent power in world politics. It was the Chinese side that initiated the Sino-Soviet split, and in the wake of the Sino-American *rapprochement*, China finally emerged as a great power with an active policy of expanding its influence in Southeast Asia.

Tensions were evident at the time of the formation of the Sino-Soviet alliance (though they were largely ignored by contemporary Western commentators). Stalin was still smarting from his failure to intimidate Tito in Yugoslavia, and suspected that Mao's nationalism would make him a 'second Tito'. Mao, for his part, resented Stalin's high-handedness towards China. But these tensions were overridden by the threat to a weak China by America's aggressively anti-Communist stance in Asia. Whatever their private reservations about their Soviet ally, the Chinese Communist leaders were aware that it provided them with urgently needed military protection and diplomatic support, as well as the aid, trade and investment funds needed for economic development. It is now ironic that when they were accused by the Americans of reducing China to colonial status by entering an alliance with the Soviet Union, the Chinese Communist press responded with indignant articles refuting charges of 'red imperialism' against the USSR.

By the middle 1950s the bargaining position of the Chinese leaders had improved dramatically. Their successful economic reconstruction within China had been widely praised. Chinese troops had performed well in Korea and in 1953 the Americans reluctantly accepted a ceasefire that allowed the survival of China's (and Russia's) ally, North Korea. In Vietnam, American-backed French forces were finally defeated by the Viet Minh in 1954. Through their roles at the Geneva Conference on Indochina and Korea in 1954 and the Bandung Conference of Afro-Asian countries in 1955, the Chinese leaders believed they had won recognition as a great power in their own right. A *People's Daily* editorial on Geneva declared: 'For the first time as one of the Big Powers, the People's Republic joined the other major powers in negotiations on vital international problems and made a contribution of its own that won the acclaim of wide sections of world opinion. The international status of the People's Republic of China as one of the big world powers has gained universal recognition. Its international prestige has been greatly enhanced. The Chinese people take the greatest joy and pride in the efforts and achievements of their delegation at Geneva.'¹¹ In addition, the easing of the extreme cold war tensions of the early 1950s gave China more room for manoeuvre.

The result was the adoption of a more assertive approach by China, which immediately produced growing strains in the Sino-Soviet alliance. The Chinese moved increasingly away from the Soviet model of socialism. Mao's collectivization drive of 1955 and the 'Great Leap Forward' are usually assessed in terms of domestic politics, but they had an important international dimension – the aim was to demonstrate China's ability to surpass the Soviets in the building of socialism. But China's economic backwardness meant that stress had to be placed on doctrinal purity and moral virtue. The cult of Chairman Mao intensified and in 1958 the *People's Daily* hailed him as the greatest living Marxist-Leninist theoretician. This implicit rejection of the Soviet leadership's claim to doctrinal authority for the whole Communist bloc was made explicit in the early 1960s, when the Chinese launched a series of increasingly open polemics against Soviet 'revisionism'.

To read the major documents of this period is to gain the impression that the split was overwhelmingly a matter of esoteric ideological disputes, but the split itself has lasted on well beyond the fall of Maoism in China. In fact the quarrel over ideology was in reality a struggle over the legitimate source of authority for the international Communist movement. The polemics of the early 1960s on the general line of the international Communist movement signalled that China and Russia had become open rivals for leadership of the Communist bloc and for influence among the newly emerging nations. China was laying claim to the position of the great power of the Communist bloc; and since the Soviets were unwilling to accept this claim, almost every international event of the period became the occasion for bitter polemical exchanges.

When Khrushchev first put forward his doctrine of 'peaceful coexistence' between the Communist and the capitalist powers in the middle 1950s, it was endorsed by the Chinese, but by the late 1950s they were becoming increasingly vocal in their criticism of Soviet 'capitulation' to imperialism. Partly, this was a response to the unwillingness of the Soviets to give the Chinese the full support they demanded in a series of crises that erupted on China's borders – the Quemoy-Formosa crisis (1958), apparently initiated by Peking in an attempt to press Moscow into a stronger commitment to Chinese unification in the face of continued American support for

Jiang Kaishek; the rebellion in Tibet (1959); and the ensuing tension with India that resulted in the Sino-Indian border war (1962).

For their part, the Soviets became increasingly exasperated with the Chinese challenge. They first entered the ideological argument by carefully marshalling quotes from Lenin in support of 'peaceful coexistence'. But within a couple of years Khrushchev was furiously castigating 'lunatics and maniacs' and 'pseudo-revolutionary windbags', and it was obvious who he was referring to. A series of Soviet actions added more fuel to the flames. In 1959, shortly before his visit to the USA, Khrushchev repudiated secret Soviet promises to help China build up an independent nuclear capability (years later, when they revealed this, the Chinese said it was 'Khrushchev's gift to the Americans'). Then, in 1960, he withdrew all Soviet technicians from China, claiming they were being mistreated. Coming just at the time of the economic crisis that followed Mao's 'Great Leap Forward', this was a blow to Chinese plans for development that would be remembered and resented for decades. The Chinese responded by raging at the 'arrogant and dictatorial' attitudes of the Soviets.

But it was the emerging triangular relationship between Peking, Moscow and Washington that lay at the heart of Chinese tirades against Soviet aspirations for 'peaceful coexistence'. The intensifying quarrel with Moscow, occurring at a time when its own relations with Washington were still bitterly antagonistic, left Peking dangerously isolated. Any sign of 'collusion' between the Soviets and the Americans was denounced as a 'betrayal' of the cause of Communism. When the USA and the USSR signed a Partial Test Ban Treaty in July 1963, the Chinese denounced it violently and a commentator in *Red Flag* charged that a 'Holy Alliance' had been formed comparable with the anti-revolutionary alliance forged by Metternich after the Napoleonic Wars, and predicted a similarly unhappy end for it.

For all the rhetorical overkill, Chinese fears of 'collusion' and a 'secret deal' between the USA and the USSR to contain Chinese influence were not unfounded. The Laos crisis of 1961 was the first occasion on which China appeared as an independent third power, and both Moscow and Washington actively tried to limit Peking's influence – even to the extent of signing a secret accord, the 'Pushkin Pact', on the matter.[12]

By the middle 1960s it was clear that China's bid to take over the mantle of leadership of the Communist bloc from the Soviet Union had failed dismally. Almost all the ruling Communist parties had sided with Moscow, apart from some (most notably North Vietnam and North Korea) who tried to remain neutral and balance the two Communist great powers against each other. Only Albania – once Stalin's favourite example of total insignificance in international politics – had wholeheartedly endorsed the Maoist version of communism. But China's ardent revolutionism was more attractive to those Communist parties still struggling to win power. Most of the Southeast Asian parties sided with China, but elsewhere they gained the support of only the New Zealand party and small breakaway sects. Attempts to win over the leaders of Afro-Asian nations, struggling to consolidate new and fragile states, to Mao's ideas also met with little success. China's first bid for great power status in its own right had proved premature, leaving China more isolated than ever.

In this context the Americans massively escalated the Vietnam war in 1965, simply ignoring Chinese outrage over the matter. Peking was again faced with large-scale American military intervention in an area vital to its security, as it had been in Korea a decade earlier. Then the Chinese had intervened themselves, but now they were no longer protected by the Russian military umbrella. The majority of CCP leaders around Liu Shaoqi and Deng Xiaoping believed that America's action had made it imperative for China to close ranks with the Soviet Union once more. But Mao had by this stage gone right out on the limb of 'anti-revisionism' and his personal prestige would have suffered if this course had been adopted. Instead, he called for the strengthening of China's 'self-reliance' and an intensified campaign against the Soviets.

Defeated inside the party, Mao and his ally, Defence Minister Lin Biao, launched a campaign of 'mass criticism' against their opponents, which snowballed into the Great Proletarian Cultural Revolution of 1966–8. This destroyed Mao's opponents, but it left the party in ruins and the country in chaos. By 1969 the army under Lin Biao had managed to restore order and was basically running the country, while Mao sought to create a ruling party more to his liking than the pre-Cultural Revolution CCP had been. This brought him closer to moderates such as Zhou Enlai once more, under whose patronage Deng Xiaoping and other veteran administrators were cautiously rehabilitated – to the great annoyance of the radicals who had suddenly risen to power during the Cultural Revolution.

Mao's 'personality cult' was exploited to the hilt in the struggle for power during the Cultural Revolution. Mao Zedong thought was proclaimed to the whole world as the supreme wisdom of the modern age. But beneath this veneer of extravagant universalistic rhetoric, the country had plunged into a self-absorbed isolationism reminiscent of the old Chinese empire. Even according to a sympathetic writer, China in this period disdained the international diplomatic community and largely abandoned state-to-state relations with the outside world.[13] Only the bearers of tribute to Mao's thought were welcome in Peking.

While it was primarily an internal upheaval, the Cultural Revolution was partly triggered off by foreign policy problems, and in turn had devastating effects on China's foreign policy. China's relations with the outside world had already reached a low point in 1965. Now, according to Mao, China had to gird itself for a final, apocalyptic confrontation with its enemies. In March 1966 Mao told a visiting delegation from Japan that a war between China and America was 'inevitable' within two years, and that the Soviets would then invade as well. China's foreign policy became increasingly xenophobic, its shrill anti-Westernism matched only by the ferocity of its denunciations of the Soviet bloc.

Indeed, Sino-Soviet relations had sunk to lower than low. In 1966 the Chinese foreign minister, Chen Yi, charged that the Russians were thieves who had stolen one and a half million square kilometres of Chinese territory, and Red Guards poured into the border province of Sinkiang to organize two million strong demonstrations demanding the return of 'lost territories'. Early in 1967 there were violent mass demonstrations outside the Soviet Embassy in Peking, and Chinese students in Moscow fought with the Soviet police.

Mao had been pressing for a re-negotiation of the Sino-Soviet border since 1963, but following Chen Yi's statement, tensions mounted as both sides built up their forces on the border, climaxing in the fighting on the Ussuri River in March 1969. The details remain obscure, although most Western writers believe it was initiated by the Chinese and the Soviets retaliated in force. The Chinese linked the border clashes to the occupation of Czechoslovakia by Warsaw Pact forces the preceding August as another manifestation of Soviet 'social imperialism', but some commentators believed that Mao and Lin Biao provoked the incident to rally support in China. In any case, the rhetoric of the Sino-Soviet confrontation now reached the point where both sides were hinting at the use of nuclear weapons. At this point, the Chinese were obliged to beat a diplomatic retreat. Having boasted in March that 'the anti-Chinese scum will end badly', they were by October reassuring Moscow that there was 'no reason whatsoever' for a border war and promising the restoration of state-to-state relations. Shortly afterwards, negotiations on the border, suspended by the Chinese in 1964, were reopened (though they made no progress in settling the dispute).[14]

The Soviet Union had secured its border with China, but only by outright coercion and at the cost of publicly humiliating and further alienating the Chinese regime. The Chinese leaders were willing to bow to superior force if necessary, but this made any subsequent reconciliation between the Soviets and even the anti-Maoist factions in Peking unlikely. Still, the fact that Mao's 'anti-revisionist' line had pushed China to the brink of nuclear war must have led to a renewed appreciation in Peking of the value of great and powerful allies. It drove home the point that by 1969 the attempts by the Chinese Communists to secure recognition as a great power had achieved very little; in the aftermath of the Cultural Revolution, the Peking regime was more isolated and vulnerable than at any time since 1949. At this point, Mao's eyes turned to America.[15] This led to a falling out between Mao and Lin Biao, who died violently in 1971 as a consequence.[16]

In the meantime, there had been some hard thinking about China going on in Washington. The USA had at first responded to the Sino-Soviet split by denying its reality, and then by favouring the more 'moderate' side, that is, Moscow. But the fact that Peking had responded to American provocation by stepping up its attacks on Moscow awakened American strategists to the possibility that it could use the 'extremists' in Peking against the Soviets. However, any immediate prospect of Sino-American *détente* was soon overwhelmed by the tidal waves of the Cultural Revolution, and in 1968 Washington still had no more communications with Peking than Moscow did. President Johnson began publicly hinting at his desire for improved relations with China, as did presidential candidate Richard Nixon. Shortly after Nixon's election to the presidency in November 1968, the Chinese proposed renewing talks over an agreement on peaceful coexistence and the Americans responded favourably. Despite some set-backs – notably as a result of Chinese apprehension when American and South Vietnamese forces invaded Cambodia in May 1970 – relations between the two countries steadily improved. This process culminated in Nixon's dramatic visit to Peking in February 1972.

By this stage the Chinese government had also taken the initiative in restoring the diplomatic links with the outside world that had been broken during the Cultural Revolution. Coupled with the obvious signs of a Sino-American *rapprochement*, this led to the United Nations General Assembly finally voting to seat the Peking rather than the Taiwan government as the representative of China. By the end of the decade, the PRC had normal diplomatic relations with most countries around the world. Ironically, once it entered the public arena, Sino-American efforts at *rapprochement* bogged down, mainly as a result of the unwillingness of either side to be seen to compromise over Taiwan. When relations were finally normalized in December 1978, their willingness to bury their differences over this issue emphasized the extent to which it was a result of the convergence of their global perspectives in opposition to the Soviet Union. At the start of the 1970s, China had been deeply suspicious of Soviet-American 'collusion', anxious to upset the *détente* between the two super-powers. By the end of the decade, Peking and Washington were competing with displays of public hostility towards Moscow; the precondition for the strengthening of Sino-American relations had turned out to be the breakdown of Soviet-American *détente*, which plunged the world into the new cold war in the late 1970s.

China's foreign relations had been revolutionized in the early 1970s. In barely three years, it had gone from a 'revolutionary' contempt for normal state-to-state relations under Lin Biao to acceptance of a permanent seat on the five-member UN Security Council, a position signifying formal international recognition of the PRC's status as a great power. After this breakthrough, China's foreign policy problems ceased to be those of an emergent revolutionary state. They became those of defining, consolidating and strengthening China's position as a great power in a world of competing powers. This inevitably meant redefining China's relations, not only with the other great powers, but also with the smaller states of the East Asian region.

The task of providing an authoritative statement of the principles of Chinese foreign policy in the wake of this diplomatic revolution fell to Deng Xiaoping, now rehabilitated after his fall from Mao's grace during the Cultural Revolution. His exposition of Chairman Mao's 'Theory of the Three Worlds' at the UN in April 1974 marked the demise of any lingering expectation that China might revert to a 'two-worlds' (capitalism versus communism) view of international politics. According to Deng: ' . . . all the political forces in the world have undergone drastic division and realignment through prolonged trials of strength and struggle. A large number of Asian, African, and Latin American countries have achieved independence one after another, and they are playing an ever greater role in international affairs. As a result of the emergence of social-imperialism, the socialist camp which existed for a time after World War II is no longer in existence. Owing to the law of uneven and combined development of capitalism, the Western imperialist bloc, too, is disintegrating. Judging from the changes in international relations, the world today actually consists of three parts, or three worlds, that are both interconnected and in contradiction to one another. The United States and the Soviet Union make up the First World. The developing countries in Asia, Africa, Latin America and other regions make up the Third World. The developed countries between the two make up the Second World.'[17]

Since the 'socialist camp' is no longer in existence 'and the imperialist camp has disintegrated' as well, China was officially freed from any residual ideological basis for distinguishing between the two 'super-powers'. Deng's speech marked the complete triumph of *realpolitik* in China's foreign policy. Indeed, while Deng had formally bracketed the Soviet Union with the United States, the Chinese believed that their main future rival for influence in the Far East would be the Soviet Union. Hence Deng argued that the USA was 'in decline' and that the USSR was the most dangerous of the two super-powers because it was still in an 'expansionist' phase. Despite the Communist ideology shared by the two powers, opposition to Soviet 'social imperialism' became the cornerstone of Chinese foreign policy for the next seven years.

Sino-Soviet Rivalry in the 1970s

China's move to the West has often been seen in terms of the threat posed to China by the growing role of the Soviet Union in East Asian affairs. Most Western commentators see this as an extension of Soviet power beyond its legitimate sphere of interest and as symptomatic of Moscow's expansionism. But a glance at the map is enough to establish a point of cardinal importance that is often forgotten – the USSR covers 8.6 million square miles, and sprawls across all of northern Asia as well as half of northern Europe. Seventy-five per cent of the territory and 29 per cent of the population of the Soviet Union are Asian. Even if the European sections are left out of consideration the Soviet Union is one of the largest and most populous of Asian states. Given this, as Geoffrey Jukes has noted, what needs to be explained is not current Soviet interest in Asian affairs so much as the lack of interest in them in the Stalin era.[18]

Current Soviet Far Eastern policy has several concerns. The first is to make its territorial boundaries, so long as to be almost indefensible, safe and secure. Here the Chinese border is a major headache: 7,500 kilometres long, it separates a large, thinly populated region with valuable natural resources from a hostile power that has traditionally dominated the area. Second, the Soviet Union has sought to promote the development of its Asian territories. Particularly in order to develop Siberia and the port of Vladivostok, it has sought a partnership with Japan – so far, without success. Japan's eyes have been on the potential of the Chinese market, and the Sino-Japanese *rapprochement* that followed the Sino-American *rapprochement* has minimized Soviet influence in North Asia. The inability to prevent the emergence of the loose but still formidable coalition of Peking, Tokyo and Washington against Moscow was the major failure of Soviet Far Eastern policy in the 1970s.

The Soviet Union has also been playing the great power game by trying to build up its diplomatic presence and its aid and trade with countries in Southeast Asia, in an attempt to counter both American and Chinese influence. Leaving the question of Indochina aside for the moment, it is evident that despite the alarm in anti-Soviet circles, Moscow has had only modest success in this regard. The facts of the matter may be conveniently summarized by quoting a recent survey article: 'Since the end of the 1960s, the Soviet Union has undertaken a major offensive to extend its influence in Southeast Asia . . . . With the opening of relations with Malaysia and Singapore in the latter 1960s, the Soviet Union has established formal diplomatic relations with all the states of Southeast Asia . . . . A major instrument in the Soviet effort to foster closer relations beyond the diplomatic level has been the familiar "carrot" of economic aid and trade offers. Here, in an area where Moscow can compete somewhat with Washington and Tokyo, and where it has a clear advantage over Peking, the Russians have had only limited successes . . . . It is only in Indonesia that a significant aid program has been undertaken . . . . Nevertheless this cooperation has been limited . . . . The Suharto regime has . . . continued to look primarily to the United States, Western Europe, and Japan for its assistance. Soviet efforts to expand trade with the countries of

Southeast Asia have also met with only limited success. Not only has total trade risen just slightly since the beginning of the 1960s, but, more significant for the Soviet Union, that country has been unable to develop a market for its goods. Moscow's balance of trade with Southeast Asia has shown a chronic deficit.'[19] Soviet diplomatic efforts in the Far East have thus borne little fruit to date. Far from Indochina forming part of a much broader pattern of rapidly expanding Soviet penetration of the Far East, it is Moscow's solitary success in the region. It is the exception, not the rule.

In the military sphere, there have been two main aspects of the Soviet Union's 'thrust' into the Far East. The first has been the military build-up on the Sino-Soviet border, especially since the fighting on the Ussuri River in 1969. The Soviets are estimated to have 400,000 troops stationed on the border, with 1.5 million Chinese troops deployed against them. The second has been the development of its Pacific Naval fleet, based in Vladivostok. 'In the last 20–25 years,' reported John Lewis in 1979, 'the Soviet Union has gone from a third-rate naval power to a first-rate naval power' and is 'now about equal in capacity' to the US Pacific fleet.[20] The Soviets have evidently aimed at parity with their super-power rival, which has involved a build-up far beyond the forces of any of the regional powers such as China and Japan, and created much apprehension among them. Both its naval rivalry with the USA and the expansion of its mercantile shipping have given the Soviet Union an important strategic interest in maintaining its freedom of navigation in Southeast Asian waters, and in access to ports and naval facilities in the region.

Concern about the Soviet 'thrust' into Asia has effectively diverted attention from the more rapid growth of Chinese influence in Southeast Asia in the 1970s. Peking's initial breakthrough was the normalization of relations with Burma in 1971, but the turning point was the opening of formal diplomatic relations with Malaysia in 1974 and with the Philippines and Thailand in 1975. Peking downplayed its support for local Communist insurgencies and formally renounced its previous claims to be the protector of the overseas Chinese communities to reassure those still suspicious of its aims. Both official and unofficial leadership consultations were used to build up friendly relations with non-Communist governments. Only Singapore and Indonesia continued to withhold formal recognition, but here, too, informal contacts multiplied rapidly. Trade relations also expanded rapidly, the value of China's trade with ASEAN countries rising to $2.4 billion US. The Chinese found a ready market for their exports in Southeast Asia. In contrast to the pattern of Soviet trade in the region, the balance of China's trade was positive. 'Chinese influence has spread rapidly in the region,' one writer sums up, 'especially among the non-Communist states, which in the past had strongly feared PRC intentions.' The cultivation of relations with Southeast Asia has been 'one of the major success stories in recent Chinese foreign policy'.[21]

The thrust of China's policies in Southeast Asia in the 1970s was directed towards the exclusion of Soviet influence from the region. Clauses pledging joint opposition to 'hegemonism' (the Chinese codeword for the Soviets) were included in the Zhao-Nixon Shanghai communiqué of 1972, and in the communiqués normalizing relations with Southeast Asian countries. After the normalization of Sino-Thai relations, the Chinese depicted this as a link in a PRC-sponsored 'anti-hegemony front' designed to 'guarantee' Southeast Asia from 'intensified Soviet expansion'. The other side of this attempt to weld Southeast Asia into a Chinese-led anti-Soviet bloc has been the encouragement of a continued American military presence in the region to give it some teeth. Whereas Peking had once proclaimed itself the most militant opponent of 'US imperialism', the Chinese now began to talk of America as 'an Asian and Pacific nation' with a 'deserved and responsible role' in Southeast Asia.[22]

The Peking leadership was thus able to view the fruits of its policies in Southeast Asia with considerable satisfaction. In broad terms, they had been successful in ensuring that Chinese rather than Soviet influence had expanded in Southeast Asia as America's presence waned after its defeat in Indochina. These were matters on which, for all their other disagreements, all the main factions in the Chinese leadership could agree. Hence the deaths of Zhou and Mao (1976), the fall of Madame Mao and the 'Gang of Four' (1976), the rise and fall of Hua Guofung (1976-81), and the rise of Deng Xiaoping (1977 onwards) had surprisingly little impact on the directions of Chinese policy. Indeed, it may be that the preoccupation of the Chinese leaders with the internal power struggle contributed to the general rigidity of China's foreign policy in this period.

Putting the Squeeze on Vietnam

From Peking's point of view, a major ground for dissatisfaction was Vietnam itself. The Peking government had aided the Communists in Vietnam, and fully expected that China rather than the Soviet Union would be the main great power beneficiary of their victory. Chinese pressure on Hanoi intensified, but the Vietnamese tried to maximize their independence from Peking by continuing to balance Chinese and Soviet influence, and by seeking an opening to the West. Especially in the light of the resounding successes of Peking's anti-Soviet policies elsewhere in the region, the Chinese leaders saw this attempt by Hanoi to continue its balancing act between Moscow and Peking as a display of 'ingratitude' that it was no longer necessary to tolerate. There had long been strains in the relations between the Chinese and Vietnamese Communist regimes, but these multiplied rapidly as Chinese pressure on Vietnam intensified.

In the polemical exchanges following the Sino-Vietnamese war of 1979, the Chinese were content to date these tensions to 1974, but there is little doubt that they went back much earlier. They explained it in terms of the growing ingratitude of Le Duan and his colleagues, who had allowed their victory over the Saigon regime to go to their heads. The Chinese polemics do not mention Peking's mounting pressure on Hanoi but they do make it clear that China expected that its wartime aid to Vietnam would be paid back in deference to China's strategic objectives in the region, specifically, by the exclusion of Soviet influence.

The Vietnamese white paper of October 1979 depicts the Chinese as consistently obstructing the Vietnamese revolution from the Geneva Conference onwards. Hanoi alleged that the Chinese were really in collusion with the French at Geneva, and that they pressured the Vietnamese into accepting a compromise solution that left Vietnam and Laos partitioned and gave no regroupment areas at all to the Khmer Issaraks, at a time when the situation on the battlefield placed total victory within grasp. When the USA subsequently intervened to shore up the anti-Communist regime in Saigon (and, one should add, Vientiane), China did its best to restrain the Communist side. China gave a 'green light' to the ensuing American escalation by making it clear that China would not respond militarily to the American actions, actively sought to prevent a united response by the Communist bloc, and then tried to avert a negotiated settlement of the conflict. All this, the white paper argued, was done with the intention of keeping Vietnam weak and divided in order to facilitate Chinese expansion in Southeast Asia.

If this was mildly hysterical, the Chinese reply was singularly unconvincing. They preferred to dwell on the volume of Chinese aid to Hanoi and the harmonious relations of the 1949–54 period (matters on which the Vietnamese white paper said as little as possible), and they tried to get over the main points of the Vietnamese indictment by bluff and bluster. On the assessment of China's role at Geneva, for example, they responded by pointing out that the positions of the Communist countries had been 'closely coordinated' without giving any more details. Because the Vietnamese, the Soviets and the Chinese were 'unanimous' in the face they presented to the outside world, Hoang Van Hoan maintains that the claims by 'Le Duan and company' of behind-the-scenes conflict must be 'very foolish': 'Were the delegations of Vietnam and the Soviet Union mere puppets to be manipulated by China during the Geneva Conference?'[23] In fact, Western analyses of the power play at Geneva confirm the Vietnamese claims.[24] Chinese interests were satisfied by a Communist state in northern Vietnam and Pathet Lao control of Phong Saly province in Laos. Beyond that, the Chinese sought a compromise with the West (hoping that in this way it could keep a hostile USA out of Indochina), whereas the Viet Minh looked forward to the complete liberation of Indochina following their military victory over the French at Dien Bien Phu; and far from having been unanimous in their actions, Zhou Enlai acted on several occasions to undercut Pham Van Dong.[25]

It is also true that in the 1960s, despite the militant rhetoric, Peking did its best to avoid entanglement in a direct military confrontation with the USA over Vietnam. Prior to 1965 China had supported a negotiated settlement, and had no obvious objections to a separate state of South Vietnam. With the American escalation of the war in that year, Peking abandoned hopes of a peaceful settlement. It sent as much aid as it could to North Vietnam's war effort but it refused to join with Moscow in a united opposition to the Americans, and did its best to obstruct the USA-North Vietnam negotiations encouraged by Moscow. It also urged on Hanoi a low-risk, long-haul strategy of protracted war, rather than any attempt to achieve a decisive victory. In their reply to Hanoi's white paper the Chinese avoid any specific discussion of these matters.

Chinese policy towards Vietnam in this period seems to have been governed mainly by national security considerations, and by the triangular relations between Peking, Moscow and Washington. On the one hand, it wanted to see the hostile American forces 'encircling' China defeated; on the other hand, it tried to prevent any direct involvement or any action by the Vietnamese that might provoke American retaliation against China itself. Finally, it also sought to avert any 'collusion' between Moscow and Washington. There is little doubt that these basic policies (not to mention the excesses of the Cultural Revolution) led to serious strains in the Peking-Hanoi relationship just as the diverging interests of the Vietnamese and Cambodian Communists led to tension in their relationships.

But Hanoi's polemicists are surely stretching things too far when they describe Peking's policies as 'giving the green light' to American aggression in a Machiavellian attempt to keep Vietnam divided. There seems no reason to doubt that, prior to the Sino-American *rapprochement* of the early 1970s, the Chinese saw US activities in Vietnam as a threat to China itself. They were able to cite the volume of their aid to North Vietnam during the war ($20 billion US, according to Peking) as evidence of genuine opposition to the US intervention. Nor is Hanoi able to produce any evidence of the master plan guiding Chinese policy towards Vietnam after 1954, apart from a string of boastful (but vague) quotes from Chinese leaders.[26] Although it is not as crude and simplistic, Hanoi's white paper shares a fatal flaw with Pol Pot's *Black Paper* – since it is unwilling to acknowledge that 'fraternal' Communist regimes may have divergent national interests, it is obliged to explain the conflicts that arise from these divergences in terms of Manichean conspiracies.

Serious Sino-Vietnamese tensions thus existed throughout the late 1950s and the 1960s. But China's *rapprochement* with the USA in the early 1970s fundamentally recast Peking's policies, leading it to adopt a much more assertive stance towards Hanoi. In the first place, the American move towards China was clearly intended to increase the pressure on Hanoi. In the 1972 Shanghai communiqué the American side promised that its forces would be progressively withdrawn from Taiwan 'as the tension in the area diminishes'. In this 'artfully crafted' statement, as Kissinger's biographers put it, 'the Americans implied that if China wanted to accelerate the US pullout from Taiwan, it had only to pressure Hanoi into a compromise settlement.'[27]

Second, once it was clear that America was on the way out in Indochina, China's main rival for influence became the Soviet Union. And after the 'ceasefire' in South Vietnam and Laos, the reliance of local Communist forces on weaponry provided by Moscow relaxed, which opened the way for renewed Chinese influence in the region. Secret Chinese internal briefings known as the 'Kunming Documents' show that the Peking leaders were preparing for a major contest with the Soviet Union for influence in Southeast Asia following the Paris Peace Agreement of 1973: 'The Vietnam armistice is . . . in our interests . . . . After the Korean Armistice, the game on the Southeast Asian chessboard became unplayable. The game has now been revived by the Vietnam Armistice. Once the United States departed, its running dogs in Asia became very uneasy. The rulers of countries like Thailand, Singapore, and the Philippines, realizing that the United States could not hang on, all wanted to enter into relationships with us . . . . In the past, Soviet revisionism intervened in Southeast Asia under the pretext of supporting Vietnam. Now that the Vietnam war has stopped, we can, by working harder, more effectively strike at Soviet revisionism.'[28]

In this situation the Chinese did not particularly want a rapid conclusion to the struggle in Vietnam. With the threatening aspect of the American presence eliminated by the Sino-American *rapprochement*, a slow collapse of the Thieu regime would give them more room to manoeuvre against Soviet influence in post-war Indochina. At this point Thieu's provocations in the Paracels provided a perfect opportunity for Peking to put the pressure on Hanoi by asserting its claims in the South China Sea. But then the Saigon regime suddenly disintegrated in early 1975, and a reunited Vietnam emerged which was, from China's point of view, far too willing to deal with the Soviets. The same applied, with only minor qualifications, to Laos. Only Pol Pot's regime had no dealings with the Soviets, and it was on it that the Chinese bestowed their favours after 1975.

Hanoi had previously tried to balance the demands of its two major patrons, but as Peking intensified its pressure after 1973 this became increasingly difficult. Hanoi responded by moving closer to Moscow, both a wealthier and a less exacting supporter, and by seeking an opening to the West that failed to materialize. By 1976 Chinese pressure had become open, with Mao declaring that the Vietnamese had not fought for forty years only to let the Soviets take the country over. But the death of Mao in September 1976 precipitated a bitter factional struggle in Peking that gave Hanoi respite for several months.

After the purging of the 'Gang of Four' there was a brief improvement in Sino-Vietnamese relations, and it looked as if China's new leaders had decided that the best approach would be to woo Hanoi rather than trying to force it away from Moscow. However, Peking evidently decided by the middle of 1977 that this was not yielding satisfactory results, and began to apply the screws again over the South China Sea. In 1978 tension mounted over the Hoa and the situation on the Sino-Vietnamese border began to deteriorate drastically. But the most explosive development was the Chinese decision to openly back Pol Pot's border war against Vietnam.

The importance of Cambodia in Peking's foreign policy was not new. China had enjoyed good relations with Sihanouk's government since the Geneva Conference. Peking's main objective at this time was to avert a US military presence, and Sihanouk's neutralist regime satisfied this aim. From 1956 they provided him with substantial economic aid and, according to one expert, gave his government a 'guarantee' of security against the Vietnamese.[29] They gave little if any practical support to the CPK, disagreeing like the Vietnamese with Pol Pot's strategy of overthrowing Sihanouk. But when Sihanouk was toppled by the right wing in 1970, it was Zhou Enlai who persuaded him to join forces with the Khmers Rouges. Both Sihanouk and the CPK distrusted the Vietnamese Communists, with whom they now became allied, and Moscow's prompt recognition of the Lon Nol regime in Phnom Penh may have unwittingly helped push both of them into the Chinese camp. In 1972 China served warning that it was opposed to a situation in which Indochina was dominated by any one country (that is, Vietnam).[30]

The ties between China and the Khmers Rouges were strengthened after April 1975. Chinese planes were reported flying into Cambodia immediately after the Khmer Rouge victory, and for some months provided the country's only link with the outside world. Indeed, China was the only country with which the new regime in Phnom Penh developed close relations. Within months, Peking was providing substantial military aid, underwriting the expansion of the Khmer Rouge army that took place with the coming of peace. In August 1975 Khieu Samphan visited Peking and signed an agreement on economic cooperation, under which China agreed to provide Cambodia with $200 million US of aid over five to six years. On the same occasion he also signed a joint communiqué condemning Soviet 'hegemony'.

In the light of these commitments, it was inevitable that the Chinese would become embroiled in Pol Pot's border war with Vietnam. It is hard to agree with Steve Heder that China's stance in the Vietnam-Cambodia dispute was one of neutrality.[31] China had established what Heder describes accurately enough as 'an anti-Soviet alliance' with the Khmer Rouge regime. But it was actively trying to pressure Vietnam into following suit, not simply seeking to prevent a 'deterioration' of its relationship with Hanoi, as Heder maintains. While Vietnam retained its Soviet connections, the Chinese were bound to oppose its attempts to develop a 'special relationship' with Phnom Penh. Indeed, encouraging Pol Pot was a useful way for China to step up the pressure on Vietnam.

In any case the Chinese 'balancing act' ended with the escalation of the Vietnam-Cambodia dispute in 1977. When Pol Pot celebrated his victory in the inner-party struggle with a visit to Peking in October, he was given an exceptionally warm welcome. Hua Guofeng, temporarily the top man in Peking politics, personally presided over his reception, which was attended by nine other members of the Chinese Politbureau. China cut all military co-operation with Vietnam on 31 December, the day Cambodia broke off diplomatic relations with Hanoi. China dropped the pretence of neutrality after the Vietnamese offensive in December 1977, openly accusing Hanoi of aggression. Peking called for a negotiated settlement, but blandly ignored the fact that it was Phnom Penh rather than Hanoi which was refusing to talk.

In January 1978 Zhou Enlai's widow, Deng Yingchao, visited Phnom Penh and signed an agreement stepping up military aid to Cambodia. Fresh shipments of ammunition and weapons arrived the following month. These included 130-mm artillery, promptly deployed to bombard Vietnam. In March Chinese engineers arrived to rebuild the Kompong Som-Phnom Penh railway line. When this task had been completed they remained in place, apparently to signal to Hanoi that any action against Phnom Penh would involve the Chinese.

All of this was part of what one American expert describes as a Chinese policy of 'restraint' towards Vietnam. This ended in May 1978, when the Chinese 'began a series of . . . moves which appeared designed to exert much stronger pressure on Vietnam'.[32] Aid projects were slashed, and the Chinese began describing Vietnam as the 'Asian Cuba'. When Vietnam, by this stage determined that Pol Pot had to go, moved to protect itself by joining COMECON, Peking's *People's Daily* responded by accusing Vietnam of annexationist ambitions, and repeated Pol Pot's 'Indochina Federation' charges. The Chinese stepped up their military aid to the Cambodian regime, cut their remaining aid projects in Vietnam, and closed the Sino-Vietnamese border. Following this the number of armed clashes on the border rose rapidly.

From this sequence of events the Vietnamese Communists concluded that the sinister hand of Peking lay behind their troubles with Cambodia. Echoing arguments that were advanced to us in Hanoi, Wilfred Burchett has written: 'Why was a negotiated solution to problems between two neighbouring states, headed by supposedly comradely Communist Parties, impossible? It is now clear that by 1977 Peking was running Khmer Rouge affairs . . . . Whereas Vietnam had stubbornly refused to be placed in China's pocket, Pol Pot had jumped into it himself. China has been charged on many occasions with being interested in fighting the United States to the last Vietnamese and was certainly no less averse to fighting Vietnam to the last Cambodian.'[33] With this assessment, we must disagree. For better or worse, it seems clear to us that Pol Pot's group had their own home grown reasons for provoking a feud with Hanoi. While Peking sought to exploit this situation to its own advantage, it was no more in control of Pol Pot than Hanoi was.

When Vietnam joined COMECON, Pol Pot's defence minister, Son Sen, was promptly dispatched to Peking to drum up more support, but the results must have been deeply disappointing to him. Since Pol Pot's visit, the power struggle in Peking had gone against the friends of the Khmer Rouge regime, and Sen had to deal not with Hua Guofeng, but with Deng Xiaoping – who doubtless remembered that he had been personally denounced over Phnom Penh Radio as an 'anti-socialist and counter-revolutionary' in 1976. Deng apparently tried to push Pol Pot's regime onto the path of moderation. It is said that he bluntly told Son Sen that while China would do its utmost to prevent a collapse of the Phnom Penh regime, all the Chinese aid in the world would be of no avail if Pol Pot continued on his current political course.[34]

Deng was as strongly committed as anybody in Peking to the notion of using the Phnom Penh regime as an instrument against Soviet-Vietnamese 'hegemonism' in Southeast Asia, but he is said to have argued that if Cambodia continued its violent provocations on the Vietnam border on the scale it was then doing, it would make a Vietnamese invasion inevitable. The outcome would be Vietnamese domination of all Indochina, rather than Deng's own personal preference, a pro-Chinese Cambodia slowly 'bleeding' Vietnam.

Son Sen thus returned from Peking with the sorry task of trying to talk Pol Pot into moderation just at the time when he was taking his final vengeance on the 'pro-Vietnamese traitors' of Cambodia's eastern region. Pol Pot allowed Sihanouk to make a few cosmetic public statements in support of the DK regime, but beyond that appears to have been unresponsive to Deng's pressure. In early

September another of Pol Pot's cohorts, Nuon Chea, made a further visit to Peking, apparently unsuccessfully seeking a commitment of Chinese troops to Cambodia. Instead, Deng urged the Khmers Rouges to start preparing for a drawn-out guerrilla campaign against the Vietnamese occupation forces. The Chinese began shipping supplies of arms, canned food and radio equipment into Cambodia, for use in such a struggle. Son Sen took charge of preparing bases in the mountains and shifting stocks of rice and other supplies up into them.

When the Vietnamese signed their friendship treaty with the Soviet Union in November 1978, the Chinese promptly sent a delegation to Phnom Penh to reassure the Khmer Rouge leaders of Peking's support. Pol Pot went on Phnom Penh Radio to praise what he described as Peking's 'unconditional support' for Cambodia's struggle against Vietnam. But the reality was much less reassuring. Deng Xiaoping had dispatched Wang Dong Xing, one of his political enemies (who he would finally sack in February 1980) to Phnom Penh, while he himself did the rounds of the ASEAN capitals to counter Pham Van Dong's earlier tour.

By this stage, Deng had apparently written off the Pol Pot regime. In Bangkok he predicted that Vietnam would invade and that Cambodia would be completely overrun. His objective was not to keep Pol Pot in Phnom Penh, but to persuade the ASEAN countries to join with China in supporting an armed insurgency in Cambodia against a Vietnamese-backed regime in Phnom Penh. He also said that China's direct response to the impending Vietnamese invasion would have to be restrained because of Vietnam's close relationship with the Soviet Union, though he added he would not rule out 'a punitive raid by China in the same way as it attacked Indian forces in 1962'.[35]

At this stage the Chinese leaders were still divided over what course to take. When Vietnam countered Chinese pressure by opting for a close alliance with Moscow in June, some, such as Hua Guofeng, apparently believed that China should immediately take drastic measures. But Deng Xiaoping emphasized the need for caution because of the danger of Soviet retaliation if China took any military measures against Vietnam.[36] In this delicately poised situation, American support for China tipped the balance in favour of war.

While relations between China and Vietnam deteriorated, rapid progress was made in the normalization of relations between Peking and Washington. The two processes were interconnected, because it was the desire to strengthen their anti-Soviet policies that induced both sides to compromise over the Taiwan issue, and the anti-Soviet hardliners in Washington encouraged China to take a tough line against Vietnam. During the visit of May 1978, which finally opened the way to full normalization of Sino-American relations, Brzezinski proclaimed that America shared China's 'resolve to resist the efforts of any nation which seeks to establish global or regional hegemony' – 'regional hegemonists' being Peking's code-word for Vietnam. China's turn to display a tough policy towards Vietnam came only four days later. America had already blocked Vietnam's first post-war endeavours to open to the West, and in the second half of 1978 it continued to reject Hanoi's increasingly desperate attempts at reconciliation.

When Vietnam signed its military treaty with the Soviet Union in November, the USA responded by announcing that it no longer opposed military sales to Peking, and in early December it came down unequivocally against Hanoi in the Vietnam-Cambodia border dispute. When the Chinese pointedly welcomed these moves as helping to limit the influence of Moscow's 'surrogate', Washington did not object. The agreement to normalize relations between Washington and Peking, announced on 15 December, duly emphasized the commitment of both sides to opposition to 'international hegemony' (the Soviet Union), and there were no US objections when Hua Guofeng added that the agreement would also be useful against 'regional hegemonism'. Ten days later Vietnam invaded Cambodia, toppling Pol Pot's regime with a speed that dismayed even those (such as Deng) who had been most sceptical of DK's military capabilities.

The Chinese began military preparations for their invasion of Vietnam in mid-January, assured that America's support would protect them against possible Soviet retaliation. But Deng was evidently not fully satisfied until after his visit to the USA at the end of the month. In private, Deng informed the American president of the planned invasion; publicly he spoke of the need to 'teach Vietnam a lesson'. Carter says that he privately advised Deng against the invasion.[37] Publicly, while they did not endorse Deng's statements on the need to 'teach Vietnam a lesson', the Americans did not object. But they did not publicly warn China against invading, or threaten any form of diplomatic retaliation if it did. They waited until Deng had left the country before declaring that these views were not necessarily America's as well as China's. Deng appears to have taken this as tacit support. The final decision to go ahead with the invasion was reportedly made the day after his return to Peking.

According to Victor Zorza, a well-informed observer, the main motivation for American policy at this juncture was to strengthen Deng's faction in the unfolding power struggle in Peking. A fortnight before the Chinese invasion, he reported: 'Senior White House officials have . . . said that one reason why President Carter had decided to move rapidly towards normalization was his wish to show support for Deng. This is one reason why Carter made the concessions on Taiwan that exposed him to the charge that he was abandoning a long-time ally. If there had been no understanding on Taiwan and no normalization with the United States, then Deng would have been unlikely to prevail against Hua . . . .'

The Americans had been alarmed by hints of a thaw in Sino-Soviet relations, and by reports that Hua favoured a partial withdrawal of troops from the Sino-Soviet border as a conciliatory gesture to Moscow before striking at Vietnam. Deng, by contrast, was especially anxious to secure American support because he wanted to maintain an antagonistic posture on the Sino-Soviet border as well as to punish Vietnam. Wrote Zorza: 'The US strategy in the Sino-Soviet dispute is designed to extract concessions from the Kremlin by threatening to build up China's power against the Soviet Union. But when Moscow and Peking come to the obvious conclusion that their interests are best served by an accommodation rather than by a continuation of the dispute . . . the United States will be left high and dry.[38]

At the very least, America's policy was one of indulging China's invasion of Vietnam while condemning Vietnam's invasion of Cambodia in the strongest terms. The Carter administration did not even slow up the process of diplomatic normalization of relations with China as a sign of displeasure, while in the case of Vietnam it rejected normalization altogether.

The Sino-Vietnamese war was the culmination of steadily mounting Chinese pressure on Vietnam following the Sino-American *rapprochement* of the early 1970s. This opened the way for a rapid expansion of Chinese influence in Southeast Asia, to which Vietnam proved the most resistant. China went to war with Vietnam because Hanoi had overthrown Pol Pot's regime in Cambodia. This was in no way a threat to China's national security (as Pol Pot's attacks were to Vietnam's security), but it did damage China's new found prestige as a great power in the Southeast Asian region. Not only had the Vietnamese persistently defied Chinese pressure to break with Moscow, they had overthrown a regime to whose protection China had committed itself. In the face of this, the fact that Deng's moderate faction, at least, regarded Pol Pot's regime as suicidally destructive was beside the point. Vietnam's actions were intolerable in the eyes of Peking; Hanoi had to be punished, and China's rapidly growing ties with the USA provided the insurance against Soviet retaliation that Deng thought necessary before China could coerce Vietnam into submission by means of military aggression. In the West, these conflicts were perceived through the prism of Soviet-American cold war antagonisms: while Vietnam was condemned and ostracized for invading Pol Pot's Cambodia, China's retaliatory invasion of Vietnam was viewed with considerable indulgence.

China's invasion of Vietnam was thus a classic exercise in power politics. Deng's announcement that China had the 'right' to teach Vietnam 'lessons' whenever it wanted was an assertion that Vietnam fell into a Chinese sphere of interest. It was an effective practical rebuttal of benign interpretations of Chinese foreign policy based on its democratic rhetoric.[39]

But China's attempt to coerce Vietnam into submission failed. On the battlefields of northern Vietnam in 1979, it was China's military weakness rather than its irresistible strength that was displayed, giving a hollow ring to Peking's threats of 'another lesson'. Vietnamese military forces in Cambodia had soon reduced Pol Pot's forces to an isolated guerrilla force once more. A pro-Vietnamese government was installed in Phnom Penh, official Chinese influence in Laos was eliminated. Hanoi remained obstinately defiant and reaffirmed its position over ths South China Sea. Given its failure to match its threats with military force, Chinese policy towards Indochina has proven counter-productive. From a position of considerable influence in 1975, Peking's policies have resulted in its influence shrinking to next to nothing, and by 1980 it was faced with the prospect of a bloc of solidly pro-Soviet states defying China's will in Indochina. The stage was set for a new struggle with Vietnam and its Soviet patron, on much less advantageous terms for China.

Notes

1. Cf. J.R.V. Prescott, J.H. Collier, D.F. Prescott, *Frontiers of Southeast Asia*, Melbourne, 1977, p. 60.

2. *Peking Review*, 4 May 1979.

3. Cf Bruce Berton, 'Contending Explanations of the 1979 Sino-Vietnamese War', *International Journal*, vol. 34, 1979 and G.D. Loescher, 'The Sino-Vietnamese Conflict in Recent Historical Perspective', *Survey*, vol. 24, 1979; Daniel Tretiak, 'China's Vietnam War and its Consequences', *China Quarterly*, no. 80, 1979, assumes that the war was the result of 'months' of conflict and attributes more importance to the immediate border tensions than to what we would consider to be the underlying causes. Li Man Kin, *et al.*, *Sino Vietnamese War*, Hong Kong 1981, is straightforward Chinese propaganda. While the text is worthless, the photographs are numerous and excellent.

4. In King C. Chen, ed., *China and the Three Worlds: A Foreign Policy Reader*, London 1979, p. 128.

5. Ministry of Foreign Affairs, Socialist Republic of Vietnam, *The Truth about Vietnam-China Relations over the Last Thirty Years*, Hanoi 1979, p. 12.

6. Cf. three articles by *People's Daily* and Xinhua commentators in *Peking Review*, 30 November – 7 December 1979. The last of these was accompanied by a lengthy article by VCP veteran Hoang Van Hoan, who defected to China in the wake of the Sino-Vietnam war. Hoan concludes that the crisis occurred because 'Le Duan is not honest and decent'.

7. C.P. Fitzgerald, *The Chinese View of their Place in the World*, London 1964, pp. 71–2.

8. In Franz Schurmann and Orville Schell, eds, *Imperial China*, vol. 1, New York 1967, pp. 107–8.

9. Truong Buu Lam, 'Intervention versus Tribute in Sino-Vietnamese Relations, 1788–90' in John K. Fairbank, ed., *The Chinese World Order: Traditional China's Foreign Relations*, Cambridge, Mass. 1968, pp. 178–9. This volume is the standard modern work on this subject.

10. Benjamin I. Schwartz, 'The Chinese Perception of World Order, Past and Present' in ibid., p. 285.

11. Quoted by Michael B. Yahuda, *China's Role in World Affairs*, London 1978, p. 67.

12. Gerald Segal, 'China and the Great Power Triangle', *China Quarterly*, no. 83, 1980, pp. 492–3.

13. Yahuda, p. 194. Not all the admirers of China were willing to admit this. In *The Second Chinese Revolution*, New York 1974, K.S. Karol wrote: 'In contradiction to some theories, China during the Cultural Revolution showed no tendency to withdraw into herself. Official statements and the entire press provide evidence that for the Chinese people these were years of great reaching out to the world, albeit in an unorthodox fashion. The very doctrine of the guiding hands of the Cultural Revolution explicitly linked the future of the "Commune of China" to the victory of the world revolution . . . . after 1966, every practical or political achievement was described as the contribution of a factory or a rank-and-file group to the world revolution' (p. 385).

But the weakness of his argument is evident from his description of how the 'Chinese people reached out to the world' in these years: ' . . . official notes from Peking's Ministry of Foreign Affairs . . . fulminated in insulting terms against "running dogs of imperialism" or "revisionist vampires". Of course, these terms normally appeared only in "strong protests" or "grave warnings", not in invitations to discussion. But the fact remains that the Ministry of Foreign Affairs sent out no other kind of notes, and had so little interest in negotiation that, from December 1966 onward it recalled all its ambassadors (with the sole exception of Huang Hua in

Cairo)' (ibid., p. 386). 'In 1967 and 1968 admittance was granted almost exclusively to delegations of militant fighters or close friends; no individual visas were granted even to men like Edgar Snow. Special consideration was shown to the "Marxist-Leninist" parties which emerged from the argument with Russia, and it was usual for Mao himself to receive their leaders' (ibid., p. 399).

14. For the best account of the Sino-Soviet dispute to this point, see O. Edmund Clubb, *China and Russia: The 'Great Game'*, New York 1971.

15. It was not the first time. Like the Vietnamese after their victory, the Chinese Communists in the 1940s had actively sought a *rapprochement* with the USA. On 13 March 1945 Mao told John Service, a political officer in the American embassy in China: 'China's great post-war need is economic development. She lacks the capitalistic foundation necessary to carry this out alone. Her own standards of living are so low that they cannot be depressed any further to provide the needed capital. America and China complement each other economically; they will not compete. China does not have the requirements of a heavy industry of major size. She cannot hope to meet the United States in its highly specialized manufactures. She also needs to build up light industries to supply her own market and raise the living standards of her own people. Eventually she can supply these goods to other countries in the Far East. To help pay for this foreign trade and investment, she has raw materials and agricultural products. American is not only the most suitable country to assist in the economic development of China, she is also the only country fully able to participate.' (Joseph W. Esherwick, ed., *Lost Chance in China: The World War II Despatches of John S. Service*, New York, 1975, p. 373.) It was even proposed that Mao and Zhou Enlai travel to Washington to explain the Chinese Communist Party's position to Roosevelt, but this idea was scotched by the American ambassador in China at this time, the anti-Communist Patrick J. Hurley. One can only speculate on the course that Asian history might have taken if there had been a positive American response to these overtures, but as it was American hostility pushed the Chinese in the direction of the Soviet Union.

16. The official version, presented at the trial of the 'Gang of Four' in Peking in November 1980–January 1981, was that Lin died in a plane crash in Mongolia, attempting to flee the country after a failed attempt at assassinating Mao and staging a coup. In 1983 an account was published by a pseudonymous Chinese author, claiming that Mao organized the assassination of Lin before the plot reached maturity, and that the story of Lin's death in Mongolia was concocted to protect Mao's reputation: see Yao Ming Le, *The Conspiracy and Death of Lin Biao*, London 1983.

17. In Chen, p. 86.

18. Geoffrey Jukes, *The Soviet Union in Asia*, Sydney 1973, p. 2.

19. Robert C. Horn, 'The Soviet Union and Asian Security' in Sudershan Chawla and D.R. Sar Desai, eds., *Changing Patterns of Security and Stability in Asia*, New York 1980, pp. 81–2.

20. John Lewis, *Far Eastern Economic Review*, 24 August 1979. This article is part of a series on 'Moscow's Thrust into Asia': see also the issues of 31 August and 7 September for further reports.

21. Robert G. Sutter, *Chinese Foreign Policy after the Cultural Revolution 1966–77*, Boulder, Colorado 1978, p. 113. Horn, p. 83, also remarks: 'Throughout virtually all of the Soviet offensive in Southeast Asia during the 1970s, Moscow has been faced with a Chinese offensive of even greater magnitude.'

22. Quoted in Sutter, pp. 55, 118–119.

23. *Peking Review*, 7 December 1979.

24. Cf. Loescher for a summary and more detailed references.

25. In its discussion of the Geneva Conference Hanoi weakened its own case by tactfully refraining from mentioning that the Soviet Union had supported China's position – although this point has doubtless been filed away for future reference and may yet appear in a white paper on Soviet-Vietnamese relations. The agreement between its two great power patrons left the Viet Minh with a choice between accepting the compromise pushed by Zhou and total diplomatic isolation. It is therefore ironic that the Cambodian Communists, supported by China, should accuse the Vietnamese of betraying them at Geneva.

26. However, some confirmation for Hanoi's analysis is given in a book by a former member of the Pakistani cabinet, Golam W. Chowdry. Chowdry played an instrumental role in developing the secret contacts between Washington and Peking in 1969–71, and went to Columbia University when he was forced to leave Pakistan in 1971. According to Chowdry, Peking's hostility towards Hanoi went back well before the 1970s, and was one of the reasons for the Sino-American *détente:* 'Chinese Vice-Foreign Minister Han Nianlong told me in July 1979 that China could foresee Hanoi's regional ambitions, or hegemonic aspirations in Southeast Asia, as early as the 1950s, yet neither Mao nor Zhou could publicly support the US cause in 1972. Just as the United States had to reaffirm its commitments for the defence of the Republic of China [Taiwan], so the Chinese leaders had to restate their position on the Vietnamese war in the Shanghai Communiqué,' (*China in World Affairs: The Foreign Policy of the PRC since 1970*, Boulder, Colorado 1982, p. 74) Frankly, we think that on this occasion Han was feeding him a line, hoping to have a favourable influence on the American position over Taiwan.

27. Marvin Kalb and Bernard Kalb, *Kissinger*, New York 1975, p. 318.

28. In Chen, pp. 149–50.

29. Roger M. Smith, *Cambodia's Foreign Policy*, Ithaca 1965, pp. 117–18.

30. Yahuda, p. 263.

31. Stephen R. Heder, 'The Cambodian-Vietnamese Conflict', in David W.P. Elliott, ed., *The Third Indochina Conflict*, Boulder, Colorado 1981, pp. 43–4.

32. Robert G. Sutter, 'China's Strategy toward Vietnam and its Implications for the United States' in ibid., pp. 175–6.

33. Wilfred Burchett, *The Vietnam-China-Cambodia Triangle*, London 1981, p. 149.

34. Nayan Chanda, *Far Eastern Economic Review*, 8 September 1978.

35. Ibid., 24 November 1978.

36. Sutter, 'China's Strategy', pp. 181–2.

37. Jimmy Carter, *Keeping the Faith*, London 1982, pp. 206–9.

38. Victor Zorza, *Guardian Weekly*, 4 February 1979.

39. In a book published shortly before the war, one expert had written: ' . . . the Chinese have not sought to act as a conventional great power, demanding exclusive spheres of influence on its periphery. Nor has China sought to dominate the lesser countries on its border.' Even at the time it was written, this blissfully ignored many facts. Chinese policy towards Indochina he summed up in these terms: 'China's relations with the countries of Indochina . . . continued to follow a strictly correct policy of total commitment and support. All these countries were independent of China and there were no attempts to cajole or dragoon them into following the Chinese line.' Yahuda, pp. 264, 262. Any commentary on this should be superfluous now, except to note that it is appropriate that the author took as proof of China's reluctance to engage in power politics its 'readiness to negotiate' over the South China Sea.

6

Indochina: Federation or Alliance?

In the early months of 1979 the Vietnamese had succeeded both in overthrowing Pol Pot's regime in Cambodia and rebuffing China's military response. The immediate crisis had been resolved in their favour, but they now faced a long struggle to consolidate their gains. The Hanoi government found itself more isolated politically than it had ever been, with its economy disrupted, and facing a long-term threat to its security from China. It had to scrap its plans for economic development and put a war-weary people in a state of military preparedness once more. It had to seek out reliable allies to support its defiance of Chinese power. Above all, it had to create a stable and sympathetic government out of the shambles of Cambodia after Pol Pot.

Vietnam under Seige

The contrast between the VCP's hopes of 1976 and the economic realities of 1979 could hardly have been more stark. The growth rate, far from rising, fell from 9 per cent in 1976 to zero at the close of the decade. Industry did expand, but only at one-third of the anticipated rate. Above all, rice production stagnated at a level of ten million tons, while the population continued to grow at 2.6 per cent per annum. The growth of exports (principally of agricultural products) anticipated by the planners failed to materialize, while foreign debt rose rapidly. At the end of 1981 it was estimated to be over $3.5 billion US, of which more than half was owed to the Soviet Union and the Eastern European countries, with France and Japan as the country's main non-Communist creditors. Earlier press reports had given a considerably higher figure, but even this revised figure meant that servicing its foreign debt was absorbing half the country's export earnings. The inability to import led to widespread shortages of raw materials and consumer goods. Put simply, Vietnam found itself unable to pay its way, and even the reduced living standard of 1979–81 was dependent on a continuing inflow of aid.

Vietnam's post-war economic strategy had been completely wrecked by the unfolding of the unanticipated conflict with the Khmer Rouge regime and China, as well as by the failure to make the expected breakthrough to the West after 1975. The measures taken by the Hanoi regime in 1977–8 in response to this crisis (the crackdown on trade and the collectivization drive in the south) had added to the economic disruption, particularly in the agricultural sector. Then, in 1978, the economy was put back on a war footing – by 1980 47 per cent of public expenditure (about 14 per cent of gross national product) was being channelled to the military.

The 1976 plan had been dependent on outside financial assistance, and left Vietnam vulnerable to outside pressures. China cut all its aid off in 1978. Japan and many Western countries followed suit after the Vietnamese toppled the Pol Pot regime. Since then Washington has also been going out of its way to obstruct any aid from international organizations flowing to Vietnam. In the case of the UN Development Project in 1981, its lobbying was unsuccessful, but the American directors of the World Bank and the Asian Development Bank are under instructions to 'actively oppose' any loans to Vietnam until it 'has withdrawn its troops from Cambodia and Laos'. To aid Vietnam, the Americans argue, is to subsidize its military expansion. France agreed to resume aid to Hanoi, and granted it credits worth $40 million in December 1981, but outside of this the major Western and international aid donors have followed the American line.

The continuing economic pressure on Vietnam undoubtedly had effect. It was evident to visitors in the early 1980s in the empty shops, the low rations, and shortages of goods of almost every kind – though many rather curiously interpret this as an expression of official puritanism rather than a product of economic circumstances. Doctors reported a rise in malnutrition-linked diseases, especially among children. The pressure was also reflected in the continuing exodus from the country, and in the changed ethnic composition of the refugees. Whereas previously most had been ethnic Chinese and many from a bourgeois background, by 1980 over 85 per cent were ethnic Vietnamese. 'There is,' reported the UN High Commission for Refugees, 'a much larger proportion than before of people, including fishermen and peasants, who are leaving for economic reasons in the hope of finding better jobs and living conditions in Western countries.'[1]

The dashing of widespread hopes for peace and a measure of prosperity has led to a sagging of morale throughout the country, afflicting the ruling party as well as the common people. A Polit-bureau directive issued in November 1980 declared: 'Our production is slumping in several ways and the livelihood of the people . . . is deteriorating and encountering many difficulties. Negativism prevails in social life. The enemy and bad elements are taking advantage of this situation to incite the masses to sow division among us and attack our leadership in order to weaken the organization of our party and state.' All this was, of course, good news from the viewpoint of China, which gleefully predicted the complete collapse of the Vietnamese social and economic fabric.

The Vietnamese responded by rethinking their basic economic strategy at the 6th Plenum of the VCP's central committee in September 1979. In contrast to the *ad hoc* decisions of 1977–8, which cracked down on private trade, stepped up the drive for collectivization in the south, and generally extended centralized controls over the economy, the strategy adopted at the 6th Plenum placed a new emphasis on market forces. Government policy was aimed at reducing the barriers to private circulation of goods and encouraging private production for the market, as well as running state enterprises more efficiently. The brakes were applied to the collectivization movement and the development of New Economic Zones in the south.

The new policies achieved their overall objectives, with help from favourable weather conditions. In the towns, thousands of petty workshops and street stalls sprang up, and people talked of the economy 'exploding'. State enterprises also appear to have increased their output sharply, despite the continuing shortages of raw materials. Even more important, agricultural production jumped. A bad season in the north was compensated by a bumper harvest in the Mekong Delta in 1980. In December 1981 Ngyuen Lam, then chairman of the state planning commission, reported that the rice harvest for that year had reached a record fifteen million tons. Further good harvests followed. In December 1983 Lam's successor, Vo Vien Kiet, was able to report that the harvest target of seventeen million tons had been 'more or less achieved' despite adverse weather conditions (including three typhoons). Exports picked up, easing the problem of external imbalance. Living standards had improved from those of 1979–80, but remained desperately low.

The Third Five Year Plan came into operation in 1981, although it was not formally endorsed until the 5th Congress of the VCP in March 1982. Compared to the Second Five Year Plan, its most striking feature was the extent to which the Vietnamese leadership had scaled down its hopes for rapid economic development. According to Premier Pham Van Dong's report to the congress, the first priority was to 'stabilize and eventually to improve' the people's living standards. Primary emphasis was placed on boosting production in agriculture and consumer goods industries, and expanding exports to reduce Vietnam's critical external imbalance. Industrialization and the 'consolidation of socialist relations of production throughout the country' remained eventual objectives, but were assigned to a secondary level, and military requirements were listed last.

There is no doubt that between them the USA and China have been able to hurt Vietnam badly through continued economic pressure. This has been in part because the Vietnamese Communists had, in the immediate euphoria of victory, adopted an economic strategy that was excessively optimistic and premissed on an opening to the West. But from 1979 Hanoi adopted a more modest and realistic approach, and by 1983 it was clear that Sino-American attempts to bleed Vietnam into submission had failed. The prospect of the Hanoi government finding itself obliged for economic reasons to capitulate over what it saw as the vital strategic interests of the country were becoming increasingly remote.

The full significance of this experiment in economic liberalization under duress has not been fully appreciated by many Western commentators. Historically, the typical response of Communist states to external pressures has been to impose tight internal political controls and to move towards a more rigidly centralized and autarchic economic system. China's response to the Sino-Soviet split, discussed in chapter V, is one example. This was the pattern Vietnam seemed to be following in 1977–8, but the 6th Plenum in 1979 broke sharply with these trends, at least in the economic sphere. It is not surprising that the new policies ran into opposition from hardliners in the party, who looked to a more Stalinist-Maoist-style approach, but in the international context of a struggle against China, the moderates were able to carry the day. The 5th Congress in 1982 marked their victory over the hardliners, and was the occasion for what Dong called 'harsh self-criticism' centred around the 'subjectivism and impatience' displayed by leading party and government bodies in the preceding years. The moderate course was re-affirmed by a meeting of the VCP's central committee in December 1983, although Le Duan's speech acknowledged that 'there are differing views' on economic policy within the party.

The immediate result of the economic pressure applied to Vietnam has been to drive it more firmly into the Soviet camp. The Soviet Union has become Vietnam's main trading partner. Nguyen Lam said that by mid-1981 more than two-thirds of Vietnam's imports of fuel, raw materials, food, consumer goods and machinery came from the Soviet Union and other COMECON members, notably East Germany. In 1980 Moscow provided Hanoi with $658 million US in economic aid and another $870 million in military aid. Unlike the 1976 plan, the Third Vietnamese Five Year Plan embodied a number of long-term agreements with the Soviet Union. The Soviets agreed to provide assistance to three electricity generation schemes and forty industrial projects, and in exchange the Vietnamese agreed to increase exports of agricultural produce and textiles to Soviet Asia. In 1982 further Soviet-Vietnamese agreements on oil and gas exploration in the South China Sea and scientific and technical cooperation were signed.

Hanoi also granted the Soviets access to the deep-water harbour facilities built by the Americans in Cam Ranh Bay. Mid-way between Vladivostock and the Indian Ocean, this was of great strategic value to Soviet naval forces in the Far East. The USSR had been seeking access to Cam Ranh Bay since 1975 but Hanoi, clearly aware of the hostility this would invite from Peking, had refused until 1979. The first visit by Soviet ships to Cam Ranh Bay was reported in April 1979, a matter of weeks after the Chinese invasion made such considerations redundant. By 1983 such visits had become commonplace. There have been numerous reports in the Western press that the Soviets have been constructing military bases at Cam Ranh Bay and other locations, but these have been denied by the Vietnamese. However, whereas prior to 1979 Hanoi said it would not allow any foreign military bases on Vietnamese soil, after the Chinese invasion it adopted the position that it might allow it in the future if the military threat from China continued.

There have been reports of persistent tensions between Hanoi and Moscow beneath the veneer of close cooperation. The Soviets, it is said, have been privately grumbling about pouring their money into Vietnam without seeing any gain for it, and complaining that Vietnamese intransigence over Cambodia has created problems for them in their dealings with ASEAN. For their part, the Vietnamese are said to complain of both the quantity and quality of Soviet aid, to resent Soviet attempts to secure some advantages for themselves from their aid to Vietnam, and to be resisting Soviet efforts to expand their influence, not only over the Hanoi government itself, but in Laos and Cambodia as well. Soviet-Vietnamese frictions were reported to be particularly acute following the abrupt dismissal of a supposedly pro-Soviet leader, Pen Sovan, in Phnom Penh in December 1981. All this is dismissed as hostile speculation by the parties concerned, but the reluctance of Communist governments to discuss their disagreements frankly makes it hard to assess the true situation. However, we would suggest that talk of serious Soviet-Vietnamese antagonism is not solidly founded.

The overriding consideration is that Vietnamese and Soviet strategic interests remain broadly congruent. While that is the case the alliance is unlikely to break up because of tensions over matters of secondary importance. Whatever private complaints they may have about the nature of Soviet aid, Vietnamese officials appear fully aware that it is of vital importance if the country is to continue to defy China's demands. On the other hand, while it is true that Vietnam's invasion of Cambodia has added to the USSR's problems in dealing with the ASEAN countries, Vietnam represents the one major success of Soviet diplomacy in Asia. Especially given the importance of Cam Rahn Bay to the Soviet Pacific Fleet, they are not likely to jeopardize it for purely hypothetical gains among the ASEAN states. And for as long as the Soviets remain at loggerheads with the Chinese, they cannot afford to abandon Vietnam to their opponent's ambitions. Thus, despite some routine frictions in the alliance, it seems clear that Vietnam will stay in the Soviet camp for the foreseeable future. It has been argued that a more generous Western approach could now woo Hanoi out of its dependence on the Soviet Union.[2] While Vietnam would doubtless be happy to accept support from non-Soviet sources, this is not likely to entice it out of the alliance with the Soviet Union unless it is persuaded that the Western powers are a more reliable anti-Chinese ally. In this context, talk of encouraging Vietnamese 'Titoism' is particularly unrealistic. This is usually envisaged in terms of independence from the Soviet Union, but it has been the Chinese rather than the Russians who have been playing the role of Stalinist bully in relation to Vietnam; indeed, it would be ironic but not misleading to describe Soviet policy as one of sustaining Vietnamese 'Titoism' *vis-à-vis* China.[3]

Forced to choose between Moscow and Peking, Hanoi had good

reasons for choosing Moscow. The USSR is both economically and militarily stronger than China, and can provide more valuable economic and military aid. In addition, its very distance affords Hanoi greater independence: the USSR is not in a position to settle any quarrel it may have with Vietnam by means of a Czechoslovakia-style operation – whereas China is, and demonstrated its willingness to use force in February 1979. However, for all the professions of socialist solidarity, experience has by now taught the rulers in Hanoi that the interests of great powers shift and change over time, and they have devoted much of their energy in the period since January 1979 to consolidating their own position in Indochina, above all in post-Pol Pot Cambodia.

Cambodia: Picking up the Pieces.

As they moved across Cambodia following the toppling of the Pol Pot regime, the Vietnamese troops found abundant evidence of the appalling brutalities that had taken place. A Polish journalist who visited Prey Veng in February 1979 gave an eyewitness account of the discovery of thousands of putrefying corpses left behind by the fleeing Khmers Rouges. Survivors of the massacre told him that 22,000 people had been killed in the town market and their bodies thrown into the town sewers; the slaughter was brought to a halt only by the Vietnamese invasion. 'Have you heard of liquid bodies?' he later asked a journalist in Bangkok. 'What we saw were the remains, which were just liquefied flesh with millions of maggots and worms.' Western journalists were soon allowed in, and confirmed this picture. The Cambodia Pol Pot left behind was described in March by AAP reporter Harish Charandola as 'a land of skulls, gore and stench'. Taken to Prey Veng, he found the stink 'unbearable'. It was not just that the town sewers were choked with rotting corpses; in the surrounding countryside, 'shallow, unmarked graves are everywhere. Bones are everywhere just below the surface'. Over the next few months such reports became commonplace, and by 1981 the discovery of more mass graves in Cambodia was no longer of any interest to the Western press. The unearthing of 60,000 bodies in September 1981, for example, barely rated a paragraph; Pol Pot's atrocities had become yesterday's headlines.

But is is impossible to understand political developments inside Cambodia under the Vietnamese occupation without keeping his legacy in mind. It was not simply that Pol Pot and his group were almost universally detested, though this was true enough. Everywhere one went in 1980–81, whether in refugee camps or inside Cambodia itself, almost all Khmers spoke of welcoming the Vietnamese invasion as a liberation from Pol Pot's tyranny – whatever their apprehensions about the ultimate intentions of the Vietnamese. 'It is true that the Vietnamese were not invited here,' an aid worker in Phnom Penh remarked to us in 1981, 'but if there had been a telephone line open to Hanoi it would have been jammed with calls.' The fear that Pol Pot would return to power and that the mass killings would resume was still an overriding concern of the population; the fact that most of the world still recognized him as the legitimate ruler of the country and expressed outrage at his overthrow by the Vietnamese was greeted with incredulity and alarm. The fear that, with foreign backing, he might be returned to power spontaneously generated a wide constituency for the Vietnamese presence despite the traditional Khmer fears of their neighbours.

Many of the traditional assumptions about the 'hereditary enemy' had been undermined by events. It was not the Vietnamese but the most ardent of the Khmer 'patriots' who had terrorized the Cambodian nation, outlawed its religion and traditional culture, and massacred its citizens. Other Cambodians, whether their political persuasions were of the left, the centre or the right had been unable to prevent this, and only the intervention of the Vietnamese had apparently brought this national self-immolation to an end. To some Khmers all the traditional groupings of Cambodian politics had discredited themselves, and the nation had to start out afresh. In this context, they were willing to go along with the new Vietnamese-sponsored authorities. The dominant mood was one of demoralization and self-doubt after the trauma of the Pol Pot regime rather than one of nationalist outrage at the Vietnamese invasion.

Vietnam's military presence made it without doubt the dominant force in the new Cambodia. By 1980 the number of Vietnamese troops in Cambodia had risen to 200,000 but travelling around the countryside one saw surprisingly little of them. It was common enough to see individual soldiers or small groups of them wandering around unarmed, sitting by the side of the road chatting with Khmer peasants, or bargaining in town markets like anybody else. Nobody seemed to take any particular notice of them. The Vietnamese soldiers built their own barracks, grew vegetables for themselves, and concentrated on their garrison duties, interfering as little as possible in the activities of the Khmer population. Basically, they were living at the same subsistence level as the Khmers, and seemed to blend into the local landscape in a surprisingly inconspicuous way. They received rations of two bowls of rice and some tinned meat, and the equivalent of 20 cents US a day as pocket money.

Cambodia certainly did not look like a country under military occupation, and the soldiers to whom we spoke showed no conquering zeal – on the contrary, they complained that they were in a foreign country and lonely, wishing they could go back to their families and girlfriends in Vietnam. They were under strict orders to behave with impeccable propriety towards the Khmer population, and local amorous liaisons were strictly forbidden. The Vietnamese authorities were obviously aware of the traditional Cambodian antipathy towards the Vietnamese, and were doing their best to neutralize it. The good conduct of the Vietnamese Communist forces in Cambodia stands in conspicuous contrast to the brutality and pillaging of the ARVN forces in eastern Cambodia in 1970–71.

We found nobody who wanted the Vietnamese to leave while there was still a chance that this would mean the return of Pol Pot. But at the same time, there was obviously widespread unease about Vietnam's long-term intentions towards Cambodia. Nobody wanted the country reduced to a colonial or semi-colonial status. In February 1980, even officials of the new Phnom Penh government would privately express fears on this point. However, it was noticeable that these apprehensions were most common in Phnom Penh, where security from the Khmers Rouges was strongest. In the provinces, especially in the west where Khmer Rouge activity was greatest, expressions of worry on this score were rare. A year later, we found that attitudes had shifted significantly in Phnom Penh. People told us that when the Vietnamese first came, they had still been fearful of what they might do, but after two years in which the Vietnamese had kept as low a profile as possible and had behaved well towards the civilian population these fears had subsided. A wider awareness of the strong international backing of the Khmers Rouges had probably reinforced this shift in attitude.

The Vietnamese concentrated their efforts on the military objective of securing the country against Pol Pot's forces. The responsibility for creating a new government apparatus in the areas they had liberated fell to their allies in the Cambodian National United Front for National Salvation (KNUFNS). The establishment of the People's Republic of Kampuchea (PRK) was proclaimed on 8

January 1979, the day after Phnom Penh fell to the Vietnamese. The new government was built up slowly, from the top down and from the centre outwards, which meant that at the village level there was a period of anarchy between the overthrow of the Khmers Rouges and the establishment of local authorities integrated with the central government. In the eastern and central regions this phase lasted for only a few weeks, but in the west of the country it was not until May or June 1979 that the new administration was able to consolidate its control, and it remained fragile for some time after that.

The resources with which the new regime was built up were pitifully few. Pol Pot's terror had decimated the ranks of Cambodia's initially small class of educated and professionally skilled people, and many of those that survived took advantage of the chaos that followed the Vietnamese invasion to flee the country. And many others probably just laid low, waiting to see what the new authorities were like before they drew any attention to themselves. But it was not just a shortage of suitable people – almost everything was lacking. Even in February 1980, when there was a clearly functioning administration, it had to do without almost all the usual paraphernalia of modern bureaucracy. There were pens and paper, but they were not easy to come by. There were no telephones, and hardly any typewriters. Officially, there was a mail service, but it did little more than link Phnom Penh and Saigon. Messages for provincial authorities were given to truck drivers and carried in the glove-box. To be certain someone got your message, it was usually advisable to see them personally.

At first the new Cambodian administration was very dependent on Vietnamese assistance. Jean-Pierre Gallois, an AFP reporter, wrote in April 1979: 'There are three Vietnamese advisers for every Cambodian official, ten Vietnamese military personnel for every Cambodian soldier.'[5] When we visited in February 1980 we expected to find the Vietnamese still shouldering most of the administrative burden, but they were not. In their anxiety to keep their profile in Cambodia as low as possible (and in response to their own pressing need for trained personnel at home), the Vietnamese were handing over administrative responsibilities to Cambodians as soon as was practicable.

By early 1980, though Vietnamese advisers continued to play a key role in many government departments in Phnom Penh, it was already essentially a Khmer administration running the country. Over the course of the year most of the remaining Vietnamese advisers were withdrawn. Some of them were replaced by Soviet technical advisers, but essentially the new Khmer authorities were increasingly reliant on their own resources.

As the new government consolidated itself, it took on the familiar contours of the Communist party-state.[6] In 1981, a new constitution was proclaimed, and elections were held for a national assembly to replace the provisional People's Revolutionary Council which had previously run the country. However, it was made clear that only candidates who supported the KNUFNS programme would be allowed to stand.

At the same time, the formation of a new Cambodian Communist party, officially entitled the People's Revolutionary Party of Cambodia, was announced. Pen Sovan was named as secretary general, and most commentators at the time emphasized the extent to which the PRPK leadership was dominated by 'veterans of the struggle' – pro-Vietnamese Communists who had spent the Pol Pot years in exile in Hanoi – rather than 'domestic' Communists such as Heng Samrin. They were therefore confounded when Pen Sovan stood down, officially 'for reasons of health', in December 1981 and was replaced by Heng Samrin. It was now argued that this reflected Soviet-Vietnamese rivalry and that, far from being pro-Vietnamese, Sovan had really been pro-Soviet. We are inclined to explain this in terms of a personal quarrel among the PRPK leaders, and have not seen any evidence that would persuade us that it really had much to do with the international alignment of the government.[7]

By the end of 1982, about half a dozen PRK functionaries had defected to Thailand. From the point of view of those who were convinced that Cambodia was languishing under a harsh foreign occupation, this was a surprisingly low number, although it was pointed out that there were doubtless others who had deserted their posts but chose to conceal their past when they reached Thailand. Still, these defectors did reinforce the picture of the PRK as a puppet of the Vietnamese when interrogated by Thai intelligence. The most prominent of them was Dy Lamthol, who had been personal secretary to the foreign minister. According to Lamthol, the VCP politbureau had established a special office, designated B-68, to oversee relations with Cambodia. He had no details of its operations (other sources claimed that the person in charge in Hanoi was Le Duc Tho), but each day the foreign ministry received telegrams from Hanoi which Lamthal interpreted as 'instructions' and 'directives'. Asked if the Cambodians ever initiated policies, he replied:

'No, everything is coming from the Vietnamese.'[8]

It seems likely that Lamthol was embellishing considerably in order to please his interrogators. But there is no doubt that as soon as the PRK was established, it took steps to set up close formal ties with the Hanoi government. The day after the government was proclaimed in Phnom Penh, it was granted diplomatic recognition by Vietnam. Diplomatic relations were established by an exchange of ambassadors on 12 January 1979. In February, a Vietnamese delegation headed by Pham Van Dong visited Phnom Penh, and a 25-year treaty of 'peace, friendship and cooperation' between the two countries was signed. They agreed to 'assist each other in all fields on the basis of respect for independence, non-interference in internal affairs, and equality'. Domestically, the cooperation envisaged would cover the economy, culture and education, public health, science and technology, the training of cadres, and the exchanging of specialists. On the border issue, there were to be negotiations to draw up a treaty delineating the frontier 'on the basis of the present borderline'; the question of the maritime border was left to future negotiations.[9]

According to this friendship treaty Vietnam and Cambodia would 'assist each other to strengthen their capacity to defend their independence' against 'all schemes and acts of sabotage by the imperialist and international reactionary forces'. The foreign policy clauses stated general principles of independence, peace and non-alignment. They also envisaged the strengthening of the 'traditional friendship between the Cambodian, Laotian and Vietnamese peoples', and also of their relations with the socialist countries. Towards Thailand and the other countries of Southeast Asia, they ambiguously promised policies of 'friendship and good neighbourliness', coupled with 'cooperation' with national liberation and democratic movements.

This treaty finally cemented Hanoi's objective of a 'special relationship' between Vietnam and Cambodia, paralleling the relationship between Vietnam and Laos. It made provisions for extensive cooperation between Hanoi and Phnom Penh in economic, cultural, political and military matters, and enabled the Vietnamese to legitimately assist in the construction of a functioning government and in the rehabilitation of Cambodia's economy. Since they were invited by the Cambodian government, Hanoi could now argue, such extensive involvement did not constitute interference in Cambodia's internal affairs. However, Pol Pot still claimed to head the real government of the country, and naturally rejected the treaty signed by the Heng Samrin government. According to his radio, the Voice of Democratic Kampuchea, the treaty was nothing but an attempt to legalize Vietnam's 'annexation' of Cambodia.

The military clauses of the Vietnam-Cambodia treaty also provided legal grounds for the presence of Vietnamese troops in Cambodia. Hanoi did not admit the presence of its troops in Cambodia at first, stoutly maintaining that the overthrow of Pol Pot was the result of a popular uprising by the Cambodian people. On 6 January 1979 the Vietnamese foreign minister even went so far as to explicitly deny their presence, and described reports of Vietnamese troops invading Cambodia as being 'an odious slander'.

But after February it could be said that Vietnamese troops had entered only on the invitation of the government, to assist in its defence, and that this did not constitute interference in Cambodia's internal affairs. On 17 March the PRK foreign minister, Hun Sen, admitted the presence of Vietnamese troops in Cambodia. By insisting that the Cambodian revolution had been carried out 'mainly' by the Cambodian people, he also admitted that the Vietnamese had played some role in the overthrow of Pol Pot. The following week a Vietnamese statement also admitted the current presence of their troops in Cambodia, but made no retrospective admissions. Under the terms of the friendship treaty, Hanoi announced, Vietnam had 'agreed to have Vietnamese armed forces help the Cambodian people to defend their country' and that their presence was 'a private matter between the two countries'. Not until July 1979 did the Vietnamese acknowledge that they had played a role in actually overthrowing the Pol Pot regime.

The PRK was recognized by countries that had friendly relations with Hanoi and Moscow, but beyond that it remained internationally isolated. The Vietnamese invasion deepened differences within the Communist bloc. While Laos, Cuba, the USSR and most of the Eastern European countries supported Vietnam and promptly recognized the PRK, both Rumania and Yugoslavia condemned Vietnam and did not recognize the new Cambodian government. The Rumanian Communist Party's paper, *Scientia*, declared on 10 January 1979 that 'no reasons and arguments whatsoever can justify intervention and interference in the affairs of another state, whatever their form, especially when two socialist countries are involved.' Yugoslavia adopted the same view, adding that Vietnam's actions had done great damage to the Non-Aligned Movement. Albania chose to remain silent over the issue.

Both China and North Korea had strongly supported Pol Pot in his war with Vietnam, and now vigorously condemned the Vietnamese invasion. The ASEAN countries issued a joint statement deploring the 'armed intervention' in Cambodia on 13 January 1979, and most Asian governments followed suit, except for Burma, which maintained a neutral stance, and India, which recognized the PRK in July 1980. The West hastened to join the chorus of condemnation of Vietnam's actions.

The conflict quickly came to a head in the United Nations. On 1 January 1979 Ieng Sary called for a meeting of the UN Security Council to condemn the Vietnamese invasion, and this was promptly supported by the United States and China. Eight days later Heng Samrin proclaimed that Pol Pot's regime had 'ceased to exist' and that the PRK was the sole legitimate representative of the Cambodian people, but the UN chose to recognize the representative sent by the DK regime on 10 January. This was none other than Sihanouk, who condemned the Vietnamese intervention as 'naked aggression from one country against another without any justification', and argued that although the Vietnamese controlled Phnom Penh and the main towns, the DK government was still functioning and controlled 'part of the territory' of Cambodia. He was followed by the Chinese delegate, who called for 'effective measures' by the UN to force Vietnam to withdraw. After an acrimonious debate a majority of the Security Council supported an alternative motion calling for the withdrawal of foreign forces from Cambodia but not committing the UN to action over the issue, but this was vetoed by the USSR.

The conflict re-emerged with the opening of the UN General Assembly in September 1979, when it was voted to reaffirm recognition of the DK regime by 71 votes to 35, with 34 abstentions. Vietnam and the Soviet bloc were, of course, the principal backers of the PRK in these debates. The Western countries as a whole threw their weight behind China and the ASEAN countries in support of DK. Not one Western country voted against the Pol Pot regime, although Austria, France, Spain and the Scandinavian countries abstained from voting for it. Pol Pot was able to repeat this diplomatic triumph annually, with the 1981 vote being 77 countries for DK and 37 against, with 31 abstentions.

For their part, the Vietnamese were philosophical about the defeat of these attempts to gain recognition for the PRK. They ignored the diplomatic pressure as best they could, and pressed on with their efforts to build a functioning government in Phnom Penh. Their attitude was summed up as follows by Nguyen Co Thach (by now Vietnam's foreign affairs minister) in a mid-1981 interview: ' . . . we were outside the UN for 33 years, and still we gained our independence. So many big events in this world have happened outside the UN, sometimes without the approval of the UN. There is a possibility Pol Pot will (win the seating question) again, just as the Guomindang were seated there for a long time when we were struggling for the People's Republic of China. Now China insists on keeping Pol Pot in the UN. It is very, very ridiculous.'[10]

The refusal to recognize the PRK might have been ridiculous, from Thach's point of view, but it was certainly not insignificant. It showed the extent to which the Vietnam-Khmer Rouge conflict had become a battleground for the great powers, and this was to have important consequences for the Khmer people. It encouraged Pol Pot and his colleagues in efforts to rebuild their smashed military machine, and it encouraged the activities of other resistance groups along the Thai-Cambodian border. It also bedevilled the attempts of international relief agencies to deal with the food and refugee crisis in Cambodia after the Vietnamese invasion.

The Vietnamese and the PRK authorities faced economic problems of staggering dimensions in Cambodia in 1979. Opponents of the Vietnamese blamed the invasion for the crisis, and some alleged that the Vietnamese were deliberately destroying food supplies to starve the Khmers into submission. The chaos that followed the collapse of the Khmer Rouge regime undoubtedly contributed to the crisis, but basically its roots went back much further than that. Cambodia was already a shattered country when the Vietnamese invaded.

In the first place, the war of 1970–75 had caused appalling devastation. Of a population of about seven million, it is believed that some six hundred thousand were killed and a million injured. More than half the population had become refugees by 1975, and the rice harvest had fallen to only a quarter of the pre-war level. Then, when the Khmers Rouges took over, they spurned outside aid and drove millions of people out into the ruined countryside to support themselves. The few outsiders allowed in found (in the words of Kaj Bjork, the Swedish ambassador to Peking, who visited Cambodia in 1976 and 1978) 'a nation under tight military control' with the entire population working 'like a people at war'. By these methods the Khmer Rouge leaders had succeeded in boosting food production to about two-thirds of the pre-war level by 1977–8, but at a terrible cost.

In the wake of the Vietnamese invasion the bonds of coercion that had held the Khmer Rouge economic system together were broken. No longer compelled to stay where they were, millions of people who had been relocated took to the road once more, returning to their old homes, or searching for family members from whom they had been separated under Pol Pot. Much of the year's main harvest stood abandoned in the fields, and was consumed by pests or trampled by wild animals and abandoned water buffaloes. Rather than work on the harvest, in many areas villagers broke into Khmer Rouge collective storehouses and feasted – often consuming seed rice as well as milled rice. In many villages livestock were also recklessly killed and eaten. Thus, for a few weeks after the invasion, many ate well, even very well – but then, as stockpiles of food were exhausted, the consequences of widespread failure to gather the year's main rice harvest began to bite home.

By February 1979 the PRK authorities warned that 'the quantity of rice available for the people is negligible.' By July they were warning of an impending famine in Cambodia and calling for urgent international aid. American officials attacked this statement as 'alarmist', but UN and Red Cross officials went to investigate the situation, and were appalled by what they found. They remarked that Pol Pot's attempt to 'turn the clock back' had turned a once-fertile land into a 'desert' and warned that two and a half million people could starve to death in the next few months unless something was done quickly. In September the British journalist John Pilger took a television crew to Cambodia to make a documentary on the state of the country. On his return he wrote: 'During twenty years as a journalist, most of them spent in transit at wars and places of contrived upheaval, I have not seen anything to compare with what I saw in Cambodia.'[11] He was accused of being sensationalist and simplistic, but the images he presented to television audiences of starvation, suffering and death did much to awaken the Western public to the scale of the Cambodian tragedy.

As Western aid workers began to go into the country they confirmed the substance of the picture painted by Pilger. Hunger and malnutrition were widespread; much of the population was anaemic and malarial, while intestinal diseases (gastro-enteritis and dysentery), parasites (such as hookworm) and tuberculosis were endemic; there had been outbreaks of anthrax and bubonic plague; and medical facilities were for all practical purposes non-existent (the few there had been having been smashed by the Khmers Rouges before the Vietnamese takeover).

Still more ominous, very little of the next season's crop had been planted. Vast numbers of people were still roaming the countryside rather than settling down to productive activity, and there were few tools and livestock. Most serious of all was the lack of seed rice. As a consequence, in the 1979 rainy season barely 40 per cent of the fields in Cambodia were under any cultivation at all, while in the fertile lower Mekong provinces (devastated in turn by the purges of 1978 and fighting in 1978–9), the figure was under 10 per cent. Even where cultivation had been established, it had been done in a haphazard fashion, and the yields promised to be low. Surveying these facts, some serious observers predicted that the extinction of the Khmer nation was a real possibility. It was painfully obvious that salvaging the situation was beyond the meagre resources of the fledgling PRK administration. International assistance was vital.

The Politics of Aid

Only Vietnam and the Soviet bloc responded immediately to the appeals of the PRK government over the food situation in Cambodia. By 1 November 1979 the Soviet Union had sent 159,000 tonnes of food to Cambodia. Vietnam, despite its own serious economic problems, had sent another 120,000 tonnes, and the remaining Soviet bloc countries had sent 2,000 tonnes. By December, about 1,500 tonnes of food from Soviet-bloc countries was being unloaded daily at Kompong Som port; in addition, medical supplies were being delivered by air, and Soviet-bloc technicians were flown in to help rehabilitate the country's shattered transport system. Soviet bloc aid played a key role in opening the docks at Kompong Som and on the Mekong River at Phnom Penh, and in restoring the road and rail links between Phnom Penh and Battambang in the west.

There were no political difficulties in Soviet aid for the latest recruit to the Soviet bloc, but it was very different for the USA. The American government was initially opposed to any Western effort to aid Cambodia at all. Immediately after the overthrow of the Pol Pot regime, the US had launched a campaign to persuade the Western countries to 'punish' Vietnam by cutting off aid. In this context, a major aid project to Cambodia amounted to breaking the siege. Officials in Washington at first refused to send any aid to Phnom Penh, and tried to discount reports from Thailand that food shortages in Cambodia were reaching crisis proportions.

As the gravity of the situation became increasingly apparent, it also became clear that an international aid effort to Phnom Penh would be mounted – without US participation, if necessary. This posed a serious dilemma for Washington: if it tried to block aid to a famine-stricken country, this could do grave damage to America's humanitarian image; but if it agreed to aid Cambodia, how could it prevent this consolidating and legitimizing the PRK government? Politically, America no longer controlled the UN and the international aid agencies, but the USA was the largest donor to these agencies, so the American government still carried a good deal of clout.

In June 1979 Washington agreed to send aid to Cambodia, but proposed sending it only to operations on the Thai border. Although much aid channelled through the border would inevitably end up in the hands of the Khmer Rouge forces, American officials cited a law forbidding American aid to Cambodia, which had originally been passed as a measure of disapproval of the Pol Pot regime, as a legal barrier to sending aid to the Heng Samrin government. Then it was argued that the requirements of 'neutrality' in the Cambodian conflict made aid to the one or two per cent of the population under Khmer Rouge control an essential precondition for giving aid to the rest. One US official explained: 'The only way we can help in Cambodia is by giving aid for both sides. If we can't find a way to help the people on Pol Pot's side it's unlikely that we'll be in a position to do anything even indirectly for those under Heng Samrin.'[12]

On 2 July 1979 US Secretary of State Cyrus Vance called for direct famine relief for Cambodia – the first senior American official to do so publicly. This reversal of the American stance opened the way for Western aid to Cambodia, but President Carter let three months elapse before he announced that America itself would make any contribution to this effort. Aid shipments from OXFAM, a British agency not dependent on the US government, began in August. But prior to the American commitment in October, shipments of Western aid to Phnom Penh were paltry compared to the flow of Soviet-bloc aid. By 12 October, when an OXFAM shipment of 1,500 tonnes arrived, Western aid to the stricken country totalled only 200 tonnes.

The basic reason for this was that the Red Cross and UNICEF, the main international aid agencies, found themselves caught in the political crossfire between Washington and Phnom Penh, and their negotiations with the PRK government got bogged down as a consequence. While Washington was withholding its funds and insisting that aid to both sides was essential, the Heng Samrin government was bitterly opposed to international humanitarian aid being channelled to Pol Pot's forces and insisted that all aid be sent to Phnom Penh.

But beggars cannot be choosers and in September 1979 the PRK needed Western aid more than it needed to deny supplies to the Khmers Rouges. Accordingly, on 26 September, Phnom Penh granted approval to the Red Cross and UNICEF for large-scale relief operations in Cambodia, even though they were still sending aid to the Thai border areas. It did not insist on stopping border aid operations, although it made it clear that it disapproved most strongly of them. Proposals to aid both sides were, said Phnom Penh Radio on 27 September: ' . . . meant to legalize aid to remnants of the Pol Pot clique to prolong the opposition to the Cambodian people and to meddle in Cambodia's internal affairs. All aid to the Cambodian people must be sent to the . . . Revolutionary Council in Phnom Penh – the only authentic and legal representatives of the Cambodian people – and all attempts at aiding the Pol Pot clique would be illegal and constitute a violation of Cambodia's sovereignty.' By emphasizing that it still regarded aid operations on the Thai border as an illegal violation of Cambodian sovereignty, the PRK government was, by implication, serving notice that it claimed the legal right to stop those operations at any time it chose.

Still, the Americans had won the tug-of-war. It was clear that, at least for the time being, the aid would flow to the insurgents, as well as to the PRK-controlled areas. On 24 October 1979, just five days after Prime Minister Kriangsak had announced Thailand's 'open door' policy towards refugees from Cambodia, President Carter announced a $69 million aid programme to Cambodia to prevent a 'tragedy of almost genocidal proportions'. He also appealed for other countries to give aid, and for a massive private charity effort as well. At a conference at the UN headquarters in New York on 5 November, aid totalling $20 million was pledged. This was to go to famine relief inside Cambodia, and also to refugees in Thai camps, and on the Thai border – as America had wanted.

From that point on, Western aid began to flow into Cambodia in increasing quantities, and by the start of December it was arriving at the rate of 1,000 tonnes a day. In fact, due to the still broken-down state of their transport system, the Cambodians were unable to distribute all the aid that now arrived. In early December a UNICEF spokesman said that food was being distributed adequately in Phnom Penh, but that only 10 per cent of that intended for the rural population was reaching its destination. On 17 December PRK foreign minister, Hun Sen, said that the bulk of Western aid was being stockpiled in warehouses, and pointed out that until a recent delivery of 600 lorries from the Soviet bloc countries, the government had only 40 trucks to shift all the aid that was delivered. As the warehouses in Kompong Som and Phnom Penh were largely filled within a month, deliveries of Western aid were cut from 30,000 tonnes a month to a more manageable level of 13,000 tonnes a month at the end of December.

Even before this the Americans had repeatedly attacked the PRK over aid distribution. In October, before America itself had agreed to give one cent in aid, the US government condemned the PRK authorities, the Vietnamese and the Soviets for failing to bring 'any discernible influence to bear to alleviate the situation'. Despite statements to the contrary by the Red Cross and UNICEF, the Americans insisted that the PRK was deliberately blocking the aid effort. It was claimed that the Vietnamese were withholding food from the population in order to starve them into submission (this was true enough with regard to the Khmer Rouge enclaves on the Thai border, but that was hardly typical). When the USA finally committed itself, after three months of foot-dragging, a government spokesman explained: 'The delaying factor all the way through has been whether we could have any assurance the food would go to where it was intended to go.' No comparable concern was shown over aid distributed on the Thai border, where misappropriations were known to be massive.

Reports that the Vietnamese were stealing aid intended for starving Khmers continued throughout November and December. 'Only a trickle of the international aid arriving in Phnom Penh reaches the Khmer people,' alleged a group of conservative French parliamentarians after a four-day visit to Phnom Penh in late November. 'There is a deliberate attempt to famish the population on Vietnam's part. The food supplies from Western countries are used as strategic arms to control the population . . . Cambodia is still a concentration camp.'

After three US senators returned from a visit to Phnom Penh, President Carter accused the PRK of 'genocide'. A month later, he was said to be 'outraged' by the latest CIA report on the situation inside Cambodia. It was revealed to the press that this 'secret' document reported that while large amounts of desperately needed supplies were reaching Cambodia, they were being diverted to the Vietnamese and PRK military. In addition, it reported that the

Vietnamese were burning crops and laying mines in paddy-fields to subdue the Cambodian population and 'verified' earlier claims that the Vietnamese were using chemical warfare against the civilian population as well as Pol Pot's forces. An anguished President Carter was reported to have cried, 'Is there no pity?' Leader-writers and editorialists took their cue. The resultant wave of self-righteous denunciations of Vietnam and Phnom Penh probably reached its zenith in the comment of Emmett Tyrell, Jr in the *Washington Post* on 24 December 1979: 'The lesson of Cambodia is the lesson of the Nazi concentration camps and the Gulag. Some people are immune to Western decency.'

Since the CIA report was 'secret', the evidence for all of this was never revealed. That aid officials and journalists in Cambodia denied these reports was ignored by the zealous champions of 'Western decency'. Jim Laurie, the Hong Kong Bureau Chief of ABC News, wrote after six weeks in Cambodia: 'It is commonly acknowledged that Cambodia's food distribution is slow and inefficient. But no competent observer, aid official or journalist who has visited Cambodia for longer than a week has concluded that the bottlenecks are the result of conscious Vietnamese or Cambodian policy. Instead, they say the delays are caused by a complex bureaucracy, inexperienced and inefficient administrators, lack of transport, and primitive communications.'[13] Investigating aid officials concluded that some aid was pilfered, but that it amounted to less than one per cent, much less than the amount lost to rats. In the end, even the US ambassador to Thailand admitted that there was no evidence that the Vietnamese or the Phnom Penh authorities were blocking the distribution of aid.

In due course the truth about these allegations filtered out. In January 1980 John Gittings reported in the British *Guardian*: 'Last November, State Department sources revealed their intention of mounting an international propaganda offensive to spread atrocity stories about Vietnamese behaviour in Cambodia. Within days, presumably on White House instructions, US journalists in Bangkok and Singapore were shown the appropriate "refugee stories" and Dr Brzezinski himself verbally briefed a distinguished foreign correspondent Washington columnist over lunch on the contents of "the latest CIA report".' Later in that year, John Pilger asked a diplomat if he had seen the CIA report that had so moved President Carter. 'Yes,' the diplomat responded, 'the State Department told us to ignore it, that it was only for the media.'[14] But the allegations had by this stage done their damage, and the myth persisted – America had managed to cast itself as the saviour of Cambodia whose humanitarian mission was being frustrated by the cruel Communists. The fact that the bulk of aid to Cambodia in 1979 had come from the Communist bloc, while America was procrastinating, was largely unknown in the West.

When we visited Cambodia early in 1980 we found the country in much better shape than we had expected. Supplies were obviously short, but there was rice, fish and fruit in local markets. Inadequate nutrition was widespread, but we saw no signs of outright starvation in the areas we visited. Children with bloated stomachs could still be seen, but there were none of the pitiful 'walking skeletons' that had attracted so much media attention a few months earlier. Many people told us that they had gone hungry in the second half of 1979, and that there had been some deaths from starvation. Conditions had been worst in the western provinces, where military insecurity was the greatest. For a few crucial months, large numbers of people had survived mainly by foraging, and it was thus the natural richness of the countryside rather than international aid that had saved them. Pressure on food supplies inside Cambodia had also been eased by the departure of about a million people from the worst areas to the Thai border.

While these conditions were terrible, there is little reason to doubt that they were better than under Pol Pot's regime. Hence we cannot agree with the estimate of the CIA, according to which: 'A conservative estimate is that for every Cambodian born during July-December 1979, 10 died. All told the first year of the Heng Samrin rule had brought an additional drop of 700,000 in the population, to an estimated 5.2 million.'[15] The CIA's 'conservative estimate' is based on the assumption that the death rate under the Heng Samrin government equalled that in the worst period of Pol Pot's rule, and is coupled in this statement in a misleading fashion with the consequences of an assumed low birth rate. Even on the CIA's own figures, the 'excess' mortality in 1979 was 130,000, rather than the 700,000 the unwary reader might assume. Our own estimate is that the number of 'excess' deaths due to food shortages in 1979 would have been no more than 36,000 – a grim figure, but far below that offered by the CIA.[16] And surely the key point, studiously ignored by the CIA study, is that the huge massacres perpetrated by the Pol Pot regime had ended.

Conditions had improved rapidly from November 1979, partly because international relief began to reach the country. But the government, as we have seen, still lacked the means of distributing aid on a large scale in the countryside, and had concentrated on feeding administrators and urban workers. By early 1980 distribution points had been established on the main highways, but it was clear that only a limited amount of aid had reached the rural population, and none at all in the more remote areas. Much of what had been distributed was Soviet-produced corn, which, the peasants complained, they did not know how to cook. The situation had improved mainly because the year's main rice crop was gathered in November-December. But it was a meagre harvest – estimated at only 300,000 tonnes, little more than a tenth of pre-war harvests – and could provide only temporary relief from famine conditions. Aid officials estimated thah the country's food supply would begin to run out in April; by July only 15 per cent of villages would have any locally grown rice left. Without outside aid, 1980 could turn out to be even worse than 1979.

In order to break out of the vicious circle of famine conditions and poor harvests into which Cambodia appeared to be locked at this point, Phnom Penh and the aid agencies decided to take a major gamble. Though large quantities of food aid would still be needed, especially to see the population through the second half of the year, they would take advantage of the breathing space provided by the harvest to bring in seed rice and agricultural implements. Over the rest of the dry season they also made major efforts to improve the efficiency of transport and distribution of aid. Government officials said that they hoped Cambodia would become self-supporting again in two years. By December 1980 more than 300,000 tonnes of food rice and 57,000 tonnes of seed rice had been delivered to Cambodia, either across the 'land bridge' on the Thai border or via Phnom Penh.

Some outside observers maintained that aid distribution was still inadequate, that supplies were being stolen by the Vietnamese and that hardly any of the seed rice had been planted, and they predicted renewed famine. Those who visited the country, however, told a different story. In September 1980, Jon Swain reported: 'Revisiting Cambodia today is like coming back into an old sickroom and finding it filled with fresh air . . . . Last January I saw suffering and hunger on every face . . . . The landscape, too, was devastated. I saw nothing but abandoned rice-fields and shattered towns and villages . . . . Today the land has become fat . . . . In parts of Kompong Cham province . . . the rice is growing as far as the eye can see. The peasants there have already harvested an early rice-crop planted in May. The big one is due in December and most people seem to be faring much better than expected.'[17]

This assessment was more accurate than those of the outside observers. The 1980 harvest turned out to be over 700,000 tonnes, more than twice that of the previous year, and enough to feed the nation until June 1981 without any outside assistance. In November 1980 a UN Food and Agriculture Organization mission to Cambodia concluded that the country had made a major breakthrough, but that the gains were still precarious. The area under cultivation was still only half that of the pre-war period. Cambodia was still well short of being self-supporting, and it could easily slip back into the cycle of famine and poor harvests from which it had emerged.

Between October 1979 and the end of 1981, non-Communist donors provided about $860 million to the Cambodian relief efforts coordinated by the UN. This went to the refugee camps and the Thai border as well as Phnom Penh. Soviet-bloc countries refused to participate in this operation, and sent their aid direct to Phnom Penh. The largest donors were the USSR, which sent aid valued at $315 million, and Vietnam, whose non-military aid was valued at $100 million. Most of this aid was delivered in 1980, and the flow of aid from both Communist and non-Communist sources fell off sharply when it became clear that the crisis situation had passed. It was hoped that by 1982–3 Cambodia would become self-sufficient in food once again, and at this point the UN operation was planned to end.

Unfortunately, Cambodia's advance in 1980 was not sustained the following year. In 1981 several regions suffered from a severe drought, and then in August heavy flooding destroyed much of the crop around the Mekong River. The aid agencies were also late with deliveries of seed, and losses of aid goods due to theft and pilferage were reported to have risen sharply. The result was that, while there was no danger of widespread starvation, the country was still dependent on relief aid during the 1982 rainy season. But 1982 saw good rains and a further doubling of production, with the harvest rising to 1.48 million tons of paddy.

In March 1983 Bob Sector of the *Los Angeles Times* reported: 'Today, after four years of comparative calm, a bounty of sorts has returned to some of Cambodia's fields. Granaries in some areas, such as Battambang province . . . are full of unthreshed rice.'[18] One visitor to western Cambodia in early 1983 told us of a significant reversal of the pattern of previous years. Traders were buying rice in local markets to sell at the Thai border. Nevertheless, as

Sector reported, important areas of the country were still food-deficient. The UN FAO estimated that in 1983 a million Khmers were still in such a situation, and projected a shortfall of between 150–300,000 tonnes for 1984.

The aid agencies came under some criticism in 1980 for becoming involved in agricultural rehabilitation programmes in Cambodia, as well as simply providing emergency relief. This, it was argued, was 'political' rather than 'humanitarian' aid, since by helping put the national economy back on its feet it inevitably helped the PRK government consolidate its control. By the same token, however, the aid channelled through the Thai border strengthened the Khmer Rouge and Khmer Serei insurgents operating in that area. Humanitarian considerations and politics cannot be easily separated.

But as the food crisis inside the country eased, the political dimension of the aid operation came increasingly to the fore. By 1982 Western donors were pressing the UN to cut off operations inside Cambodia altogether, and to channel all aid through the Thai border. United Nations aid officials were accused of making 'doomsday predictions', while the UN secretary-general, Javier Perez de Cuellar, responded that his mandate was to help 'the Cambodian people as a whole' and implied that the attitude of the donor countries was making this impossible. Of the $87 million needed for its Cambodian operations in 1982, the UN was able to raise only $49 million. Furthermore, all the new donations, except for that of Finland ($230,000), were earmarked for the Thai border rather than the interior of Cambodia. In short, the donors were insisting that UN aid benefit the anti-Vietnamese insurgents rather than the PRK.

Understandably, the Soviet bloc continued to refuse to participate in the UN project and to send all its aid direct to Phnom Penh. In June 1982 Moscow agreed to provide the PRK with a further $60–65 million worth of assistance, mainly road-building equipment, fertilizer, and other inputs to boost agricultural production. East Germany was also reported to have given Phnom Penh a grant of $10 million and a loan of $10 million.

In 1975 the Democratic Kampuchea leaders had sought salvation for their war-shattered country in an economic strategy of 'self-reliance'. In 1979 the leaders of the People's Republic of Kampuchea pursued a diametrically opposite strategy – they appealed for large-scale international aid. The aid effort to Cambodia was, inevitably, plagued by political problems at every step, but by 1982 the situation seemed to have stabilized. With international assistance, a functioning economy had been re-created, and the control of the PRK over most of the country had become secure. It was essentially a Khmer administration, but it was protected by Vietnamese arms and, increasingly, supported by only Soviet bloc aid. It is not surprising that it was closely aligned with Vietnam and the USSR. The West concentrated its energies increasingly on building up the Khmer Rouge and Khmer Serei guerrillas seeking to overthrow the PRK. The seeds of a new war were thus being sown, this time on the Thai-Cambodian border rather than the Vietnam-Cambodian border.

'Standing Shoulder to Shoulder'

The Lao People's Democratic Republic was the second government to recognize the Heng Samrin regime.[19] In an attempt to legitimize this, on 30 January 1979 *Sieng Pasason* confirmed for the first time earlier reports of clashes along the Lao-Cambodian border. Despite this it appears that the Lao had little appreciation of the magnitude of the catastrophe in Cambodia under Pol Pot. The burden of Vientiane's explanation of Pol Pot's aggressive policies followed Hanoi's – he was 'following another country's lead' in attacking his neighbours: the reference was obviously to China. But the flood of reports on the brutality of Pol Pot's rule, followed by China's invasion of Vietnam, served to strengthen Vientiane's support for Hanoi's actions.

Prince Souphannavong headed a LPDR delegation to Phnom Penh in March 1979 and signed a five-year agreement with the Heng Samrin government providing for economic, cultural and technical cooperation between the two states. Though there was no military clause in the formal agreement, the presence of the military commander for southern Laos in the delegation implied the possibility of informal military cooperation. Reports from Bangkok claimed that the Lao were joining with the Vietnamese in military campaigns against Pol Pot's forces in northern Cambodia. A joint communiqué of the three governments welcomed the overthrow of the 'dictatorial and fascist regime of the Pol Pot-Ieng Sary clique' and declared: ' . . . it is entirely legitimate for the peoples of Cambodia, Laos and Vietnam to build their solidarity by standing shoulder to shoulder and giving one another mutual support and

assistance in defending their countries against aggression and interference by the imperialists and Peking reactionaries.' Thus the
three Indochinese countries had come together into a politico-
military bloc under Vietnamese leadership to resist Chinese pressure. Rather predictably, Pol Pot's radio denounced the Lao
government as a 'puppet' of the Vietnamese the day after the LPDR
delegation left Phnom Penh.

China could hardly be expected to overlook the stance Vientiane
had taken. From January 1979 Peking began to criticize Laos
openly, accusing it of being a client-state of Hanoi's. 'Vietnam,'
announced the *People's Daily* 'has placed Laos under tight control
with its 50,000 troops and thousands of advisers.' But it was the
Chinese invasion of Vietnam in February that swung the remaining
neutralists in Vientiane into the pro-Vietnamese camp. When the
strike into Vietnam failed, Chinese troops were reported massing
on the Sino-Lao border, and it looked as if they were preparing for a
thrust through northern Laos. This possibility even drew the former
neutralist prime minister, Souvanna Phouma, into the fray with a
public expression of fear that the Chinese might invade Laos in
order to strike into Vietnam via Dien Bien Phu.

The Chinese military build-up on the Lao border was first
reported in *Pravda* on 2 March, then by the Vietnamese on 4
March, and the Lao on 6 March. The Chinese seized on this
sequence with glee, as proving that Laos was indeed a puppet of
Moscow. Western intelligence sources said that there was no
Chinese build-up on the Lao border beyond that connected with the
invasion of Vietnam. Whether the Soviet report was true, or a piece
of 'disinformation' published to panic the Lao into the Vietnamese
camp is impossible to tell (at least for those like us who regard
unverifiable intelligence reports from both Moscow and Washington as untrustworthy). Certainly, the government in Vientiane was
in no immediate position to verify or disprove it, and with full-scale
war in northern Vietnam and in Cambodia it was an alarmingly
plausible scenario.

But it did not happen, and further reflection reveals that the
Chinese had good reason to desist. The Chinese army had got into
trouble in northern Vietnam, and it was not obvious that it would
necessarily make the situation any better by embroiling itself in a
wider war. Western opinion had been willing to view China's attack
on Vietnam indulgently, given Vietnam's preceding attack on
Cambodia. But an invasion of Laos, which had clearly done little to
provoke the Chinese, would surely have been greeted differently.

Furthermore, it would do irreparable damage to China's relations with the ASEAN countries. The Thais have even less interest in seeing Chinese soldiers staring at them across the Mekong than they do in seeing Vietnamese soldiers on their border.

Unease in Vientiane over the influence of the Chinese in northern Laos had been evident since early 1978. The mountainous terrain of the country meant that northern provinces such as Phong Saly formed part of a natural economic region with southern China, with relatively few linkages with the Vientiane lowlands. For eighteen years the Chinese had been aiding the integration of these areas into the Lao national economy by using PLA troops to construct an extensive road network through the mountains of northern Laos. By 1978, this network ran from the provincial city of Mong La in China's Yunnan province to Dien Bien Phu, near the Lao-Vietnam border, and almost to Luang Prebang in the centre of northern Laos. In the changing political circumstances of the time, this could only take on an increasingly sinister aspect. This road network would give the Chinese military tremendous mobility, which is one of the main reasons why the Vietnamese were so concerned about the political allegiance and military security of their neighbour.

The LPDR asked most of the 18,000 Chinese troops in Laos to leave in 1978, after a major section of the road was completed, and the day after it received reports of Chinese war preparations on the border, Vientiane then asked the rest to leave 'for their own security'. A week later, the LPDR charged that the Chinese troops had been making military preparations by digging trenches, and accused China of making armed incursions into Lao territory, and of supporting anti-government rebels.

By mid-1979 the Chinese embassy in Vientiane had to divest itself of military personnel and limit its staff to twelve – that is to say, it was placed on a par with the US mission in Laos. From this time onwards the propaganda war between Laos and China has become increasingly maledictory and spiced with fewer hints of former good times. Yet the rhetoric has not been marked by the bitter invective that passes between the Vietnamese and the Chinese. The quarrel with China was not of Laos' making, and Chinese pressure on Laos is directed at the Vietnamese-dominated 'Indochina bloc' rather than at Laos as such.

Even so, Sino-Lao relations continued to deteriorate. Serious armed clashes were reported on the Sino-Lao border in 1981, and on 16 September, Peking Radio proclaimed that Vietnam had colonized Laos and turned it into a base for its anti-China operations, but that the Lao people were resisting vigorously: 'At present the flames of anti-Vietnam guerrilla warfare of the Lao people are blazing up, and they are attacking the aggressors everywhere. Laos, like Cambodia, has become a heavy burden for the Vietnamese aggressors. This burden will certainly drag them to defeat in the end.' In fact the Chinese-backed insurgency in Laos appears to be ineffective, but China's stance has served to strengthen the Lao commitment to the Soviet-Vietnam camp. In 1982 officials in Vientiane reiterated the Vietnamese line that China was the 'direct and most dangerous' enemy of the Indochinese countries, and a menace to peace in Southeast Asia.

An 'un-Lao' Laos

The Lao and Thai governments managed to keep their bilateral affairs immune from the wider regional power struggle for some eighteen months after the Vietnamese invasion of Cambodia. This followed Thai Prime Minister Kriangsak's policy of trying to maintain some Thai influence in Vientiane to counterbalance that of Vietnam. However, the solidification of an Indochinese bloc of states over 1979, and then the fall of Kriangsak in February 1980, made it increasingly difficult for either state to isolate bilateral issues from regional ones. Thus a mid-June 1980 shooting incident on the Mekong border, of the sort that had been ignored under Kriangsak, was linked to a Vietnamese incursion across the Cambodian border into Thailand on 23 June, and led the Thais to close their border with Laos. Hence Bangkok sought to reassert its traditional power relationship with Vientiane. As one of the main Thai dailies put it, the purpose of the closure was 'to make Laos realize that it is more dependent on Thailand than on Vietnam. Although it is under the political domination of Vietnam, it cannot obtain economic relief from that country'.

But in contrast with the past the Lao were now unresponsive to Thai whip-cracking. 'The Thais have always found the Lao willing to compromise, but in the past few weeks they have found their stand to be very un-Lao,' commented one ASEAN diplomat at the time. 'They say that they have felt that it was no longer Lao but Vietnamese who were coming to talk to them.' In many ways this statement summed up Thai reluctance to recognize the changing power relationship in the region, and the fact that Laos, whatever its problems, is becoming relatively stronger. Laos has now broken the Thai monopoly over its access to the outside world: part of the country is served by a Vietnamese-built oil pipeline; and Route 9 linking the city of Savannakhet to the Vietnamese port of Danang can apparently be used almost all year round because of sixty-eight bridges built by Sweden. 'Thailand closes the border anytime it wants,' Soulivong Phatsihideth, general secretary of the Lao foreign ministry complained. 'The significance of this road is our independence. When Route 9 is finished . . . the Thai can close the border or open it whenever they like.' To the Thai this will make the Lao even more 'un-Lao'.

The importance of breaking the Thai stranglehold on Laos was acknowledged by the three Indochinese states at a meeting of foreign ministers in February 1981. Lao road and rail access to the sea through Vietnam and Cambodia was set as a top priority for the three states. The existence of a friendly and cooperative government in Phnom Penh has given the Lao a retrospective and uncontemplated stake in the overthrow of the Pol Pot regime, as the more access routes it has to the sea the greater its independence. Close ties between Phnom Penh and Vientiane give them jointly greater leverage with their powerful neighbours. Under Pol Pot this was impossible. But the new regime in Cambodia offers greater scope for cooperation under the umbrella of an Indochinese military alliance.

Another result of the July 1980 border closure was the veiled threat by both Vientiane and Hanoi to revive their support for insurgency in Thailand. In the midst of the blockade a shadowy group called the Democratic Alliance of Thailand broadcast the Lao version of the incident over Vientiane Radio, adding that the incident proved 'that Thailand is not acting of its own free will and is already subject to the command of the Peking regime'. Reporting the existence of this group, Hanoi Radio posed the question of what the Thai reaction would be if 'someone organizes overseas Thais, including subversive forces, close to the Thai border or even backs their acts of sabotage inside Thailand'. It would provide some people in Bangkok with food for thought if Laos in the future was able not only to ignore any Thai blockade but also support Thai insurgents. This would be a truly significant readjustment of the traditional power relationship between the two countries.

In 1981 the Soviet Union decided to establish a direct relationship with Vientiane, whereas previously it had been content with working via Hanoi. The Soviets promised substantial economic and technical assistance for the Lao five-year plan (1981–5), and Brezhnev himself awarded Prime Minister Kaysone the Order of Lenin. Some commentators saw this as a sign of Soviet-Vietnamese rivalry for influence in Indochina. At the congress of the LPRP in April 1982, Kaysone explained Vientiane's relations with Moscow and Hanoi in these terms: 'In foreign policy, we advocate relying decidedly on the Soviet Union and the other fraternal countries, strengthening the special militant alliance of our people with the Vietnamese and Cambodian peoples.' Lao officials explained to Nayan Chanda that this meant 'a regional security alliance with Vietnam within the framework of strategic reliance on Moscow for material support.'[20] Chanda saw this as a Lao attempt to balance between rival Soviet and Vietnamese ambitions on Laos, but to us it looks more like a practical division of labour – Moscow is hardly in a position to send troops to Laos, while Vietnam is hardly best placed to advise the Lao on economic planning and technological matters.

In view of America's policies towards Hanoi and Phnom Penh, it has pursued a surprisingly lenient policy towards Vientiane. Washington has continued to recognize the LPDR, although the relationship has been plagued by the same problems about property and MIA's that were given as grounds for not opening relations with Hanoi. While until 1981 the USA gave no aid to Laos, it did not go out of its way to obstruct important loans from the Asian Development ment Bank and the International Monetary Fund - bodies on which American opinion carries a great deal of weight. In October 1981, US Assistant Secretary of State for Asia and the Pacific John Holdridge declared: 'Laos does retain at least some degree of autonomy and many officials there appear to welcome closer relations with the West . . . . We maintain our embassy in Vientiane to contribute to this effort and to offer some small counterbalance to the Soviet-Vietnamese influence.' Then, in December, the Reagan government made a donation of medical supplies to Laos, and promised more in the future. Of course, the Americans could make similar statements about both Phnom Penh and Hanoi any time they chose to, but it is unlikely that throwing a few sops to Vientiane in this fashion will succeed in splitting Laos off from Vietnam and Cambodia; presumably the basic US approach is to keep a foothold in Indochina via Vientiane while venting its displeasure against Hanoi and Phnom Penh.

Nevertheless, this has led Lao officials to make a distinction between Chinese and American policies, whereas the Vietnamese continue to emphasize their collusion. In an interview in February 1982, the Lao minister for information, Sisana Sisane, said that American and Chinese policies toward Indochina were 'not identical'. He argued that the USA was fearful lest its interests be jeopardized by the expansion of Chinese influence in Southeast Asia, and that the Americans favoured a 'dialogue' between Indochina and ASEAN over Cambodia.[21] However, America failed to confirm Sisana's optimistic reading of the situation.

The overall pattern of Lao foreign policy as it emerged from the Indochina crisis of the late 1970s was authoritatively summed up in Kaysone's political report to the 3rd National Congress of the Lao People's Revolutionary Party in April 1982. Its 'cornerstone' was Laos's 'special solidarity with Vietnam and Cambodia', buttressed by 'solidarity and all-round cooperation with the great Soviet Union and the other socialist countries'. He declared that the ruling circles in Peking had made themselves the 'direct and dangerous enemies of our people'. Nevertheless, he went on, 'we persevere in our efforts and will do all we can to maintain and consolidate the neighbourly friendship between our people and the Chinese people while resolutely opposing the hostile policy of the reactionary clique in the Peking ruling circles. In the interests of peace in Southeast Asia, and the world, we are ready to normalize our relations with the People's Republic of China.' He also said that Laos was 'eager' for improved relations with the USA, and called for the strengthening of dialogue and peaceful coexistence between the Indochinese and ASEAN countries, and the further development of economic and cultural ties with Thailand.

The 'Indochina Federation' revisited

Vietnam had thus succeeded in its basic strategy for resisting Chinese pressure. It had created a viable ally in Cambodia and consolidated its close relationship with Laos. This regional alliance was underpinned by substantial material support from the USSR, and this Soviet commitment placed a further constraint on Chinese actions against the Indochinese states.

The emergence of an Indochina political bloc was driven home to the rest of the world in February 1980 when the foreign ministers of Vietnam, Laos and Cambodia met in Saigon. While the foreign policies of the LPDR and the PRK had been closely aligned with those of the SRV, and the governments had been bound together by 'treaties of friendship', they now issued a joint communiqué stressing 'the identity of their views on international problems'. There was, they declared, no room in Cambodia for Pol Pot's group or for 'other reactionaries including Sihanouk' who were working to subvert the PRK government. China was described as the most dangerous enemy of the Indochinese people, and while China, the USA and 'other reactionary forces' maintained their hostility towards the Indochinese states, the presence of Vietnamese troops in Laos and Cambodia was 'very necessary' for their defence. This uncompromising statement made it clear that the three countries were digging in for a long struggle with China, and that they would negotiate with the ASEAN states and other countries over the Cambodia issue only as a bloc, not separately.

It was immediately charged by hostile critics that the formation of an Indochina bloc amounted to the complete subjugation of Laos and Cambodia by Vietnam. Many saw it as a vindication of Pol Pot's allegations of Vietnamese designs for an 'Indochina Federation'. When an article in a Vietnamese Communist Party journal in early 1982 referred to the relationship between the Indochinese states as a 'strategic alliance', a Chinese commentator responded: 'During the past three years, the Vietnamese authorities have denied charges by others that Vietnam is pursuing an "Indochina Federation" strategy. But now the Vietnamese authorities have admitted that a "regional strategic alliance in Indochina" has been established. Is there any real difference between this belligerent new term, and the old term "Indochina Federation"? It only helps to reveal Vietnam's strategic plot to dominate Indochina.'[22] Since this writer deliberately 'put aside the article's anti-China tone', it is hardly surprising that he could find no convincing reason for the 'strategic alliance'. From this, he concluded that it was a smokescreen for the consolidation of Vietnam's control over Indochina 'before they expand it to other areas'.

Faced with this sort of reasoning, some very elementary points have to be made. The difference between a 'federation' and an 'alliance' is considerable, even if the Chinese and many Western commentators cannot see it. An alliance is an agreement between sovereign states. No matter how close the alliance may be, its members remain in charge of the conduct of their own foreign relations and are regarded as independent states in international law; and any institutions created by that alliance (the supreme command of the NATO pact forces, for example) are not recognized as states. By contrast, a federation involves the formation of a *federal state*, which assumes full responsibility for the conduct of international relations. Authority over internal affairs is divided between the member states and the federal authorities, but these member states are not regarded as states for the purposes of international law. [23]

In the case of Indochina we are clearly dealing with an alliance, as the Vietnamese maintain. No federal state has been formed. Diplomatically, Vietnam and Laos are recognized by China, the USA and other countries as sovereign states, responsible for the conduct of their own foreign affairs - including the right to form alliances. The main objectives of Indochinese diplomacy has been to gain the same recognition for the PRK. One of the more balanced appraisals of the relationship was offered by journalist Richard Nations, commenting on the treaties signed between Vietnam, Cambodia and Laos in 1979: ' . . . they provide the sturdy legs of a simple diplomatic structure dominating Indochina with its apex in Hanoi. The technical accords between Vientiane and Phnom Penh now furnish a cross-beam - a necessary, if not a load-bearing part of the whole structure . . . . The treaties and accords which have been wrapped around the backbone of the Vietnamese troops in Indochina over the past few years in no way subordinate national sovereignty to a federation, at least from a legal point of view. With the structure of these agreements, Hanoi hardly needs such a federation.'[24] He concludes that so long as there is unity in their basic foreign policies, 'Laos and Cambodia would be allowed to follow their national interests according to their own lights'.

None of this is to deny that the Vietnamese have provided the military backbone of the alliance and are clearly the dominant force within it - as, for example, the USA is in the case of NATO, and China would be in any regional bloc it succeeded in establishing. But the Vietnamese have gone to some lengths to emphasize that the alliance is one based on mutual consent and that Hanoi is not dictating policy to its junior partners. Thus Laos was chosen as the official spokesperson for the Indochina bloc, and the Vietnamese have insisted that they will not negotiate any settlement of the Cambodia question over the heads of the PRK authorities. The Indochina bloc has emerged, argue the authorities in Vientiane and Phnom Penh, not because of Vietnamese dreams of a federal state of Indochina, but because, in the face of Chinese hostility, the interests of Laos and Cambodia are best served by the alliance with Hanoi. Of course, other states in the region were alarmed by the expansion of Vietnamese and Soviet influence, but that is a separate question, and one to which we will now turn.

Notes

1. On the other hand, it should also be noted that the existence of Western refugee programmes gave the outflow a certain self-generating character. Despite its technically illegal character, it increasingly came to resemble a migration rather than a refugee flow. One student of the problem adds the sombre remark: 'Much of the Third World's population would also seek to emigrate in a similar fashion if they were given international assistance and resettlement opportunities of the kind afforded the Vietnamese and Lao.' (Astri Suhkre, 'A New Look at America's Refugee Policy', *Indochina Issues*, no. 10, September 1980) This is confirmed by cases of locals seeking to smuggle themselves into refugee camps in Thailand in the hope of getting to the West. The problem has been quietly recognized by the US. In March 1981 authorities under the aegis of the State Department suddenly deferred hundreds of entry applications from Vietnamese because of doubts about whether they were genuine refugees. This move was successfully staved off for 1981 by right wingers in the administration who insisted that all refugees were fleeing from Communist tyranny; but by September of that year the numbers for 1982 had been cut.

2. For a good example of an argument of this type, see Derek Davies 'Bleeding Vietnam White', *Far Eastern Economic Review*, 25 December 1981; see also the response by US Assistant Secretary of State for East Asia and the Pacific John Holdridge in the issue of 4 June 1982.

3. The break between Yugoslavia and the Soviet Union was marked by bitter recriminations similar to those which passed between Vietnam and China in 1979. Tito charged that Stalin's support for the Yugoslav partisans during the Second World War had been tardy, and that he was more concerned with cultivating good relations with the great powers (Britain, the USA) than with helping comrades in smaller countries. Stalin directed his sharpest invective against Tito's attempts to counterbalance Soviet domination by building up an alliance of Balkan Communist states. A 'Balkan federation', argued Stalin, would enable Yugoslavia to dominate her neighbours. This attempt to turn Balkan nationalism against Tito succeeded with a vengeance in Albania. After the break, Tito reacted against Stalinism by experimenting with more moderate versions of Communism; while in Albania the moderates were purged and Enver Hoxa built up a xenophobic little police-state every bit as repressive as the Stalin regime he modelled it on. The Indochina parallel is, of coure, Pol Pot. Such parallels can be taken only so far. For all his hostility to Titoism, Hoxa did not launch military attacks on Yugoslavia. While Stalin seriously considered invading Yugoslavia, he decided against it. In this he showed more restraint than the 'moderates' in Peking. The affair ended in 1955 with a public apology by Khrushchev to the Yugoslavs for Stalin's behaviour. It is unlikely that Deng Xiaoping's successors will follow this example. The irony is that these parallels are not appreciated in either Hanoi or Belgrade. In the 1940s, the Viet Minh leaders had unhesitatingly backed Stalin, and relations with the Yugoslavs have been prickly ever since.

4. For a more extended account of the new administration, see Ben Kiernan, 'National Rehabilitation in the Eye of an International Storm', *Southeast Asian Affairs 1982*, Singapore 1982. See also the special issue of *Southeast Asia Chronicle* on Cambodia under Heng Samrin (no. 77, 1981), with useful articles by Kiernan, Steve Heder and others.

5. Jean-Pierre Gallois, 'Inside the Silent City', *New Statesman*, 13 April 1979.

6. This is no doubt the principal basis for the complaint of Elizabeth Becker *(Washington Post,* 1 March 1983) that there has been 'no country-wide equivalent of de-Stalinization . . . . Rather than dismantle Pol Pot's party, the Vietnamese want to rebuild it.' It is true, of course, that both Heng Samrin's and Pol Pot's governments are Communist; for Becker, that is apparently all that matters. However, 'de-Stalinization' did not mean the over-turning of Communist rule *per se* – Khrushchev ended the system of rule by police-state terror that was characteristic of the Stalin years, but he certainly did not 'dismantle' the Communist Party - on the contrary, whereas Stalin had used the security apparatus to exercise a personal dictatorship over a terrorized party (and general population), Khrushchev restored the party to a dominant position in Soviet political life. The actions of the Vietnamese, in over-turning a terroristic personal dictatorship and re-establishing 'the leading role of the Communist Party' under the PRK. was precisely analogous to 'de-Stalinization'. Of course, this was deeply disappointing to those who hoped that the overthrow of Pol Pot would overturn Communist rule completely and restore the Cambodian right to power.

7. For the background to this incident, see Ben Kiernan, 'The New Political Structure in Kampuchea', *Dyason House Papers*, vol. 8, December 1981.

8. Quoted by John McBeth, *Far Eastern Economic Review,* 15 October 1982.

9. On 31 July 1982 the PRK council of state issued a decree on territorial waters. In keeping with the usual practice, it proclaimed a 12-mile zone of territorial waters and a 200-mile economic zone, offering to settle 'by means of negotiations . . . on the basis of mutual respect' any problems this created. In the West it took the Franco-Siamese Treaty of 1907 as marking the border. In the east it promised negotiations 'in line with the spirit and letter' of the 1979 treaty.

10. *Asiaweek,* 5 June 1981.

11. John Pilger, 'Letting a Nation Die' in John Pilger and Anthony Barnett, *Aftermath: The Struggle of Cambodia and Vietnam,* London 1982, p. 63.

12. Quoted by Elizabeth Becker, *Far Eastern Economic Review,* 20 July 1979; see also her articles in the *Guardian Weekly,* 2 December 1979 and 24 February 1980 (both reprinted from the *Washington Post*). Two *Indochina Issues* also deal with the aid question: Murray Hiebert and Linda Gibson Hiebert, 'Famine in Kampuchea: Politics of a Tragedy', no. 4, December 1979, and Linda Gibson Hiebert, 'Kampuchea: Breaking the Cycle', no. 5, April 1980.

13. Jim Laurie, *Far Eastern Economic Review,* 18 January 1980.

14. John Pilger, 'Only the Allies are New' in Pilger and Barnett, p. 99.

15. CIA, *Kampuchea: A Demographic Catastrophe,* Washington, May 1980. For a further distortion of these figures, see Stephen J. Morris, 'Vietnam under Communism', *Commentary,* September 1982, p. 45, where the 700,000 figure is quoted to show that Hanoi's ruthless imperial drive *killed* [our emphasis] is one year as many Cambodians as died in *five* years of war, 1970-75.'

16. There are few studies of demographic catastrophes to provide guidelines here. However, one such study, dealing with the impact of civil war, famine and an exodus of refugees in Bangladesh found that the overall death rate increased from 15.3 to 21.0 per thousand, an increase of 26 per cent (Georg T. Curlin, Lincoln C. Chen, and

Sayed Babur Hussain, 'Demographic Crisis: The Impact of the Bangladesh Civil War (1971) on Births and Deaths in a Rural Area of Bangladesh; *Population Studies*, vol. 30, 1976, p. 91). This is well below the increase of 33 per cent we assumed to arrive at the figures in the text. Furthermore, we know that the population was closer to six million, rather than 5.2 million postulated by the CIA. There is little doubt that the CIA's estimates exaggerate the seriousness of the situation in Kampuchea in 1979.

17. Jon Swain, *Sunday Times* (London), 31 August 1980.

18. Bob Sector, *Age*, 22 March 1983.

19. For a useful overview, see Martin Stuart-Fox, 'Lao Foreign Policy: The View from Vientiane', *Journal of Contemporary Asia*, vol. 11, (1981).

20. Nayan Chanda, *Far Eastern Economic Review*, 28 May 1982.

21. Ibid., 26 March 1982.

22. *Beijing Review*, 19 April 1982.

23. For a summary of the relevant issues, see, for example, Michael Akehurst, *A Modern Introduction to International Law*, London 1970, pp. 73-5.

24. Richard Nations, *Far Eastern Economic Review*, 6 April 1979.

7

ASEAN: The Dominoes Push Back

The non-Communist country most immediately affected by these developments in Indochina was Thailand. The Thai government had played a central role in America's struggle to 'contain' Communism in Asia – when SEATO was formed in 1954, its head-quarters had been established in Bangkok. After the fall of Indo-china to Communism, and the visible retreat of American military power in the region, many of Thailand's political and military leaders believed that they faced a serious danger of invasion from Vietnam, and that support from Laos and Cambodia for the communist-led insurgents operating in the north and northeast of Thailand would make it almost impossible for the government to defeat the insurgents.[1] The smiles from Hanoi after 1975 were welcomed, but the fear and the mistrust did not go away. The fall of Pol Pot's regime to Vietnamese troops in 1979 only intensified these feelings. The belief that Thailand would be the next 'domino' to fall was shared by many on the left as well.[2]

For twenty years after the coup led by Sarit Thanarat in 1951 the Thai military leaders had relied on the 'threat' of Communism to attract unconditional support from the USA and to justify the sup-pression of their domestic opponents. The cold war served them well, and they had welcomed the intensification of America's involvement in Indochina with enthusiasm. But when the USA began seriously searching for a way out of Vietnam, from 1968 on, the Thais were, in John Girling's words, 'left stranded with a militant anti-Communist commitment, but deprived of the means to fulfil it'.[3]

They responded by moderating their reliance on America; as early as 1969, Bangkok announced the scaling down of the American military presence in Thailand, and began cautiously seeking a dialogue with Peking. However, the aim was a neutralist policy of equidistance from all the great powers rather than subservience to another one. The Thai policy that crystallized as the war in Indochina reached its conclusion was well summed up in a speech by the Thai foreign minister in January 1974. The Thai government would, he said, continue to have friendly relations with the USA but would correct 'the over-emphasis on military co-operation'. Thai policy aimed at achieving a 'balance' between all the powers with interests in the region; in this context, not only did he predict developing relations with China, he also described the Soviet Union as being in a 'strong position' to contribute to the stability of Southeast Asia.

Like Vietnam, Thailand was seeking to balance Moscow and Peking against each other – though Bangkok's aim was to bring as much restraining influence as possible to bear on a reunited Vietnam. Hanoi proved receptive to this policy, which was in keeping with the general relaxing of tensions in the *détente* of the early 1970s. But Thai policy was to fall victim to the escalation of the Vietnam-Cambodia and Vietnam-China conflicts, especially as these coincided with the breakdown of *détente* and the shift towards the new cold war.

Even before this happened, however, the policy of 'balance' proved unacceptable to influential right-wing elements in the army. To them, Thailand was accepting the loss of its influence in Vientiane, Saigon and in Phnom Penh without demur. This 'capitulation to Communism' they linked to their loss of influence after the establishment of a civilian government in Bangkok in 1973, and the 'disorder' of the democratic politics it ushered in. In October 1976 the Thai military staged a coup which they claimed saved the country from an impending Communist takeover. The government they installed, headed by Thanin Kraivichien, adopted a militantly anti-Communist stance with the intention of reviving the American alliance. But Washington was anxious not to jeopardize the emerging Sino-American *détente*, and quickly made it clear that it had no intention of being drawn into a military commitment to Thailand. In this context, Thanin's opposition to improving relations with China and the Indochinese countries was driving Thailand into dangerous isolation. Disillusioned, the military overthrew Thanin in another coup in October 1977.

His successor, General Kriangsak Chomanan, reverted to a more pragmatic approach. Accepting the retraction of American power, he looked to Communist China as a great power that would help maintain stability in Southeast Asia and moved to improve relations with Indochina. In this regard, Kriangsak was discomfited by the belligerence of the Khmer Rouge regime towards Thailand. Even more important, when he visited Peking in March-April 1978, he found that Deng Xiaoping's main objective was to push Thailand into a regional alliance with Pol Pot against the Vietnamese. While there is no evidence to suggest that Kriangsak actually agreed to this, his acceptance of a 'constructive relationship' with China at this critical juncture no doubt excited the worst suspicions in Hanoi.

Another thread of Thai foreign policy in the 1970s was the attempt to weld the non-Communist countries of the region into an effective counter-balance to Vietnam. This was only achieved in 1979, in response to the crisis over Cambodia and the 'boat people'. The emergence of ASEAN as a regional anti-Communist bloc has matched the emergence of the Communist Indochina bloc, although this aspect of the situation has attracted relatively little comment.

ASEAN: an anti-Communist Bloc

Originally formed in Bangkok in 1967, ASEAN brought together the Philippines, Thailand, Malaysia, Singapore and Indonesia, but for several years conflicts and rivalries between member states ensured that it was of little practical significance. When ASEAN was formed, Singapore had only recently broken away from the Malaysian Federation. Malaysia had also faced the armed challenge of Indonesia's *konfrontasi* policy until the coup against Sukarno in 1965, and a territorial claim by the Philippines on the east Malaysian state of Sabah, which was finally abandoned only in October 1982. Both Thailand and the Philippines were members of SEATO, while Malaysia, Singapore and Indonesia leant more towards neutralist policies.

America's débâcle in Vietnam strengthened neutralist tendencies in ASEAN. As early as 1971, a Malaysian proposal for a 'zone of peace, freedom and neutrality' was given general endorsement, although nothing was done to eliminate the American military presence. In 1974-5 the ASEAN countries began to open up diplomatic relations with China and North Vietnam, and recognized the new governments in South Vietnam, Cambodia and Laos. SEATO was phased out, and the American bases in Thailand (though not those in the Philippines) were closed down. Western commentators feared that the decline in American influence would open the way for a major expansion of Soviet influence in Southeast

Asia, but the main outcome of this shift in the direction of neutralism was to strengthen ASEAN as a regional bloc. Soviet diplomatic efforts achieved little and, as we have seen, Chinese rather than Soviet influence has increased in Southeast Asia.

Fears that a weak and divided non-Communist Southeast Asia would be threatened by a vigorous and united Indochina spurred the ASEAN countries to bury their differences after 1975. The first summit conference of the ASEAN heads of state at Bali in February 1976 was thus very much a response to the Communist victories in Indochina. Agreements signed at this meeting laid the basis for political, economic and cultural cooperation between the five countries. To avoid provoking their new Communist neighbours unnecessarily, it was emphasized that ASEAN was not a military pact.

But after 1975 the ASEAN countries experienced an economic boom while Indochina was gripped by economic and political crisis. The ASEAN countries found themselves being wooed by all parties to the conflict as the Cambodia-Vietnam-China dispute unfolded. Singapore's foreign minister, Sinnathamby Rajaratnam, commented in 1978: 'The dominoes have not fallen. It seems to be working the other way . . . instead of the consolidation of the Communist wave that was foreseen after their victory, we see the disintegration of Communist solidarity. ASEAN is consolidating instead of disintegrating.'

This situation, so favourable to the ASEAN countries, came to an end when the Vietnamese toppled Pol Pot's regime. The speed and effectiveness of Vietnam's military intervention was in itself alarming to non-Communist Southeast Asia, which knew that it did not possess such military capability. Moreover, the main consequence of the intervention was to create the unified Communist Indochina bloc that the ASEAN countries had feared would emerge in 1975. It is not surprising, therefore, that they condemned the Vietnamese action, with scant regard for the details of the Vietnam-Cambodia dispute. Given the shift in the regional balance of power, the rights and wrongs of the conflict were, from their point of view, immaterial. It was better to have a murderous dictator like Pol Pot as a neighbour than a united Indochina bloc.

The ASEAN foreign ministers met in Bangkok on 11 January 1979 to discuss how they should respond to the Vietnamese invasion of Cambodia. The following day they issued a joint statement deploring 'the armed intervention threatening the independence, sovereignty and territorial integrity of Cambodia', affirming 'the right of the Cambodian people to decide their own future without outside interference or influence from outside powers', and calling for the 'immediate withdrawal of all foreign troops from Cambodian territory'.

Despite the display of unanimity on this occasion, there were serious differences between ASEAN members over the Cambodia issue. Thailand was in the uncomfortable position of a 'front-line state'. With the fall of Pol Pot's regime, it found itself facing superior Vietnamese forces along all of its northern and eastern border, from Chiang Saen in the north to Klong Yai in the southeast. The arrival of the Vietnamese on the border opposite Aranyapratet was particularly alarming to the Thai government, for it meant that Vietnamese troops were only a few hours from Bangkok itself, across flat, easily traversed and thinly defended country. It became a standard joke that if the Vietnamese invaded Thailand, they would be stopped only by traffic jams in Bangkok – but for those responsible for the country's security, this was no laughing matter. While the anxiety about Vietnam's intentions were naturally strongest in Thailand, Singapore shared it, and also pushed a strong anti-Vietnamese line. In January 1979 Rajaratnam declared that 'the implication of what has happened in Cambodia is that we have moved into an era where imperialism is no longer associated with Western imperialism but with Communist imperialism'. However, Malaysia and Indonesia were inclined towards a more accommodating position. The Jakarta government declared that the events in Cambodia did not mean that there was a Vietnamese threat to the ASEAN countries, because Vietnam was too busy with its internal problems.

These divergences were in part a reflection of differing attitudes towards China. The old fears of the southward expansion of Chinese Communism had been allayed by Peking's courting of the ASEAN countries in the 1970s, but they were by no means completely extinct. China's insistence on maintaining relations with 'fraternal' Communist parties leading insurgencies was one source of friction in its relations with the ASEAN governments. Another was its influence in the overseas Chinese communities in these countries. Distrust over these matters was particularly sharp in Malaysia and Indonesia, which were inclined to sympathize with the idea of an independent Vietnam as a barrier to Chinese influence. As ex-colonies themselves, they also had more sympathy for the nationalist aspirations of the Vietnamese Communists. By contrast, in both Singapore and Thailand, the local Chinese business community exerted a strong influence on the government in favour of friendly relations with Peking, and there were not the same memories of a struggle against Western imperialism. Bangkok's attitude was further influenced by the consideration that Thailand had traditionally competed with Vietnam for influence in Laos and Cambodia.

From the beginning the other ASEAN states publicly followed the lead of Thailand, as the country most directly affected by the Cambodia crisis. But even in the Bangkok government opinion was divided over what practical measures should be taken. Counsels of caution suggested that, while the Vietnamese invasion should be vigorously condemned, the Heng Samrin government would have to be quietly accepted as a fact of life unless a direct threat to Thailand itself emerged: there was no point in becoming involved in an attempt, probably futile and certainly dangerous, to try and force the Vietnamese out of Cambodia. These views were reinforced by the Malaysians and the Indonesians, who favoured the opening of a 'dialogue' with Hanoi rather than a confrontation. Behind the scenes, the Indonesians in particular tried to undercut the hard-liners and to reach an accommodation with Vietnam.

But the hardliners in Bangkok and Singapore prevailed over these counsels. Kriangsak flew to Washington, where Jimmy Carter assured him of American support if Thailand's security was threat-ened. Then the Chinese attacked Vietnam. On 22 February, five days after the Chinese invasion, Kriangsak said that Thailand would continue to recognize the Pol Pot government as the legitimate government of Cambodia. He warned 'potential aggressors' of the strength of Thailand's armed forces, and said that they were capable of checking the threat of any expansionist movement. He also took steps to build up Thailand's border defences and to rally ASEAN support for this stance. Kriangsak had made what would prove to be a crucial commitment for Thailand: the basis of a balanced foreign policy had been destroyed by the decision to side with China and the Khmers Rouges in the Indochina conflict.

Over the next few months the situation on the Thai-Cambodian border became increasingly tense. Disorder, fighting and food shortages in western Cambodia resulted in a stream of refugees fleeing into Thailand. As this exodus of 'land people' coincided with the flood of 'boat people' from Vietnam, they were part of a refugee problem for the ASEAN countries of alarming dimensions. At the same time, Pol Pot's forces were retreating to the Thai border with the Vietnamese hot on their tails and it was feared that the fighting between them would spill over into Thailand. The Thai government rather inconsistently proclaimed its neutrality towards the conflict inside Cambodia while condemning the Vietnamese and supporting Pol Pot's DK as the legitimate government of the country. They could not deny it very convincingly when Sihanouk, quoting Han Nianlong, the Chinese vice-foreign minister, declared in May 1979: 'To the outside world, the Thais say they are neutral, but they are not neutral in fact. They are with Pol Pot.'

When the foreign ministers of the ASEAN countries conferred over the refugee crisis at Bali in June 1979, the meeting was dominated by the anti-Vietnamese hardliners. The most outspoken was once again Singapore's Rajaratnam, who said that Vietnam was an expansionist power aiming at domination of all Southeast Asia, which had 'declared war' on ASEAN and was 'carrying out a policy of genocide'. 'Today it is the Chinese-Vietnamese. The Cambodians have already been added to the list of those who are going to die . . . . Why not Thailand tomorrow, and Malaysia, Singapore and others who stand in the way of Vietnam's dreams?' In Rajaratnam's view, Vietnam was already menacing Thailand with 180,000 troops, and was deliberately driving refugees out of Indochina in an attempt to de-stabilize non-Communist Southeast Asia. He said that ASEAN had reached the limits of its patience, urged a tough line on refugees, and advocated that ASEAN provide arms and material support to Cambodia's patriotic struggle against Vietnamese domination (that is, concretely, to Pol Pot's forces). He warned his fellow ASEAN members against any policy of accommodation with Hanoi, arguing that Vietnam could not be treated as 'an essentially peace-loving neighbour'.

The final communiqué adopted at Bali condemned the Vietnamese and called for 'international support' for Cambodia's 'right of self-determination', equating this with the DK regime. It re-affirmed the ASEAN countries' support for Thailand, and declared that any escalation of the fighting in Cambodia or any incursion into Thailand would directly affect the security of the ASEAN states as a group. No military pact was drawn up at Bali, but this made it clear enough that if Thailand came under attack, the others would go to its aid. Following this conference, the American Secretary of State, Cyrus Vance, pledged that the USA would come to the assistance of any ASEAN country attacked by an outsider. The June 1979 Bali conference thus represented a significant step in the direction of turning ASEAN into a *de facto* military alliance backed by the USA.

Military cooperation among the ASEAN states accelerated after

Bali, but on a bilateral rather than a multilateral basis. They made exchanges, joint exercises and attempts at standardizing their equipment. This was underpinned by a sharp increase in military spending, supported by military aid from the USA. For the ASEAN countries as a whole, defence spending rose to $5.466 million US in 1980 – an increase of 47 per cent on 1979 and 2,849 per cent on 1975.

Even so, in any direct comparison of their military forces, the regional balance of power favoured Vietnam. By 1980, the ASEAN countries had 693,400 men under arms, compared to Vietnam's one million. Furthermore, the armies of several of the ASEAN countries were tied up with domestic insurgencies or heavily involved in administration. ASEAN remained a collection of militarily weak states, heavily dependent on the protection of the USA and China in dealing with any Vietnamese threat.

The reasons ASEAN evolved in the direction of a military alliance were well understood by Western commentators, and there were none of the half-baked theories that were characteristic of discussions of the Indochina bloc. No attempts were made to characterize ASEAN as a 'federation', or to depict it as an instrument of the 'colonialism' of one of the dominant member states, or of the USA. Partly, of course, this is a reflection of the fact that no single country dominates ASEAN to the same extent that Vietnam obviously dominates the Indochina alliance. It is also a reflection of the much more extensive military cooperation in Indochina, of which Vietnam bears the main burden. In the main, however, it is because Western observers had no difficulty perceiving a Vietnamese threat to Thailand, and in understanding ASEAN's response as a defensive reaction. They were quite capable, in this connection, of perceiving how the exigencies of current political events could submerge the 'historic enmities' and cultural differences between states. The celebration of ASEAN unity was not marred by recalling old (and not so old) disputes between its members, or any emphasis on the gap between Islamic and Buddhist cultures in ASEAN (which is at least as great as the cultural gap between the Indianic and Sinitic traditions evoked by some as the underlying cause of the Vietnam-Cambodia dispute).

The same commentators were usually unable to perceive that the Indochina bloc was also defensive in character. They saw a Vietnamese threat to Thailand in the invasion of Cambodia but were incapable of seeing the Chinese threat to Indochina, despite China's invasion of Vietnam. If the Indochina bloc was more tightly knit, this was in large part because the threat it was facing was much more real. But despite these parallels ASEAN and the Indochinese countries were fundamentally at cross purposes over Cambodia: for ASEAN the prime concern was ending the perceived threat to Thailand by bringing about a Vietnamese withdrawal from Cambodia, while China was a secondary issue; for Indochina, however, the Chinese threat was the primary concern, and the Vietnamese presence in Cambodia was secondary. The possibility of a diplomatic solution that would satisfy both sides was remote.

Negotiations between the ASEAN and the Indochinese countries simply never got off the ground. In 1980 the Vietnamese stated repeatedly that they would not negotiate on the future of Cambodia over the head of the government in Phnom Penh, but the ASEAN countries would not be party to any negotiations that included the 'puppet' Heng Samrin administration. The Vietnamese also made it clear that their troops would remain in Cambodia as long as the 'Chinese threat' to the Indochinese states remained. They offered to withdraw *some* of their troops in exchange for Thailand denying sanctuary and supplies to the Khmers Rouges, but would not accept a *complete* withdrawal while China's stance remained hostile. However, it was on a complete withdrawal that the ASEAN countries insisted. Hanoi tried to mollify Bangkok's fears of Vietnamese 'expansionism' by offering Thailand a non-aggression pact. But in Thai eyes, such a pact had little meaning in the light of Vietnamese actions in Cambodia, and Bangkok rejected the offer. Vietnam proposed a demilitarization of the Thai-Cambodian border, which Thailand rejected because this would implicate it as a party to the dispute in Cambodia. It countered with a proposal for a demilitarized zone between the warring factions inside Cambodia, which the Vietnamese rejected because it meant a *de facto* partitioning of Cambodia.

Over this issue the ASEAN countries found themselves in an alliance with the USA and, rather more uneasily, with China. They followed their diplomatic victory over the seating of Pol Pot at the United Nations by calling for an international conference on Cambodia under UN auspices. They proposed a total withdrawal of Vietnamese troops, the establishment of a UN peacekeeping force to maintain law and order in Cambodia after the departure of the Vietnamese, and UN-sponsored elections to create a new government. On 22 October 1980 the UN General Assembly passed Resolution 35/6 on Cambodia. This followed the ASEAN draft on all but one point – the call for a UN peacekeeping force was deleted. This excision, which would leave the Khmers Rouges as the only organized military force in the country (whatever the results of the election), was reportedly made on the insistence of China. The Indochinese countries rejected this proposal because the UN had accepted the legitimacy of Pol Pot's DK regime and rejected that of the PRK, and was thus in no sense an impartial body.

The UN conference proposed by ASEAN went ahead in July 1981. Vietnam and Laos refused to participate while Pol Pot's regime was still accepted as officially representing the Cambodian people. The PRK government was invited to attend as an observer, it being emphasized that this in no way involved legal recognition. Invitations were issued to Sihanouk and Son Sann's anti-Communist Khmer People's National Liberation Front (KPNLF) on the same terms. Sihanouk sent a letter to the conference; but neither the PRK nor the KPNLF participated.

Without the participation of the Indochinese countries, a conference on Cambodia was, as one diplomat put it, like clapping with one hand. However, it was notable for the gap that opened up between the ASEAN position and that of China and the USA. As with UN Resolution 35/6, ASEAN tried to write in clauses assuring Vietnam that its security would not be threatened. Singapore's foreign minister, Suppiah Dhanabalan (the inimitable Rajaratnam having become deputy prime minister for foreign affairs) emphasized that ASEAN did not want to see the Khmers Rouges returned to power by force, and that they recognized that any solution to the Cambodian problem should take into account 'Vietnam's legitimate concern that Cambodia should not be used to threaten its security'. He was supported by the other ASEAN ministers.

The emergence of this conciliatory line in ASEAN alarmed the Chinese. Prior to the conference Peking publicly attacked the ASEAN proposal to invite the different Cambodian political factions as observers. According to the Chinese, only the two conflicting parties – Vietnam and DK – should have been invited. The PRK should not have been asked in any role; nor should Sihanouk or Son Sann unless they were willing to align themselves with DK, Cambodia's sole legal representative. China's response to talk of Vietnam's 'legitimate security interests' was to insist that the conference focus on the 'main issue' – forcing the Vietnamese into withdrawing all their troops from Cambodia. At the conference itself, Han Nianlong, as acting Chinese foreign minister, proposed that only *after* the Vietnamese had withdrawn should the members of the UN Security Council and the countries of Southeast Asia undertake to respect Cambodia's independence and neutrality.

China's hardline stance was supported by the USA. The objective of American policy in Indochina was to bring maximum pressure to bear on Hanoi, to escalate the Cambodian crisis rather than find a solution to it. In 1979 a 'senior Western diplomat' in Bangkok with 'access to Washington's thinking' told Nayan Chanda that the USA was opposed to any attempt to reach an agreement with Vietnam because that would 'only encourage Hanoi's expansionism, not restrain it'. The Americans preferred to force a confrontation, which, they hoped, would enable them to 'crack' the will of the Hanoi leadership, even if it took five to ten years.[4] Apart from a desire for vengeance, the Americans were also anxious to please the Chinese. Said one American source at the time of the UN conference: 'If anybody thinks Democratic Kampuchea is an alternative (to the PRK), he's crazy . . . . The only reason we're supporting the DK's credentials is that the Chinese want us to.'[5] This American stance left little scope for flexibility on ASEAN's part.

Secretary of State Alexander Haig told the UN conference that 'the United States has no intention of normalizing relations with a Vietnam that occupies Cambodia and destabilizes the entire Southeast Asian region.' In Peking, shortly before the conference, Haig's assistant secretary, John Holdridge, had given his stamp of approval to increasing 'the political, economic and, yes, military pressures on Vietnam' to bring about 'some changes in Hanoi's attitude'. Two days after the conference, Holdridge spelt out American policy towards Indochina in testimony before the Senate Sub-committee on East Asian and Pacific Affairs in these terms: ' . . . the central issue in US policy toward Vietnam is the occupation of Cambodia, and that is why we will continue to keep pressure on Hanoi. In this we and ASEAN are in full agreement: the course of action most likely to result in the removal of Vietnamese troops from Cambodia is to make the occupation as costly as possible for Hanoi. We will continue a process of diplomatic isolation and economic deprivation until Hanoi . . . (agrees) to troop withdrawal, free elections, and an end to outside interference.'[6]

As a result of this divergence in views between ASEAN and China and the USA two draft declarations were submitted to the conference, one by Singapore and one by Peking. The differences were the same as those that had emerged over Resolution 35/6, but now they were out in the open. The final version adopted by the conference accepted China's demands that the Pol Pot group remain fully armed. The *New York Times* commented: 'The document implicitly permits the return of the Pol Pot group to administer

Phnom Penh if and when UN-supervised elections are ever held there. . . . China's success in defending the rights of the Pol Pot faction, which it backs with weapons and aid, was all the more remarkable because China was backed only by Chile and Pakistan . . . . The final draft . . . only urges "appropriate measures to ensure that armed factions" will not disrupt the elections . . . . This would give the Pol Pot faction, with about 25,000 guerrillas, a great advantage . . . . Instead of Singapore's call for a neutral administrator in Phnom Penh during elections, the final document merely urges "appropriate measures for the maintenance of law and order". That could let an armed Pol Pot group be present in the capital during the vote.'[7] Thus, even when the moderates in ASEAN seemed to have gained the upper hand, Sino-American pressure ensured that, in practice, they continued to throw their weight behind Pol Pot. While they did not wish to see a military solution to the Cambodian crisis, this made a diplomatic solution extremely difficult.

The Indochinese countries responded to these ASEAN initiatives by setting out their basic negotiating position in a statement by the foreign ministers of Vietnam, Laos and the PRK on 28 January 1981. They blamed tension in the region on China's policies of expansionism and hegemonism, and argued that 'the basic factor for restoring peace and stability in Southeast Asia at present is that China must terminate its hostile policy towards the three Indochinese countries and its policy of interfering with other countries in this area'. The three governments declared their readiness 'to sign bilateral treaties of peaceful coexistence with the People's Republic of China on the basis of the principles of absolute respect for each country's independence, sovereignty and territorial integrity, nonaggression, non-intervention in each other's internal affairs; equality; mutual benefit; good neighbourly relations and the settlement of all bilateral disputes through peaceful means'. This was dismissed by the Chinese premier, Zhau Ziyang, at a press conference in Bangkok on 1 February. There was, he said, 'nothing new' in the Indochinese proposals, and he stated that China would be prepared to take part in a conference with Vietnam and other countries concerned for an international guarantee against foreign interference in Cambodia only *after* Vietnam had withdrawn all its troops.

The Vietnamese followed this up in April 1981 with an offer to withdraw all their troops from Cambodia if China was willing to sign a non-aggression pact with Vietnam, Laos and the PRK. Thach told a reporter from the Japanese paper *Yomiuri Shimbun*: 'The only condition for the Vietnamese forces to pull out of Cambodia is for China to conclude a pact of non-aggression with the Indochinese countries.' But this Peking adamantly refused to do. The Chinese *People's Daily* depicted the Vietnamese withdrawal offer as a 'trick' to 'put all the blame on China'. China would be willing to sign a non-aggression pact with Vietnam only after it had halted its 'aggression and expansion', stopped 'intruding' into Chinese territory, and withdrawn all its troops from *both* Cambodia and Laos. In short, they demanded total capitulation before any talks could begin.

In relation to the ASEAN countries, the Indochinese statement of 28 January 1981 advocated an ongoing 'dialogue' between ASEAN and Indochina. It advanced a proposal for a regional conference involving the ASEAN and Indochinese countries, and perhaps, Burma, to discuss 'the problems concerning them'. After these countries had concluded a treaty on peace and stability in Southeast Asia, the statement called for an enlarged international conference to recognize and guarantee this treaty. This differed from the ASEAN proposal principally in that it called on the countries of the region to work out their own negotiated solution to the Cambodian problem without the involvement of outside powers, which would then be presented to the great powers (China, in particular) as a *fait accompli* for their endorsement. The Indochinese statement also emphasized that the PRK should be taken as 'the sole genuine and legal representative of the Cambodian people', while offering a partial withdrawal of Vietnamese forces 'if Thailand stops allowing the Pol Pot army and other reactionary Khmer forces to use Thai territory as a base to supply them with weapons and provisions, and if it concentrates them in separate camps far from the border areas'.

ASEAN's official response was given through the Philippine foreign minister, General Carlos P. Romulo, on 6 February – five days after Zhao Ziyang had spelt out China's opposition. The Indochinese proposals, he said, 'ignore the root cause of the problem, the blatant breach in Cambodia of the fundamental principles of the non-aligned movement and the principles of the UN Charter' and 'seek to justify and perpetuate Vietnam's continued military occupation of Cambodia and to deny the right of the people of Cambodia to determine their own future, free from outside interference and coercion'.

The diplomatic impasse continued into 1983. Essentially, neither side was willing to make a real compromise and each was waiting for the other side to make the first major concession. The Indochinese approach was to assure the ASEAN countries of their peaceful intentions, and to offer them friendship and cooperation in exchange for acceptance of a pro-Vietnamese government in Phnom Penh. As part of this basic strategy, Vietnam began defining the conditions under which it would withdraw its troops from Cambodia, and announced a modest reduction of its troop strength there in July 1982. A further withdrawal followed in May 1983, reducing Vietnam's troop strength in Cambodia to about 150,000, according to Western intelligence sources.

The ASEAN stance was to try and pressure the Vietnamese into withdrawing by supporting DK, while assuring Hanoi that they recognized Vietnam's security interest in Cambodia. This has left ASEAN saddled with the task of sustaining DK as a credible alternative government to the PRK. The ASEAN countries also found that they had seriously misjudged Chinese policies towards Cambodia in 1979. Peking was not, rhetoric notwithstanding, concerned primarily with the defence of Cambodian sovereignty, but with 'bleeding' Vietnam into submission. Both ASEAN and China supported DK, but for different reasons. Whereas the ASEAN countries, Thailand above all, genuinely wanted to see the Vietnamese withdraw from Cambodia, the Chinese preferred to see them bogged down in a protracted war in Cambodia. As Deng Xiaoping frankly explained to the Japanese prime minister in December 1979: 'It is wise for China to force the Vietnamese to stay in Cambodia because in that way they will suffer more and will not be able to extend their hand to Thailand, Malaysia and Singapore.'[8] China therefore used its influence to block any moves that might lead to a compromise solution of the Cambodian crisis. The ASEAN countries thus found that, having committed themselves to the cause of DK, they were unable to resolve the crisis without coming into open conflict with China, whose stance was backed by the USA at critical moments such as the 1981 UN conference on Cambodia. They were thus locked into the commitment they had made in February 1979.

With a negotiated settlement seemingly impossible at this stage, the outcome of the dispute depended on political and military developments that substantially altered the balance of forces in the region. It was to achieving this, rather than diplomacy, that both sides devoted most of their energies after early 1979. Vietnam concentrated on consolidating the Heng Samrin government, strengthening its 'special relationship' with Laos and Cambodia, and building up its defences on the Sino-Vietnamese border.

Thailand, backed by ASEAN, tried to step up the pressure on Hanoi by manipulating the refugee crisis and covertly supporting the anti-Vietnamese insurgents operating on the Thai-Cambodian border.

The Vietnamese Invasion and International Law

Vietnam's military intervention in Cambodia was condemned by ASEAN, China and the West for basically strategic reasons, but the grounds given officially were legal ones. The Vietnamese were accused, not of shifting the regional balance of power against Thailand and ASEAN by their actions, but of flagrantly breaching international law. As a corollary of this, the ASEAN countries have maintained that, while they deplored the crimes perpetrated by the Pol Pot regime, they are legally bound to recognize Democratic Kampuchea rather than the People's Republic of Kampuchea as the legitimate government of Cambodia – to do otherwise, they argue, is tantamount to 'legalizing aggression'. To this, the Vietnamese respond that Pol Pot was the aggressor, and that their presence in Cambodia is a legitimate act of self-defence. The two conflicting views were succinctly summed up in an exchange between Nguyen Co Thach and Malaysian Prime Minister Mahathir Mohamed in July 1982. Thach declared: 'The Vietnamese presence in Cambodia is a right of self-defence, as Cambodia was used to threaten the security of Vietnam.' To which Mahathir responded: 'You don't go into a neighbouring territory, just as you don't want others to go into your territory.'

The basis for the position adopted by ASEAN is Article 2(4) of the UN Charter, which reads: 'All members shall refrain in their international relations from the threat or use of force against the territorial integrity or political independence of any state, or in any other manner inconsistent with the purposes of the United Nations.' The UN Security Council is empowered to determine whether 'threats to the peace', 'breaches of the peace' or 'acts of aggression' have occurred, and to take action to maintain international peace and security, including the use of international military forces if necessary. However, the drafters of the Charter were aware that countries subjected to armed aggression could hardly be expected to wait for the UN Security Council to decide what it would do before taking effective action in their own defence. Article 51 of the UN Charter therefore provides: 'Nothing in the present Charter shall impair the inherent right of individual or collective self-defence if an armed attack occurs against a member of the United Nations, until the Security Council has taken the measures necessary to maintain international peace and security. Measures taken by members in the exercise of this right of self-defence shall be immediately reported to the Security Council and shall not in any way affect the authority and responsibility of the Security Council under the present Charter to take at any time such action as it deems necessary to maintain international peace and security.' In fact almost all the armed conflicts since World War II have been resolved without effective involvement by the Security Council, and the deployment of UN peace-keeping forces has proven successful only where it has had the consent of all parties to the dispute. Furthermore, while fighting is in progress, the countries involved have rarely 'immediately reported' their actions to the Security Council.

Quite clearly, Vietnam has used military force against the 'territorial integrity and the political independence' of Pol Pot's regime – indeed, it tried to wipe it out of existence entirely. On this point, ASEAN rests its case. But Article 2(4) must be read in conjunction with Article 51 of the UN Charter, which makes it clear that the Charter does not automatically condemn all recourse to military force by states, but rather makes the distinction between aggressive and defensive operations fundamentally important. Unfortunately, in the heat of battle this distinction is often difficult to apply (unless one of the states involved is reckless enough to openly proclaim itself the aggressor). Nevertheless, some important points can be made. The question of which side *initiated* 'armed attacks' on the other side is central. The 'right of self-defence' exists only in response to armed attacks that have already occurred, and the Charter makes no general provision for what has been termed 'anticipatory self-defence'. In the second place, it is generally agreed that the force used in self-defence must be proportionate to the scale of the attack, so that trivial border incidents cannot be used as a pretext for launching an all-out war. In the third place, most writers on the question point out, it does not include a right of armed reprisals. As Akehurst puts it: ' . . . if terrorists enter one state from another, the first state may use force to arrest or expel the terrorists, but, having done so, it is not entitled to retaliate by attacking the other state.'[9]

These are the criteria by which Hanoi's actions in its conflict with the Pol Pot regime should be judged under international law. From the evidence in chapter four, it seems clear that it was the Khmer

Rouge regime that initiated armed attacks on the other side. The case against Vietnam thus rests on the argument that its response was disproportionate to the attacks to which it was subjected, and, in particular, that the incursion of December 1977 and the invasion of December 1978 were reprisals that cannot be justified in terms of the UN Charter's 'right of self-defence'. The case for Vietnam is that Article 2(4) cannot be used to provide legal impunity for a regime guilty of repeated, large-scale acts of aggression.

In considering the issue of reprisals, a further point needs to be borne in mind. The distinction between acts of 'self-defence' and 'armed reprisals' is one that applies to armed clashes between countries that are basically at peace with one another – for example, the prohibition on armed reprisals should be applied in relation to clashes on the Thai-Cambodian and Thai-Lao borders. But, according to the authorities on international law, once the threshhold has been crossed into a state of 'war-like operations' or a 'state of war' the prohibition no longer holds. Although these terms cannot be defined precisely (now that the old-fashioned practice of making formal declarations of war has fallen into general disuse), and although the states involved tried at first to conceal it, relations between Cambodia and Vietnam in 1977–8 were clearly ones of at least 'war-like operations'. The legal consequences of this are so great that it is worth quoting a leading authority, Professor D.W. Greig, at some length: 'Prior to the Charter it was by no means clear how far a war undertaken in self-defence could justify action directed against the territorial integrity and political independence of the aggressor. The view of the states which defeated Germany and Japan in the Second World War was that they were entitled to occupy the territory of the enemy states and to take over the administration of those territories in order to establish democratic government and institutions on a firm foundation. It is believed that this principle, that an aggressor is not entitled to claim the benefit of what is now contained in Article 2(4) of the Charter, is also accepted by the Charter . . . . Article 2(4) is no barrier to action against an aggressor which has mounted an armed attack against any state . . . . A state which has reasonable grounds for believing that its existence is threatened, is entitled to protect itself even to the extent of launching an attack into the territory of the state from which the threat emanates. A state's "territorial integrity" does not extend so far as to enable it to prepare, free from all interference, an invasion against a neighbouring state . . . . Territorial integrity does not denote inviolability if what a state is preparing is a breach of the peace or act of aggression.'[10]

In short, if it is accepted that a state of war or 'war-like opera-tions' existed between Vietnam and DK; that the DK government was the aggressor; and that Vietnam had 'reasonable grounds' for believing that this state of affairs constituted a grave threat to the government of Vietnam; then Vietnam was justified in eliminating the threat by invading and occupying Cambodia – just as the Allies were justified in invading and occupying Germany and Japan in 1945.

Greig continues: 'However, territorial integrity and political in-dependence would obviously be applicable to prevent a state, initially acting in self-defence to meet a threat from another state, from annexing, whether in whole or part, the territory of that other state . . . . A *threat* of an attack will never justify the threatened state from taking over the government of the alleged "aggressor" in order to oblige it to "mend its ways". It will seldom, if ever, justify the seizing of territory belonging to the "aggressor".' Thus there would be no justification for annexing territory from Cambodia or for placing it permanently under a Vietnamese administration; the invaders would be expected to hand over power to a new Cambodian government, administering the country within its exist-ing borders. And this, of course, is precisely what the Vietnamese did by installing Heng Samrin's PRK administration. The fact that the PRK is friendly to Vietnam and that this makes Thailand unhappy is an inevitable consequence of this but, legally, it is beside the point.

The ASEAN case against the Vietnamese invasion of Cambodia on legal grounds is thus weak. The view that military intervention by one country in another country is always unjustifiable is simplistic and untenable. Judgements about the culmination of a conflict cannot be meaningfully separated from the genesis and develop-ment of the conflict, and the side that ends a war should not necessarily be branded as an 'aggressor'. In any case, the ASEAN response to China's invasion of Vietnam showed that in practice they are willing to accept military intervention – when it coincides with their interests.

Even so, ASEAN won the propaganda battle over the Cambodia issue. They were helped by the fact that the Vietnamese, no doubt anxious to avoid anything that could justify Chinese intervention, also adopted the principle that military intervention in another country can never be justified. This made a forthright defence of their own actions in Cambodia impossible. Instead, Hanoi tried at first to deny that it was involved in the Cambodian fighting, depicting it as a 'popular uprising', and then claiming its troops had been 'invited' by the PRK government. This transparent dishonesty only brought discredit on Hanoi – and the Chinese invaded Vietnam anyway.

The issue of the legality of Vietnam's intervention in Cambodia is closely linked to the question of whether the PRK should be granted international recognition. ASEAN's argument for continuing to recognize Pol Pot's regime is that recognition of Heng Samrin's government would be tantamount to 'legalizing aggression'. With Chinese and American backing, ASEAN's arguments have held sway over those of Vietnam and its Soviet-bloc allies. In September 1979 the UN General Assembly voted by 71 to 35 with 34 abstentions to reaffirm recognition of DK. Although the ASEAN countries were worried that support for this position would subsequently crumble, diplomatic recognition of Pol Pot's group of desperadoes in the jungle as the legal government of Cambodia has become stronger rather than weaker. In 1980 the UN vote was 74 for Pol Pot and 35 against with 32 abstentions; in 1981 it was 77 for and 34 against with 31 abstentions.

Recognition of a new government, such as the PRK, means a willingness to accept it as a legitimate member of the international community. In principle, most countries base recognition on effective control of territory and population, not on approval of a government's policies. This approach was classically stated by the British ambassador to the USA, Sir Roger Matkins, in 1954: 'If a government is in effective control of the country in question; if it seems to have a reasonable expectation of permanence; if it can act for a majority of the country's inhabitants; it it is able (though possibly not willing) to carry out its international obligations; if, in short, it can give a convincing answer to the question, "Who's in charge here?" then we shall recognize that government.'

However, the USA has followed a different approach. In 1931 US Secretary of State Henry L. Stimson argued that the Japanese puppet state of Manchuko in Manchuria should not be recognized because it had been created by an illegal act of aggression, and urged that the League of Nations (the predecessor to the UN) should adopt this as a general principle. However, the Stimson doctrine proved ineffective, breaking down the first time it came to the test – over Mussolini's conquest of Abyssinia in 1936. As diplomatic postures have to bow to politial realities sooner or later, the main effect in trying to apply the Stimson doctrine has been to defer recognition, not to prevent it. Inevitably, it is applied in an arbitrary and politically selective fashion. While this moralist's approach to the question of diplomatic recognition has therefore been generally abandoned in favour of the realist approach spelt out by Matkins, the USA still holds to the view that granting recognition involves giving a stamp of political approval to a regime.

In the case of Cambodia, by the end of 1979 the answer to the question 'Who's in charge here?' had become clear. Heng Samrin's PRK government was in control of most of the country, and was consolidating its position. The DK 'government' controlled only enclaves in remote and isolated parts of the country. We invite those who think otherwise to try travelling around Cambodia on a visa issued by DK.

Perhaps it could be argued that international recognition of the PRK would be premature until it has demonstrated its capacity to survive without Vietnamese military protection but by the usual criteria of control of territory and population, there is no case for continuing to recognize the DK regime. Far from continuing to be the legal government, it has become a legal fiction. The argument that to recognize the PRK is to legitimize Vietnamese aggression appears to be an appeal to the Stimson doctrine. However, if this is accepted, then the other side of the coin should also be accepted – recognition of DK involves giving the stamp of approval to its policies.

The inconsistencies of the ASEAN countries' position on Cambodia is thrown into relief by their attitude towards events in Africa at the same time. In 1978 Idi Amin's loathsome regime in Uganda was overthrown by a Tanzanian military intervention, after Amin had invaded Tanzania. Although the parallels with the Vietnam-Cambodia situation are quite close, there was no controversy over international recognition of the regime the Tanzanians installed in Kampala, although it proved to be much less stable than the PRK. The ASEAN countries, along with the rest of the world, did not hesitate in accepting the Tanzanian intervention as legitimate and in recognizing the new regime. There was no hypocritical attempt to maintain that Amin still had to be recognized as the country's legal ruler even by those who abhorred his crimes.

The USA found itself in a particularly anomalous position over Cambodia. It had refused to recognize DK in the first place. In 1978 President Jimmy Carter had denounced it as the 'worst violator of human rights in the world', and human rights were supposedly the linchpin of Carter's foreign policy. Then, after the regime had been toppled, America found itself voting, with much embarrassment, for the DK delegation as the country's legal representative in the UN. American officials argued that to support DK in the UN in no way involved recognition or support for the DK regime itself. After the American representative on the UN credentials committee had voted for the Pol Pot delegation in 1979, someone grabbed his hand and shook it. 'I looked up and saw it was Ieng Sary,' he later recalled, 'I felt like washing my hands.'[11]

Other Western countries were embarrassed by their diplomatic support for the deposed Communist dictator, and sought to distance themselves from him, at least in public. Unlike the USA, the British government had granted full recognition to DK, on the grounds of its control of the territory and population of Cambodia. After the Vietnamese invasion these grounds were no longer valid, and recognition of DK was withdrawn in December 1979. After much hesitation, the Australian government followed suit in February 1981.

However, neither Britain nor Australia were willing to grant recognition to the government that did control the population and territory of Cambodia. They both hastened to reassure China and the ASEAN countries that they would refuse to recognize the PRK, on grounds that it was dependent for its control on the Vietnamese. No such considerations had been involved, for example, in recognizing the new regime in Kampala, although its dependence on the Tanzanians was evident. The hope of these governments was that a viable alternative to both Heng Samrin and Pol Pot would emerge, that a non-Communist contender for power in Cambodia could be found.

The new government in Phnom Penh was a political reality, regardless of how this had been accomplished. The reasons for the refusal to recognize it had more to do with power politics than legal arguments: Vietnam was aligned with the USSR and had overthrown a pro-Chinese regime in Cambodia and shifted the regional balance of power against Thailand, while the West and the ASEAN countries opposed any expansion of Soviet influence and hoped to cultivate China as an ally against the Soviet Union. Given this, the rights and wrongs of the Vietnamese intervention itself were immaterial. In the atmosphere of a renewed cold war in the late 1970s, no pro-Soviet regime, no matter how secure and well-behaved it might be, and no matter how brutal its predecessor had been, could expect to be accepted as a legitimate government by the Western powers.

Uganda was an entirely different matter, not because of any point of law, but because the interests of the great powers were not involved.

Thailand's Refugee Crisis

During 1979–80 there was a massive influx of Cambodian refugees into Thailand. Some chose to present this as a flight from Vietnamese domination, but the reality was more complex. The exodus was a product of several factors – the economic collapse inside Cambodia, Vietnamese military campaigns against the Khmer Rouge base areas near the Thai border, and the policies pursued by the Bangkok government and the international relief agencies themselves. The refugee crisis placed Thailand under heavy strain, but it also provided it with an unexpected major lever of influence in the political struggle over Cambodia.

Let us begin by describing the movement of refugees into Thailand in some detail. The flow had begun in 1975, with the Khmer Rouge takeover, but it remained at a relatively low level until 1979. From April 1975 to December 1978, a total of 34,000 Cambodian refugees had entered Thailand, 19,000 of whom had been re-settled in other countries, leaving a residual of 15,000 refugees in Thailand. Contrary to a widespread impression, the Vietnamese invasion did not trigger off an immediate, large-scale flight of Khmers across the border. By mid-April 1979, only a further 5,000 refugees had entered Thailand. These were mostly survivors from the Phnom Penh middle class, former Lon Nolists, and others who had strong political objections to living under any Communist government. They took advantage of the disorder prevailing in Cambodia at that time to flee the country, and they left primarily for political rather than economic reasons.

But the situation altered dramatically in April 1979 when the Vietnamese attacked Khmer Rouge strongholds near the Thai border. Tens of thousands of people, including several thousand Khmer Rouge soldiers, streamed into Thailand. The Thais allowed them to enter – officially, only if they laid down their arms – but denied the Vietnamese/Heng Samrin forces any right of pursuit into Thai territory. The government in Phnom Penh responded to this Thai policy by angrily charging that Thailand's proclaimed neutrality in the Cambodian conflict was fraudulent – by providing sanctuary for the Khmers Rouges, the Bangkok government was

clearly 'standing with Pol Pot and Peking'. There was much speculation in the Western press that the Vietnamese would pursue their
enemies across the border even if this brought them into armed
conflict with the Thais.

Many of the Cambodians who entered Thailand at this time
returned more or less immediately to Cambodia, but large numbers
sought more permanent refuge. By the end of May 1979 there were
80,000 to 90,000 Cambodians on Thai soil, and it was estimated by
the Thai government that as many as 150,000 had entered Thailand
between mid-April and the end of June. By this time the fighting on
the border had died down and the crisis had eased off.

The Thai government refused to grant refugee status to most of
the Cambodians entering the country. The convention adopted by
the UN in 1951 defines a refugee as a person who leaves the country
of their origin 'owing to a well-founded fear of persecution for
reasons of race, religion, nationality, membership of a particular
social group or political opinion'. It has been accepted as a general
principle that people in this situation should be given sanctuary, and
should not be forcibly returned to their country. But the Thais
would only accept as 'refugees' those who were able to provide firm
guarantees that they would be re-settled in a third country – and as a
rule this was something that only a lucky minority of upper or
middle-class background could do. While most commentators still
continued to refer to the rest as 'refugees', they were officially
classified by the Thai government as 'illegal entrants'. The implication of this was that the Thais had the right to repatriate them to
Cambodia when the situation 'normalized', and that in the
meantime these people would remain under the control of the Thai
military and not the international agencies such as the UN High
Commission for Refugees (UNHCR) – which was refused access to
the border region. Not to be deterred, UNHCR and other aid
agencies went ahead and organized a programme of assistance for
the 'illegal entrants' even though under these circumstances all they
could do was give supplies to the Thai military. They had no way of
controlling, or even of monitoring, how these supplies were distributed by the military, and Phnom Penh alleged that international
humanitarian aid was being channelled into supporting Pol Pot's
army.

In mid-1979 the Thai government was still not reconciled to the
presence of so many Cambodian refugees on its soil, and by June
only 11,000 had been accepted for resettlement. The government
decided to deal with the rest of them by forcibly repatriating them.

On 8 June they began an operation to send more than 42,000 refugees back. They were trucked to the frontier of the northern Cambodian province of Preah Vihear, where there was little fighting in progress, given food for eight days, and pushed across the border. All of them faced a trek of over a hundred kilometres through uninhabited, trackless forest, and some found that they had been forced into minefields. For many, repatriation of this sort was nothing but a sentence of death.

There was an international outcry at this action, including representations to the Thai government from the UN secretary-general, Kurt Waldheim. At first the government responded by arguing that the refugees were a burden that a poor country like Thailand could not be expected to bear, but on 18 June it announced its decision to postpone the forcible repatriation of another 42,000 refugees. Distressed by the plight of the Cambodian refugees, to which the action of the Thai government had attracted a blaze of publicity, governments and international organizations promised to provide greater humanitarian aid – without looking too closely at how it was being handled in Thailand.

In the second half of 1979 the situation on the border deteriorated alarmingly. During the rainy season, there was only a trickle of refugees out of the Khmer Rouge zones, but by September they were arriving in greater numbers, in much poorer physical condition. 'These people tell us that as they walk through the forests towards Thailand, they see bodies lying everywhere,' said one relief official after 1,500 emaciated refugees were admitted to Mai Rut camp in mid-September.

With their food stocks exhausted, the Khmer Rouge forces were being starved out by the Vietnamese, who had cut off all their access to food-producing areas in Cambodia. This attempted siege by the Vietnamese was the context in which the distribution of humanitarian aid along the Thai-Cambodian border began. In June 1979, the Thais had allowed the Catholic Relief Service to distribute food to people in need on the border, and over the next few months most of the other agencies followed suit. The agencies tried to maintain that they gave aid to civilians only, but they admitted that they had no control over the situation. Inevitably, a significant amount of the aid went to Pol Pot's soldiers.

The trickle of refugees into Thailand turned into a flood again in October 1979. On 10 October, with the rains easing off, the Vietnamese launched a series of heavy attacks on Khmer Rouge positions around Phnom Malai, to the south of Aranyapratet. Pol Pot's troops had little choice but to retreat right to the Thai border, and even here they continued to come under artillery and mortar attack. The Thai government agreed to give them asylum on condition that they laid down their arms, and some 80,000 people crossed the border. Though hungry, the soldiers were still relatively healthy, but most of the people under their control were emaciated and riddled with disease. Many others camped around the food distribution points hastily established by the Thai army, and here reporters watched Khmer Rouge porters hauling off sacks of rice provided by the UN's World Food Programme, by UNICEF, by the Red Cross and the Australian government; while in the hospital tents the sick and wounded Pol Pot soldiers were treated by Western doctors.

Reporters visiting the border were now able to get a first-hand glimpse of conditions in the Khmer Rouge zones. Michael Richardson crossed the border into one encampment in the Phnom Malai sector and described conditions there in these terms: 'Much of it is forest. To penetrate this gloomy world . . . is to take a long walk through hell. We followed a track that winds for several kilometres past towering limestone mountains . . . . On either side, far into the malaria-infested forest, people were huddled in groups under crude shelters of plastic, matting, branches and grass. The air was acrid with smoke from countless small fires as women crouched over pots cooking rice, corn, dried fish and green papaya. The vast majority of these jungle hermits are women and children with just a sprinkling of old folk. Some appear to be reasonably well-fed and healthy. But many, stricken with malnutrition, malaria or beriberi, were lying on beds of leaves or straw mats. Apart from this listlessness, the thing I remember most clearly was not the sound of subdued voices or wood being chopped, but of children wailing and people coughing.'[12] AP reporter Denis Gray visited another Khmer Rouge encampment, where he found similar conditions. Most people refused to talk to him, and those that did explained everything in terms of *angkar* ('the organization', that is, the CPK). He concluded that 'even while the ultra-revolutionary movement may be preparing for its last stand, it makes no concessions to these under its control. The savagery and iron discipline remain.'

By 27 October some 30,000 starving and sick people had been deposited in a hastily established 'holding centre' at Sa Kaeo, sixty kilometres back from the border. Initially, this was nothing more than a fenced-in enclosure of sixty acres of badly drained paddy. People were transferred there from the border so hastily that no housing or sewerage had been established, and before supplies of food and medicine had been organized. About half the people had dysentery, and three-quarters of them had malaria. To cap it all, shortly after the camp was established it rained again, and the camp was flooded. With the help of volunteer workers, the aid agencies worked frantically to dig latrines, to set up tents and huts, and to organize food, water and medical services. Conditions at Sa Kaeo in the first few weeks were horrific, and the death rate was more than thirty-five per day.

By January 1980 conditions in the camp had improved greatly, and the death rate had fallen to only one or two a day. Perhaps half the camp population were Pol Pot supporters – the others having been a captive labour force – and about 7,000 were soldiers. Theoretically, they had laid down their weapons before they entered Thailand, but in Sa Kaeo they were equipped with machetes for building huts – 'tools not weapons' according to the Thai camp commander, and none of the hundred Thai soldiers responsible for maintaining order in the camp felt like investigating things too closely.

The camp leader, appointed by the Thais shortly after the camp opened, stalked around with a squad of half a dozen bodyguards, shouting orders to the refugees through a megaphone provided by the Thais. He was Colonel Phak Lim. He had organized the purges in the northwest region (Battamburg and Pursat provinces) for Pol Pot in 1978, and thereafter held the post of security chief for the region. In Sa Kaeo, he had those who disobeyed *angkar* beaten, staked out on hot tin roofs in the sun, or buried up to their necks in the ground. Nor were Western aid officials who displeased him exempt: one had to be transferred from the camp after a death threat.

The Vietnamese military offensive in Western Cambodia in October 1979 brought them right to the Thai border at many points, and led to renewed tension between Vietnam and Thailand. As they attacked Khmer Rouge forces straddling the border, Vietnamese shells sometimes landed on Thai soil, and from time to time Vietnamese and Thai patrols exchanged shots. On 16 October the Thai government called on the UN secretary general to send observers to the border, and warned that Thailand might retaliate against flagrant violations of its territory by warring factions in Cambodia. Three days later, Ngyuen Co Thach flew to Bangkok and assured the Thai government that the Vietnamese forces would not enter Thailand, but the Thai prime minister dismissed this as 'pure diplomatic deception to divide us and ASEAN'. Thach responded by making it clear that the Vietnamese assurances would be dependent on Thailand halting aid to Khmer Rouge forces.

By early November 1979 Pol Pot's remaining forces in western Cambodia appeared to be on the brink of defeat, dispersing in the face of the Vietnamese attacks and abandoning much of their territory. Their bases in the Cardamons were captured, only scattered groups (most straddling the Thai border) survived south of Pailin, and the mining town itself fell to the Vietnamese. On 5 November they were driven out of their main strongholds in the Phnom Malai area. Their main organized forces, estimated by the Thais to have fallen to only 12,000, were holed up in the rugged limestone hills between Phnom Malai and Pailin. Even though the Khmer Rouge military shed many of their civilian followers in October, their food problems continued.

It was widely expected that the Vietnamese would try and deal a knockout blow to the Khmers Rouges in the 1979-80 dry season. But given the rugged terrain and the fact that they were straddling the Thai border, this would not be easy. There was speculation that Vietnam would launch a massive strike into eastern Thailand, to cut around behind the mountains and completely encircle Pol Pot's army. In October 1979, Deng Xiaoping pledged that China would come to Thailand's assistance if it was attacked by the Vietnamese.

But the expected Vietnamese offensive never materialized. The fighting continued around Phnom Malai for the rest of the dry season, but on a much reduced scale after mid-November. In January 1980 the Vietnamese occupied the Khmer Rouge base at Phnom Chat, to the north of Aranyapratet, for a week. They then withdrew, and the base was promptly reoccupied by the Khmers Rouges. Essentially, the situation had reached a stalemate: Pol Pot's forces sat on the border and retreated into Thailand when attacked, while the Vietnamese avoided encroachments into Thailand.

From Hanoi's point of view, there was no need for a thrust into Thailand, with all the international repercussions that would follow. Although they had not been eliminated totally, Pol Pot's forces had been reduced to little more than a nuisance. The Vietnamese aim at this point was to keep them bottled up in the mountains and to concentrate on building up the PRK into a viable government. For their part, despite their dire condition at the end of 1979, the Khmers Rouges showed no sign of surrendering. What they wanted was time to regroup and reorganize their forces on the ground, and to rally international support for their cause. In the 1979–80 dry season, therefore, both sides were playing for time.

On 19 October 1979 the Thai government announced a decision that transformed the border situation. Kriangsak declared an 'open door' policy towards all displaced people from Indochina who sought asylum in Thailand. This immediately opened the way to a major international effort to aid them. On 1 November Kriangsak made a formal request to the UNHCR to provide care and maintenance for up to 300,000 Cambodians in Thailand, at a total cost of $59.7 million US. Two days later, the UNHCR agreed to the proposal, and at a UN conference in New York on 5 November $46 million was pledged to this project.

As a result of the new policy a huge holding centre, designed to house 200,000 people, was opened at Khao-I-Dang, twelve kilometres to the north of Aranyapratet, on 21 November. But the heavy fighting expected in Cambodia at this time did not eventuate. In addition, when the Thais tried to transfer refugees from encampments that spilled over the Cambodian border into Thailand to the camp, most chose to return to their own country despite political and economic instability – asked why, they said they were afraid of the Thai army. As a result, although it had been expected that the camp would be filled to capacity by the end of the year, at the start of 1980, its population was still only 84,000. Khao-I-Dang's population peaked at 130,000 in May 1980, at which point it was the largest concentration of Khmer people outside Phnom Penh.

Compared to Sa Kaeo, Khao-I-Dang was a model refugee camp. Facilities turned out to be more than adequate, and many of the refugees who came here were of middle-class background. They were better able to deal with Western officialdom than most Khmers and often had good prospects of being accepted by a third country. There were practically no Pol Pot supporters in Khao-I-Dang, and the main political problem was occasional fighting between different right-wing factions. However, the black market was in operation and crimes such as robbery and rape were reportedly common.

When the international agencies began distributing food aid to those in need at points along the border not controlled by the Khmers Rouges conditions were deteriorating in the interior of Cambodia, and there was a large-scale movement of people to these sections of the border. Though they recounted stories of hardship, suffering, and sometimes famine conditions in PRK zones, aid workers noted that they were in better physical condition than those who came across from the Khmer Rouge zones. It was the 'walking skeletons' who staggered out of Pol Pot's mountain strongholds who created the images of famine in Cambodia for the Western media. With the encouragement of American 'genocide' claims, this image was inaccurately applied to the masses of refugees from the PRK zones and, by extension, to the Cambodian population as a whole.

By December 1979 there were perhaps one million Khmers – nobody knew the precise number – encamped along the border in the flat country to the north of Aranyapratet. Sprawling shanty towns sprang up across miles of what had once been paddy-fields and thin forest, and the whole area became a crowded shambles of dusty straw huts, primitive trading stalls, flies and faeces. Local Thai farmers watched helplessly as the refugees scavenged their fields for food and building materials, turning them into a barren waste and destroying their meagre livelihoods. Most of the refugees here looked in good health. Signs of malnutrition were rare, but sores and eye infections were common – an indication of a dangerously unsanitary environment. Health workers thought that the lack of sanitation was the major problem, and worried that an epidemic of disease could sweep through this teeming mass of humanity like wildfire.

All of these people were themselves unproductive, and mainly dependent on aid from the international agencies operating along the border. Like the peasants on whose land many of them were squatting, their only potential source of livelihood was trade. And so the refugee settlements became huge trading centres. One of the chief items of trade was the aid delivered to the border camps. This was supposed to be distributed to the refugees as rations, but much of it was commandeered for trading purposes by armed groups. In early 1980 a Red Cross official said that this happened to up to 80 per cent of the food the ICRC delivered at the border, and the picture was much the same for the other agencies. 'We've had problems in many parts of the world trying to help people in need, but I have never seen anything like what is happening right now on that border' commented another official.

Private enterprise was quick to respond to the opportunities this situation presented. Thousands of Thai traders streamed to the Cambodian border, carrying goods for sale – fruit and vegetables, medicines, bicycle parts, tape cassette players, clothes, cartons of cigarettes, crates of beer bottles. The trade was immensely profitable, for the price mark-up between nearby Thai towns and the border camps was four or five-fold. Aranyapratet was temporarily transformed from a sleepy provincial market town into a hectic boomtown whose streets were jammed with stalls selling everything conceivable. The Thai government attempted to suppress this trade, but it was ineffective, for the Thai military itself was deeply involved. The Thai army commander in the Aranyapratet region at this time was said to have personally commandeered a ton of rice per convoy as the price for army cooperation.

From the other side of the border, thousands of Khmer traders arrived in the encampments every day, on foot or on bicycles, bringing gold and jewellery, or whatever valuable trinkets they could find in Cambodia (some were even rumoured to have dug up some of the mass graves in search of gold fillings). After resting for a few days, they set off down the dusty trails, carrying incredibly heavy loads into the interior of Cambodia. The border settlements became the centre of a huge network of trade stretching right across Communist Indochina, and at every step the prices were marked up. At its peak, in August 1980, the volume of the border trade was said to be 30–60 million Thai baht ($1.5-3 million) per day. By 1981, not only were Thai goods abundant in Phnom Penh, at least for those who had money, they were also readily available in the streets of Saigon, and luxury items such as quality tape recorders were reportedly doing a brisk trade in Hanoi. Technically, this 'black marketeering' was illegal, but the authorities in Phnom Penh and Vietnam seem to have largely turned a blind eye to it. Whatever threat it might have posed to a socialist economic order in the long run, in the short run it played a vital role in bringing food and other urgently needed consumer goods into a devastated Cambodia (and a besieged Vietnam).

The 'open door' policy towards refugees adopted by Kriangsak never had the wholehearted endorsement of the ruling elite in Bangkok. Officially, the Thai government had maintained that its stance was motivated by humanitarian concern, but the far-reaching political ramifications could hardly have escaped its attention. Thailand had succeeded in getting international funding for a programme that drew hundreds of thousands of Khmers out of the PRK-controlled zones into the sphere of influence of the Thais and the anti-Vietnamese insurgents on the border. It was reasonable to expect that these masses of refugees, saved from famine and foreign conquest by the Thais, could be moulded into a base of support for the insurgents, providing Thailand with a major level of influence in Cambodian politics.

Critics of Kriangsak's policy could point to the risk that as soon as world attention and world funding was drawn away from Cambodia by the next international crisis, Thailand would be left saddled with an intolerable financial burden in maintaining the refugees. The result could be a chronic problem approaching the magnitude of the Palestinian refugee problem in the Middle East. This could be guarded against by denying refugee status to the mass of Cambodian entrants, so that the Thai government would always have the option of repatriating them if need be. But this strategy would require the cooperation of the government in Cambodia (the real government, not the fictional one warming the UN's Cambodian seat), and so it was likely to turn the refugee question into a liability for the Thais and a potentially useful bargaining point for the PRK and Vietnam.

Repatriation and Reaction: Vietnam's Incursion into Thailand, June 1980

As the refugees in Khao-I-Dang and the other camps consumed the funds committed to them in November 1979, some of Kriangsak's critics' fears began to be realized. As the next donors' conference in March 1980 approached, it became clear that Thailand would not get the scale of funding it wanted – many of the donors were attracted by the proposition that the best way to assist Cambodians was to send money to Cambodia rather than to Thailand. The Thais threatened to boycott the meeting and used the occasion itself to call for an overall political solution to the crisis (that is, for a Vietnamese withdrawal and the replacement of the PRK) and for third countries to admit more Cambodian refugees.

Noting the Thai government's discomfort, Phnom Penh had offered in February 1980 to open talks with Bangkok on the refugee question. This was rejected by the Thais because they maintained that to negotiate with the PRK would amount to a *de facto* recognition of its sovereignty over Cambodia, and this was what they wanted above all else to avoid. Instead they decided to go ahead with a *unilateral* repatriation of the refugees, thus turning the issue into a direct challenge to PRK control of Cambodia.

On 26 March 1980 the Thai military supreme command announced that 1,345 people from Khao-I-Dang camp had been repatriated to an encampment at the village of Mak Mun, which was under the control of right-wing Khmer Serei guerillas. Downplaying the political dimension of the action, the supreme command went on to emphasize the humanitarian aspect of what they were doing. The returnees were all volunteers (unlike those sent back in June 1979), they had been provided with food and were being sent back to a 'battle-free' part of the border, and most sought to be reunited with family members. The whole operation had been carried out with the full knowledge of officials from international organizations. Phnom Penh Radio responded on 30 March with a propaganda blast against the Thais for forcibly repatriating 'reactionary Khmers' to assist the Khmer Serei, but there was no retaliatory action.

Through April and May the Thais quietly repatriated small groups of refugees. Specifically, Colonel Lim and the senior Khmer Rouge leaders at Sa Kaeo were secretly trucked back to the border at night. In May the Thai government began to talk publicly about new large-scale repatriations. On 26 May the Thai foreign minister, Air Chief Marshal Siddhi Savetsila, told a UN-sponsored conference that 'the most natural and desirable situation would be for the Cambodians, most of whom are farmers, to return to their fields and engage in food cultivation for their own sustenance, as well as for the country's economic reconstruction'. The Thais proposed that a safe zone for refugees be established under UN supervision in western Cambodia – thus raising the prospect of a partitioned Cambodia, with UN protection for anti-Vietnamese insurgents in the western zone.

In an attempt to forestall any moves in this direction, Phnom Penh on 6 June proposed to hold talks with Bangkok 'at any level and in all appropriate forms' to discuss 'questions of mutual interest', specifically, causes of tension on the border. The importance of this offer was emphasized by barrages of follow-up propaganda from Hanoi, Vientiane and Moscow, but the Thais refused to talk to the government in Phnom Penh and pushed ahead with their scheme.

On 10 June the Thai supreme command announced that refugees who wished to return would shortly be repatriated, beginning with those at Sa Kaeo. Singapore's Rajaratnam praised the announcement, and exhorted the refugees to 'go back and fight'. Phnom Penh Radio responded three days later with a very tough statement describing the proposed repatriation as a 'vile manoeuvre', an attempt to smuggle Pol Pot combatants back to the fighting zone under the guise of a humanitarian gesture. The statement told Thailand 'not to play with fire' and warned that the PRK 'will not allow such an importune violation of Cambodian territory'. Hanoi repeated these warnings. The UNHCR tried to talk the Thais into postponing the operation, but they refused.

In a politically calculated move the repatriation began on 17 June 1980 – just one week before an important conference of ASEAN foreign ministers was due to meet. At Khao-I-Dang only 1,600 out of 128,000 refugees volunteered to return. The great majority of those who did go back (7,464 out of 9,090) came from Sa Kaeo camp, where, as elsewhere, the repatriation was nominally voluntary, but the process of 'volunteering' was overseen by Khmer Rouge cadres. *Le Monde* correspondent Roland-Pierre Paringaux visited Sa Kaeo at this time, and described the situation there: 'The Khmer Rouge, who at most amount to a third of the camp, are proud of membership in the Angkar (CPK) and have lately been openly chafing to get back into Cambodia and have it out with the Vietnamese. They lord it over thousands of distressed civilians, many of whom do not dare talk openly to foreigners. A group of young peasants spoke to me of the pall of terror that settles over the camp at night . . . . Hundreds of people sleep in the camp pagoda every night fearful of the physical violence to which the Khmer Rouge subject refractory persons. Unlike the refugees in Khao-I-Dang, the people in the Sakeo camp feel – and not without good reason – they have been abandoned.'[13] As the first batch of returnees left Sa Kaeo, a UN official commented to John Pilger: ' . . . they're ready to fight . . . we're sending back a whole division of the bastards. This is like a declaration of war.'[14] When they arrived on the border more than 250 Khmer Rouge troops crossed into Thailand to welcome them. At their head was a familiar face – Colonel Lim.

For a week Phnom Penh and Hanoi complained loudly while the repatriations went on but did nothing. Then, early in the morning of 23 June 1980, the Vietnamese retaliated by attacking the refugee settlements at Mak Mun and Nong Chan, to the north of Aranyapratet. Warned by their scouts of the approaching Vietnamese, most of the Khmer Serei soldiers at Mak Mun melted away into the forest and left their camps exposed and defenceless, while those at Nong Chan dug in to resist the attack. At Mak Mun the Vietnamese took the camp over in half an hour and closed it down, sending 25,000 back into the interior of Cambodia. When they ran into resistance at Nong Chan, they plastered the settlement with an artillery and mortar barrage that took uncounted scores of lives, sent 60,000 panic-stricken refugees fleeing into Thailand and thousands of others running into the Cambodian forest. Khmer Serei sources later told reporters that the Vietnamese carried out mass executions and other atrocities at Mak Mun and Nong Chan, but they were unable to produce any concrete evidence (bodies, for example) to support these allegations.

Then about two hundred Vietnamese troops crossed the border into Thailand. They occupied three villages, warning the inhabitants to leave, and set up ambushes for Thai troops on the roads approaching the border. The Thais were caught off balance – they had been expecting the Vietnamese to respond with a new offensive against the Pol Pot forces in the Phnom Malai region, not an incursion into Thailand through the Khmer Serei areas – and the first troops they rushed to the border were caught in the Vietnamese ambushes. There were two days of skirmishes between the Thai army and the Vietnamese, and then the Vietnamese withdrew. The Thais gave the number of dead at twenty-two Thais and seventy-five Vietnamese. The Vietnamese government stoutly maintained that its troops had never entered Thailand, and was universally disbelieved.

The Vietnamese then sealed off a fifty-kilometre stretch of the border to the north of Aranyapratet for a month, bringing a halt to the cross-border relief operations, shutting down the black market and bringing the repatriations to an end. UNHCR had gone along with the Thai project unhappily in the first place, but it refused to continue after this Vietnamese show of strength. 'We agree with the Thai government that we are not going to send refugees into a war zone,' a senior UNHCR official announced, 'the repatriation is off until further notice.'[15]

There was an immediate protest that Vietnam's incursion into Thailand was an act of aggression, and that it was in violation of Thach's assurances to the Thai government on 19 October, 1979. On the second issue, it is important to note that Thach expressly withdrew these assurances after they had been rejected by the Thai government. In other words, the Vietnamese had clearly implied in October 1979 that if Thailand persisted in actively supporting anti-Vietnamese Khmer forces, they might retaliate against Thailand itself. In relation to the first issue, the Vietnamese presumably denied what they were doing because it was not defensible under international law – the PRK and its Vietnamese allies were justified in taking action against Khmer Rouge groups entering Cambodia from Thailand, but not in retaliating against the Thais themselves; despite the tensions, there was nothing approximating a 'state of war' between Thailand and the PRK.

Occurring as it did just before the ASEAN foreign ministers' conference, the Vietnamese incursion into Thailand had important diplomatic consequences. Over the previous six months, the Vietnamese had been diligently cultivating the divisions among the ASEAN countries and trying to isolate the hardliners in Singapore and Thailand. In December 1979 they had gratefully received the Malaysian foreign minister, who had been sent to Hanoi to foster a 'dialogue' between ASEAN and Vietnam. They had also been pleased by the results of the talks at Kuantan in March 1980, when Malaysia and Indonesia agreed that a settlement in Cambodia would be easier if China as well as Russia ended its involvement in Southeast Asia – a thinly veiled attack on Thailand's pro-Chinese stance. In May, Thach (who had taken over the position of Vietnamese foreign minister in February 1980) had visited Malaysia, where he said talks had gone favourably, and Thailand, where they led to a bout of public vituperation. In short, it looked as if the hawks from Bangkok and Singapore would come under heavy pressure on the Cambodian question at the meeting of ASEAN foreign ministers in June. They were saved at the last minute by the Vietnamese incursion of 23 June. As one reporter put it: 'If Vietnam had deliberately set out to cast itself as an international villain, it could not have arranged things better.'[16]

Indeed, it looked suspiciously as if Vietnam's diplomatic hand did not know what its military hand was doing. At the time of the incursion, Thach was in Jakarta, lobbying the Indonesians for the ASEAN foreign ministers' conference. He was warning them of China's ambitions and blaming tension over Cambodia on the Thais – and reportedly impressing his audience. He had made no attempt to prepare them for any action by the Vietnamese, and when first told of reports of the incursion in the press, denied them. 'It is not possible,' he said, 'it is not our policy.' After the reports were confirmed (and, presumably, after he had been in contact with Hanoi) Thach changed his line – the fighting had taken place after all, but it had been in response to Thai provocations, and the fighting had all taken place on Cambodian soil. This was unconvincing (the Vietnamese later obliquely admitted that they had crossed into Thailand on this occasion), and it looks like the one occasion when this sophisticated diplomat was caught off balance.

But the damage had already been done, and Thach's efforts were not enough to save the situation. Malaysia and Indonesia closed ranks with Thailand and Singapore, and the ASEAN foreign ministers' conference was another victory for the anti-Vietnamese hardliners. The meeting adopted a statement condemning the 'act of aggression by Vietnam' as 'irresponsible and dangerous'. It reaffirmed continued recognition of DK as the Khmer people's legal government and full support for Thailand's repatriation scheme. The USA responded by condemning Vietnam's action as a threat to the peace, called on the Soviet Union to restrain its protégé, and announced it was launching a special airlift of weapons to help defend Thailand. The Chinese responded with a barrage of propaganda denunciations of the incursion, offers to help Thailand, coupled with renewed violent clashes on the Sino-Vietnamese border and threats of military action against the Vietnamese 'trouble makers'.

But contrary to American, Chinese, and ASEAN rhetoric, there was little danger of a full-scale war between Vietnam and Thailand. The Vietnamese incursion was a limited one, a response to Thailand's unilateral repatriation scheme, and they all knew it. But by launching the repatriation on the eve of an important conference the Thais were able to put the Vietnamese in the position of choosing between their diplomatic efforts over the previous six months and the security of the PRK on the ground in Cambodia itself. What internal conflicts there were over this in Hanoi we do not know. But by taking retaliatory action against the Thais on 23 June 1980, the Vietnamese served notice that they judged the security of the PRK as more important than good relations with ASEAN.

The Shifting Great Power Triangle

The Indochina crisis of 1978–80 effectively demolished the 'balanced' foreign policy Thailand had adopted in the wake of America's military disengagement from Indochina in the early 1970s. The Thais now moved towards a policy that was pro-Chinese and pro-American, and anti-Vietnamese and anti-Soviet. Rather more hesitantly, the other ASEAN states followed the lead of their 'front-line' member. The basic premiss underlying this commitment was that the great power alignment of the 1970s – growing bonds between Washington and Peking, hostility on the part of both towards Moscow – would continue. But this had already proved false by 1983.

In America, the election of Ronald Reagan as president in November 1980 consolidated the trend towards a new cold war in

Soviet-American relations.[18] In June 1982 Reagan declared that, as far as he is concerned, 'the Soviet Union is at war with the United States.' In March 1983 he said the USSR was the 'focus of evil in the world' and that 'we are enjoined by scripture and the Lord Jesus to oppose it with all our might.' The Soviet response was tough. In his last speech, in October 1982, Leonid Brezhnev accused the American president of 'adventurism, rudeness, and undisguised egotism'. He said Reagan's policies were 'threatening to push the world to a nuclear war', and that the Soviet Union would 'spare nothing' in its efforts to meet the challenge of the American military build-up under Reagan.

Brezhnev's death in November 1982 did nothing to improve Soviet-American relations. His successor, Yuri Andropov, was pledged to continue the same foreign policy. In a speech to the central committee of the CPSU shortly before his election as general secretary of the party, Andropov declared: 'We know well that peace cannot be gained from the imperialists by begging for it; it can be defended only by the invincible might of the Soviet armed forces.' By 1983 both Soviet and American experts were agreed that relations between their two countries were worse than at any time since the Korean War.

Reagan's attitude towards the Soviet Union's main ally in the Far East was one of unremitting hostility. A Reagan official said of the Vietnamese in late 1981: 'Let them stew in their Soviet juice. Hanoi hasn't paid its dues; we aid those countries we defeat, not those that defeat us.'[19] This American attitude effectively undercut concili-atory currents within ASEAN, and strengthened the hand of the hawks.

Since the Chinese had frequently called on the Americans to take a tougher stance against the Soviets in the past, one might expect that this stance would only strengthen Sino-Soviet ties. And, indeed, at first this seemed to be the case. Following the recognition of the People's Republic of China by the Carter administration on 1 January 1979, trade relations between the two countries expanded rapidly. Agreements for scientific and technological cooperation were signed, and the Americans began building an atomic particle accelerator and a satellite ground receiving station for the Chinese. In 1980 the Americans announced their intention to sell military support equipment to Peking, and their willingness to sell weapons the following year. In 1981 it was also reported that the two countries were cooperating in establishing an electronic spy station in western China to monitor Soviet missile tests (both Peking and

Washington would neither confirm nor deny these reports).

Moscow watched these developments with undisguised alarm. Doubtless recalling their own unhappy experiences with the Chinese, the Soviets argued that arming China would prove to be in the interests of neither the USSR nor the USA, since China had its own ambitions, which it would pursue at the expense of both the super-powers. An article in *Pravda* on 27 June 1981, under the name 'I. Alexandrov' – a pseudonym for top Kremlin officials – commented: 'The danger of China's militarization – and this is the path that has been chosen by the Reagan administration – lies in the fact that American weapons in the hands of the Chinese will be used in the first place against relatively small neighbouring countries, among which, incidentally, there are American allies as well . . . . It seems that China is being pushed towards the realization of its territorial claims in Southeast and Southern Asia . . . . If Washington counts on using the rabid anti-Sovietism of the current Chinese leadership for the advance of the United States in its global anti-Soviet strategy, Peking has its own interests to pursue, viz, to set the United States and the Soviet Union against each other so as to dominate the world after a nuclear conflict which, according to Peking's plans, will annihilate America and Europe but, possibly, spare some dozens or a few hundred millions of Chinese . . . . The teaming up of the USA and China on an anti-Soviet basis will be taken into account in an appropriate way in the USSR . . . '[20] But it was precisely at this point that the alignments of the great powers began to undergo a new mutation.

The Sino-American *rapprochement* of 1979 had involved a fragile compromise over Taiwan. Peking continued to insist that it was part of China, and would eventually be reunified with the mainland. But in 1978–9 Peking was anxious to get American protection against the Soviets for its invasion of Vietnam, and so the Chinese pledged that they would not reunify Taiwan with the mainland by force. On the other side, Brzezinski was anxious to play 'the China card' against the Soviets, but did not wish for the USA to be seen to be abandoning its allies on Taiwan. The Americans did agree to de-recognize the Taipei government, to end their mutual defence pact with it, and to withdraw all American troops from the island. But they then passed the Taiwan Relations Bill, by which the USA maintained unofficial relations with the Taiwan government through the American Institute in Taipei, and continued with arms sales to the island. The consequences were that Peking went ahead with the invasion of Vietnam, while America's concessions over

Taiwan alienated Taipei without placating Peking. As soon as Chinese fears over Soviet retaliation began to fade, Peking was ready to take a tougher line over Taiwan once more, and the *rapprochement* began to unravel.

The old 'China Lobby' was still very influential in the right wing of the Republican Party, and Reagan attacked Carter's policies as a sell out. After he came to office, he stepped up arms sales to Taiwan, a line of action that drew sharp criticism from Peking as 'interference in China's internal affairs'. The disagreement over this festered on for two years, with neither side budging. On 17 August 1982 a joint Sino-American communiqué on the problem was issued, but it resolved none of the disagreements. Peking continued to issue schemes for the peaceful takeover of Taiwan, which were all instantly rejected by Taipei. The Americans endorsed a 'one China' policy – which brought Reagan under fire from his own right wing – and agreed that they would eventually end arms sales to Taiwan. However, they refused to set a cut-off date and in March 1983 Reagan announced that the USA would send $800 millions' worth of arms to Taiwan that year, and $780 millions' worth in 1984. He said: 'We do not believe that to make one friend, we should discard a long-term ally and friend – the people of Taiwan.' To this, Peking's English-language *China Daily* responded: 'It is sheer mockery to profess interest in the peaceful reunification of Taiwan with China while all the time militarily supporting the Taiwan authorities.'

Reagan was also unhappy at the prospect of Communist China emerging as a major regional power in its own right. As a State Department spokesperson put it in 1981: 'We are not asking China to be the regional policeman. We want to play an active role here.' Concern in the Reagan administration about China's independent regional ambitions mounted as the dispute over Taiwan intensified. American policy began to place more emphasis on Japan and, to a lesser extent, South Korea, as the main US allies in the region. This shift of emphasis was finally made explicit on 5 March 1983 when Haig's successor as secretary of state, George Schultz, made the first comprehensive statement of US policy in Asia for six years. Japan was up-graded to America's main ally, while China was treated as a regional power only, not as a world power. This approach further antagonized Peking, by delegating it to a lower place in the international order than it desired, and by strengthening an anti-Communist alliance that could be directed against it as readily as against the Soviets.

Central to American thinking at this time was an assumption that the Sino-Soviet antagonism could not be undone. Peking had turned to the West to safeguard itself against Soviet bullying, it was reasoned; if pressured by the West, therefore, it would have little choice but to make concessions. This was a serious miscalculation. As we showed in chapter five, Peking's independent great power ambitions had played a major role in precipitating the Sino-Soviet split, and China held more of the initiative in Sino-Soviet relations than is usually assumed. China's turn to the West had been motivated more by opportunism than by fear of the Soviets, and it could easily be reversed if Peking thought its advantages had been exhausted. This point had been reached in 1981.

The Soviets have always maintained that the Sino-Soviet split is an aberration, a 'nationalist deviation' from the true path of 'proletarian internationalism', and have always looked forward to an eventual reconciliation between the great powers of the Communist world. This seemed out of the question while Mao dominated Chinese politics, but after his death in 1976 the Soviets suspended their anti-Chinese polemics and began hinting broadly at their desire for friendship. But at that time Peking's eyes were still cast firmly in the direction of Washington, and the Chinese responded by reaffirming Mao's view of the Soviet Union as a 'social-imperialist' country. By 1978 Sino-Soviet relations were, if anything, worse than they had been in the latter years of Mao's life.

However, the progressive demolition of Maoism in China over the next few years gave the Peking leadership greater scope for flexibility. Articles in the Chinese press in 1979–80 made it clear that Mao's critique of the Soviets as well as his domestic policies had fallen into disfavour. On 20 April 1980 the *People's Daily* publicly repudiated the famous series of articles it had carried in 1963–5, in which Mao had detailed his critique of Soviet 'revisionism'.

It is probable that as early as 1979–80 a majority of the Chinese leaders were in favour of winding down their quarrel with the Soviets, but there were still important differences between them (specifically, between Deng and Hua, as we saw in chapter five) on the question of timing. Nevertheless, while the Vietnamese and the Khmers Rouges were fighting what Brzezinski fondly imagined to be a 'proxy war' between the Soviets and China, Peking was initiating a modest thaw in Sino-Soviet relations. In April 1979 Peking announced that the 1950 treaty of friendship between the two countries would not be renewed. While this came as a surprise to nobody, Peking also took advantage of the occasion to offer to negotiate a normalization of relations with the USSR. The talks began in September, but were suspended by the Chinese in January 1980, in the wake of the Soviet intervention in Afghanistan. Sino-Soviet relations then remained frozen over for another eighteen months.

Chinese policy began to shift once more in the middle of 1981. When Alexander Haig visited Peking in June, he gave the Chinese strong support over Indochina, and offered them arms. But, instead of reciprocating, they gave him a torrid time over the Taiwan issue. Then, on the day he left the Chinese capital, the *People's Daily* published an article by Li Huichuan on the Sino-Soviet border dispute. Though it attacked the Soviets in strong terms, it called for a reopening of the talks suspended by China in 1980. In addition, the Chinese conspicuously refused to join the American-orchestrated chorus of condemnation of the Soviets over the Polish crisis. From this point on, Chinese statements began emphasizing the 'independence' of Chinese policy.[21]

These hints were not lost on the Soviets. In February 1982 they proposed a reopening of the border talks. Then, in a major speech at Tashkent on 24 March, Brezhnev made an emphatic appeal to Peking for a normalization of Sino-Soviet relations. He maintained that although the Soviets had openly criticized Chinese policies, 'there has not been and there is no threat to the People's Republic of China from the Soviet Union.' He also sought to exploit Sino-American disagreements by emphasizing that the USSR 'fully recognized' China's sovereignty over 'Taiwan island'. This doubtless pleased the Chinese, but they played hard-to-get. They responded that what they wanted from Moscow was 'deeds, not words'.

A first round of talks between the Chinese and the Soviets was held in October 1982, and a second round in March 1983. The Chinese demanded that the Soviets end their hegemony over Mongolia (a country which Peking sees as belonging rightfully to its sphere of influence), withdraw their forces from Afghanistan, and halt all aid to Vietnam until it withdrew all its forces from Cambodia. The Soviets insisted that the talks concentrate on bilateral issues, specifically the Sino-Soviet border, and made no concessions over relations with third countries.

Nevertheless, the change of mood in Peking was clear, as was Moscow's willingness to encourage it. Trade, cultural and sporting exchanges between the two countries multiplied, despite the lack of progress on the diplomatic front. When the Americans claimed there was a threatening new Soviet military build-up in the Pacific this was ignored in Peking, where once it would have been pounced on as an occasion for fulminations against 'social-imperialism'. When the Soviets shot down the South Korean airliner KAL-007 in September 1983 the Chinese studiously avoided contributing to the torrent of denunciations.

Before flying to Moscow for Brezhnev's funeral in November 1982, Huang Hua declared: 'President Brezhnev was an outstanding man.' Hua was the most senior Chinese leader to visit Moscow since the early 1960s, and Andropov went out of his way to make it clear that he was welcome. Before returning to Peking, Hua said that he was looking forward to a gradual but steady improvement in Sino-Soviet relations.[22] By the end of 1983 this is exactly what has happened – neither more, nor less.

It is too soon to say what the consequences of this shift in global politics will mean for Indochina and ASEAN. But there is no doubt that they will prove considerable. Paul Quinn-Judge reported from Bangkok late in 1982: 'Though the only result of last October's first round of Sino-Soviet talks seems to have been discreet diplomatic activity, news of the meeting has had the unsettling effect of an earth tremor in this part of the world. Sino-Soviet hostility has been one of the foundations on which much of the region's politics has been built in recent years. Now the foundations are shifting, and people are waiting to see whether things will return to normal, or whether policies will be reduced to rubble.'[23]

So far, at any rate, present alignments have held intact. The Chinese, of course, are hoping to drive a wedge between Moscow and Hanoi. Vietnam has welcomed the Sino-Soviet thaw as reducing tensions in the region, and has expressed confidence that the Soviets will not abandon it. The Soviet deputy foreign minister, Mikhail Kapitska, was given an especially warm welcome in Bangkok in February 1983. It is too soon to know whether this was simply a follow-up on China's initiative, or whether the Thais were taking the opportunity to move towards a 'balanced' foreign policy once again. In the meantime, however, the local cold war between ASEAN and Indochina continues.

Notes

1. For the reaction in Bangkok to the Communist victories, see M. Ladd Thomas, 'The Perceived Impact of Communist Indochina on Thailand's Security' in Clark D. Neher, ed., *Modern Thai Politics: From Village to Nation*, 2nd ed., Cambridge, Mass. 1979, pp. 398–402. For recent general accounts of Thai foreign policy, see

John L.S. Girling, *Thailand: Society and Politics*, Ithaca and London 1981, ch. 6, and Leszek Buszynski, 'Thailand: Erosion of Balanced Foreign Policy', *Asian Survey*, vol. 22, 1982.

2. See, for example, Malcolm Caldwell, 'Thailand and Imperialist Strategy in the 1980s', *Journal of Contemporary Asia*, vol. 8, 1978.

3. Girling, p. 239.

4. Quoted by Nayan Chanda, *Far Eastern Economic Review*, 21 December 1979.

5. Quoted by J. M. van der Kroef, 'Kampuchea: The Diplomatic Labyrinth', *Asian Survey*, vol. 22, 1982, p. 1020.

6. 'Diplomacy of the Kampuchea Conflict: Key Documents', *Indochina Issues*, no. 21, November 1981.

7. *New York Times*, 18 July 1981.

8. Quoted by Nayan Chanda, *Far Eastern Economic Review*, 21 December 1979.

9. Michael Akehurst, *A Modern Introduction to International Law*, London, 1970, pp. 317–18.

10. D.W. Grieg, *International Law*, 2nd edn, London 1976, pp. 849-95.

11. Quoted by Gareth Porter, 'Kampuchea's UN Seat: Cutting the Pol Pot Connection', *Indochina Issues*, no. 8, July 1980. The credibility of America's position on Cambodia was further undermined by the justifications it offered for its own military intervention in Grenada in 1983. These were summed up by Assistant Secretary of State Kenneth Dam in an interview in Paris as follows:

'Q: What are the legal bases, according to you, for the invasion?

'A: There are three: the first is the call for aid from the Governor-General which is in itself sufficient since, according to the constitution of 1973, he has the power to appoint the government and, in the absence of a government, we think that he has the right to act to re-establish order, which he did by demanding the intervention of the forces of Jamaica, Barbados, and the United States.

'Second reason: the UN Charter recognizes the right of regional collective security, and the Organization of American States (OAS) forsaw certain conditions in which an intervention, undertaken within a regional framework, is not forbidden. The Organization of Caribbean States decided to act. It estimated that not only was there a power vacuum that constituted a menace to regional security, but also that the introduction of foreign military advisers and large quantities of armaments constituted a de-stabilizing factor. This problem held all our attention, and that is why, when the Organization of Caribbean States asked for our aid on Friday, 21 October, we dispatched our special envoy, Ambassador McNeil, to see if they had accurately presented the situation and if their demand for our assistance was serious.

'Third reason: a humanitarian action to assist American citizens in difficulty is recognized by international law. Finally, I would like to say it is also important to consider the situation of the President. By waiting he would have sparked a debate. But we were coming up the fourth anniversary of the taking of hostages in Teheran, and we had every reason to think, according to information received by Dominica, Barbados, and Jamaica, that waiting would have entailed grave risks. The President had to take a decision and could not allow himself to wait for a wide international debate before acting. He took responsibility, and has been largely supported by the United States, the region, and even Grenada, as you will come to see.' (*Le Monde*, 9 November 1983)

If these were to become accepted principles of international law, the case justifying Vietnamese intervention in Cambodia is many times stronger than the case for the US actions in Grenada. After all, Pol Pot was threatening Vietnam with something more substantial than a 'power vacuum'.

12. Michael Richardson, *Age*, Melbourne, 22 October 1979.

13. Roland-Pierre Paringaux, *Guardian Weekly*, 6 July, 1980.

14. John Pilger, 'Only the Allies are New', in John Pilger and Anthony Barnett, *Aftermath: The Struggle of Cambodia and Vietnam*, London, 1982, p. 95.

15. In fact, after a few months, the repatriation was quietly resumed. It proceeded quietly, rather than as a public challenge to the PRK, and refugees were not sent to the Khmer Rouge bases. By early 1983 the Thai army had transferred most refugees in Thai camps to Khao-I-Dang (population, 56,000), and was hoping to close down the others. At Khao-I-Dang, those who had little chance of repatriation were coming under increasing pressure to return to the border. In April, when the Vietnamese attacked Nong Chan and Phnom Chat, the refugees were transferred to another point on the border rather than admitted to camps inside Thailand.

16. Richard Nations, *Far Eastern Economic Review*, 27 June 1980.

17. Buszynski, p. 1046. See also his 'Thailand, the Soviet Union and the Kampuchean Imbroglio', *The World Today*, February 1982. Golam W. Choudri writes: 'China was pleased with the outcome of the Vietnam-Thailand border conflict in June 1980.' (*China in World Affairs*, Boulder, Colorado 1982, pp. 228–29.)

18. See Fred Halliday, *The Making of the Second Cold War*, London 1983, ch. 9.

19. Quoted by Derek Davies, *Far Eastern Economic Review*, 25 December 1981.

20. *Keesing's Contemporary Archives*, 30 July 1982, p. 31621.

21. For authoritative statements of Peking's present policies, see Hu Yaobang's Report to the 12th CCP Congress (*Beijing Review*, 13 September 1982) and Huang Hua's Address to the UN General Assembly (ibid., 11 October).

22. For analyses of the thaw, see William E. Griffith, 'Sino-Soviet Rapprochement', *Problems of Communism*, March-April 1983; Donald Zagoria, 'The Moscow-Peking Deténte', *Foreign Affairs*, Spring 1983; O. Edmund Clubb, 'The World View From Peking', *Nation*, 19 March 1983.

23. Paul Quinn-Judge, 'Sino-Soviet Thaw', *Indochina Issues*, no. 33, January 1983.

8

Coalition of Lost Causes

Cambodia became the focus of a confrontation between Vietnam, intent on keeping the PRK government in place, and the ASEAN countries, who sought to restore Pol Pot's Democratic Kampuchea. Overarching this conflict was China's determination, backed by the USA, to exploit the situation in order to 'bleed' Vietnam. The key to the strategies of both ASEAN and China was the growth of the military capabilities of the anti-Vietnamese resistance forces on the Thai-Cambodian border. Non-Communist groups also operated here, but the Khmers Rouges were undoubtedly the most effective.

Rebirth of the Khmers Rouges

Pol Pot's forces were in a desperate state in the closing months of 1979. Vietnamese attacks had captured or destroyed most of their base camps, and their people had been reduced to a nomadic forest existence, with no idea where their next meal would come from. Starvation and disease were rapidly reducing their numbers, and their organizations were disintegrating. The army had fallen to a total strength of about 20,000, but half of them were isolated and dispersed, totally cut off from the main force. Some units of the latter were breaking up into roaming bands of armed predators. In a force that had prided itself on its discipline, robbery, rape and murder had become commonplace. In this situation of general social breakdown, only rigid discipline managed to hold things together – but even the CPK organization was riven by desperate struggles over food, and by bitter mutual accusations of treachery. The party leaders were still blaming all the set-backs they had suffered on 'traitors among the ranks of the party, the army and the people'. Many people lived with the fear that, on top of everything else, their rulers would launch a new round of sweeping purges to eliminate 'traitors' and restore their crumbling authority.[1]

It was foreign support that relieved the pressure on Pol Pot's forces. With the commencement of large-scale food distribution across the Thai-Cambodian border in October 1979, the Khmer Rouge leaders were assured, at least for the time being, of a regular supply of food for their supporters. As the health of their workforce began to improve, they were able to organize the construction of more permanent base camps, the clearing of forest and the planting of crops and vegetables. When we visited their model village at Nong Pru in January 1981, the Khmer Rouge cadres were able to show us extensive fields of vegetables, and claimed that this settlement of 1,000 people was self-sufficient, except for rice. How true these claims were, or how typical this was of the Khmer Rouge base areas as whole, we cannot judge. But what is certain is that this situation was radically different from what reporters saw in the same area in 1979.

Economic rehabilitation had major political consequences. The aid agencies had little choice but to hand food over to the cadres for distribution, which meant that the distribution of food within the Khmer Rouge zones was controlled by the party organization. Control over food supplies had been one of the key methods used by the Pol Pot regime for controlling the population, and economic stabilization inevitably meant consolidating the CPK's power again. Although food aid across the border undoubtedly saved thousands of lives, one of its major consequences was the political revitalization of the Pol Pot forces.

Needless to say, this was also true of the military aid the Khmer Rouge forces received from China. This reportedly began flowing through Thailand in January 1979, as soon as Phnom Penh fell, but Khmer Rouge cadres expressed bitter disappointment at the paltry quantities of aid they received in the course of 1979. However, in November or December of 1979 a major shipment of military aid from China reached Pol Pot's forces, and further supplies followed in 1980. They included ammunition, rifles, machine guns, mortars, rockets and land-mines, medical kits and new uniforms (from this point on, increasing numbers of Khmer Rouge soldiers were seen wearing green, Chinese-made uniforms in place of the traditional black Khmer peasant garb). Although Thailand officially maintained that it was neutral in the conflict, the Thai military took responsibility for transferring the Chinese supplies to the border (and Khmer Rouge cadres complained about the extent of pilfering by Thai soldiers).

Over the first half of 1980 the Khmer Rouge leaders made major efforts to rebuild their armed forces. Not only did units that had been cut off manage to rejoin their main forces, new recruits were pressed into service. By mid-year, they claimed to have 60,000 men under arms (and many more 'irregular' units supporting them throughout Cambodia). Thai intelligence sources, however, put the figure at 40,000, while Western observers in Bangkok thought even this was an inflated figure, and that between 25,000 and 30,000 was a more realistic figure. While even the lowest of these figures indicated a marked improvement on the situation in October 1979, nothing suggested that they had grown enough to be a serious threat to the Vietnamese in conventional warfare.

However, the Khmer Rouge leaders knew that the support they were receiving came not because of any positive enthusiasm for them and their policies, but because it was hoped that they would be a major military threat to the Phnom Penh government. Accordingly, their propaganda depicted a major military effort in a Cambodia still torn by heavy fighting, and claimed that they had inflicted huge casualties on the Vietnamese. (These figures were so inflated that they were obvious fabrications. For example, on 15 May 1980 the Voice of Democratic Kampuchea claimed that 70,000 out of the 200,000 Vietnamese troops had been put out of action over the preceding dry season. According to a statement by Khieu Samphan on 21 October another 63,000 were killed or wounded during the rainy season – that is to say, two thirds of the Vietnamese forces in Cambodia had been put out of action in one year! Claims of this order of magnitude are repeated annually.)

When we talked with him in January 1981, Khieu Samphan was at pains to stress that Khmer Rouge actions had brought about 'a qualitative change in the military situation in Cambodia'. The initiative had passed from the Vietnamese, who were said to be 'worn out, exhausted and without morale', to the Khmer Rouge forces. He gave us a map allegedly showing the military situation in August 1980, apologizing for not being able to provide a more up-to-date one. 'Hot battlefield areas' covered about a quarter of the country and most of the rest was depicted as 'guerrilla fighting zones' – less than 10 per cent was depicted as securely in the hands of the Vietnamese-PRK.

In fact, though their forces were stronger than in the second half of 1979, there was relatively little military activity by the Khmers Rouges in 1980. They did succeed in re-taking their basecamps in Phnom Malai early in the year, and held off renewed Vietnamese attacks later in the year. But most of their forces were deployed to defend their own base camps, and they had little offensive capacity. Visitors to the country found little evidence of insurgent activity even in the western provinces. Nor was this picture basically altered by the 'monsoon offensive' of 1980, to which much publicity was given. The Khmers Rouges were unable to attack large Vietnamese forces and operated as small guerrilla bands, making night raids on bridges, isolated army outposts and vehicles. Their largest operation was a daylight attack on the train from Battambang to Phnom Penh on 10 June. One hundred and fifty people were killed, most of them unarmed traders bringing goods back from the Thai border. Towards the end of the year *New York Times* correspondent Henry Kamm summed up the situation: ' . . . Vietnamese occupation troops control all of populated Cambodia – the towns and villages, as well as the roads, railroads and waterways that link them. . . . The Pol Pot forces control only enclaves in formerly uninhabited areas. . . . They control no roads and own no vehicles. Their leaders cross into Thailand to travel from one enclave to another'.[2] He concluded that the essential activity of the Pol Pot forces was to stay in action in Cambodia in order to justify political pressure blocking diplomatic recognition of the PRK government. A military fiction was required to sustain the diplomatic fiction.

However, the lack of impact of their 1980 'monsoon offensive' revealed the inability of the Khmers Rouges to mobilize support among the peasantry – the class that had provided their mass base in the war of 1970–75. Their chief appeal was strident nationalism, but to most people living peacefully under PRK rule and perfectly capable of recalling the terror of the Pol Pot years, Khmer Rouge propaganda against the Vietnamese 'racial exterminators' inevitably rang hollow. In almost every village or town, the Khmer Rouge cadres found that the mass of the population was opposed to them and, worse, a substantial section were willing to actively cooperate with the new authorities against them. Except in the most remote parts of the country, they could not even rely on the willingness of the peasants to look the other way, let alone their support. As a result, Steve Heder concluded on the basis of interviews with Khmer Rouge soldiers at this time, 'most of the populated countryside was off limits to the Democratic Kampuchea fighters and agents'. The conditions for launching a successful guerrilla war against the Vietnamese occupation were not present.

One consequence of this was that the Khmer Rouge leaders had little chance of expanding their forces after about mid-1980. Unable to recruit from populated areas inside Cambodia, their armed forces could draw its manpower only from the base camps on the Thai border and from refugee camps inside Thailand. Once these reserves had been mobilized, the process of expansion came to a halt, and at the end of 1981 the Khmer Rouge armed forces were still about the same size as they had been eighteen months earlier (25,000–30,000).

Pol Pot's group was aware that their effectiveness was limited by their unpopularity, and early began efforts to broaden their appeal. In an interview in June 1979 Ieng Sary said that the Khmers Rouges were willing to cooperate with Sihanouk, the right-wing Khmer Serei groups, Lon Nol, and even Heng Samrin, to drive the Vietnamese out. In another interview, he conceded that there had been some 'excesses' in the past, but promised a 'gentle and liberal regime' if the Khmers Rouges were restored to power once more. 'We are willing to forget the past,' he announced, 'and I hope that others too forget the past, to join in a national patriotic united front.' In September 1979 the Khmers Rouges launched a new 'Patriotic and Democratic Front', whose draft programme promised free elections, freedom to form political parties, freedom of speech, the press, and of religion. The economy would be based on individual or family productive activity, and the rights of private property would be guaranteed. However, no politically significant figure joined this new front. Invited to become its president by Khieu Samphan, Sihanouk refused.

In December 1979 Pol Pot stood down as prime minister of DK, to be replaced by Khieu Samphan. Thereafter Pol Pot was not seen in public again, but he retained his positions as commander-in-chief of the Khmer Rouge armed forces and as general secretary of the CPK. With Pol Pot still in personal control of the army and party, Khieu Samphan, as prime minister, could be little more than a figurehead. Most observers concluded that Pol Pot's stepping down was no more than a cosmetic operation, probably urged on the Khmer Rouge leadership by China.

However, it was more than just a face-lift. It did signal an important political shift in the political line of the Khmer Rouge leaders. They announced at the same time that they would 'cease to implement' the 1975 constitution and adopt the draft programme of the 'Patriotic and Democratic Front' as the fundamental law of the land. In the new situation, they announced, 'our present task is no longer to make the socialist revolution and to build socialism. Our present task is not an ideological one, it is a struggle for the defence of the territory and race of our beloved Cambodia.' Cambodians of all classes and creeds would be 'warmly welcomed' into the new front. When we questioned Khieu Samphan on this in January 1981, he emphasized that nationalist rather than Communist ideology had always been the driving force of the movement: 'No more socialism. No more socialist revolution . . . . Our ideal is the survival of Cambodia. As for Communism, we saw it as the way to lead Cambodia to independence and survival – *a means only*, not the ideal. Now, through the flesh and blood of people, we have been given the experience to know we cannot follow this way.'

The rejection of socialism was no doubt intended mainly to open the way to an alliance of the Khmers Rouges with right-wing forces against the Vietnamese. But it did signify a shift away from the extreme policies previously pursued in the Khmer Rouge zones. The new purges in the air in October 1979 never materialized. Total collectivization was abandoned and the base camp population was organized into low-level cooperatives. Collective work was continued, but at an easier pace. The cultivation of private gardens was allowed, and family life was restored. But this was still socialism of a sort, and the Khmer Rouge settlement at Nong Pru was a model of disciplined serenity compared to the chaos of Nong Chan and Nong Samet.

These moves, along with the dramatically improving living conditions made possible by international aid, apparently did much to restore faith and morale among Khmer Rouge supporters. In August 1980 one of them, a former intellectual, told Heder of life in the base camps: 'Life here is not too bad. We can't do what we want but we can use our brains and contribute. We don't spend all our time planting vegetables, criticizing each other and worrying who's going to disappear next like we did after '75. This is the sort of regime we can support. Nobody could support the regime that existed after '75.'

Yet even among the party faithful, many were uneasy because they perceived that there was no guarantee that things would not go off the rails again. This is how one defector summarized what he said was a widespread feeling in the base camps: 'The cadres who were responsible for the ultra-left line and the killings still grasp all power. Now suddenly they've changed 100 per cent. . . . But these guys do just what they want according to their subjective analysis of the situation. They could change back just as suddenly. Furthermore, no one can question them about what went wrong before. They don't accept any criticism or admit that they were wrong. They blame everything on others. How can you trust them? They say everything depends on the concrete situation, but they're the ones who conclude what the concrete situation is and sometimes even create the concrete situation, like after '75 when they screwed everything up. It could be like that again. Nobody could stop them.'[3] If such fears were common among those who had stuck with Pol Pot's group through everything, one can imagine the problems they faced in trying to win over wider support. Very few Khmers were willing to accept Ieng Sary's invitation to 'forget the past'.

At the end of the dry season in 1981 the Vietnamese withdrew their forces from some of their more remote and vulnerable outposts. This was apparently because of difficulties they had experienced in keeping the backroads of Cambodia open during the previous rainy season, but some interpreted it as a sign that the Vietnamese were in serious military trouble in Cambodia. As might be expected, the Khmer Rouge leaders hailed this as a great victory, and in May Ieng Sary claimed that they would be ready to liberate some district and provincial towns by early 1982. The Vietnamese withdrawal did allow Khmer Rouge forces greater mobility, and they were more active than in the previous rainy season. Visitors to Cambodia reported an evident deterioration in security in the northern and western provinces.

But any expectation that the Khmers Rouges might be building up to a military breakthrough was soon dashed. The Vietnamese took the initiative once more in the 1981–2 dry season, and inflicted a series of devastating defeats on the Khmers Rouges. With the central provinces now largely peaceful, the Vietnamese could concentrate more of their troops on the battlefronts, and for the first time PRK troops appear to have played a major role in the fighting. For the first time, too, the Vietnamese made regular use of Antonov-26 transport aircraft for ferrying troops and supplies. This liberated their logistics from dependence on Cambodia's ramshackle road system, and gave them much greater mobility and striking power. Having suffered from shortages of ammunition in some of the previous fighting, the Vietnamese now ensured that ample supplies were stockpiled close to the combat zones before sending their troops into action. New weapons were deployed. Heavy artillery, including 133-mm field pieces, were used to devastating effect against Khmer Rouge encampments. An-26s were also rigged up for bombing raids, and Mi-8 helicopter gun-ships were reportedly used for the first time. Against these new weapons the Khmers Rouges had no effective defence except mobility.

In mid-December the Vietnamese captured a jungle camp near the junction of the Thai, Lao and Cambodian borders, where Pol Pot's defence minister, Son Sen, had his headquarters. They inflicted heavy casualties on the 10,000 troops under Sen's command, captured field hospitals and major ammunition and supply depots established before the Vietnamese invasion, and neutralized the whole command structure of the Khmers Rouges operating in the northeast of Cambodia. This camp had also been used to supply Lao guerrillas and apparently anti-government forces in the Vietnamese central highlands, as well as the Khmers Rouges themselves.

In January 1982 the Vietnamese launched a new assault on the main Khmer Rouge base area at Phnom Malai. They succeeded in driving the Khmers Rouges out of their front line defences, and pinned them down in a narrow strip of land, twenty-five kilometres long, straddling the Thai border. The Khmers Rouges were left with only one hilltop observation post still in their hands, and were forced to destroy large quantities of supplies to prevent them falling into the hands of the Vietnamese. The 5,000 Khmer Rouge troops in this sector suffered heavy casualties. Another offensive in the mountains to the south of Phnom Malai inflicted still more. Overall, there is little doubt that the Vietnamese offensive of 1982 resulted in the worst set-backs the Khmers Rouges had experienced since 1979. While Vietnamese losses are said to have been considerable, the reserves of military manpower on which they could draw were vastly greater than those of the Khmers Rouges.

As usual, in public the Khmer Rouge leaders looked resolutely on the bright side of things. In the judgement on the dry season's campaign he gave to a *Peking Review* correspondent, Khieu Samphan maintained that things were still going well - the 'combat effectiveness and military quality' of the Vietnamese forces had been reduced. But, reading between the lines, even Samphan admitted that the Khmers Rouges were losing ground: ' . . . the Vietnamese aggressors recaptured a number of areas we liberated during the monsoon season in May-October 1981. . . . We are concentrating on conserving our effective strength, not on winning land. We sometimes temporarily give up an area to preserve our strength . . . '[4]

The defeats suffered by the Khmers Rouges in the 1981-2 dry season led military analysts to conclude that many earlier estimates of the size of Khmer Rouge forces had been too high. Whereas previously this figure had been put as high as 45,000, most people agreed that a figure of 25,000 was more likely in December 1981. And given the casualties they suffered in this period, it is probable that their numbers had fallen to 20,000 or less by the end of the dry season. Heavy casualties made their lack of recruitment base more critical than ever. As one Bangkok analyst said at this time: 'Every soldier they lose is irreplaceable.'

During the 1982 rainy season the Khmers Rouges regained much of the territory they had lost in the previous dry season. There was a modest upsurge of guerrilla activity, mostly in the far west of Cambodia, although in August they staged an ambush in Kompong Cham province that took the lives of a PRK vice-minister for agriculture and two Vietnamese advisers. Guerrillas also continued to harass the main highway in Kompong Thom province. One commentator summed up: 'The Khmer Rouge attacks served to prove that they were not yet extinct as a military force, but did not pose any threat to the survival of the Heng Samrin regime.'[5]

Outside support was able to rebuild Khmer Rouge military strength to some extent after 1979. However, it could not create the political conditions for effective guerrilla warfare in Cambodia. Pol Pot's supporters were detested by the Cambodians because of their conduct in the 1975–8 period, and no amount of outside support could offset this fundamental handicap. It may be difficult, in the present international context, for the Vietnamese to annihilate them completely, but it is clear that they have almost no prospect of ever capturing power in Cambodia again.

For eighteen months after the Vietnamese toppled Pol Pot, the ASEAN countries, China and the USA had all based their policies on the assumption that the Khmers Rouges' nationalism and fighting capabilities made them a potent opposition force, despite their reputation for brutality. But the débâcle of the 1980 'monsoon offensive' showed how weak and politically isolated the Khmer Rouge leaders really were. China stuck by its Cambodian allies, but the ASEAN countries had always been embarrassed to find themselves in alliance with a deposed Communist dictator, and they were uncomfortably aware that if the Khmers Rouges' defeat at the hands of the Vietnamese came to be seen as permanent rather than temporary, the PRK would gain increasingly wide recognition. Unless it could be endowed with a more attractive public face than Pol Pot's group could provide, diplomatic support for DK would crumble. In this context, ASEAN's attention turned increasingly to the non-Communist resistance groups operating on the Thai-Cambodian border, to the Khmer Serei.

The Khmer Serei and the Rise of the KPNLF

Banditry and smuggling had long been common along the Thai-Cambodian border, and right-wing Khmer Serei ('Free Khmer') guerrillas had operated here in the 1960s. In the 1970s the Khmer Serei had joined forces with the Lon Nol regime, but after 1975 many of the surviving remnants of these groups had returned to smuggling and sporadic guerrilla operations on the Thai border. They were given a new lease of life by the influx of politically minded, anti-Communist refugees after the overthrow of the Pol Pot regime. Most of the new groups that sprang up at this time were led by former Lon Nolists, but the term Khmer Serei stuck.[6]

The strongest and best organized of these groups was the 'Khmer People's National Liberation Front' (KPNLF). It had been formed in Paris in March 1979, but its existence was not proclaimed until 9 October 1979, after it had managed to bring several other anti-Communist splinter groups under its wing. The leader of the KPNLF was Son Sann, a frail, bespectacled man in his seventies. Of mixed Khmer-Vietnamese ancestry, Sann studied in Paris in the 1930s, and was one of the few Khmers to have served in the French Indochinese administration (in which he rose to the level of provincial governor). Under Sihanouk he had founded the Cambodian National Bank in 1955 and served as prime minister in the rightist government of 1967–8. When Sihanouk was overthrown in 1970 Sann went into exile in Paris, where he tried unsuccessfully to create a 'third force' opposed to both the Lon Nol regime and the NUFK.

Most of the groundwork for the emergence of the KPNLF was done on the Thai-Cambodian border by Dien Del. Vietnamese by birth, Del had moved to Cambodia in his teens and served as a divisional commander in the Lon Nol army. Sann appointed him commander-in-chief of the KPNLF's military forces, and he was highly regarded by the Thai military, who gave their backing to the KPNLF in Khmer Serei faction fights.

While the KPNLF was militarily the strongest of the Khmer Serei groups, with about 2,000 men under arms in 1980, Son Sann and Dien Del were aware that their small force was in no position to launch a direct military challenge to the Vietnamese. They concentrated their energies on establishing control over the border encampments, with their rapidly expanding populations, on distributing anti-Vietnamese propaganda, and on building up a network of sympathizers and informers inside Cambodia. Their political line was one of opposition to Pol Pot and to Sihanouk, as well as to the

Vietnamese and Heng Samrin. They tried to persuade other Khmer Serei leaders to avoid entanglement in dubious black market operations, but in vain.

Politically, their most serious rival was the Movement of National Liberation of Cambodia, commonly known as 'Moulinaka'. This was a slightly smaller but highly active group formed in August 1979 by Kong Sileah, a former Lon Nol naval lieutenant. With about 2,000 men but only arms for a few hundred, Moulinaka maintained that the anti-Vietnamese struggle could rally wide support only if it was led by Prince Sihanouk and if the non-Communist groups were willing to collaborate with the Khmers Rouges to take immediate military action against the Vietnamese. On the other hand, the KPNLF regarded the Khmers Rouges with loathing and Sihanouk with suspicion. However, both groups agreed that the Khmer Serei should concentrate on the struggle against the Vietnamese rather than on smuggling, black market activity and banditry.

But it was on precisely these activities that the Khmer Serei groups that were the most successful in the short run based themselves. Wan Sarin, a former Lon Nol soldier who had turned to banditry and teak smuggling in the Pol Pot period (after a short spell as a Buddhist monk in Bangkok), had established control of the settlement at Mak Mun. The influx of refugees brought some 200,000 people into the small area his forces controlled. Now calling himself Vong Atichvong, he announced the formation of a Khmer National Liberation Movement, with himself as commander-in-chief of its armed forces. With about 1,000 armed men under his command, he adopted the titles of 'Marshal' and 'Prime Minister'.

Sarin's camp was joined by Andre Okthol, who had spent the 1970s in France as a political science student but now attracted a following by calling himself Prince Norodom Soriavong and claiming to be a cousin of Sihanouk's. Wearing a neat safari suit, dark glasses and the wispy beginnings of a Zapata-style moustache, he held 'press conferences' at which he called on the West to provide him with the $800 million needed to liberate Cambodia from the Communists. A religious fanatic, he wore Buddhist amulets to ward off evil spirits and bullets, captivated the most despairing of the refugees with his mystic incantations, and terrified the rest with his violent outbursts of temper. His followers were untrained and utterly undisciplined, strutting around showing off their shiny new weapons and smoking marijuana. He was quickly nicknamed the 'Mad Prince' by reporters.

To the north of Mak Mun, the encampment at Nong Samet was

controlled by an uneasy coalition of former Lon Nolists led by In Sakhan and a group of defectors from the Khmer Rouge settlement at Phnom Chat led by Mitr Don. With about 2,000 men under arms, they ruled over about 200,000 refugees, but the main focus of their activity was black market profiteering rather than politics.

From late 1979 to early 1981 the struggle among these groups for control of the people and trade along the border repeatedly flared up into violence, aggravated by the occasional intervention of the Thais, the Vietnamese and the Khmers Rouges. When violence did erupt, the resultant shoot-outs between groups armed with automatic weapons and rocket-grenade launchers occurred in the middle of densely populated refugee settlements and took an appalling toll of life.

The outcome was that by early 1981 most of the border to the north of Aranyapratet was controlled by the KPNLF, or at least by camp warlords who gave their allegiance to the KPNLF. Wan Sarin's group at Mak Mun was smashed; he himself fled to Thailand, where he was reportedly murdered. The 'Mad Prince' disappeared without trace, and the KPNLF took over the camp. At Nong Samet a bloody struggle resulted in Mitr Don driving In Sakhan's followers out of the camp. At this point Don enjoyed KPNLF backing, but in February 1981 he was ambushed and killed after falling out with Dien Del. Kong Sileah resisted KPNLF control, but he died of cerebral malaria in August 1980. His followers quickly reached an understanding with Dien Del, and for two years they continued to operate as an independent group out of the KPNLF-controlled Nong Chan camp. (Sileah's successor, Nhem Sophon, was reported to also have succumbed to cerebral malaria in August 1983.) Minor clashes between Moulinaka and KPNLF supporters were common occurrences. In Sakhan resurfaced in 1981, at first swearing loyalty to the KPNLF, and then switching to Moulinaka. This so annoyed the Moulinaka military commander at Nong Chan, Chea Chutt, that he responded by switching over to the KPNLF.

Once KPNLF dominance had been established, an uneasy peace settled over the border camps, although they remained lawless places. Yet though they had made their peace with the KPNLF, many of the camp leaders still seemed more interested in profiteering in the black market than in the political struggle. This was highlighted by an incident in October 1982, when the KPNLF commander at Ban Sa-Ngae camp, Siem Sam On, was killed in an ambush. He was on his way home from a meeting with Dien Del, at which the two men had quarrelled fiercely. Del thought that On was more interested in his highly profitable video café at Ban Sa-Ngae, where he was showing pornographic movies to appreciative refugee audiences twice a day, than he was in fighting the Vietnamese. Many of the other KPNLF commanders were outraged by On's death – which they blamed on Del, though he denied all knowledge of the killing – and Son Sann had to fly back from the UN in New York to patch things up. He was obliged to force Dien Del to stand down as supreme military commander of the KPNLF, although he kept him on as an 'adviser'.

Del was replaced by a joint military command, consisting of Sak Sutsakha, Thang Reng, Hing Kamthorn, and Chea Chutt. The first two were leading Lon Nolists, who had been persuaded to rejoin the struggle a few months earlier – Sutsakha had been the last commander of the republican army in 1975, Reng the commander of a 'Special Forces' brigade. Kamthorn was a leading political figure in the KPNLF, one of Sann's lieutenants, while Chutt was the commander at Nong Chan. The meteoric rise of Sutsakha and Reng indicates the substantial continuity of the KPNLF forces on the Thai border with the defeated Lon Nol regime.

The KPNLF also had an important base camp at Sokh Sann, to the south of Pailin. This was the headquarters of Prom Vit, one of the non-Communist leaders held in high regard by Bangkok observers. Vit was said to be adept at guerrilla warfare, whereas the other Khmer Serei leaders still thought in terms of conventional military tactics. Sokh Sann was a complex of four villages with a population of 8,000, relatively remote from the corrupting influences of the black market.

On the whole, the right-wing forces remained very weak in 1981, despite the opportunities presented by the collapse of the Pol Pot regime. The Khmer Serei groups were the linear descendents of the Lon Nol regime, and inherited its weaknesses – chronic disorganization, paralyzing corruption, and a lack of any positive political direction – in exaggerated form. Their main support came from the dispossessed Cambodian middle class, but that was small to begin with and had been decimated by Pol Pot's terror. Few of its surviving members had any heart left for counter-revolutionary struggle; they hoped for a ticket to the USA, France or Australia rather than a gun and a chance to have a crack at the Communists. The peasants remained indifferent to the political appeals of the Khmer Serei, even though the influx of refugees to the border in search of food brought many thousands under their control and influence.

Son Sann never failed to impress Western commentators with his conservatism and personal integrity. To Elizabeth Becker, for example, 'he sounds like the leader Graham Greene's "quiet American" died searching for.'[7] But in fact, he can be taken as a symbol of the weakness of the right: an elderly banker is unlikely to be the successful leader of a guerrilla war.

Lacking a mass base, the Khmer Serei groups also failed to build a modern political movement. They developed no effective organizational structures and no ideology with mass appeal. Only the KPNLF showed any understanding of the importance of organization, but its ideological appeal was vague. The various other Khmer Serei 'fronts' were little more than personal cliques, and their politics quickly degenerated into warlordism and banditry. The resultant wave of bloody in-fighting among the Khmer Serei groups also helped to disillusion and alienate their potential support.

The emergence of the KPNLF as the dominant force on the border restored some stability to rightist politics after 1981. Nonetheless, the problem of how to expand their forces was a critical one for the KPNLF leaders, especially as the number of people on the border was dropping off rapidly as the food situation inside Cambodia improved. At this point the Khmer Serei (and the KPNLF in particular) found itself the repository of ASEAN and Western hopes of 'saving' Cambodia. External support tremendously enhanced their powers of patronage, and led to a substantial growth in the numbers of their followers. By 1983 the KPNLF reportedly had 9,000 men under arms, and Moulinaka had 3,000. By this stage, according to Tim Carney, first secretary in the American embassy in Bangkok, they were strong enough to send small sabotage and propaganda teams 'deep into the interior, of Cambodia.[8] Heartening as this was for the anti-Communists, it was not, realistically, making much of a dent in the Vietnamese-PRK position in Cambodia.

The Politics of a 'United Resistance'

For three years the left-wing and right-wing oppositions to the Vietnamese presence in Cambodia remained at odds. Then they were brought together in a 'united resistance' – as a result of their own weaknesses and under heavy pressure from their foreign patrons, China and the ASEAN countries. Moulinaka and the KPNLF had no military strength or diplomatic recognition, while the

Khmers Rouges had found that their military prowess was vitiated by their unpopularity. Each side detested the other, but hoped to exploit it.

ASEAN played a major role in bringing the coalition partners together. Following the failure of the Khmers Rouges' 1980 'monsoon offensive', Lee Kuan Yew described Pol Pot as a 'butcher', and said: 'We [the ASEAN countries] do not want to see Pol Pot restored in Cambodia.' What Cambodia needed, he announced, was for someone like Sihanouk to take over the DK forces. But ASEAN would continue to champion the cause of recognition of the DK regime in the UN. Those who thought that this stance was contradictory he dismissed as 'silly and simplistic'. He elaborated on ASEAN's new proposal in a subsequent interview: '(China) is now the sole supporter of the Khmers Rouges . . . ASEAN does not want Pol Pot back in Cambodia, although it supports Democratic Kampuchea for tactical reasons . . . . There are leaders who have not been associated with the atrocities of Pol Pot, like Sihanouk, Lon Nol, Sonn Sann, and Im Tam, who can command the respect and the loyalty of Cambodians and who can win their support in any secret, freely expressed ballot . . . . ASEAN does not want Pol Pot and the Khmers Rouges to be in power ever again; to achieve this we must preserve the Democratic Kampuchea seat in the UN and alter the nature of the government of Democratic Kampuchea. Both the Chinese and Khmer Rouge leaders must recognize that the alternative to this is the eventual legitimizing of a Vietnamese puppet regime in Cambodia.'⁹ Lee's basic proposal was that the right-wing groups join a coalition with the Khmers Rouges so that they could take over the mantle of 'legality' from Pol Pot and eventually be installed in power in Phnom Penh.

This solution to the Cambodian problem was quickly endorsed by the other ASEAN countries, but the Chinese were not persuaded. They did not think that the non-Communist groups really had the strength to play a leading role in a coalition, and argued that it was essential that the leadership and army of DK should not be weakened by any rash changes. The Thai prime minister, Prem, went to Peking in October 1980 to try and sell the idea, and he was followed by Lee in November. The Chinese finally endorsed the scheme at Zhao Ziyang's press conference in Bangkok on February 1981.

For their part, the Pol Pot group made it clear that they would welcome others joining them in a coalition, but that they had no intention of standing down for them. They viewed a coalition primarily as a way of gaining respectability and widening their own recruitment base. They showed no interest in being used to bring other groups to power.

The prospect of a coalition with the Khmers Rouges was not attractive to the non-Communist groups. The KPNLF responded by making a bid for power in its own right. In January 1981 Sonn Sann trudged across a mountain trail from Thailand to Sokh Sann, where he was given an enthusiastic ceremonial welcome. He announced to his followers (and to the reporters who accompanied him) that he would form his own provisional government before the next UN General Assembly. He attacked the idea that the KPNLF was a 'third force' (that is, in competition with the Khmers Rouges and the Sihanoukists) and claimed it was the true representative of 'all Cambodian patriots'. He claimed to have 60,000 followers and called for foreign economic and military aid for the KPNLF.

Nor was the other leading candidate for an alternative to Pol Pot, the exiled Sihanouk, enthusiastic about a coalition. While he had acted as DK's representative at the UN in January 1979, he had subsequently tried to distance himself as much as possible from the Khmer Rouge leaders. From mid-1979 to the end of 1980 Sihanouk had lobbied for an international conference modelled on the Geneva Conference of 1954 to work out an acceptable compromise among the great powers, and he modestly proposed himself as a leader who was loved by the Cambodian people and acceptable to all parties to the conflict. He was also relying on Chinese backing. As he explained to a reporter in 1979: 'The Chinese are very intelligent. Things are getting worse for Pol Pot, so if they go bad for Pol Pot they still have Sihanouk. I am the Sihanouk card. First they deal Pol Pot, and if that doesn't work they deal Sihanouk.'[10] At this time he was also emphasizing that the essential condition for any wider compromise was the elimination of any chance of Pol Pot's group returning to power.

When he was invited to head the Khmer Rouge 'Patriotic and Democratic Front' in September 1979, he wrote to Khieu Samphan: 'The new front and the new political programme presented by the Khmers Rouges are incontestably a new deception. Only idiots and imbeciles will fall into the trap of your new delusions.' His initial response to Lee Kuan Yew's coalition proposal was negative. In an article published in November 1980, he argued: 'According to certain Westerners, the Khmer Rouge wolves are perfectly capable of transforming themselves into lambs. Such wishful thinking is dangerous, above all for the Cambodian people still in Cambodia.

These people are hoping the free world can find some means of saving them other than by supporting the so-called legitimacy and legality of the infernal regime of Pol Pot, Ieng Sary and Khieu Samphan.'[11] And in December 1980, in a tape-recorded message distributed to his followers on the Thai-Cambodian border, Sihanouk described the Pol Pot group as 'arch-criminal, anti-national and anti-people', and said that the Vietnamese were being 'shamefully dishonest' in accusing him of being an accomplice of Pol Pot's.

But when Zhao Ziyang gave China's imprimatur to the idea of a united resistance, it was Sihanouk who was first off the mark with a proposal for a united front between himself and the Khmers Rouges. He announced his willingness to cooperate with the Khmers Rouges on 8 February 1981, and met with Khieu Samphan on 10 March in Pyongyang, the North Korean capital. Samphan agreed to some of Sihanouk's demands but rejected others – notably the disbanding of the Khmer Rouge army after the Vietnamese had gone. This was a matter of no little significance; as Sihanouk later commented, 'the Khmers Rouges do not want to give the slightest guarantee that they will not again begin their massacres.' He said that the Cambodian people would prefer Vietnamese domination to the risk of a return to genocide. Nevertheless, he agreed to meet again with Samphan for further discussions on joining forces.

Sihanouk was driven into an alliance with the Khmers Rouges by the weakness of his own position. His attempts to find a diplomatic solution to the Cambodian crisis in 1979–80 had been rejected by all parties. By 1980 he had concluded that his only chance of having any say in his country's future was to field an army. He succeeded in rallying Moulinaka and a few small Khmer Serei factions, but they remained very weak. Sihanouk himself claimed a membership of 5,000 for his army in early 1981, but observers on the Thai-Cambodian border said the real figure was 600–800. Sihanouk claimed a wide following among his 'little people' and Western commentators who thought of him as a 'charismatic figure' were inclined to agree.

But Sihanouk was a traditional ruler who had been stripped of his power. And with political power he lost much of his sacred aura and popular following. Our own impression inside Cambodia was that he seemed like a figure from a remote past – remembered with a vague fondness, but irrelevant to present problems. However, a visitor's impressions on such a sensitive matter could easily be misleading. In 1983 a Vietnamese official told reporter Paul Quinn-Judge: 'Ten years ago Sihanouk's name was strong enough to rally a country against the Americans. Now his name can cause us some problems, but they are tolerable. Ten years from now he'll be forgotten.' However, Quinn-Judge believes that 'the Sihanouk name still works its magic among the peasants.'[12] In support of this, he relates that a Vietnamese soldier who had worked as a military adviser in western Cambodia told him that, though the peasants hate the Khmers Rouges, if the guerrillas say they are working to restore the prince, the peasants will listen to them.' They will listen, yes; but their response will doubtless be shaped by memories of the outcome of the last Khmer Rouge-Sihanouk alliance. As for Sihanouk's 'magic' appeal, if our understanding of kingship in Therevada Buddhist societies is correct, the peasants will wait for a practical demonstration of the return of Sihanouk's powers before they rush to support him.

Sihanouk acknowledged that he was motivated not only by a sense of obligation towards his 'little people', but also by personal pique. He explained to Nayan Chanda that he resented critics 'from coffee shops in Paris, Montreal and Los Angeles' who accused him of doing nothing. According to Sihanouk, it was pressure from anti-Communist, anti-Vietnamese exiles – the 'blue Khmers', he called them – that was forcing him into an alliance with Pol Pot: ' . . . since I could no longer live in peace and tranquility, even here in Pyongyang, because of these letters and telegrams arriving from them insulting me, calling me a pro-Vietnamese traitor and a selfish do-nothing, I said, "All right, I launch myself into war." . . . The Blue Khmers, carried away by their Vietnamese phobia, refuse to see reality. They have lost all notions of the Cambodian people's misery. They don't realize that the people now have a much better life than under the Khmers Rouges, and they absolutely don't want the return of the Khmers Rouges. The whole policy is totally unrealistic. To go to war in Cambodia now is madness. But I have to participate in this madness because otherwise I will be called a traitor.'[13] Whatever they might say about him joining forces with the Khmers Rouges, the exiles could no longer accuse him of doing nothing. Most were outraged, but in due course many found themselves obliged to follow suit.

Sihanouk soon found that the mere possibility of forming the united front was not enough to attract the sponsorship he wanted. In April he conferred with the Chinese foreign minister, Huang Hua, who told him that China would give him weapons only if he could resolve his differences with the Khmers Rouges. Then he turned to America. On 25 April he met the US chargé d'affaires in Peking, J. Stapleton Roy, and asked him if America was willing to provide the weapons. But Roy also insisted he join forces with Pol Pot. 'After that,' said Roy, 'it will be easier for friendly countries to help you.' Finally, in May, Deng Xiaoping offered him weapons for an army of 3,000 if he promised that they would fight the Vietnamese and not the Khmers Rouges.

Son Sann found himself coming under similar pressures. To get weapons, he had to agree to a coalition. Having earlier denounced Sihanouk for negotiating with Khieu Samphan, he now found himself forced to do the same. He tried desperately to assure his followers that there was no danger in this – in order to make a 'turn to the right', he argued, it was necessary to 'veer a little to the left first'. He evidently agreed in principle in April 1981, because a shipment of Chinese arms for the KPNLF arrived on the border on 23 April. By May it was clear that Sann had been forced to drop the idea of establishing his own government, and to work through the framework of DK. But he would not budge from his demand that the entire Khmer Rouge leadership stand down in his favour. 'We can't accept a coalition with them,' one of his aides explained. 'They would murder us in our sleep.'

A 'summit conference' between Samphan, Sann and Sihanouk in Singapore on 2–4 September resulted in an agreement to form a coalition government, but it broke down almost immediately. Sihanouk explained on 5 September that he had signed the agreement 'without happiness . . . . For me to get aid from China I must integrate my movement into a united front. China has told me that I have to be a member of the proposed coalition if I want to get any arms.' He criticized both Samphan and Sann for their 'intransigent and unrealistic approach'. The same day Sann declared that the KPNLF would drop none of its preconditions for forming a coalition and that he would attend the next UN General Assembly as prime minister-designate of Cambodia. Samphan then produced a statement of 'clarification' denying that Sann was prime minister-designate and denouncing the other parties' attacks on the Khmers Rouges as a violation of the agreement.

The quarrels continued for another nine months. There was another round of talks in November, to consider a Singapore proposal for a 'loose coalition' in which each faction would retain its own separate political identity. This was accepted by Sihanouk and Sann, and rejected by the Khmers Rouges. A further round of talks was held in Peking in February 1982, but Sann refused to attend. The Chinese blamed Sann for the failure of the talks, and suspended their aid to the KPNLF in March. Malaysia, Singapore and Indonesia blamed the Khmers Rouges, and hinted that if their intransigence continued, ASEAN would withdraw support from the coalition proposal.

There were more talks in Peking in May 1982. The Thai foreign minister, Siddhi Savetsila, flew there to try and persuade the Chinese to pressure the Khmers Rouges into making concessions to Son Sann, but the Chinese refused. Siddhi flew back to Bangkok and declared that he was ready to 'wash his hands' of the coalition. A senior Thai official explained: 'We found the Chinese leaders extremely firm in their conviction. ASEAN believes in a political solution, but China is convinced that only military pressure – and eventually military victory – would oblige Vietnam to change its approach. We must consider new options besides the coalition. We have asked Prince Sihanouk to keep the issue alive. There is not much more we can do. And ASEAN cannot afford another failure.'[14] At this point, several European countries were considering dropping support for seating Pol Pot's regime at the UN, and Indonesia was ready to opt for an accommodation with Hanoi, even if it meant accepting the status quo in Cambodia.

In desperation, the Thai foreign ministry drafted a new coalition proposal, and secretly called for a new round of talks between the Khmers Rouges and the KPNLF. If the Chinese would not force the Khmers Rouges to give way, they would have to pressure Son Sann into submitting. But it was not until 12 June, one day before Siddhi was to fly to Singapore for the ASEAN foreign ministers' conference, that Sann finally agreed to sign the coalition agreement.

Sann was forced to submit because, for all the numerical growth claimed for it, the KPNLF was still politically and militarily weak. In March the Vietnamese had captured the KPNLF's main base camp at Sokh Sann with ease; its 2,000 defenders, the cream of the KPNLF's fighting forces, had fled after putting up only nominal resistance. Morale was bad and funds were running low. Yet such strength as the KPNLF possessed was based on foreign patronage, and it was becoming politically isolated. The Khmers Rouges, Sihanouk, China, and now the ASEAN countries, were all blaming the failure of the coalition talks on Sann's 'intransigence'. 'We cannot afford a lonely position any more,' admitted a senior KPNLF figure in May.

The coalition agreement was ceremonially signed in Kuala Lumpur on 22 June 1982. Norodom Sihanouk (who now became president of the Coalition Government of Democratic Kampuchea), Khieu Samphan (vice president in charge of foreign affairs) and Son Sann (prime minister) gave each other cheek-to-cheek embraces. Both Sihanouk and Sann described their decision to join with the Khmers Rouges as 'agonizing', but they said 'we have no other choice', since the key issue was 'the survival of Cambodia'. When Sihanouk was reminded of his 1980 statement that it was dangerous to imagine that the Khmer Rouge 'wolves' could be 'transformed into lambs', he observed: 'I am a lamb. Son Sann is a lamb. We have to choose between being eaten by Khmers or eaten by Vietnamese. As Khmers, we prefer to be eaten by Khmers, because we are nationalists.'

It was a united front formed on the wolves' rather than the lambs' terms. Although the coalition document was written by the Thai foreign affairs ministry, it reads, commented one American diplomat in Bangkok, 'like a Khmer Rouge document'. It states that the working of the Coalition Government of Democratic Kampuchea shall be guided by the principles of tripartism, equality und non-preponderance.' This meant that, contrary to ASEAN's original hope that the non-Communist elements would gradually take the coalition over and get rid of the old Khmer Rouge leaders, the latter were now given a formal guarantee that they were accepted as a fully equal partner in the coalition. They retained control of their own military and security forces. As a concession to Sann and Sihanouk, Ieng Sary did stand down from the post of foreign minister, but the foreign policy making process remained in the hands of the Khmers Rouges. The government would operate 'by the principle of consensus' on all matters of importance, but if the consensus broke down the coalition was to become 'inoperative'. In that case, 'the current state of Democratic Kampuchea led by H.E. Mr Khieu Samphan will have the right to resume its activities as the sole legal and legitimate state of Cambodia.'[15] In other words, if the non-Communist groups were not willing to go along with the Khmers Rouges, they would be dismissed from the 'government'.

Yet there were some concessions to the non-Communist groups. They were allowed to retain their own 'organization, political identity and freedom of action, including the right to receive and dispose of international aids specifically granted it'. This gave Sihanouk and the KPNLF a chance of getting aid from sources that would refuse to aid the coalition as a whole, while leaving China free to channel aid to the Pol Pot group. Sihanouk immediately embarked on an international tour to rally support (and aid) for the coalition. Singapore promptly came forward with an offer, and Sihanouk said that Australia, Canada, Malaysia and Japan were all considering sending aid earmarked for the non-Communist groups because they did not want them to become dependent on Chinese support.

In reality, the independence of the parties was so great that the coalition did not exist on the ground. The first outsider to visit the 'capitals' of the new coalition was Japanese journalist Isao Oglso, who wrote in *Manchini Daily News* that the anti-Vietnam coalition was an illusion that existed only on paper. According to Oglso, there was no communication between the Khmer Rouge, KPNLF and Sihanoukist forces. He was told by one of Sihanouk's aides: 'There isn't any such thing as an anti-Vietnamese coalition government. We are acting independently. The only thing we have for the Polpotians is antipathy and hatred.'

There had always been a curious air of unreality about the attempts to create a unified resistance, which probably reached a peak with Son Sann's statement in April 1981 that a united front would drive the Vietnamese out of Cambodia within four years. It had been an attempt to bring the most disparate elements – monarchists, anti-monarchist bourgeois republicans, and ultra-left Communists – together under the common banner of nationalism. The hope was that, somehow, the whole would not have the failings of the individual parts. Each group was driven to seek out allies not because of any convergence of objectives, but simply because of their own weakness, and because of foreign pressure. Given the accumulated suspicions and hatreds produced by a decade of incredibly brutal civil war and revolution, it was surprising that even the façade of a coalition was created.

Hanoi did not seem greatly alarmed. It argued that the coalition was dominated by the Khmers Rouges and that Sihanouk and Sann had lent themselves to a US-China plot to give the Pol Pot group greater international respectability. But the situation in Cambodia was irreversible, and the formation of the coalition did not alter that. 'A corpse is a corpse, no matter how dressed up,' commented *Nhan Dhan*. Some interpreted Vietnam's announcement of a troop withdrawal from Cambodia in July 1982 as a calculated display of contempt for the military potential of the coalition.

There were many for whom the illusion was all that was needed. Before the announcement of the coalition, the ASEAN countries had been fearful that diplomatic support for DK was beginning to crumble. But on 25 October 1982, following an address by Sihanouk as president of the coalition government – since Khieu Samphan was in charge of foreign affairs, strictly speaking he should have given the speech, but this was not an occasion for reminding the audience of political realities – the UN General Assembly gave its largest ever vote in favour of recognition of the DK government. There were 90 votes in favour of DK (compared with 77 in 1981), 29 against (compared with 34), and 26 abstentions (compared with 31). The performance was repeated in 1983.

The purpose of the coalition, as ASEAN had originally conceived it, had been to strengthen the non-Communist groups by putting the coalition (including the Khmer Rouge army) under their control, and displacing the discredited Pol Pot group. But the Khmer Rouge leaders, with the support of China, had refused to let themselves be phased out in this convenient fashion. In the end, ASEAN had to force the unwilling non-Communist groups into the coalition on largely Khmer Rouge terms.

From ASEAN's viewpoint, perhaps the best that could be said for the coalition agreement was that it created a tenuous legal basis for providing military aid to the non-Communist groups. Yet the prospect of openly aiding armed insurgency in Cambodia only aggravated the divisions within ASEAN. At a meeting of ASEAN foreign ministers at the beach resort of Pattaya in Thailand in December 1981, it was agreed that the non-Communists had to be helped to build up their strength to a level comparable to that of the Khmers Rouges. Otherwise, as a Malaysian official put it, they would become a 'third farce' instead of a 'third force'. But a Singapore proposal that ASEAN send military aid to them was rejected, on the grounds that ASEAN was a non-military organization. If aid was to be sent, it could only be by countries acting on an individual basis and not by ASEAN as a whole.

The idea of overt military aid to armed forces in Cambodia was also reported to have run into strong opposition from some top Thai army leaders, who were said to be alarmed at Thailand's deepening involvement in supporting the insurgents. This, they argued, was probably futile, and likely to provoke Vietnamese retaliation. These reports seemed confirmed in January 1982, when the supreme commander of the Thai armed forces made a thinly veiled attack on China in a televized speech. He warned that a 'superpower' that supported Communist activity in Thailand (the Communist Party of Thailand was pro-Chinese) had tried 'openly and subversively to lead Thailand into a near-war situation with neighbouring countries ruled by different ideologies and ultimately into a bitter and barbarous proxy war'. The Thai armed forces would act with 'extreme caution' to prevent such a situation arising.

Following the formation of the coalition government in June 1982, Sihanouk made a tour of ASEAN capitals, seeking promises of military and economic aid for his cause. Singapore, in fact, was already reported to have secretly begun supplying the KPNLF in early 1982. A shipment of light infantry weapons for about 2,000 KPNLF troops and 1,000 Sihanouk troops arrived in September. Sihanouk said that Australia, Canada, Malaysia and Japan were all considering sending aid earmarked for the non-Communist groups because they did not want to see them dependent on China. Lee Kuan Yew was reported to have urged Sihanouk to bring about a merger between his army and the KPNLF 'to create a receptacle for aid from potential donors' and to reduce the Khmers Rouges' 'decided military advantage in the partnership'.

When Sihanouk got to Bangkok, he was given a friendly reception by the king and by the Thai prime minister, Prem Tinsulanond, but it was made clear that the Thai government would not be providing him with any weapons. He then visited Khao-I-Dang, where he persuaded thousands to return to the border encampments of the Khmer Serei. He claimed that 40,000 people volunteered to join his armed forces, but that he had had to turn them away because he had not been given sufficient aid to supply them with food and weapons.

There is little doubt that Sihanouk was able to strengthen his forces considerably once the Thais let him go on a recruiting drive in the refugee camps. According to refugee officials, 13,000 people left Khao-I-Dang to join 5,000 other Sihanoukists at the newly established camp of O-Smach, over the border from Thailand's northeastern province of Surin. Many of these recruits were, of course, civilians who probably had little understanding of the militarily exposed position into which they were being led. The KPNLF also received a booster as a result of Sihanouk's visit, but it was Sihanouk himself who made the most immediate gains as a result of the formation of the CGDK.

The KPNLF had often been criticized for avoiding combat with the Vietnamese. In fact, it had concentrated almost exclusively on propaganda and intelligence gathering. Like the Khmers Rouges in 1980, it now had to try and impress actual and potential backers with its fighting ability. Early in October, shortly before the annual UN debate on the recognition of DK, it was announced that the KPNLF had taken the offensive against the Vietnamese in several operations. A number of small Vietnamese outposts had been attacked and overrun, and the KPNLF claimed to have killed forty-two Vietnamese soldiers and wounded more than fifty, suffering four dead and twenty-seven wounded itself.

Son Sann was in Singapore appealing for more aid when his troops captured a string of Vietnamese guard posts near the Nong Chan camp in December 1982. The Vietnamese twice failed to re-take them, withdrawing as soon as they ran into fire. KPNLF morale soared. A jubilant Son Sann declared in early January 1983, after meeting with the Pope and thanking him for the Vatican's 'broad support' for the KPNLF, that his forces would allow the Vietnamese 'no truce' in Cambodia. 'The Vietnamese,' he said, 'must never eat, sleep or travel in tranquility in our country.'

But the Vietnamese and PRK forces struck again on 17 January and quickly re-took their positions. On 31 January they launched a direct assault on the KPNLF stronghold of Nong Chan. The Vietnamese quickly took the camp, inflicting heavy casualties on KPNLF forces commanded by Chea Chutt. They withdrew two weeks later. This was followed by assaults on the Khmer Rouge stronghold of Phnom Chat and the Sihanoukist camp at O-Smach in March and April. Western commentators were surprised at the ease with which the hardened Khmer Rouge forces at Phnom Chat were overrun. The Vietnamese occupation of O-Smach was a heavy blow to Sihanouk's position. Not only did it inflict heavy casualties on his forces, it left them without a base camp.

This fighting was right on the border, and led to the most serious encounters between Thai and Vietnamese military forces since June 1980. There were artillery exchanges and troop clashes all along the stretch of border north of Aranyapratet. According to the Thais, some Vietnamese shells landed in the Thai township of Ta Praya, and on one occasion the Thais napalmed a Vietnamese force, which they said was well inside Thai territory.

Once again, thousands of refugees fled from the fighting on the border into Thailand. These were mostly relocated to KPNLF base areas to the north of Nong Samet, of which Ban Sa-ngae was the most important. A new camp was opened up at Phnom Dongrek, located where the Thai-Cambodian border curves to follow the Dongrek mountains. The Vietnamese-PRK forces were also reported to be building a barricade parallel to the border, presumably to restrict access to the interior for hostile forces on the border. Some writers suggested that, having failed to establish a demilitarized zone along the border by diplomacy, the Vietnamese were now attempting to establish it by force.

There was little change in the situation over the rest of 1983. With the coming of the rainy season, Khmer Rouge guerrilla activity was stepped up as usual. They had just received a new shipment of arms from China, and claimed once again to inflict astronomical casualties on the Vietnamese. Analysts in Bangkok discounted these figures, but some claimed that Khmer Rouge fighters were ranging through the country more freely than any time since 1979. At the start of the year Khmer Rouge commanders told a journalist that they intended to cut access to Angkor Wat and then bring the township of Siem Reap under attack. But this scheme went the same way as Ieng Sary's 1981 promise to begin 'liberating' towns. The Khmers Rouges continued to wage a low-level guerrilla campaign. In August ten Soviet cotton experts were killed in an ambush in Kompong Chnaang province, and in September the Phnom Penh-Battambang train was attacked again.

The Khmers Rouges driven out of Phnom Chat in April were transferred to the Phnom Dongrek camp, along with 12,000 refugees from Nong Samet (the Thais hoped to eventually resettle more than 25,000 Khmers at this site). When John McBeth visited the camp in September he found it under a KPNLF commander, who maintained that Khmer Rouge and KPNLF families were living together amicably. Built by the UN Border Relief operations at a cost of $1.8 million, it was hoped that its inaccessible location would protect it against Vietnamese attacks.[16] The same consideration, of course, made it an excellent base of operations for both the Khmers Rouges and the KPNLF.

The KPNLF received a shipment of arms from Singapore, and also stepped up its activities in the rainy season. Their objective was to establish permanent bases in the forest surrounding the Tonle Sap, but they did not succeed. The soldiers who were to carry out this mission were graduates of a special camp the KPNLF had established to train its guerrillas with Malaysian advisers, but more than half the trainees deserted rather than undertake such a dangerous mission.[17]

One result of the increased KPNLF activity in the Cambodian interior was a sharp rise in the number of clashes between its forces and the Khmers Rouges. In October 1983 both the KPNLF and the Sihanoukists complained that the Khmers Rouges were avoiding combat with the Vietnamese, but subjecting their forces to a deliberate campaign of harassment and intimidation. In the interests of coalition unity, they said, they had been obliged to be restrained in their response. The Khmer Rouge leaders indignantly denied these accusations. When Sihanouk, Sann and Samphan went to Peking at the end of the year seeking more aid, they made a special show of their unity.

The KPNLF's intelligence network inside Cambodia also received a heavy blow in May, when the Vietnamese and the PRK launched a major crackdown on suspected collaborators with the insurgents in western Cambodia. According to the KPNLF more than 300 PRK officials, ranging from village chiefs to a provisional governor, in the three northwest provinces of Siem Reap, Oddar Meanchy and Battambang, were arrested. A number of villages suspected of harbouring the KPNLF were forcibly relocated, precipitating an exodus of over 10,000 people to the border. In August the KPNLF produced a list of some of the high-ranking officials arrested in the purge, which, it rather hopefully added, 'proves the seriousness of the deteriorating situation of the Vietnamese' in Cambodia. At one point they were claiming that Heng Samrin himself had been arrested, but they soon had to drop this claim. The KPNLF claims are almost certainly exaggerated, but it is likely that a purge of some sort did indeed take place. What remained of the KPNLF and Khmer Rouge intelligence networks is, of course, unknown.

With less than 5,000 men, refused arms by both Singapore and China, with his main base camp destroyed, and his men harassed by the Khmers Rouges, Sihanouk found that his fortunes had taken a sudden, bad plunge. He responded by threatening to withdraw from the coalition, arguing for the need to reach some accommodation with Hanoi, and accusing the Khmers Rouges of inflexibility. In New York in October 1983 he told journalists that the Khmer Rouge leaders believed that they could oust the Vietnamese and regain total power in Cambodia. To achieve this, he complained, they were willing 'to go on fighting until the end of the earth'. And if they ever achieved their objective, he added, they would 'kill all of Heng Samrin's supporters 'and us too'. But he still remained their partner in the CGDK.

The Vietnamese attacks on CGDK bases in early 1983 were intended to demonstrate to the ASEAN countries that they were backing a coalition of lost causes on the Thai border. The ASEAN countries had supported, first, the Khmers Rouges, and second, the coalition, in the hope that they could force Vietnam to withdraw from Cambodia without making any significant concessions themselves. They hoped to wear Hanoi down with a strategy of attrition. ASEAN thinking at the start of the coalition venture had been summed up by Rajaratnam on 20 September 1980: 'They must crack under the strain. ASEAN has to keep the pressure up.' In this spirit, they had rejected Vietnamese offers of a non-aggression pact, of a demilitarization of the Thai-Cambodian border, and of a partial troop withdrawal.

But by 1983 it was clear that they had played their cards wrongly. The Vietnamese had been able to handle pressure exerted by means of the Khmer resistance groups. If we ask how ASEAN's strategy of attrition has fared after four seasons of fighting, even a sympathetic observer such as Michael Liefer agrees: 'The simple answer is – not very well.' Indeed, he observes, the Vietnamese have applied 'an effective counter-strategy of attrition' against the Khmers Rouges – and, over the 1982–3 dry season, against the non-Communist groups as well.[18] But, having chosen this strategy, the ASEAN countries found themselves locked into a position that seemed to serve China's aims of squeezing Vietnam rather than their own interests in regional security.

Following the border fighting in the 1983 dry season, Vietnam embarked on a new round of diplomatic activity. In Bangkok, critics of the rigid stance of the Thai government became more vocal, and in May, the Thai foreign minister promised a 'more flexible policy' that would 'respect the legitimate interests' of the Vietnamese in Cambodia. The ASEAN countries also dropped their references to settling the dispute by means of an international conference on Cambodia. One ASEAN diplomat even referred to this formula as 'an embarrassment'. This implied the possibility of ASEAN agreeing to a regionally negotiated settlement, without the participation of China, as the Vietnamese had been demanding.

On 20 September 1983 the ASEAN foreign ministers issued a statement which confirmed that they were willing to consider a settlement of the Cambodian problem that by-passed the framework of the UN. They maintained that the essential element of a settlement should be the withdrawal of the Vietnamese forces. They suggested that this could take place on a territorial basis, with the Vietnamese troops being replaced by peace-keeping/observer forces, to be followed by an overall political settlement.

Thach did not reject this scheme. He said that it was interesting, and that he would study it closely. But there was little chance of Vietnam agreeing to withdraw its forces before the achievement of an overall political settlement involving the disarming of the Khmers Rouges and, presumably, the acceptance of the PRK government in Phnom Penh. And these conditions ASEAN was still unlikely to accept, especially as this would incur the wrath of both Peking and Washington.

The anti-Communist Resistance in Laos and Vietnam

If the non-Communist resistance groups in Cambodia were too weak to be used as an effective lever against Hanoi, the resistance movements in Laos and Vietnam itself were in an even more parlous state. Yet the notion that Laos is, along with Cambodia, languishing under an oppressive foreign occupation, has led some commentators to an exaggerated idea of the potential nationalist appeal of the resistance groups in Laos. For example, in the most detailed account of anti-government activity in Laos to date, Geoffrey Gunn concludes: 'Clearly it is the Soviet-backed, armed Vietnamese domination of the Indochinese peninsula that supplies the *raison d'être* of resistance movements in Laos and Cambodia. The corollary is that as long as Hanoi pre-empts by military suasion alternative political arrangements or alignments in Laos or Cambodia, the popular appeal of these resistance fronts can only expand.'[19] This judgement is not supported by the available evidence.

The main opposition to the new government in Vientiane was based on tribal rather than class or national loyalties. Its backbone was the Hmong hill tribes of central Laos, who had traditionally resisted lowland Lao control. Many of them had served with General Vang Pao's CIA-funded 'Secret Army' prior to 1975, and were fearful of Communist retaliation. Government attempts to encourage the hill tribes to resettle in the lowlands, confused attempts at collectivization, and a series of poor harvests all helped fuel Hmong resentment of the Pathet Lao government. But this resentment found expression in flight into Thailand rather than armed resistance inside Laos. And the tribal loyalties that gave the movement some basis among the Hmong severely restricted its appeal to other sections of the population.

There was some military resistance to the new regime after 1975, but on an ever-diminishing scale. The number of Vang Pao supporters who remained in Laos after 1975 is unclear, but it was probably no more than a few thousand. The organizational framework of the old 'Secret Army' had disintegrated, and they were totally disorganized. Scattered fighting was reported throughout

1976 and 1977, and in the closing months of 1977 there was a major clash with government forces in the vicinity of Phu Bia, near the Plain of Jars. This battle appears to have broken the back of what resistance there was, and many of the remaining Vang Pao supporters either fled to Thailand, turned to simple banditry, or returned to their villages. Since then, what few Pathet Lao military operations there have been appear to have been no more than local mopping up operations. As Geoffrey Gunn puts it, the main opposition to the LPDR was a 'constellation of rightists' drawing their support from 'the refugee population in the camps in the north and the northeast of Thailand' – not from inside Laos at all.

The scale of the problem would not appear to warrant resort to drastic military measures such as the use of poison gas against the Hmong rebels, as has been claimed by refugees in Thailand. These claims have led in turn to accusations of 'genocide' against the Pathet Lao by journalists and some of the relief workers involved with the Hmong refugees. These accusations were pounced on and heavily publicized by the US State Department, but a UN team sent to investigate the issue late in 1981 concluded that there was a 'lack of hard evidence'. When the investigation closed in December 1982, the hard evidence was still lacking. The UN team concluded that the allegations had not been proven, although 'circumstantial evidence, could not be disregarded.[20] From Luang Nam Tha in northern Laos also came reports of a resistance movement based on the Yao hill tribe and led by one Chao La. So far, at any rate, nothing is known of their operations. In addition, an even more shadowy guerilla band led by a 'General Champa' is said to be operating in Phong Saly province. None of this adds up to a very impressive popular opposition to the pro-Vietnamese government of the LPDR.

After the Vietnamese invasion of Cambodia in December 1978, these northern Lao resistance movements could draw on Chinese support. Until then the Chinese had restricted themselves to recruiting members of the hill tribes for intelligence purposes. From that point on, however, the Chinese provided supplies for the Hmong and Yao guerrillas; and 'General Champa's' group is said to be Chinese-trained and Chinese-directed.

In 1981 it was reported that the Chinese were running a training camp for Lao insurgents at the town of Sumao, in Yunnan province. There were alleged to be some 2,000–3,000 newly trained Lao insurgents there under the command of Kong Le, a former Lao neutralist leader. They were being trained not by the Chinese, but by about 100 Thai right-wing activists. Many of the Thais were believed to be mercenaries who had earlier fought with the CIA's 'Secret Army' in Laos. Others were thought to be members of the Thai fascist Red Guar organization, which had carried out the massacre of students at Bangkok's Thammasat University in 1976, and which has since been playing an important role in the struggle against the Thai Communist Party in the hill tribe areas of northern Thailand adjacent to Laos.[21]

Yet these efforts by the Chinese have had little impact on the Lao political scene. Gunn suggests that this is because the Chinese have provided 'less support than might be expected', Peking being reluctant to cut all ties with Vientiane. The ferocity of Chinese polemics against the 'puppets of Le Duan' in both Phnom Penh and Vientiane make this unlikely. We would suggest two other considerations are probably more relevant. In the first place, the hill tribe resistances always had a very limited base, and militarily their backbone had been broken before 1979. While the Chinese doubtless wished to encourage them to continue the struggle, whatever the consequences might be for the people concerned, there was little point in sinking money into a lost cause. Despite some Chinese support, these groups do not appear to have undertaken any significant military operations since 1979. Second, Peking may have been wary of encouraging separatist tendencies among the hill tribes of northern Laos, because with many (including the two key groups, the Hmong and the Yao) the majority of their population lived in China, not Laos. An upsurge of tribal separatism could have uncontrollable consequences for China itself.

There were also some reports of resistance in the southern parts of the country, a traditional stronghold of aristocratic rivals to the royal house of Luang Prabang. Appealing to lowland Lao, the southern Lao resistance had a potentially wider basis than a tribal movement. This 'White Lao' resistance had disintegrated by mid-1977, but revived in early 1980. 'Until about eight months ago,' one diplomat in Bangkok told reporter Marcel Barung in late 1980, 'the so-called resistance in the south was little more than a bunch of free-booters, but there is evidence that they have tried to become more organized and more politically credible by claiming to fight in order to rid Laos of the Vietnamese presence rather than against the Pathet Lao regime.' In September 1980 the formation of a Lao People's National Liberation Front (LPNLF) was announced.

The revival of the southern resistance in 1980 was partly a result of the disaffection produced by a bungled collectivization drive by the Pathet Lao in 1978–9, but the White Lao appear to have had little success in linking their cause to local peasant grievances, or recruiting inside Laos. Their reinvigoration appears to have been lagely a result of the support they got from the Khmers Rouges, via Son Sen's base near the junction of the Thai, Lao and Cambodian borders. Gunn quotes reports that up to 1,500 Lao were being trained by the Khmers Rouges. 'While there is no unified command structure,' he writes, 'liaison between the Lao guerrillas and the DK forces is said to extend to the organizational and supply requirements of the Lao *maquisards* as far north as Savannakhet.' Or, to put it somewhat differently, the organizational incapacity of the White Lao resistance was such that throughout their entire field of operations they were heavily dependent on Khmer Rouge backing.

The dependence of the southern Lao anti-Communists on the Khmers Rouges could hardly have enhanced their appeal to peasants resentful of the Pathet Lao's attempts at collectivization. Nor did it overcome the endemic factionalism among right-wing Lao. Chinese and DK-encouraged efforts to bring about a united front of all anti-Vietnamese resistance groups had little result. Despite Gunn's claim that joining forces with the Khmers Rouges was a 'landmark event' in the development of the southern Lao resistance, the White Lao movement sank out of sight once more after 1980.

The Lao resistance groups could, as a rule, count on the support of sympathetic Thai government and army officials in the provinces, but Bangkok would have nothing to do with them despite its support for the Khmer resistance. Apparently encouraged by the enthusiastic reception given to the Cambodian coalition, a former RLG prime minister, Phoumi Nosovan, announced in August 1982 that he would establish an anti-Communist liberation government in Laos on 10 October. The Thais quickly declared that they would neither recognize nor support such a government. The situations in Laos and Cambodia were quite different, they said; whereas in Cambodia, ASEAN recognized not the Heng Samrin government but DK, in Laos they recognized the LPDR and would not support armed insurgents against it.

The Khmers Rouges had also tried to build up links with the main armed resistance inside Vietnam, the 'Front Uni pour la Lutte des Races Opprimées' (FULRO). This operated among the hill tribes of the central highlands of Vietnam, exploiting their resentment at political control by lowlanders. The tribes that provided the main basis of FULRO, the Rhade and the Jarai, spread over the border into Cambodia's Ratanikiri and Mondulkiri provinces, so it is plausible that Khmer Rouge groups operating in northeastern Cambodia had established links with them. Son Sen's base camp was said to be the main conduit of supplies from the outside world for FULRO.

Little is known of FULRO's operations. Visitors to Vietnam's central highlands in 1981 reported that the local Vietnamese authorities still faced serious security problems. FULRO forces 'and other armed groups' frequently extorted money from passengers on local buses, and from time to time Vietnamese army vehicles were ambushed on remote roads.[22] On the whole, however, fighting appears to have been small-scale and infrequent, certainly by comparison with the pre-1975 period. Also, in assessing such reports, it should be remembered that banditry is endemic in this part of the world.

In September 1982 the Vietnamese paper *Saigon Giai Phong* published an account of the demise of FULRO. According to this source, FULRO had been weakened by a series of purges and assassinations associated with an internal power struggle in 1976–8. In 1980 the Khmers Rouges began claiming they had joined forces with FULRO. Other sources reported that Chinese weapons were being channelled to FULRO via the Khmers Rouges. The Vietnamese government responded by launching a series of military operations against FULRO's forces. By mid-1981 its forces were said to have been broken, and a number of the movement's leaders captured. But several key figures had evaded the Vietnamese, so the victory was by no means total. But there are few outside visitors to this remote part of the world, so we are not aware of any independent reports that would confirm *Saigon Giai Phong's* account.

From time to time in the early 1980s Hanoi announced military operations against 'bandits' in the mountains of northern Vietnam. An article in *Nhan Dan* in 1981 asserted that in Son La and Lai Chau provinces 'the Chinese reactionaries have colluded with and instigated former bandits to form reactionary groups in an attempt to stir up anti-revolutionary rebellion.' Some officials in border provinces were accused of 'double-dealing' – professing loyalty to Hanoi, but secretly coming to terms with the Chinese.

The apparent background to this was Hanoi's decision in 1976 to abandon the autonomous zones for minority peoples in these strategic areas. While this strengthening of central authority was motivated by security concerns, it apparently created much local dissatisfaction, which the Chinese have been doing their best to exploit. But there is nothing to suggest that the problem is of such a scale as to be a major worry for Hanoi. Once again, the tribal basis of these groups ensures that they have little wider class or national appeal. The main area of mass dissatisfaction with Communist rule in Vietnam is in the south, especially in Saigon. But any opposition movement here was effectively decapitated by sending most of the leading figures of the old regime to 're-education camps'.[23] And a considerable part of its constituency subsequently fled the country as 'boat people'. Some ARVN units supposedly went underground to continue the struggle after 1975, but nothing has been heard from them since. For all practical purposes, then, the bourgeois opposition has become an emigré opposition.

To sum up, there is little sign of a nationalist resistance to Vietnamese influence in Laos, or of organized opposition to Communist rule within Vietnam. Such resistance as exists is atomized and based on tribalism. We are dealing with traditional communities resisting the encroachments of the centralizing state, rather than a modern nationalist movement. Failure to recognize this point underlies most of the exaggerated assessments of their potential strength. While the Chinese and the Khmers Rouges have given some support to these groups, the ASEAN countries have wisely kept their distance. But the chief problem has not been, as emigré leaders sometimes assert, lack of external support. It has been lack of a popular constituency within Laos or Vietnam.

The Chinese, in a curious inversion of the 'Indochina Federation', have been trying to bring all of these disparate groups into an Indochina-wide united front 'struggling against hegemonism'. In the unlikely event of such a venture getting off the ground, given the weakness of all the other groups, such a united front would be effectively dominated by the Khmers Rouges. They, not the motley assortment of non-Communist groups, are offering the real alternative to the existing pro-Hanoi governments.

Notes

1. This section draws heavily on an unpublished paper by Steve Heder, 'The Democratic Kampuchea Military'. This is based on extensive interviews and covers the period from October 1979 to August 1980; for an analysis of the December 1978-October 1979 period in the Khmer Rouge zones by the same author, see *Kampuchea:*

Occupation and Resistance, Asian Studies Monographs no. 027, Chulalongkorn University, January 1980. The earlier study is weakened by the curious assumptions that the Hanoi government and 'their' Salvation Front in Cambodia 'promised' an anti-Communist 'counter-revolution' to the Cambodian middle class, and that the Khmers Rouges still retained much of their earlier popularity among the peasantry.

2. Henry Kamm, *New York Times,* 25 November 1980.

3. Quoted by Heder, 'The Democratic Kampuchea Military'.

4. *Beijing Review,* 10 May, 1982.

5. *Asia 1983 Yearbook,* Hong Kong 1983, pp. 127–8.

6. There is no satisfactory survey of the non-Communist resistance in Cambodia in print. Bernard Hamel's *Resistances en Indochine 1975–80,* Paris 1980, is devoted mainly to a tendentious diatribe against the 'Tonkinese' and contains little information on the resistance groups themselves.

7. Elizabeth Becker, 'The Quiet Cambodian', *New Republic,* 20 January 1982.

8. Timothy Carney, 'Cambodia in 1982: Political and Military Escalation', *Asian Survey,* vol. 23, 1983, p. 76.

9. *Far Eastern Economic Review,* 26 September 1980.

10. Quoted by Jay Matthew, *Washington Post,* 30 October 1979.

11. *Far Eastern Economic Review,* 7 November 1980.

12. Paul Quinn-Judge, *Far Eastern Economic Review,* 26 May 1983.

13. *Far Eastern Economic Review,* 6 March 1981.

14. Jacques Bekaert, 'The Khmer Coalition: Who Wins, Who Loses?', *Indochina Issues,* no. 28, September 1982; for a discussion of the earlier stages of the negotiation by the same author, see 'Cambodia's "Loose Coalition": A Shotgun Wedding', *Indochina Issues,* no. 22, December 1981.

15. The text of the coalition agreement was published in *Peking Review,* 5 July 1982.

16. John McBeth, *Far Eastern Economic Review,* 18 September 1983.

17. Paul Quinn-Judge, ibid., 13 October 1983.

18. Michael Liefer, 'The Balance of Advantage in Indochina', *The World Today,* June 1982, pp. 233, 236.

19. Geoffrey C. Gunn, 'Resistance Coalitions in Laos', *Asian Survey,* vol. 28, 1983, pp. 337–8. For an extreme version of the same argument, see Hamel.

20. For a full discussion of the poison gas allegations, see Grant Evans, *The Yellow Rainmakers,* London 1983.

21. John McBeth, *Far Eastern Economic Review,* 31 July 1981.

22. Nayan Chanda, ibid., 30 October 1981.

23. The number of political detainees in Vietnam is a matter of much controversy. The American right wing claims that there are at least 200,000. Stephen Morris quotes as 'credible' a figure of 340,000 ('Vietnam under Communism', *Commentary,* September 1982, p. 40). Releasing the US State Department's annual review of human rights in 1983, Reagan's Assistant Secretary of State, Elliott Abrams, singled out Vietnam as the 'worst country to live in' in the entire world. By contrast, he said, the human rights situation was improving in countries such as El Salvador.

The Vietnamese government told Amnesty International in September 1980 that there were then 20,000 people in re-education camps, and that the number had peaked at 40,000. In early 1983, Phan Hien (by now justice minister) told Michael Richardson that there were 'no more than 10,000', held in 'a few dozen camps away from the cities, mainly in southern Vietnam'. (*Age,* 26 March 1983).

9

Conclusion: the Red Brotherhood at War

One of the central claims of supporters of the regimes in Saigon, Phnom Penh and Vientiane during the Second Indochina War was that they were fighting to protect the independence of their nations from conquest by 'international Communism'. The Vietnamese Communists were accused of being lackeys of either Moscow or Peking, rather than nationalists, and the Khmer and Lao Communists were in turn accused of being puppets of Hanoi. Events after the Communist victory have shown how totally misconceived these ideas were. Triumphant nationalism has torn asunder the international solidarity of the 'Red Brotherhood' within three years.

Some commentators have tried to explain this as the triumph of 'traditional' nationalist passions over the ideology of proletarian internationalism, but this is not very persuasive. In Indochina, as elsewhere, nationalism is a modern phenomenon. Nor was Communism the creation of an internationalistic proletariat. The Communist movements of Indochina have their roots in the nationalist revolt against Western colonialism, and the Third Indochina War has its basis in the dynamics of that revolt rather than in a mysterious revival of ancient antagonisms. Viewed from this angle, the events since 1975 are less surprising: this is by no means the first occasion on which victorious nationalists have turned on each other once foreign domination has been overturned.

The main driving force for revolutionary change in Indochina as a whole was the cataclysmic upheaval in the most developed and populous country, Vietnam. It was inevitable that Vietnamese influence was deeply imprinted on the Communist movements of Laos and Cambodia after these countries gained independence. But Communism in Laos and Cambodia was never simply controlled by Hanoi – rather, they were indigenous movements, which, especially in their early stages, looked to the Viet Minh as a model for their own revolutionary movements. But, as they developed a social and political base of their own, they adapted to different national political environments, and their paths diverged. The Communists in Laos and Cambodia found themselves operating in a milieu that was much less touched by modernizing forces than Vietnam, and this in turn rebounded on their relations with Hanoi.

As a consequence of the strength of royalism in Cambodia in the 1950s and 1960s, Hanoi's main concern was to cultivate good relations with Sihanouk's regime. The strains this created between Hanoi and the handful of Sihanouk 'ultra-leftists' in the CPK seemed of little importance at the time – but they were to boomerang on the Vietnamese after Pol Pot's group came to power in 1975. By contrast, in Laos the weak RLG provided Hanoi with no comparable temptations. The interests of Hanoi and the Pathet Lao leadership never diverged significantly, and the result was that their alliance endured well beyond 1975.

The conflicts that erupted after 1975 were an outcome of the dynamic established by these divergent but intertwined paths of nationalist-communist revolution. The view, popular among Western and Chinese commentators, that Vietnam embarked on a course of 'expansionism', seeking to subjugate Laos, Cambodia, and beyond that, perhaps all of Southeast Asia, is no more than propaganda. What positive evidence there is points in the opposite direction. The leadership in Hanoi wanted to concentrate on the internal tasks of economic development and modernization.

But, the exponents of this view claim, the proof of the pudding is in the eating: the proof of the 'hegemonistic' ambitions of Vietnam lies in its subjugation of Laos and Cambodia. If Hanoi did not will this, they ask, why did it happen? The answer to this is that the realities of international relations are considerably more complex than these theorists assume – Hanoi's decisions were not made in a vacuum. In the wake of the victories of 1975, instead of the peaceful international context it had assumed, Hanoi found itself under increasing pressure from China, and with its expected opening to the West blocked by the United States. As the pressure mounted, the Vietnamese leadership reacted by switching its attention from economic development to national security. And as this became the preoccupation in Hanoi, the geography of the region ensured that the Vietnamese would become increasingly concerned over their relations with the governments in Phnom Penh and Vientiane.

In the case of Laos the outcome was the signing of the 1977 treaty of friendship with the Lao People's Democratic Republic. This is often depicted as the climax of Hanoi's 'colonialist' drive to 'subjugate' Laos. In reality, it simply represented a strengthening of the long-standing close relations between the Pathet Lao and the Vietnamese Communists. The claim that it was imposed on an unwilling Laos by its Vietnamese masters has never been backed up with evidence. It appeals to common Western prejudices about Communism and serves to blacken an alliance inimicable to Western interests in the region, but it has little basis in fact. As we have seen, while Vietnam was seeking to strengthen its hand against China, Laos was trying to strengthen its hand against Thailand.

The basis of the charge of Vietnamese 'colonialism' is simply that Vientiane has opted for a close political and military alliance with Hanoi, whereas Western critics would prefer to see it neutral or aligned with Bangkok. But such a realignment was one of the most predictable outcomes of the Communist victories in 1975, and has nothing to do with colonialism. Classic colonialism involves the imposition of direct foreign rule, which is clearly not the case in contemporary Laos. So-called 'neo-colonialism' involves the substitution of economic domination for direct political controls. Neither can be taken very seriously as a model of Lao-Vietnamese relations. The administration in Laos is a Lao administration, notwithstanding Vietnam's troop presence – just as, for example, the West German government is undoubtedly a German government, notwithstanding the American troop presence. And if we turn to the question of economic dependence, the Lao have been, and still are, more dependent on Thailand than on Vietnam. In this context, developing relations with Hanoi and the Soviet bloc has actually widened Vientiane's options – hence the annoyance of many of Bangkok's rulers at what they regard as the 'un-Lao' behaviour of the Pathet Lao leadership.

For a state in the midst of a turbulent region, as Laos is, the option of neutralism and non-alignment is an attractive one. But such a policy can easily prove an expensive luxury for a small state, leaving it vulnerable to outside intervention. The principal alternative is to opt for a protective alliance with one regional power or another. In the case of Laos, this amounted to a choice between Bangkok, Peking, or Hanoi. Forced to take sides, the Pathet Lao leaders had no good reason to turn against their long-term allies, the Vietnamese Communists. There is no reason to assume that this cut across widespread popular feeling – though this is the cherished myth of Lao anti-Communist emigré groups.

It is in this wider context that the presence of Vietnamese troops in Laos should also be viewed. As a militarily weak state at the geographic centre of the conflicts of more powerful states, it is not surprising that Laos has relied on the military presence of allied forces to deter intervention by hostile forces. Many other governments in a similar situation have pursued the same strategy. According to the government in Vientiane, Vietnamese troops are deployed in Laos to deter Chinese aggression. The exponents of the 'Vietnamese colonialism' theory maintain that they are there to coerce the local population, but they have not produced evidence to support this claim. What is known of the actual deployment of the troops on the ground is consistent with the claims of the government, not those of its Western critics. Certainly, Vientiane does not have the atmosphere of a city under foreign occupation.

It is also worth recalling that many of those who now insist so loudly that Laos is a Vietnamese 'colony' insisted with equal vehemence before 1975 that the Khmers Rouges were no more than 'puppets' of Hanoi. It is evident that their certainty often arises more from the requirements of propaganda rather than from firm knowledge.

It was in relation to Cambodia rather than Laos that the post-1975 crisis in Indochina erupted, and here the critics of Vietnam appear to be on stronger ground. After all, Pol Pot and his colleagues explain the Vietnam-Cambodia war in terms of their heroic resistance to Vietnam's drive to 'colonize' Cambodia. But are they truthful witnesses?

Once again, a closer examination of the available evidence undermines the thesis of a Vietnamese expansionist urge. Hanoi undoubtedly wanted friendly relations with the new regime in Phnom Penh, just as it had sought them with Laos – and, for that matter, with Sihanouk. To this end, Hanoi was willing to turn a blind eye to the atrocities perpetrated by the new regime, both within Cambodia and on the Vietnam border. When Pol Pot spurned the offer of a treaty of friendship, the Vietnamese reluctantly accepted this. While Hanoi preferred a sympathetic government in Phnom Penh, it was willing to accept an unsympathetic one provided it did not constitute a threat to Vietnam itself.

The immediate catalyst of the Third Indochina War was not any expansionist drive on the part of Vietnam, but the violent and provacative conduct of Pol Pot's regime – if Hanoi can be criticized on any count in this connection, it should be for its willingness to acquiesce to the most barbaric behaviour just across the border in the sacred name of 'national independence'. But in the quest for an unattainable 'perfect sovereignty', Pol Pot's regime not only slaughtered its own citizens, it also turned issues of no intrinsic importance into the basis of a major confrontation on the Vietnam-Cambodia border. No government can reasonably be expected to tolerate military actions of the sort to which Vietnam was subjected by Pol Pot's regime in 1977–8. Hanoi was especially sensitive because of the disruptive impact of Phnom Penh's assaults on an already fragile situation in southern Vietnam.

Nevertheless, Hanoi's initial response was moderate. While it made no concessions to Phnom Penh's unilateral demands over the border, it did try to contain the conflict and find a diplomatic solution. It was in the face of Pol Pot's repeated rejections of such a solution that the Vietnamese escalated their military response, and eventually decided to overthrow the Pol Pot regime by force of arms. Perhaps the decision to invade can be criticized as an excessive response to Pol Pot's border war. But it is clear that it was the actions of the regime in Phnom Penh that started the war; Hanoi's actions ended it.

It is thus on the nature of the DK regime rather than on the alleged regional ambitions of Vietnam that we have to focus if we wish to understand the genesis of the Third Indochina War. Here the arguments advanced by Hanoi and the Heng Samrin government it installed in Phnom Penh are politically convenient and not very persuasive. They argue that the leadership of an authentic people's revolution was 'usurped' by a group of Maoist fanatics, led by Pol Pot. These usurpers then smashed all urban life because of their 'anti-working class, poor peasant line' and proceeded to turn Cambodia into a forward base for Chinese expansion in Southeast Asia. All in all, it stands as a terrible warning to any Communists inclined to adopt a sympathetic attitude towards China.

But the Vietnamese are unclear on just how it was possible for the leadership of an authentic people's revolution to be usurped in this fashion. Nor is it very clear what Cambodia's 'true Communists' were doing all the while. Precedents can be found in Maoist theories for the anti-urban orientation of Pol Pot's regime, but hardly for their utter extremism. The thuggery of Mao's Red Guards was child's play compared to the actions of the death squads unleashed by Pol Pot. Nor were Pot Pot and Ieng Sary puppets dancing on strings pulled in China – although it was their regime's main supporter, Peking probably had little more control over them than Hanoi did.

The standard clichés of Western commentary are not very helpful either. Journalists usually describe the internal politics of Communist regimes in terms of a conflict between 'pragmatists' (the moderates and rightwingers) and 'ideologues' (the extreme left wing). But Pol Pot does not seem to have been an ideologue; rather, like Stalin, he prided himself on his pragmatism. In 1978 he boasted of building 'socialism without a model', based on 'the experience gained in the course of the liberation struggle'. Considerations based on general theories or the experiences of other countries in building socialism were contemptuously dismissed.

If the extremism of Pol Pot's regime thus has pragmatic roots, it is in the practical circumstances of the Cambodian revolution that its explanation is to be found. In the chaos that followed the overthrow of Sihanouk, the Khmers Rouges rose from extreme isolation to state power in only five years. The essence of Pol Pot's ideology was the glorification of the self-sacrifice and military heroism that had made this possible. After his victory in 1975, the entire nation was to be remade on the spartan model of an isolated guerilla encampment.

When they came to power in 1975 the Khmers Rouges lacked the educated cadres needed to staff the administrative apparatus of a modern state. The backwardness of the social structure as a whole, and the rapidity of the growth of the movement, meant that the cadres of Khmer Communism were drawn heavily from the ranks of poorly educated peasant soldiers. Most were young and inexperienced, with little understanding of the world beyond the village and the war, easily manipulated by those who were more sophisticated, and ready to use brute force to solve problems they did not understand. Perhaps, with a united, flexible and sophisticated leadership, the CPK would have been able to overcome these problems with time. But all these things, too, were lacking in Cambodia in 1975.

It was the inability of such a political apparatus to deal with the problems of running Cambodia's refugee-swollen cities that explains the extraordinary decision to disperse the urban population and subject it to a campaign of terror. As in earlier revolutions, the resort to terrorist methods of rule was a symptom of weakness and insecurity rather than strength. By these 'pragmatic' methods Pol Pot was able to by-pass the whole problem of constructing a modern bureaucratic state.

The Khmer Rouge movement was by no means united in 1975, and the course pursued by the Pol Pot leadership only added to its internal tensions. Then Pol Pot used the secret police and loyal military factions to carry out an ever-widening series of purges to crush his opponents, both in the central government and in the entrenched regional structures of the party and government. Out of this there emerged a highly centralized military-police-state, headed by a small family clique, which cultivated nationalist delirium in a desperate attempt to establish its legitimacy.

An extreme backwoods chauvinism could be 'pragmatically' exploited in terms of Cambodian internal politics. But externally it locked Pol Pot and his group on a dangerous course. They probably did not have clear-cut expansionist ambitions, but they were certainly irascible neighbours. Incidents erupted all around the country as the Khmers Rouges tried to seal Cambodia's ill-defined borders to stem the flight of refugees and the infiltration of 'enemy agents'. The fact that the most obvious external influence on Cambodian Communism was Vietnamese meant that Vietnam became the main focus of Pol Pot's xenophobia. Thus the campaign to annihilate rival groups within Cambodia went hand-in-hand with escalating violence against Vietnam.

Nothing comparable happened in either Vietnam or Laos. In Vietnam, a more developed society gave rise to a Communist system dominated by modernizing bureaucrats. In Laos, the most backward of all the Indochina countries, the outcome was similar. This was the result of the Pathet Lao's long and complex path to power, and the extent to which they were influenced by the Vietnamese along the way. This enabled them to gradually build up a body of experienced cadres, and a more sophisticated version of nationalism than that which prevailed in Cambodia. The Khmers had the misfortune to be the unhappy medium.

Pol Pot exploited the 'traditional fear' of Vietnamese expansion embodied in Sihanouk's nationalist ideology for his own ends – as Lon Nol did before him. His demands to readjust the Vietnam-Cambodia border rested on 'historical' grievances borrowed from Sihanouk's account of Cambodia's decline. But Pol Pot never accepted the traditional notion of a border as a porous and shifting zone of contact between states that ruled over diverse populations (nor, for that matter did Lon Nol or Sihanouk). He insisted on a territorial state with sharply demarcated borders and a homogeneous, united population, hallmarks of modern nationalism. Nor did he accept the emphasis of traditional statecraft on compromise and the submission of small states (no matter how absolute their internal despotism may be) to more powerful ones. On the contrary, he was motivated by the distinctly modern ideal of 'perfect sovereignty' for a small state. Realism had made the traditional Khmer kings adept at balancing the demands of their neighbours, and playing them off against one another to maximize their own freedom of manoeuvre. Sihanouk tried to continue this style of diplomacy, but like Lon Nol, Pol Pot believed that it was a failure, and was responsible for the decline of Cambodia. He attempted to meet the demands of all his neighbours with force. Pol Pot's excursions into history were not those of a political leader steeped in traditional lore – they were attempts to bestow legitimacy on present policies by re-writing the past. In short, Pol Pot was not a prisoner of Cambodia's traditions. He was a modern nationalist, albeit a particularly crude and brutal one.

Thus it was neither Vietnamese expansion nor the tragic traditions of Cambodia that made the Vietnam-Cambodia war inevitable. It was the actions of Pol Pot as the leader of a modern revolution that destroyed itself. The revolution succeeded in smashing the framework of Sihanouk's patrimonial traditionalism, but not in establishing a new institutional framework in its place. The war with Vietnam was in a sense simply the external projection of the instability, bellicosity and violence of the Pol Pot regime within Cambodia. The war was not precipitated by any expansionist acts on the part of the Vietnamese; they merely had the misfortune to be standing nearby – preoccupied with their own problems – when Cambodia's revolution blew up in their faces.

This is not to say that they did not have an abiding interest in what happened in a neighbouring country. They were deeply interested in Cambodia and Laos, just as the Thais were. Our point is simply that the available evidence indicates that the Vietnamese sought to peacefully develop friendly relations with Phnom Penh, and that it was Pol Pot's forces that started the war between the two countries.

It might be objected that it was suicidally irrational for Pol Pot's regime to provoke a war with a more powerful state such as Vietnam (or Thailand, with which it came close to war in 1977). This is true, but what it proves is not that Pol Pot could not have attacked Vietnam, but that his foreign policy was irrational. In fact, as Anthony Barnett has pointed out, this is only one of a number of recent wars precipitated by unstable dictatorships in an attempt to create internal unity, with similarly disastrous consequences: Somalia's invasion of Ethiopia; Uganda's invasion of Tanzania; Iraq's invasion of Iran; Argentina's occupation of the Falklands.[1]

It is clear that those commentators who emphasized the local roots of the Vietnam-Cambodia war are right. It is not to be understood, as President Carter's secretary of state, Zbigniew Brzezinski, depicted it in 1979, as a 'proxy war' between the Soviet Union and China (in turn, of course, the USA itself was an innocent party). Yet the local conflict was aggravated by, and exploited by, great powers outside the region. Of these, the most important has been China. Without a consideration of this global dimension as well as the local roots, it is impossible to understand the outcome of the conflict.

During 1977–8 the view was expressed that the abuses of human rights in Pol Pot's Cambodia were so great as to justify external military intervention. When such intervention did come, however, it was almost universally condemned. Indeed, it was those who had been most vociferous in their condemnation of the DK regime who now insisted most loudly that it was the 'legitimate government' of the country and called for the overthrow of Heng Samrin's government – even though it was generally admitted that its human rights record was incomparably superior to that of its predecessor. It is evident that genuine concern for the Cambodian people has been subordinated to the propaganda requirements of great power politics.

The Communist victories in Indochina in 1975 fundamentally recast the balance of power in the whole Southeast Asian region. American power was on the retreat – with Thailand, and even the Philippines to some extent, rethinking the whole question of American military bases on their soil in the wake of the débâcles in Cambodia, South Vietnam and Laos. As the 1973 'Kunming Document' reveals, Communist China aspired to establish itself as the dominant power in the region as American influence waned, and saw the USSR as its main rival. China's drive to open diplomatic and trade relations with Southeast Asian nations met with considerable success – more so than the parallel efforts by the Soviet Union. As an ally to which Peking had given substantial support, Vietnam was naturally expected to submit to Chinese hegemony. The pressure on Hanoi began even before the fall of Saigon, with the occupation of the Spratly Islands in 1974, and intensified rapidly thereafter.

Yet most Western commentators have been curiously blind to China's assertive policies from 1975. In the 1950s there had been much talk of Peking's 'expansionist policies' – at a time when China was actually weak and cautious in its behaviour. It was in these terms that American intervention in Korea and Indochina had been justified at the time. Of course, China was then an ally of the Soviet Union – on the wrong side in the cold war, from Washington's point of view. But one of the first consequences of China's assertion of its aspirations to independent great power status was the shattering of the Sino-Soviet alliance; and by the late 1970s American leaders were anxious to play the 'China card' against the Soviet Union. In this context, Western commentators benignly overlooked a considerable growth of Chinese influence, while flying into a panic over any sign of Soviet 'expansionism'. Thus a major shift in the international balance of power occurred with surprisingly little comment. But it was a shift of the first order of importance for Indochina.

It was, ironically, in Communist Vietnam that Chinese hegemony met with the most resistance. Hanoi's leaders had long struggled to maximize their own freedom of manoeuvre by carefully balancing the demands of their Chinese and Soviet patrons. In this way they had managed to carry on a war about which neither of the Communist great powers were happy through to a victorious conclusion. But from 1975 China's new assertiveness made such a balancing act increasingly difficult. While the non-Communist countries of Southeast Asia were able to balance Chinese influence with American influence, this course was not open to a government that had only recently defeated American military intervention. Hanoi's efforts to develop an opening to the West were frustrated by US hostility. As its options diminished, Hanoi had little choice but to align itself with Moscow and gird itself for a long struggle with China.

Faced with a stark choice between Moscow and Peking, Hanoi had sound reasons for choosing Moscow. For a leadership anxious to modernize a backward country, Peking could offer little by way of sophisticated technology, economic aid, or successful development planning. And, for a country plunging once again into a perilous international situation, Moscow could offer more sophisticated weapons. Unable to compete with Moscow's blandishments, Peking resorted to crudely coercive measures – threatening Hanoi, cutting off aid, and stepping up the military pressure on the Sino-Vietnamese border. At each step, Peking's influence in Hanoi shrank; by 1978 the VCP leadership had decided that China had become 'the main enemy of the Vietnamese revolution'. At the same time, Peking was becoming increasingly apprehensive about the ties between its southern neighbour and its antagonist to the north, the Soviet Union.

The outcome was bitter rivalry between Vietnam and China for influence in Indochina. Vietnam began pressing Laos and Cambodia for a 'special relationship' that would, in effect, exclude

Chinese influence. Laos went along with this, but in Cambodia it only inflamed the antagonism of Pol Pot's regime towards Vietnam. In non-Communist Southeast Asia, ties with China had already become considerable, and no one wished to jeopardize them by siding with Vietnam. And Hanoi's sudden enthusiasm for excluding great power influences from the region was inevitably viewed with scepticism, given its growing relationship with Moscow.

Pol Pot's group provided China with its only diplomatic triumph in Indochina. From 1975 Peking became the main foreign patron of the DK regime, and used it to step up its pressure on Hanoi. As the Vietnam-Cambodia war unfolded, Peking openly threw its weight behind Phnom Penh. China's preference was for a protracted conflict, sufficiently low-key to 'bleed' Vietnam without provoking effective retaliation, but such subtleties were beyond the capabilities of the Pol Pot regime. Peking appears to have sought to restrain some of DK's most suicidal excesses in 1978, but in vain. While characters like Pol Pot were unloved in Deng Xiaoping's Peking, Deng could hardly stand by idly when the Vietnamese overthrew a regime to whose protection China had committed itself. On this, if nothing else, the Maoists and the 'pragmatists' were agreed. Such an action was a damaging blow against China's new-found prestige throughout Southeast Asia. But, given Soviet backing for Vietnam, military intervention by China was a dangerous option. The Peking leadership was divided over the issue, and in this context America's attitude proved decisive. By strongly condemning Vietnam's actions in Cambodia and making it clear that an attempt to 'teach Vietnam a lesson' would not interrupt the process of Sino-American *rapprochement* in any way, Washington helped tilt the scales decisively in favour of intervention. But, even so, the final decision was made only after Deng had been reassured by his visit to the USA in January 1979.

China's invasion of Vietnam in February 1979 proved unsuccessful. Much damage was done to northern Vietnam, but the Chinese troops performed poorly, and sustained heavy casualties. Hanoi was able to rebuff the invasion without either supporting action from the Soviets or without withdrawing troops from Cambodia. Far from being cowed by China's actions, the Hanoi leadership became more resolute than ever. And, after the first failure, threats of 'another lesson' rang hollow.

While keeping the situation tense on the Sino-Vietnamese border and giving backing to the anti-Vietnamese guerrillas operating in Cambodia, China concentrated on bringing maximum diplomatic pressure to bear on Vietnam. In this it had the backing of the USA, and achieved considerable success. The Vietnamese intervention was almost universally condemned by countries outside the Soviet bloc (and by some within it). What Western aid had been flowing into Vietnam was cut off, adding to the economic disruption and the demoralization within the country. In 1979 Hanoi found itself under more effective siege than at any time during the Second Indochina War.

Vietnam responded to these pressures by moving further into the Soviet orbit, by readjusting its economic policies at home, and by consolidating its ties with Laos and the new regime it had installed in Phnom Penh. The economic ties between the Soviet bloc and Vietnam were further strengthened, and the Soviets were granted access to Cam Ranh Bay – to the great annoyance of Peking and Washington. The more moderate economic policies adopted in 1979 meant scaling down the VCP's plans for rapid modernization, but they did succeed in lifting the Vietnamese economy out of the acute crisis situation of 1979–80. In this, they were helped by more favourable weather conditions in the early 1980s. By 1983 it was clear that the strategy of economic coercion had failed – Vietnam remained mired in acute poverty, but the prospect of the Hanoi leadership capitulating on matters it regarded as vital to the country's security because of economic pressures was becoming more remote than ever.

Meanwhile, Communist Indochina was emerging as a political and military bloc under Vietnamese leadership. Laos quickly established relations with Heng Samrin's PRK government, and in February 1979 Vietnam signed a treaty of friendship with Cambodia paralleling its 1977 treaty with Laos. The 'militant solidarity of Laos, Vietnam and Cambodia' became a stock phrase in political rhetoric, and the three countries adopted a common stance on the Cambodia issue. To Chinese commentators, this was a vindication of Pol Pot's charge that Hanoi aspired to establish an 'Indochina Federation'. In reality, Chinese pressure was a major factor in catalysing Hanoi's drive to strengthen its regional alliances.

In Cambodia, the Vietnamese faced immense problems. Contrary to some claims, military resistance was not one of them. The Khmers Rouges did not surrender, but within six months they had been largely confined to remote and unpopulated areas of the country, where the Vietnamese attempted to starve them into submission. With Chinese and Western aid, Pol Pot was able to rebuild his forces in enclaves along the Thai-Cambodian border but he was not able to mount any serious challenge to the Vietnamese military presence in Cambodia, either by conventional or guerrilla warfare. The wholesale brutality of his regime in power meant that his forces did not have the minimum level of popular support (or even tolerance) necessary for effective guerrilla warfare.

Behind the protective shield of the Vietnamese military, their Cambodian allies attempted to build up a new administration. Here they faced problems of staggering dimensions. After Pol Pot's terror, there was little left of the educated middle class needed to run the government; and those willing to work with the PRK were frequently still traumatized, dispirited, and of uncertain political loyalties. Inevitably, the new administration was at first heavily dependent on Vietnamese advisers. However, as the number of trained Khmer officials rose, the PRK became increasingly capable of standing on its own feet, and the Vietnamese advisers were largely withdrawn. Not surprisingly, the new government was dominated by Khmer Communists who had fled to Vietnam to escape Pol Pot's purges, and was organized along the lines of the Vietnamese bureaucratic model.

The collapse of the Pol Pot dictatorship left behind an uprooted and exhausted population, and a devastated economy. The country urgently needed a massive injection of outside aid to stave off famine. But the effort to aid Cambodia was quickly embroiled in the international conflict surrounding Vietnam's intervention. Soviet bloc aid came quickly, but the Americans were reluctant to send aid that would shore up the PRK and ease the pressure on Vietnam – and the USA was a major donor to the international aid agencies through which most Western aid would be channelled. In the end, they agreed to send aid to Phnom Penh, but engaged in a campaign to blacken the PRK's handling of aid, and insisted that much of it be distributed on the Thai-Cambodian border. Here, under the guise of 'humanitarianism', aid could be channelled to the Khmers Rouges and other insurgents, and used as a magnet to attract population from the PRK-controlled zones into the insurgent-controlled zones.

Over the next three years, conditions within Cambodia gradually returned to normal. This was due in large part to the 1980 decision of the aid agencies to concentrate during the dry season on bringing in seed rice and agricultural implements, thus facilitating the rehabilitation of the country's productive capacity. This inevitably rebounded to the benefit of the PRK and was heavily criticized as 'political' rather than 'humanitarian' aid. Western aid via Phnom

Penh was cut back and eventually stopped, and the West concentrated its 'humanitarian' efforts on the areas in the hands of anti-Vietnamese insurgents on the Thai-Cambodian border.

Thus, by 1983, Vietnam's Khmer allies had built up a stable administrative structure, with effective control of most of the territory and population of Cambodia. But it faced insurgency on the Thai border, sustained by Chinese and Western aid efforts, and it remained dependent on the military shield provided by the presence of 150,000 Vietnamese troops. It had become a pillar of Hanoi's anti-Chinese Indochina bloc, and the focus of international controversy.

The presence of Vietnamese troops in Cambodia has been widely condemned as a 'foreign occupation', and this is the usual argument given in demands that they be withdrawn. At a practical level, it is clear that they are deployed to deal with the insurgents on the Thai border, rather than to coerce the general population, and that (whatever worries people may have about them in the long run) there is considerable support for them in that role. Their presence was 'legalized' by the 1979 treaty between Vietnam and the PRK, an agreement that was, of course, condemned by DK. Since a sovereign government has the right to form whatever military alliances it chooses, and to invite allied troops to defend its soil if it chooses, the legality of Vietnam's military presence in Cambodia is dependent on whether one decides to recognize Pol Pot's or Heng Samrin's PRK as the legal government of the country.

Outside the Soviet bloc, countries have almost universally refused to recognize the PRK, on the grounds that the Vietnamese invasion that installed it was an illegal act. But this is a shaky argument, for it ignores the fact that it was aggression by Pol Pot's regime that precipitated the Vietnam-Cambodia war. The notion of the inviolability of national sovereignty cannot be used as a shield to protect a regime guilty of repeated violations of another nation's sovereignty. The condemnation of Vietnam's actions by the West and the ASEAN countries rings hollow when heard against their endorsement of the Tanzanian invasion of Uganda, their acquiescence to China's invasion of Vietnam (a classic exercise in power politics, incidentally, in no way a defence of Chinese sovereignty), Indonesia's invasion of East Timor, or the American invasion of Grenada.

Of course, the opposition to Hanoi's action was not really based on these half-baked notions of international law. It sprang primarily from the fact that it settled the issue of who would be the dominant power in Indochina in Vietnam's favour. China lost its main lever against Hanoi. Thailand lost a buffer state between it and Vietnam, the culmination of its loss of influence in the region. The USA lost another struggle to restrict the spread of Soviet influence. Cambodia has thus had the misfortune to become a focal point of the new cold war as well as a regional struggle for spheres of influence.

While the emergence of an Indochinese Communist bloc dominated by Vietnam has attracted much attention, and condemnation, the solidification of ASEAN into an anti-Communist regional alliance has drawn less comment. Yet this has been one of the most important outcomes of the conflict in Indochina. When it is acknowledged, it is usually presented as a natural reaction to the perceived threat to the security of ASEAN countries, specifically Thailand, from Vietnam. This is accurate enough, but it is rarely pointed out that this parallels the way in which Hanoi, Vientiane and Heng Samrin's government in Phnom Penh closed ranks in the face of Chinese threats – real ones, too, not merely 'perceptions'. One is seen as natural, the other as illegitimate. As we noted earlier, many commentators have a huge blind spot when it comes to China's role in the Indochina conflict.

The ASEAN countries could have reacted to Vietnam's invasion of Cambodia by applauding the overthrow of Pol Pot's reign of terror, recognizing the PRK, and continuing relations of *détente* with Communist Indochina. Such a policy would have had a good basis in both humanitarian considerations and international law. There was a significant current of opinion within the ASEAN governments that favoured such a course. But, instead, they attempted to mobilize international opinion against Vietnam, manipulated refugees and aid, and threw their weight behind anti-Vietnamese insurgents on the Thai-Cambodian border, in an attempt to overthrow the new government in Phnom Penh.

They embarked on this course because the dominant groups in ASEAN (specifically, in the Bangkok and Singapore governments) feared that the Vietnamese invasion of Cambodia posed a serious threat to the security of Thailand, and of the ASEAN countries more generally. To accept the Vietnamese action as a *fait accompli* would be, they believed, to acquiesce to a serious weakening of Thailand's international position. They also assumed that the Vietnamese would face widespread popular resistance in Cambodia, and that the outcome of the invasion was by no means as 'irreversible' as the Vietnamese were proclaiming.

The backlash against Vietnam's actions was reinforced by the crisis over refugees, pouring out of Indochina by land and by sea at the time, and by the hostile stance of China and the United States towards Vietnam. This ensured that, in taking a stand against Vietnam, the ASEAN countries would have powerful backing. In fact, it is probable that this backing was a major factor influencing the path chosen by the ASEAN countries in 1979.

The campaign spearheaded by ASEAN was successful in isolating Vietnam diplomatically, but beyond that it proved a failure. Given the ability of the Vietnamese leadership (with the backing of the Soviet bloc) to withstand the diplomatic, economic and military pressures exerted by China and the USA, it rested on the ability of the insurgents on the Thai-Cambodian border to transform themselves into a fighting force. This has not happened, despite considerable (if covert) external support, because these groups have been unable to build up a base of popular support within Cambodia.

The largest and most organized of the insurgent groups are the Khmers Rouges, whose wholesale brutality while in power has effectively isolated them from their original peasant base. The next largest group is the KPNLF, which is in effect the surviving rump of the Lon Nol regime. Plagued by weak organization and factionalism, it represents essentially the emigré middle class. There is nothing to suggest that it has a significant appeal for the Khmer peasantry. Finally, there are Sihanouk's supporters – the smallest and the most disorganized of these groups, but with the potential for tapping traditional loyalties to the monarchy among the peasants. The precise extent of these loyalties in present-day Cambodia is unclear, but there is little doubt that they have been widely broken down by the impact of the events of the 1970s. Thus, none of these groups has served as an effective magnet to rally 'patriotic' opinion (that is, anti-Vietnamese opinion – the PRK is also nationalist, and is also promoting its version of patriotism in Cambodia, rather more effectively than its opponents).

Nor has this situation been substantially altered by the formation of the Coalition Government of Democratic Kampuchea. This has been largely for foreign consumption, and it did serve to avert a collapse in international diplomatic support for DK. But on the ground, cooperation between the anti-Communist republicans, monarchists and Communists participating in the CGDK remains minimal. The ideological differences and mutual antagonisms generated by past events are too profound to be overcome by a document written in the Thai foreign ministry. Despite ASEAN's attempts to promote the KPNLF and Sihanouk, the Khmers Rouges remain the main force in the resistance, and would doubtless be the main beneficiaries if, through ASEAN and Western support, the CGDK should find itself in Phnom Pehn. The extreme remoteness of such a possibility was, however, shown by the crushing success of the Vietnamese attacks on the main base camps of the non-Communist groups in the 1983 dry season campaign.

While ASEAN has been struggling to hold together a tattered and divided coalition with only a precarious toe-hold on Cambodian soil, the PRK administration has been steadily consolidating its hold on the country as a whole. The limited withdrawals of Vietnamese troops since 1981 have been the result of Hanoi's growing confidence in the capabilities of the PRK administration, rather than a sign of weakness. Thus, the reductions in troop numbers in no way indicate a diminution of Vietnamese (or, more accurately, pro-Vietnamese) influence in Cambodia. This is why the ASEAN countries, which had been calling for Vietnamese troop withdrawals, did not welcome them when they came. Instead, the troop withdrawals were greeted with frustrated rage, and denounced as a 'fraud' – for, of course, the real issue was not getting Vietnamese troops out of Cambodia; it was overturning a pro-Hanoi government in Phnom Penh.

If ASEAN remains committed to 'rolling back' Vietnamese influence, rather than coming to terms with a pro-Vietnamese government in Phnom Penh, the 'Cambodian problem' will remain a point of friction in the region. While they continue to enjoy Thai support and protection on the border, the anti-PRK insurgents can be contained but not eliminated by the Vietnamese – and while this is the case, the Thai-Cambodian border will remain a focus of instability and violence. This does not enhance Thai security, which is the objective of ASEAN's policies towads Cambodia.

In their attempts to bring maximum pressure to bear on Hanoi, the ASEAN countries have associated themselves closely with Chinese and American policies towards Vietnam – despite suspicions about China's long-term objectives in some ASEAN governments. Since Hanoi's policies over Cambodia were formulated largely in response to Chinese pressure, the main consequence of this was to make the Vietnamese more intransigent towards ASEAN. Once again, it is a policy that has proved counter-productive in terms of ASEAN's interests in regional peace and stability. But it does serve the interests of Chinese and American policies towards Vietnam, and any attempts on ASEAN's part to change course now can be expected to incur the displeasure of Peking and Washington.

In this context, the search for a 'solution' to the Cambodian problem is mainly a search for a face-saving formula for ASEAN. Vietnam's 'solution' to the Cambodian crisis is in place in Phnom Penh and, in practice, there would seem to be little that ASEAN can do about it – short of launching a full-scale invasion, which would doubtless prove as disastrous for Thailand as for Cambodia and Vietnam. Given this, finding a way out for ASEAN means finding a way of letting it extricate itself from the increasingly bankrupt policy of promoting the CGDK, and coming to terms with the government in Phnom Penh – as it has, reluctantly, come to terms with a pro-Vietnamese government in Vientiane. It also means finding a way of reaching a *détente* with Communist Indochina without antagonizing Peking and Washington. This would undoubtedly be the most difficult part of the exercise.

If the situation on the ground in Indochina appears increasingly stable, the relationships between the great powers are in flux. The international conjuncture prevailing at the time of the Third Indochina War has now passed. But there is little comfort for ASEAN's present policies in this. Since the election of President Reagan in 1980, Sino-American relations have deteriorated almost continuously, and since 1981 the Chinese leadership has been slowly but steadily improving its relations with Moscow. This has undermined some of the key assumptions on which ASEAN's overall approach to Indochina since 1979 has been based on. No change in Peking's policies towards Hanoi has yet resulted, but neither has Peking succeeded in persuading Moscow to cut its support for Hanoi's policies in Indochina. China would have to be bargaining from a position of considerable strength to persuade Moscow to abandon its allies in the region, and it is not in such a position.

Yet it is probably the changing imperatives of these great power relationships that will open up a 'solution' to the Cambodian problem. It is unlikely that Peking will continue with futile attempts to coerce Moscow's allies in Indochina while pursuing *rapprochement* with Moscow itself. No doubt China's rulers will still aspire to exercise influence in Indochina, as in the rest of Southeast Asia. But they will have to come to terms with the fact that their crudely coercive approach in Indochina since 1975 has set their cause back years, probably decades.

If a slow *rapprochement* between the two great powers of the Communist world led to a softening of Peking's attitude towards Hanoi, this would open the way to *détente* between Indochina and ASEAN. When a conciliatory current surfaced in the ASEAN bloc in

1981, it was Chinese intransigence that frustrated it. If China came to adopt a more relaxed policy, this could mean that future moves in a similar direction would be likely to be more successful. But at this point, we are moving into the realm of speculation, and guessing about the future is always a hazardous venture.

Turning to more general considerations, it is evident that the interpretations of events in Indochina since 1975 offered on both sides of the great ideological divide of the cold war are seriously inadequate. Anti-Communist circles in the West and in ASEAN have usually couched their arguments in terms of Vietnamese 'expansionism'. This brings back memories of the domino theory and the analogies with Munich that were thrown around with abandon during the First and Second Indochina wars. It is no doubt useful for propaganda purposes, but it ignores the complexities of regional politics and is altogether misleading. Vietnam's intervention in Cambodia is treated in isolation from the actions of the DK regime that provoked it, and from Peking's drive for dominance in post-war Indochina. In their eagerness to compress facts into a convenient cold war mould of 'patriots' opposing 'Communist expansionism', some of these theorists have been inclined to almost overlook the point that China and DK are also Communist states. In fact, the conflicts of post-revolutionary Indochina cut right across the old bipolar cold war alignments.

If the clichés of Western anti-Communism look pretty thread-bare, so too do those of the other side. Mao proudly told General Montgomery in 1961: 'We are Marxist-Leninist, our state is a socialist state not a capitalist state, therefore we wouldn't invade others in a hundred years or even ten thousand years.'[2] His successors had proven him wrong within three years of his death. For their part, the Vietnamese did no good for their cause in Cambodia by appealing to the same rhetoric of 'internationalism' that the Soviets had used to justify their intervention in Czechoslovakia in 1968. The situation was in fact quite different: Pol Pot did attack Vietnam, but no one has ever suggested that Alexander Dubcek's government attacked the Soviet Union.

Nor were the responses of the Western left to the conflicts in Indochina very satisfactory. One section put its main emphasis on the pernicious role of US imperialism, the legacy of destruction before 1975 and the obstructive pattern of American diplomacy since then. Another section of the left deplored these events as a further illustration of the nationalist deviations produced by 'bureaucratically deformed' socialism. Both of these lines of argument seem to us to evade rather than confront the basic problems. They keep alive a wistfully utopian vision of socialism by insulating it from the practical problems of post-revolutionary societies. Neither approach provides a good guide to what happened in Indochina after 1975.

In this book we have argued that the motive force of the revolutions in Indochina has been state-building and political mobilization; nationalism is not a 'deviation' but an expression of the central aspiration, the creation of a sovereign nation-state. Khieu Samphan was probably speaking for many Third World radicals when he declared that socialism was only a means to this end.

Where the sovereignty of the nation-state is the overriding principle of international politics, its corollary is international anarchy. In such a situation, the basic rules of statecraft are those of power politics. And where Communists win power in the course of nationalist revolutions, it is these rules that regulate relations between them – the security of the state takes precedence over ideological purity.

But Marxist-Leninist theory has emphasized the 'class' nature of the state, offering a theory of capitalist imperialism and a theory of socialist internationalism by way of an explanation of international relations. Internationalism is not, as the cold warriors maintain, a formula for Communist military expansion and conquest. Communists are, in theory, committed to world revolution, but then, American Christians are also committed to turning the other cheek. In Soviet foreign policy, revolutionary zeal gave way to *raison d'état* as long ago as the 1920s, and this has also happened in China, Vietnam and other Communist states. The achievement of power exerts a strong conservatizing influence on politicians of all political persuasions, their rhetoric notwithstanding.

Internationalism commits Communists to friendly and co-operative relations with all states who are willing to reciprocate, and especially other Communist states, and to the pursuit of the good of all mankind rather than the selfish pursuit of their particular *raison d'état*. It is an idealized picture of how the world should be, not one of how it really is. The 'Brezhnev doctrine' of 1968, justifying Soviet intervention in Czechoslovakia is, of course, an abuse of these ideas, not an expression of them.

One can understand why Communist leaders are attached to theories that depict them in such a favourable light (just as leaders on the other side of the cold war divide cling to their equivalent theories). But these theories do not provide a satisfactory basis for dealing with conflicts and disagreements when they do arise. They pass over the questions of territoriality, sovereignty and defence against external attack that lie at the heart of many international political issues. Like the state itself, these issues have conspicuously failed to wither away under Communism. These theories also fail to recognize the forces of nationalism and power politics in Communist international relations. In practice, as in Hanoi's relations with Pol Pot, it means that Communist leaders steadfastly refuse to admit that there are any problems until they finally erupt into the open, charged with all the accumulated resentments built up before the split. This pattern is evident in both the Sino-Soviet and the Sino-Vietnamese splits, not to mention Pol Pot's *Black Paper*.

There have been conflicts between Communist states before – the break between Tito's Yugoslavia and Stalin's Russia, the Sino-Soviet split is another – but in Indochina these reached a new level of intensity. In one of history's fateful turns Ho Chi Minh's dying hope that Vietnam would heal the rift in the 'Red Brotherhood' was dashed by the eruption of the Third Indochina War, which illustrated just how deep differences between Communist nation-states can be. But these cannot be explained away simply as unfortunate deviations from the straight and narrow path of 'proletarian internationalism'. Where they are not purely rhetorical, appeals to internationalism in the Communist bloc (as in the West) usually turn out to be appeals for international support for the policies of one particular nation-state.

The weaknesses of socialist internationalism are particularly evident in dealing with the Communist revolutions in Asia where, as we argued earlier, the forces of state-building and mass nationalism are central aspects of the drive to modernity. The Third Indochina War was a product of these forces. Stripped to its essentials, it is a story whose ingredients are familiar from other parts of the world that have undergone the experience of modernization; and no doubt variations on it will be repeated elsewhere in the future.

The Communist victories of 1975 were the culmination of nationalist revolutions that destroyed Western domination in Indochina. But the new states were insecure and unstable, and the hierarchy of power in the region was by no means clear. China, in its drive for great power status, sought to establish its own dominance and exploited the adventurism of Pol Pot's regime to that end. Vietnam's reaction was not that of fanatical 'Communist expansionists' bent on world conquest, or of pure-minded 'proletarian internationalists' – it was the typical reaction of a middle-ranking power intent on maintaining its independence by forming a protective alliance with a friendly great power, the Soviet Union, securing its rear by destroying Pol Pot's regime, and building up a regional bloc to help it withstand Chinese pressure.

The Third Indochina War settled the question of which was to be the dominant power in Indochina in Vietnam's favour – but it also provoked a reaction from another regional power, Thailand. In a response paralleling Vietnam's, Thailand swallowed its ideological scruples, formed an informal alliance with China, and secured regional support in ASEAN. It then sought vainly to reverse what had been accomplished through the Third Indochina War.

It was a sequence of action and reaction that Machiavelli, well-versed in the problems of new states in early modern Europe, would have understood very well. However, he would have been unfamiliar with the rhetoric of revolution and nationalism in which conflicts between states have become enveloped. That is the mark of the modern era of mass politics. The peoples of Indochina have undergone a particularly traumatic initiation into that era, and there is no sign that the ordeal is over.

Notes

1. Anthony Barnett, 'Iron Britannia', *New Left Review*, no. 134, July-August 1982, pp. 65–6.
2. Quoted in Dick Wilson, *Mao: The People's Emperor*, Melbourne 1979, p. 362.

Select Bibliography

As a work of contemporary history, this book is based primarily on current reportage rather than published research. The best coverage is to be found in the Hong Kong weekly, *Far Eastern Economic Review*. In its *Asia Yearbook*, the same office produces a valuable reference work. For most of the period we are concerned with, Nayan Chanda was its Indochina correspondent and John McBeth reported from Bangkok. *Asiaweek*, also published in Hong Kong, is the *Review's* main competitor, but its coverage is not as thorough. *Indochina Issues* and *Southeast Asia Chronicle* are also useful specialized publications. One general publication that brings together information on current affairs from a wide range of sources is *Keesing's Contemporary Archives*, published in London. Many important statements are broadcast over radio and are most accessible in the BBC's *Summary of World Broadcasts* (London). There are many books dealing with the pre-1975 period, and with the various powers that have been involved in Indochina. Here, the following list can provide no more than a beginning. On the other hand, very few works of scholarly merit have been published on the post-1975 period, and here we can lay claim to greater comprehensiveness. Even so, this is still a select list of what we see as the most useful of the secondary sources.

Adams, Nina, and McCoy, Alfred W., eds., *Laos: War and Revolution*, New York, 1970.
Ambrose, Stephen R., *Rise to Globalism: American Foreign Policy 1938–80*, 2nd edn., Harmondsworth 1980.

Berton, Bruce, 'Contending Explanations of the 1979 Sino-Vietnamese War', *International Journal*, vol. 34, 1979.
Burchett, Wilfred G., *The Vietnam-China-Cambodia Triangle*, London 1981.
Buszinski, Leszek., 'Thailand: Erosion of a Balanced Foreign Policy', *Asian Survey*, vol. 22, 1982.

Caldwell, Malcolm, and Lek Tan, *Cambodia in the Southeast Asian War*,

New York and London 1973.

Chang, Parris, H., *Power and Policy in China*, 2nd edn., Pennsylvania University Park and London 1978.

Chen, King C., *Vietnam and China 1938–54*, Princeton 1969.

Chen, King C., ed., *China and the Three Worlds: A Chinese Foreign Policy Reader*, London 1979.

Chesneaux, Jean., *The Vietnamese Nation: Contribution to a History*, Sydney 1966.

Chomsky, Noam, and Herman, Edward S., *After the Cataclysm: Postwar Indochina and the Reconstruction of Imperial Ideology*, Boston 1979.

Clubb, O. Edmund., *China and Russia: The 'Great Game'*, New York 1971.

Deutscher, Isaac, *Russia, China, and the West, 1953–66*, Harmondsworth 1970.

Duiker, William J., *The Rise of Nationalism in Vietnam, 1900-1940*, Ithaca 1976.

Duiker, William J., *The Communist Road to Power in Vietnam*, Boulder, Colorado 1981.

Elliott, David W.P., ed., *The Third Indochina Conflict*, Boulder, Colorado 1981.

Emerson, Rupert, *From Empire to Nation: The Rise to Self-Assertion of the Asian and African Peoples*, Cambridge, Mass. 1960.

Evans, Grant, *The Yellow Rainmakers: Are Chemical Weapons Being used in Southeast Asia?*, London 1983.

Fall, Bernard, *The Two Vietnams: A Political and Military Analysis*, 2nd edn., London 1963.

Fitzgerald, Frances, *The Fire in the Lake: The Americans and the Vietnamese in Vietnam*, New York 1972.

Fitzgerald, Stephen, *China and the Overseas Chinese: A Study of Peking's Changing Policy 1949-70*, Cambridge 1972.

Funnell, Victor C., 'Vietnam and the Sino-Soviet Conflict 1965-76', *Studies in Comparative Communism*, vol. 11, 1978.

Girling, J.L.S., 'Indochina' in Mohammed Ayoob, ed., *Conflict and Intervention in the Third World*, London 1980.

—— *Thailand: Society and Politics*, Ithaca and London 1981.

Gittings, John, *The World and China, 1922-72*, London 1972.

Grant, Bruce, *The Boat People: An 'Age' Investigation*, Melbourne 1979.

Hammer, Ellen J., *The Struggle for Indochina 1940-55*, Stanford, 1955.

Harrison, Selig S. *China, Oil and Asia: Conflict Ahead?* New York 1977.

Jeffrey, Robin, ed., *Asia: The Winning of Independence*, London 1981.

Jukes, Geoffrey, *The Soviet Union in Asia*, Sydney 1973.

Keyes, Charles F., *The Golden Peninsula*: *Culture and Adaptation in Mainland Southeast Asia*, New York 1977.
Kiernan, Ben, 'Kampuchea 1979-81: National Rehabilitation in the Eye of an International Storm', *Southeast Asian Affairs 1982*, Singapore 1982.
Kiernan, Ben, and Chanthou Boua, eds., *Peasants and Politics in Kampuchea 1942-81*, London 1981.

LaFeber, Walter, *Russia, America and the Cold War 1945-80*, 4th edn., New York 1980.
Lewis, John W., ed., *Peasant Rebellion and Communist Revolution in Asia*, Stanford 1974.
Loescher, G.D., 'The Sino-Vietnamese Conflict in Recent Historical Perspective', *Survey*, vol. 24, 1979.

Marr, David, *Vietnamese Anti-Colonialism 1885-1925*, Berkeley and Los Angeles 1971.
——,*Vietnamese Tradition on Trial 1920-45*, Berkeley and Los Angeles 1981.
Marwan, S. Samuels, *Contest for the South China Seas*, London 1982.
McAlister, John T., *Vietnam*: *The Origins of Revolution*, New York 1971.

Nguyen Khac Vien, *Histoire du Vietnam*, Paris 1974.
Nogee, Joseph L., and Donaldson, Robert H., *Soviet Foreign Policy since World War II*, New York 1981.

Osborne, Milton, *The French Presence in Cochin-China and Cambodia 1895-1905*, Ithaca and London 1969.
——,*Power and Politics in Cambodia*: *The Sihanouk Years*, Melbourne 1973.
——, *Before Kampuchea: Preludes to Tragedy*, Sydney 1979.

Pao Min Chang. 'The Sino-Vietnamese Conflict over the Ethnic Chinese', *China Quarterly*, no. 90, 1982.
Ponchaud, François, *Cambodia Year Zero*, Harmondsworth 1978.
Prescott, J.R.V., Collier, D.F., and Prescott, D.F., *Frontiers of Southeast Asia*, Melbourne 1977.

Segal, Gerald, 'China and the Great Power Triangle', *China Quarterly*, no. 83, 1980.
Shawcross, William, *Sideshow*: *Kissinger, Nixon, and the Destruction of Cambodia*, London 1979.
Stuart-Fox, Martin, ed., *Contemporary Laos*: *Studies in the Politics and Society of the Lao People's Democratic Republic*, St Lucia, Queensland 1982.
Sutter, Robert G., *Chinese Foreign Policy after the Cultural Revolution 1966-73*, Boulder, Colorado 1978.

Taylor, Jay, *China and Southeast Asia: Peking's Relationships with Revolutionary Movements*, New York 1974.

Thion, Serge, and Kiernan, Ben, *Khmers Rouges! Materieux pour l'histoire du Communism au Cambodge*, Paris 1981.

Toye, Hugh, *Laos: Buffer State or Battleground*, London 1968.

Tretiak, Daniel, 'China's Vietnam War and its Consequences', *China Quarterly*, no. 80, 1979.

Turley, William S., ed., *Vietnamese Communism in Comparative Perspective*, Boulder, Colorado 1980.

Wain, Barry, *The Refused: The Agony of the Indochina Refugees*, Hong Kong 1981.

Woodside, Alexander B., *Community and Revolution in Vietnam*, Boston 1976.

——, *Vietnam and the Chinese Model*, Cambridge, Mass. 1971.

Worsley, Peter, *The Third World*, 2nd edn., London 1967.

Yahuda, Michael B., *China's Role in World Affairs*, London 1978.

Zasloff, Joseph J., and Brown, MacAlister, *Communist Indochina and US Foreign Policy: Postwar Realities*, Boulder, Colorado 1978.

Index

308